The Critical Practice of Film

The Critical Practice of Film

An Introduction

Elspeth kydd

First published 2011 by
PALGRAVE MACMILLAN

Palgrave Macmillan in the UK is an imprint of Macmillan Publishers Limited, registered in England, company number 785998, of Houndmills, Basingstoke, Hampshire RG21 6XS.

Palgrave Macmillan in the US is a division of St Martin's Press LLC, 175 Fifth Avenue, New York, NY 10010.

Palgrave Macmillan is the global academic imprint of the above companies and has companies and representatives throughout the world.

Palgrave® and Macmillan® are registered trademarks in the United States, the United Kingdom, Europe and other countries

ISBN 978–0–230–22975–4 hardback
ISBN 978–0–230–22976–1 paperback

This book is printed on paper suitable for recycling and made from fully managed and sustained forest sources. Logging, pulping and manufacturing processes are expected to conform to the environmental regulations of the country of origin.

A catalogue record for this book is available from the British Library.

Library of Congress Cataloging-in-Publication Data
Kydd, Elspeth.
The critical practice of film : an introduction / Elspeth Kydd.
    p. cm.
Includes index.
ISBN 978-0-230-22976-1 (pbk.)
1. Film criticism. 2. Motion pictures--Philosophy. I. Title.
PN1995.K93 2011
791.4301--dc22
2011008066

Printed in China

For UT/FV
'It's eye opening'

Contents

PART III   TECHNIQUES OF FILM

PART IV ANALYSIS AND CRITICAL PRACTICE

Illustrations

Acknowledgements

A number of people have helped and supported the writing of this book; I am particularly grateful for the assistance of Jeffery Heydinger, also to Douglas Hawley, Sandy Kydd, Nora Kydd, Pajil Wiggins, Maggie Welty, Gabriel Gomez, Jane Buchbinder and Brian Forney. I am indebted to the colleagues I worked with at the University of Toledo: Bob Arnold, Dyrk Ashton, Jamie Barlowe, Jane Bradley, Alexander Clarkson, Deb Davis, James Hill, Ruth Hottell, Tammy Kinsey, Ed Levy, Marrietta Morrissey, Joan Mullin, Kaye Pope, Sue Ott Rowlands, Steven Marc Weiss, Carter Wilson and the Arts and Sciences Master Teachers. Thanks also to those at the University of the West of England: Jane Arthurs, Charlotte Crofts, Seth Giddings, Kathrina Glitre, Steve Presence, Vicky Smith and Greg Tuck. Thanks also to the editorial staff at Palgrave: Francis Arnold, Rebecca Barden and Joanna St Mart. And, as always, thanks to my family for their support.

Every effort has been made to trace all copyright holders, but if any have been inadvertently overlooked, the publisher will be pleased to make the necessary arrangement at the first opportunity.

PART I

Critical Practice

The Critical Practice of Film

Learning objectives

After completing this chapter you will be able to:

- Develop an appreciation of the critical-practice approach to film;
- Distinguish the different types and genres of film;
- Recognize the characteristics of **Classical Hollywood Cinema**;
- Identify the different phases in the production of a film.

Critical practice

So you want to make films. Or maybe you love watching them and want to learn more about how they are made. Perhaps you want to expand your knowledge and understanding of critical analysis and theory and how these relate to the practical aspects of filmmaking. Whatever your interest in film, you have turned to this book for further information. This book introduces you to both the production and the critical analysis of film. Throughout you will discover the techniques that go into making films and will examine how film functions as a part of the larger culture and society in which we live.

The approach this book takes is that of 'critical practice'; a process that explores the integration and intersection between the critical analysis of films and the practical aspects of filmmaking. In other words, this book is both an introduction to the ways in which we watch films, as well as an introduction to how films are made. It stands to reason that the more you know about how films are made, the more you can appreciate the artistry involved in a film. Likewise, the more you appreciate the cultural context and critical ideas that inform how films are viewed, the more interesting and engaged your creative work will become. Thus, critical-practice filmmaking and analysis guide you towards both creative expression and an active role as both a viewer and a critic.

The separation between thinking and doing is a problematic binary we need to interrogate; it is based on the absolute distinctiveness of both categories, and a division of labour between those who do, and those who think about and theorize. Theorist-practitioner Mike Wayne in *Theorising Video Practice* questions this division between theory and practice:

> Rather than seeing theory and practice as distinct and separate activities, we need to see them as part of a continuum. The terms 'theory' and 'practice' refer to those circumstances and contexts in which either reflection on practice (theory) or the implementation of theory (practice) predominate. (Wayne, 1997: 13)

Throughout this book we will embrace the idea of a continuum between theory and practice rather than absolute categories, breaking down these distinctions, in order to see writing criticism and theory as practical and creative, and practice as critical and theoretical. As we will see throughout the book, but particularly in Chapter 12, this integration is not new, filmmakers have always engaged with critical and theoretical ideas, just as critics have explored and experimented with creative practice.

Critical practice also means that we debate and discuss our own practice and see theorizing as practice: writing and producing new knowledge and ways of engaging with the world. Thus, although this book deals with conventions of filmmaking, it also has the goal of questioning, disrupting and experimenting with the normative models of practice and challenging the restrictions of conventional forms. Throughout the book, the aim is to find a creative practice that goes beyond the limitations imposed by industrial structures and conventional thinking. Likewise, we aim to overcome any stigma associated with the notion that theory or theorizing limits creativity. Sometimes, instinctive doing without critical reflection, has a romantic appeal grounded in the notion of the genius of the individual artist, but what it frequently fosters is the reproduction of traditional models of practice that are trained into us by our viewing and consumption of conventional media. Critical reflection allows for a breaking of this pre-programming and a licence to experiment with form. Thus, throughout the following chapters we will explore some of the conventions of filmmaking and the so-called 'rules' that have developed from the dominant traditions of **Classical Hollywood** style. From the basis of understanding these conventions, we will then question the dominant style, disrupt the so-called rules and experiment with alternative ways of filmic communication.

Before we continue with the process of critically engaging with film, let's first explore how we have already become involved in the world of film through theorizing, criticism and practice. Most of us have used a camera at some time in our lives – snapshots from a family holiday, a videotape of a cousin's wedding or the amateur horror flicks you made with your teenage friends. Even if you have never used a video camera, if you have taken still shots and arranged them in a photo album or online display, you have gone through a filmmaking process: first composing and shooting the snapshots, then a type of editing process, selecting and placing images together in a sequence. What you have done here is similar to the way that a filmmaker first shoots, then edits: taking pictures, then selecting different shots. On some level, we are all filmmakers. Through closer study and analysis we can come to appreciate how different techniques of camera operation, or placement of items in the **frame** can make even your amateur productions more interesting.

What then links our intuitive ability to make media with the powerful structures of the creative industries? How can we come to an understanding of our role as amateur film producers and theorists in relation to the systems of industrialized media production? How can we understand the differences between our own home movies, or even our student productions and the world of 'professionals': artists, filmmakers and multiplex cinemas? Like many of the issues of representation that this book addresses, these questions about our role in media practices are **ideological** questions and lead us into the area of theory and criticism: an awareness of the cultural context in which media representations exist. How we address these issues in the coming chapters, relates to the process of critical practice, by fostering an understanding of how the film work we produce fits into the larger world of cultural production.

Just as all of us can be filmmakers, so all of us are critics of film. We watch films, we are influenced by them, and we have opinions and reactions to what we see. We enjoy and analyze film in our daily lives. Woody Allen reminds us of this in a famous scene from *Annie Hall* (1977) when the two main characters are waiting in line at a cinema and have to listen to the opinions of another of the patrons. Although hopefully you are not as rude and overbearing as the character in *Annie Hall*, still, when you go to the cinema with your friends, you talk about the film afterwards. You say whether you liked it or not, and what you particularly enjoyed, and maybe how you sympathized with one character or another. If you have seen other films by the same director, or with the same actors, you might make comparisons. You discuss the elements of story and character, sometimes you talk about the techniques: the special effects, the music or the acting. These discussions are the basis of critical analysis of a film, a key part of the critical-practice approach. Your analysis of a film will become deeper with a stronger appreciation of the techniques and styles that go into its creation.

There is a further level of analysis to consider beyond the critical discussion of an individual film. Film theory places creative practice within its cultural context, giving a fuller understanding of how representation works. Adding this to our analysis or creation of individual films, we gain a deeper knowledge: not just of the artistry of film or the entertainment industry which produces it, but also of the society in which we live. Throughout the analyses that follow, we will return to the concept of **ideology**: the interpretation of a film in relation to how it reflects certain ideas or assumptions about the cultures in which it is made and seen. Thus, through analysis of films, we can see how the world of social, political and economic ideas is reflected in the imagination of a culture. On another level, if you continue to make films yourself, an understanding of theory and ideology will help you produce work that is critically informed, sophisticated and able to communicate ideas on a number of levels.

So to get started on this process, let's look at some of the basic divisions and types of filmmaking practice, then we will introduce the dominant conventions of Classical Hollywood Cinema, before exploring the phases of production that go into the creation of a film.

Types of film

If you have visited the cinema recently you may have felt that there is a wide selection of films on offer. With so many screens in an average multiplex, there should be a suitable choice of films to view, something for every taste. There are, however, many types of films made that are not shown on your multiplex screen, and that are interesting and challenging examples of film art. In this book we will be considering many different types of film, comparing and contrasting the kinds of movies you may already know from mainstream cinema, with less well-known styles of filmmaking.

Most of us are familiar with mainstream Hollywood **narrative** cinema. These are the films we go to see in the cinemas, rent to watch on DVD or download to view. Chapter 4 will introduce you to **documentary**, a form you will have also seen on television, in an educational context or occasionally at mainstream cinemas. A third type of film production is **experimental film**, often associated with art and exhibited and viewed within that context. We will look more closely at experimental film in Chapter 5.

When we consider the contrasts between narrative, documentary and experimental film, one difference is the context in which these types of films are viewed:

- Narrative films are seen in cinemas, downloaded, rented on DVD (often from national chains) or seen on television. When we go to the cinema, download, rent a DVD or watch a film on television, we are looking for diversion, pleasure and a way to spend our free time.
- We view documentaries on television or on the internet: we watch them in courses at university and on loan from the library. When we watch a documentary, we are usually looking for information, often we are interested in the subject and want to know more about the content of the film.
- Experimental film is perhaps the least commonly viewed style of filmmaking; these films are often seen in art galleries or festivals and are produced as part of the culture of contemporary art. As the name suggests, experimental films challenge our ideas about what film is and 'experiment' with both form and content. Although they may be less popular, and seen by fewer people, experimental films are nonetheless influential in shaping the development of narrative and documentary styles as well as inspiring other forms of media such as music video and advertising.

Just as these three types of films are seen in different contexts, they are also produced by different groups:

- The average narrative cinematic feature film is created by a multinational corporation with global interests. Such a film's production cast and crew all work for this large company. The film is part of a business: a commercial enterprise designed primarily to make money.
- In contrast, documentaries are often funded from a number of public and private sources, including television commissions. Documentary production teams are groups of filmmakers, including researchers and historians, who create films for a variety of reasons, but often to serve as a record or an educational tool.
- Experimental films, by contrast, are made by individual artists or groups of artists working outside the commercial mainstream. They are expressions of the individual's artistic vision of the world.

Within these broader categories of film practice, films can also fall into particular **genres**. Genre is a term for a category or type of film, usually one that is identifiable by a set pattern of tropes, character types, style or subject matter, for instance. It is common for the audience to mention genre when talking about film. When deciding what to go and see at the weekend, you might use certain terms to describe the films playing at the cinema. These terms assign the films to their respective genres; for example, *Austin Powers: International Man of Mystery* (1997) is a comedy, *Star Wars* (1977) is a science-fiction film. Some films, of course, cross different genres, and are described using multiple terms. For example, a film such as *Men in Black* (1997) is a science-fiction, comedy and action film, all at the same time.

Genre is both a critical category and part of the structure of the film industry. As industry terminology, genres are shorthand methods for describing a film to potential backers, and can be employed as a marketing strategy to draw an audience. These terms are used by DVD rental outlets to sort their shelves and by critics to describe a film to their readers as succinctly as possible. The studios that produce films, target certain genres towards certain audiences. So, an animated adventure cartoon, such as *Finding Nemo* (2003) is geared towards children, or a broader family audience, and marketed that way. Horror films are mostly marketed to a young, teen audience, whereas romance films such as *The Time Traveller's Wife* (2009) have a target audience of women in their twenties and thirties. In film marketing, the genre of a film is part of an understanding between audience and producers. This means that if you go to see a film advertised as a horror film, such as *Drag Me to Hell* (2009), you expect certain types of action: suspense, murder and stylized violence. You also expect to see a certain **iconography**, which can include deformed monsters, bloody death scenes and screaming teenagers.

In discussing genre as critical category, theorists and critics look at the different elements that link a group of films together, and analyze the common features. So if we define *Star Wars* as a science-fiction film we have to ask the question; what is it that makes it science fiction? Setting is one of the elements that define a genre; in the case of *Star Wars*, the galaxy 'far, far away', indicates science fiction (with the flavour of fairy-tale fantasy). Science fiction also uses elements that do not exist in the contemporary world that we know. Thus in *Star Wars* there are light sabres, blaster guns, androids, alien creatures and super-fast space travel. These are all things that are fictional to our current science. On another level, films within the same genre often feature similar themes. In science fiction, the conflict between technology and humanity is a strong theme. In *Star Wars*, Darth Vader (David Prowse) himself embodies this theme, as he is physically part human and part machine, in conflict with himself. A similar theme underlies films such as *The Terminator* (1984) or *The Matrix* (1999), both of which include the struggle between the technology and individual human heroes.

Genre studies then, look at the common features that unite a group of films, including the setting, the iconography, character types, plot situations, underlying structures and thematic concerns. It is important to remember that genres are mutable and a film can belong to a particular genre without adhering to all its conventions. Each genre film is different, and genres change stylistically over time, developing new approaches to their central thematic concerns. For example, during the early days of sound film in Classical Hollywood, a **musical** involved a simple translation of theatrical stage shows to the screen. As film musicals grew over time they developed a clear sensibility of their own, reaching a period of sophistication and popularity during the 1950s. They then declined in popularity to return, in a different form, after the growth of the music-video culture of MTV. Certain genres are also culturally specific, in the sense that distinctive genres emerge from various parts of the world and reflect an aspect of a country's culture. The **Western** is a good example of this, as it is a particularly American phenomenon, relating to a part of US culture. Likewise the Japanese samurai film is a genre specific to Japanese culture.

Many of these examples of genre are drawn from popular mainstream narrative film. It is important to remember, however, that other filmmaking traditions utilize different styles of practice. Likewise, we have been using genre as a way to talk about narrative films, but other types of filmmaking also fall into broad types or styles. In Chapters 4 and 5 we will discover how documentaries and experimental films both engage with different genres or types: such as the rhetorical or observational style of documentary or the structuralist/materialist or the personal film of the experimental tradition. Like narrative genres, these particular types emerge out of a specific cultural context, often connected to different movements in the historical trajectory of the style.

The critical-practice approach to film engages with different types and genres by fostering an understanding of cultural context. Genre filmmaking, for example, is a mode of practice based on how the generic styles and techniques arise from the particular structures of the entertainment industry. These structures lead to a codification of style, created within the limits of the generic form. Genre study becomes a way of exploring how style and modes of production are intricately linked. On another level, genre conventions become of interest to critical practice, as they can be explored, imitated, parodied or undermined creatively as a way to a deeper critical understanding of the medium. As with many other conventions, genre is a key part of the development of Classical Hollywood and is one of the many ways in which the industrial structures of Hollywood defined their cinematic product. Today's entertainment industry is still grounded in this generic approach to film. So to continue, let's explore the Classical Hollywood style and its legacies.

The conventions of Classical Hollywood

Classical Hollywood conventions were developed within a specific cultural context, a dominant mode of practice and a set of industrial structures, which affected film techniques and aesthetics. Thus, the films that were produced within the Classical Hollywood style, and the conventions that developed from it, were, at least on some level, a reflection of the context of creation within the entertainment industry. Therefore, before we are introduced to the styles and techniques of filmic practice in the upcoming chapters, let's review the cultural context in which many conventions of film style emerged. Throughout this it is important to remember that these Hollywood conventions only represent one filmmaking tradition and we will study examples of others before returning to a closer analysis of critical-practice traditions in Chapter 12.

The period known as Classical Hollywood Cinema ranges from the 1920s into the 1960s and the characteristics of the Classical style influenced cinematic storytelling in many ways. The Classical Hollywood system developed a particular set of industrial practices under a structure known as the **studio system**. The studio system arose in the 1920s when the most successful production companies consolidated their economic power and developed a series of creative practices that would assure an output of financially successful products. One of the characteristics of the studio system was **vertical integration**. This meant that the five dominant studios owned all elements of the film business from its creative production, through the channels of distribution, to the cinemas where the audiences watched the films. This virtual monopoly lasted until the late 1940s, allowing these studios to exercise an unprecedented control over the US film industry.

A key feature of the studio system was how the films were produced: a method which defined the style of the films made during this period. The studios developed a factory-like approach to production. This means, in effect, that the workers in a studio film followed a strict division of labour. Each job in the process was clearly defined and each participant had his or her own duty to perform. Under the studio system the workers had long-term contracts: making film after film with the same studio, without any choice about which films they made. This included the studio's actors; the films they made were decided on by the studio. Ranging from the **extras** performing small roles to the studio's stars, all were controlled by long-term contracts. The studio's control over the stars meant that the stars' images were cultivated and publicized over a number of films and film roles were created especially for them. The **star system** was one of the studio's methods for promoting and marketing a film. The stars were products of the studio system; their film roles, as well as the publicity that surrounded them, was carefully engineered by the studio to create their image. One of the questions that this factory system raises is how the films made by the studios reflect this approach. Factories generally produce a standardized product: one Ford car coming off an assembly line should be exactly like another. In film this is not the case, as each film has to be distinctively different. Yet through genre style the studios attempted to create similar products that could be sold to an audience based on the commonalty between them. Genre allowed the studios to create films that were a standardized product, yet at the same time each film was individualized with its own story to tell.

During the studio period in Hollywood, a self-regulating method of censorship developed that also had a significant effect on film style. The **Hays Code** was introduced in the early 1930s and defined how films dealt with controversial subjects such as sex and violence. The process of regulation mandated by the Hays Code had an interesting effect on the storytelling of the films produced under its rubric. For example, the Code stipulated, 'crime need not always be punished, as long as the audience is made to know that it is wrong' (reprinted in Mast, 1983: 328). Thus, Classical Hollywood films always have endings that show the bad guy being caught or killed, endings designed to enforce the Code's moral ideals. Although the Code was replaced with the rating system in the 1960s, the ways in which it affected film storytelling continue to have implications for film style. The structures of film narratives still often require an ending (or **closure**) that restores the moral order. A film such as *The Player* (1992) is so effective because of the surprise ending that shows a murderer profiting from his crime: something that the Classical system would not have allowed. This type of ending is particularly unexpected to an audience trained by the conventions of Classical Hollywood to expect a certain moral resolution. In addition to moral closure, the Code was very specific about the methods of portraying sex. These regulations meant that filmmakers in this period developed metaphorical images to express passion and/or sexual activity. Often scenes would **fade to black** just as characters kissed and would then return to the scene at a later point in time, implying sexual activity that could not be shown on screen.

Classical Hollywood style is a form of narrative filmmaking. The films of this period are designed to entertain and tell stories. In fact, the Hays Code opens with this assertion: 'Theatrical motion pictures … are primarily to be regarded as *Entertainment*' (Mast, 1983: 321). During this period, the narrative form of film was consolidated, and techniques for communicating stories through cinema became standardized. Under the Classical system, writing for the screen developed along formulaic lines. This is not to say that all these films were the same, only that there was a system in place for structuring stories in a similar manner. Classical Hollywood films had strongly defined character types, recurring plot situations and structures that fitted neatly into the time span of ninety minutes to two hours. Despite the formulaic structure, Classical Hollywood produced many great films. In Chapter 3, when we discuss story form in detail, we will see how some of these structures operate.

Classical Hollywood also refers to the style of filmmaking that developed at this time and under these institutional conditions. One of the principles of the Classical style is the invisibility of the cinematic techniques. In other words, when you are watching a Classical film, you are drawn into the story world and forget that you are watching a film. This invisible technique led to the development of unobtrusive lighting and camerawork; camera angles and movements were designed so as not to call the viewer's attention to the apparatus of production. In addition, as we continue to study film techniques, we will frequently return to the **continuity** style of staging and editing. This is a Classical technique of shooting and editing film that creates a particular view of narrative space, where the viewer can clearly understand the relationship between the different characters by where they are placed in a scene. We will return to how this system works in Chapters 7 and 9. The practices of Classical Hollywood defined the conventions of filmmaking for a considerable time and still influence contemporary style in a number of ways. As we will see in upcoming chapters, this invisible technique, what Bordwell, Thompson and Staiger (1985) have called 'an excessively obvious cinema' (3) is an illusionistic practice with ideological ramifications. In concealing its own status as filmic fantasy, the Classical model also hides its ideological work. Film theory and criticism seek to interpret the ideological **subtexts** in films that claim to be just entertainment. On the other hand, alternative methods of filmmaking (explored in later chapters) often use **reflexivity** – a film's awareness of its own status as a film – to expose the process of production, or to break the illusion and make the ideological nature of film visible.

It is important to keep in mind the context of development and the basic conventions of Classical Hollywood practice, in order to effectively critique the limitations of this model. From this critique it is then possible to use the critical-practice approach to explore what is effective in this style, as well as to experiment with alternative forms of creative expression. Hollywood's method of production, with its strong division of labour, led to a particular process of creation: the stages of making a film that we will now survey. These stages need to be critiqued from their basis in an industrial division of labour but they are also, to some extent, a viable approach to film practice that can be adapted to alternative types of film.

The stages of making a film

It is quite possible that you are a film student who will soon be embarking on a creative project for the first time. You have an idea of what you want to make: maybe a spoof horror film or a music video for your garage band. You have developed a short script and a plan for how you are going to shoot the project. Then you call some of your friends to perform in the project, arrange to have a video camera, and maybe more friends to help out with the technicalities. You tell your friends to meet you at a certain a place, at a certain time. What you have done here is the same as most filmmakers do in arranging and planning to shoot a project. In the filmmaking business this stage is known as **preproduction**. Now, if you are lucky, all your friends have shown up and you can get the serious business underway. You shoot your short video with the video camera, which records the sound from the scene at the same time. Perhaps to make things look a bit better, you turn on extra lights, or move some lamps around the room. Maybe you shift the furniture to best suit the scene or bring in extra props that are needed for the action. You have your friends perform the scene and they interpret your idea. Setting up and shooting are parts of the **production** phase of the film. In the next phase, after everything is shot and your friends have gone home, you watch what you have created. If you are fortunate enough to have an editing program on your computer, you might capture the images and sounds from the camera and rearrange them, selecting the best shots and constructing the project from this. You may want to add some music or record an extra voice track to edit into what you have created, and put titles at the beginning or the end. This is the **postproduction** phase of a film. Now that you have created the 'film', you call all your friends again and invite them over to watch the final product. You might even make copies and give them to your friends or upload them to YouTube or Facebook; this is the **distribution** and **exhibition** phase.

Within the structures of the film industry, these are the phases of creation of a film. The production processes, and the roles that are required to perform them, are codified and clearly delineated. In **preproduction**, the preparation for filming takes place: the development of the idea, the writing of the script, the casting of the actors, the search for a location or the building of a set, the rehearsals and all the preparation for shooting. In this phase, the key personnel include the **screenwriter(s)** who works on the script, often through many drafts and revisions. The producers are also at work securing funding and making the necessary arrangements for production. One of the important functions of the preproduction stage is this acquisition of funding, as the size of the budget often defines how a film will be produced. Funding works differently for different types and levels of filmmaking. A studio-funded feature film, for example, would receive money based on the development of its script within standard studio practices, whereas independent filmmakers acquire funding by collecting sponsorships and investments. The **director** is involved in the process from this early stage, participating in the casting (supervised by a **casting director**) and having input in the search for and choice of locations (the job of the **location scouts**). During preproduction, the director also works with the **cinematographer** to break down the script into shots, which are then produced as a **storyboard**. Once the script and the storyboard are prepared, the **production manager** can then schedule the shoots, so that a plan is in place to film all the necessary scenes of the script, with the relevant cast, crew, equipment, **props**, costume and make-up all at the correct location at the scheduled time.

The production stage is perhaps the best known. It is when the cameras roll and sound is recorded; the action is captured on film. This includes elements we will study in detail in the first three chapters of Part III: **cinematography**, **mise-en-scène** and sound recording. The production crew works in teams, with the cinematographer supervising the camera operator and assistants, and the lighting crew. The **production designer** and the art crew are involved with all elements of design, from the construction of the set to the smallest details of the props. The sound team is responsible for production audio, choosing and placing microphones, recording and mixing sound at appropriate levels. Also on the production team is a **script supervisor**, who assures that all the necessary shots are taken and that continuity is maintained from shot to shot. The director oversees every part of production, and works particularly with the actors to interpret the script through the dialogue and performance. Finally, on a large-scale feature, there could also be a **second unit**, which is another production team that is scheduled to shoot scenes at different locations while the main unit continues working.

Once the shooting is completed and the sound recorded, a very large part of the process of making a film still has to be undertaken; the film enters the postproduction stage. The film is edited, the special effects are added, parts of the soundtrack are **dubbed**, the music is composed and recorded and the audio track mixed and all the extensive work done to bring the finished film together. In the last two chapters of Part III we will look at editing and music in more detail. Finally, the film is distributed to the cinemas, where the audience gets a chance to see it. This stage also includes the business of marketing, advertising, merchandizing and all the tricks of the trade that are used to bring in an audience.

The preceding description of the stages of film relates to both the large-scale industrial practices of the entertainment industry or the smaller-scale independent productions that imitate these models. These stages of filmmaking apply in different degrees to the various types of filmmaking. Smaller crews are often used for documentary, for example a production team of three, one person to operate the camera, one for sound and a director to oversee the production or to ask questions of interview subjects. Experimental filmmakers' work can be done in a variety of ways, from the individual practice of an artist such as Stan Brakhage, who we will study in Chapter 5, to a variety of crew and production methods. In general, however, an overlapping three-part stage of preparation, shooting and editing is a useful model for many types of practice.

Before we finish with the first chapter, let's see what is coming up later, and look at how the book takes on the task of introducing and exploring the critical practice of film.

How to use this book

The book is divided into four parts. Part I introduces the idea of 'critical practice'. This chapter has explored the integration of critical analysis with the creation and critique of film. The next chapter introduces motion picture, film and video technology: the way in which still images are transformed into moving images. As an extension of this idea, we will explore animation as it is a particularly apt illustration of this principle.

Part II examines different types of film in more depth. First we start with a detailed study of narrative film and how stories are constructed and developed in script form. This involves working with both the process of screenwriting, as well as the study of narrative structure and theory. The next two chapters continue with other non-narrative film forms: Chapter 4 introduces documentary conventions and Chapter 5 experimental film and the related areas of **Expanded Cinema** and **video art**.

Part III then breaks a film down into its different elements. Here we will analyze the creative use of film techniques; cinematography, mise-en-scène, sound, editing and music. This part of the book is structured around the process of making a film, introducing the elements of production first: cinematography, mise-en-scène and production sound. The next two chapters deal with aspects of postproduction: editing and music. There is also a distinction here between the study of sound and music, although both constitute parts of the auditory experience of a film (as cinematography and mise-en-scène are both part of the visual scheme). This is done in order to first introduce the possibilities of the sound environment of a film then to explore film music in some depth as a creative force, drawing on a distinct artistic practice with its own conventions, expectations and emotional impact.

Part IV develops further the critical-practice ideas that have underpinned previous chapters. Chapter 11 introduces writing as practice: presenting some of the ways of writing about film, including critical analysis, theoretical interpretation and creative reflection on your own practice. The book then concludes with a chapter offering concrete examples of successful critical/theoretical practitioners who embody the engagement between artistic creation and critical dialogue.

Each chapter begins with the learning objectives. These will guide you to the key points that will be covered and the aims you can achieve once you have read and engaged with the material. The chapter ends with summaries in the form of questions which will allow for discussion with peers, or for you to assess your understanding of the chapter. One goal of this book is to move beyond passive consumption, so that after reading each chapter there are exercises and experiments that allow you to take your knowledge one step further, by actually trying out some of the concepts presented. The exercises at the end of each chapter give you the opportunity to think critically as well as to explore filmmaking practice: things to think about and things to try. You can try these exercises on your own, or you can work on them in the context of a film studies education. Finally, the section 'Want to Learn More?' guides you to resources to deepen your knowledge and understanding of any given area.

Throughout the chapters there are a number of examples from various films. For the sake of consistency many of these films are the same. This means, for example, that when we study a scene from the classic Western *Stagecoach* (1939) for the ideology of camera position and technique in Chapter 6, we return to that scene again in Chapter 10 to integrate the study of music and see how different techniques work together to create various levels of meaning. The number of films selected as examples for study are purposely limited so as not to overwhelm any reader with a variety of films that incorporate different techniques. Instead there are fewer examples, enough to make up a reasonably achievable core of recommended films for viewing. This selection is representative of styles, eras and movements but does not constitute an overview of film art in any way. Other examples are equally valid, or may better exemplify film techniques or theoretical concepts. The hope is that after studying the topics, the engaged reader will apply the concepts learned when viewing other examples. To that end, there is a list of suggested further viewing at the end of each chapter.

Unlike most novels, a book like this is not meant to be read cover to cover. If you read it in the order it is presented, that's great, you will see how many of the ideas and concepts progressively build on each other. However, the book is also designed so that you can read it out of order and still follow the logic of the ideas being developed. To facilitate reading the book in this way, some words or ideas that may be new to you are in bold and defined in the glossary. There are also cross references in the text to the chapters where one idea will be elaborated on from a different perspective. There are many film studies classes at colleges and universities throughout the world and every instructor has a different way of presenting the material. The features in this book will hopefully facilitate reordering and presenting the various topics as necessary to accommodate different learning approaches.

Summary and key questions

As the starting point in your study of film, take this opportunity to check your understanding of the key ideas introduced.

- What is 'critical practice'? How does critical practice integrate production, criticism and theory?
- What are the distinguishing characteristics of the three types of film?
- How are genres of film defined and categorized?
- What are the key features of the conventions of Classical Hollywood? How are these conventions part of the ideological project of entertainment?
- What do the different phases of filmmaking involve?

Want to learn more?

Think about this ...

Film genres

Objective: To distinguish the different types and genres of film.

Choose a genre or style of filmmaking that you particularly enjoy; do you like action films, romances or comedies, etc.? What films are made in this style? What are the characteristics of this genre or style? What themes, character types and plot situations recur in this type of film? What stylistic elements define this genre?

Classical Hollywood

Objective: To recognize the characteristics of Classical Hollywood Cinema.

View a couple of examples of films from the Classical period of Hollywood. What aspects of style, structure and technique can you identify? How are they reflective of the time and place in which they were made?

Phases of creation of a film

Objective: To identify the different phases in the production of a film.

Think about the times and places you have been involved in the creation of visual media in the broadest possible way – still photography, photo albums, online picture sites, amateur video, etc. Having identified examples of your own media practice, think through how you went about the creation of this work. What were your phases of production? How did your working method relate to the standard practices of preproduction, production, postproduction, and distribution and exhibition?

Try this ...

Analysis of your own media work

Objective: To develop an appreciation of the 'critical-practice' approach to film.
You will need: A group of friends and somewhere to show them your work.

Using any of the media work that you have discovered in the last exercise, show that work to a group of friends. Take the opportunity to discuss your work and to solicit their reactions to it as an example of media communication. Have them compare your media practice to their own experiences of making media. What do you learn from how your media communicates with this audience?

Further reading

A good introduction to how theory and practice integrate is Mike Wayne's *Theorising Video Practice*. This book combines analysis of different parts of technique with examples drawn from student productions to explore how ideas can be put into practice in the experimental environment of a media studies education. An equally key text in this area is Jean-Pierre Geuens, *Film Production Theory*, which includes analysis of technique and a critique of conventional modes of practice. A more theoretical reading of the relation between theory and practice can be found in Noël Burch's *Theory of Film Practice*. For ongoing debates around the integration of theory with practice in both a professional and a higher educational context, *The Journal of Media Practice* includes a number of articles on the topic and keeps up to date on debates in both the theoretical and the creative fields.

There are a large number of theorists working in the area of genre studies, I will just mention a few of the most significant. Steve Neale's edited collection *Genre and Hollywood* is a good core introduction to the topic, as is Thomas Schatz's *The Genius of the System*. The conventions of Classical Hollywood are critically explored in numerous writings. Key texts include David Bordwell, Kristin Thompson and Janet Staiger, *The Classical Hollywood Cinema* on the formal aspects of Hollywood style and Richard Maltby, *Hollywood Cinema* on the critical and contextual elements of Hollywood.

To get a better sense of film production there are a number of technical guides that explore the filmmaking process from beginning to end. It is important to read these critically and to be aware of how they reproduce conventional ways of thinking about the industrial structures of filmmaking. Mike Wayne's *Theorising Video Practice* contains a useful chapter 'Art and Industry' which includes a critique of how technical texts are often steeped in certain ideological perspectives about filmmaking.

Films studied in this chapter

Annie Hall 1977 Woody Allen (director)
Austin Powers: International Man of Mystery 1997 Jay Roach (director)
Drag Me to Hell 2009 Sam Raimi (director)
Finding Nemo 2003 Andrew Stanton and Lee Unkrich (directors)
The Matrix 1999 Andy Wachowski and Larry Wachowski (directors)
Men in Black 1997 Barry Sonnenfeld (director)
The Player 1992 Robert Altman (director)
Stagecoach 1939 John Ford (director)
Star Wars 1977 George Lucas (director)
The Terminator 1984 James Cameron (director)
The Time Traveller's Wife 2009 Robert Schwentke (director)

Other examples to explore

Chapter 12 looks at the work of critical practitioners from a variety of different movements and styles of filmmaking. Any of the recommended viewing from there would serve as a strong introduction to critical practice. There are also numerous examples of Classical Hollywood, from a variety of genres, many suggested in later chapters. One particularly interesting film is *Sunset Boulevard* (1950 Billy Wilder director) that is set at the height of the Classical period and reflects some of the aspects of the style.

Motion Pictures

Learning objectives

After completing this chapter, you will be able to:

- Explore the operating principles of a camera and a projector;
- Define the distinctive features of film and video;
- Experiment with the principles and techniques of animation;
- Analyze and evaluate examples of the art of animation.

A darkened room

We often think of a camera as a complex piece of technology; after all, the latest digital cameras have so many features they can be intimidating. Despite all the fancy things you can do with today's cameras, the basic concepts behind how they operate are surprisingly simple. In fact, you can create a version of a film camera in its most basic form within an enclosed space with a small number of accessories. Let's try a quick experiment turning a 'darkened room' into a 'camera'. If you place a dark blind over the window of a room, with a small incision in it, you would produce the conditions to turn that room into a type of camera. Then, hold up a white surface to serve as a screen opposite the hole in the blind, and you will see an image of the world outside the window reflected on your screen. The image will be upside down, but you will have created a **camera obscura**. You can make your camera obscura more sophisticated by placing a **lens** in the space of the hole. This is a shaped piece of glass that will focus the light rays coming into the room and give you a clearer projected image.

The phrase 'camera obscura' comes from the Latin for 'darkened room', and it is from this phrase that we get the word 'camera'. The principles of physics that give us the camera obscura have been known for a long time, with experiments in the movement of light made by the Arabian scientist Alhazen in the tenth century. In sixteenth- and seventeenth-century Italy, camera obscuras became a form of public entertainment, while the Jesuit scholar, Athanasius Kircher explored their workings in his study on optics, *Ars Magna Lucis et Umbrae* (*The Great Art of Light and Shadow*) (Mannoni, 2000: 15–17). Today, camera obscuras are popular tourist attractions in various cities, such as the one in Edinburgh, Scotland, built in the 1850s and placed high up

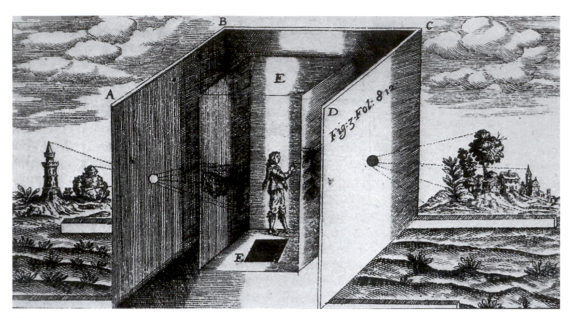

Figure 2.1 Camera obscura, Athanasius Kircher, 1646

on the castle hill. The room is dark, without windows, and the hole is in the ceiling. It has a movable periscope, with a series of lenses built inside, stretching up. The image is then projected onto a screen on the floor and the spectators can get a clear view of what is going on in the city below.

There is another simple piece of technology that will help show the next concept needed to create a moving-image camera. Bored students sometimes amuse themselves by drawing doodles on the corner of the pages of a book. Maybe you remember a time when you have drawn such a series of images, each drawing slightly different and each illustrating a moment within a sequence. So, when you flip the pages of the book you can watch as these still images combine to create motion: a ball bouncing or a stick figure running. These **flipbooks** are an amateur form of animation and they also demonstrate one of the basic principles on which film is based: film works through a series of still images combined to create motion.

Thus, a film camera captures a series of rapidly photographed still shots. Each of these shots is known as a **frame** of film. A standard film camera shoots 24 frames per second (**fps**), but this number can vary with different types of camera (video cameras range from 25–30 **fps**). Inside a camera, a complex operation is occurring repeatedly:

- A strip of film passes through the camera;
- A **shutter** opens to allow light on to the frame;
- The film pauses for 1/48th of a second;
- The shutter closes;
- The film moves on to the next frame and the cycle is repeated.

This process is known as **intermittent motion**. It can also be seen at work in mechanisms other than the motion-picture camera. In the nineteenth century, a number of devices and experiments, the forerunners to film technology, demonstrated the working of still images in motion. These included the **Zoetrope**, a cylindrical device built on a turning mechanism. The drum has a series of slits in it and the images are placed on a strip inside. The images are created on a cycle, ending where they begin. Thus, when you look at the Zoetrope turning you can see the continuous motion of the animated strip inside. In the Disney film *Tarzan* (1999) there is a scene with a Zoetrope. As Tarzan is exploring the world of his new human friends he looks into a Zoetrope and the shot transforms into his own movement through the jungle: making the link between this old-fashioned piece of technology and the animated film you are watching, both of which operate on the same principles of movement.

Motion-picture film is also based on the earlier invention and development of still photography, which took place throughout the nineteenth century. Key photographic precursors were the **series photography** experiments of Eadweard Muybridge and Étienne-Jules Marey. Series photography involved placing a group of still cameras in front of the path of a person or an animal in motion. As the person moved they tripped wires that activated the shutters of the camera taking a series of pictures of the subject's movement. These photographs could then be viewed sequentially to give the impression of a subject in motion. As an invention, series photography was looked upon as a scientific experiment: exploring the biology of human and animal motion. But it also gives us the first basic experiments in film and we can see how motion-picture photography grew out of these innovations.

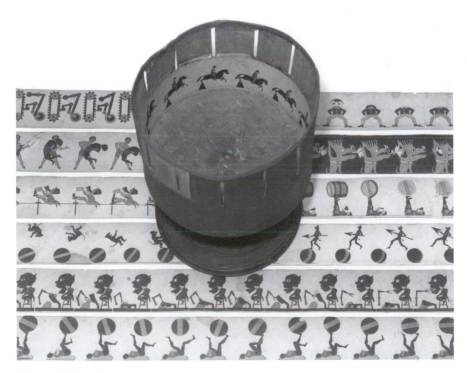

Figure 2.2   A Zoetrope

Figure 2.3 Series photography: *The Horse in Motion*, Eadweard Muybridge, 1878

So, before the invention of motion-picture film we have three separate processes that were identified and came together during this time: the camera obscura, intermittent motion (demonstrated by toys such as the Zoetrope) and photography. Each of these provides a necessary ingredient to the development of film. Thus, if we put the concept of intermittent motion together with the darkened room and photographic film we can imagine ourselves inside a working model of a camera.

- On the outside of the main chamber we have the lens: a series of optics that focus the light entering the camera.
- Then, we have the small hole through which the light enters; this is known as the **aperture**.
- In front of the aperture is the shutter, which opens and closes to allow the light to enter when necessary.
- Then we have the **film**, which moves through the camera and captures a still frame twenty-four times each second.
- A mechanism on each side of the film **gate** – where the film is held in front of the aperture – moves the film so that it can stop and start (intermittent motion).
- Finally, there are two **reels** on each side of the gate: the first to hold the **unexposed** film and the second to hold the film that has been **exposed** to the light and therefore contains the images.

This gives an idea of how moving images are captured on film. But how do these images get translated into the experience of watching a film in a cinema? Once the film has been exposed to the light it is then **processed** in a lab, before being edited into a final film. When it is finished it is projected onto a screen to be viewed by the audience. Thus, the next thing we need to understand about motion pictures is **projection**. The camera obscura is a model of a camera without the film, it also demonstrates projection as the fundamental principle of the cinema. The light entering the room passes through a lens and is focused onto the surface of the screen. In this way the camera obscura is a camera and a cinema in one. Projection allows for a large group of people to see a film at once, and is therefore a key ingredient in the cinematic experience.

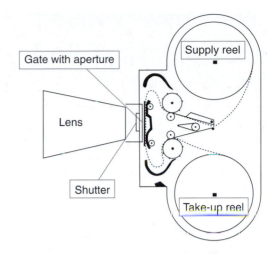

Figure 2.4   Camera

Film, however was not always projected; the motion-picture camera was invented before the projector, therefore allowing films to be created before there were the means to watch them in a large group. In 1893 the inventor Thomas Edison first started making short films with the **Kinetograph**, a camera developed in his workshop. These films were under a minute long, such as *Fred Ott's Sneeze* (1894), which was only a few seconds and was seen in a continuous loop. These short films were viewed on the complementary **Kinetoscope**, designed for screening the Kinetograph shorts. A single viewer stooped over the box and viewed the image through a peephole. Inside the machine, a strip of film was looped around a series of wheels in a box, passing a light source at the point where the film was viewed.

Before the development of cinema, forms of entertainment grew that were parallel to the camera obscura, demonstrating projection. These inventions include the **magic lantern**, a popular nineteenth-century toy, which was essentially a primitive form of slide projector. It used a light source and images painted onto glass slides, the light then passed through a lens that projected the images onto a screen. These inventions were used as parlour entertainment for those who could afford them. They were also popular with magicians in carnival sideshows and impressed the audiences with their trickery. For audiences watching before the invention of film, these tricks were interesting and entertaining. In *Tarzan* we also see this technology at work as Jane and her father show Tarzan images of the world outside the jungle by projecting them through a magic lantern.

The motion-picture projector is a development of the magic lantern and works similarly to a camera in reverse:

- The light source is inside the body of the projector as a bright bulb is placed behind the gate where the film passes through;
- The film passes the gate, as it does with the camera, through intermittent motion;
- There is a shutter in front of the film that opens and closes;
- Allowing the light to pass through the aperture;

Figure 2.5 *Fred Ott's Sneeze*, W. L. K. Dickson, 1894

Figure 2.6 Thomas Edison's Kinetoscope

- Outside the body of the projector is a lens. In this case the lens enlarges the image;
- So that it shines onto the screen.

The simultaneous development of both the means for photographing the film image and the process of projection of that image, allowed for the birth of cinema as the spectacle we know today. This all came together in the last decade of the nineteenth century. Some of the earliest projected films were the by the French brothers Louis and Auguste Lumière, who showed their first films at a public screening in 1895. Unlike the Edison Kinetoscope, these films were projected on a screen for an audience and were short records of a moment in time, for example *Leaving the Lumière Factory* (1895).

Now that we have seen how film developed and some of its fundamental principles, let's clarify the differences between film and the related technology of digital video.

Film and digital video

So far we have been discussing the development and workings of film technology, we will now expand our attention to look at the related area of video. For your own critical practice you are more likely to use video technology than film, mostly due to cost and availability. Although they are often used interchangeably today, the terms 'film' and 'video' or 'DV' refer to very specific things. It is important to understand clearly the differences between them, as this is key to fully appreciating the growth and change in contemporary technology as film and digital video become increasingly convergent.

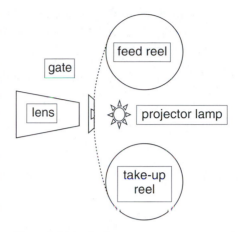

Figure 2.7   Projector

Film is created through a photochemical process, light enters the body of a camera through the lens and makes contact with the film. The film is composed of light-sensitive chemicals placed on a plastic coating. The chemicals create an imprint that is then processed to give us an image. Processing takes place in a laboratory where the exposed film is treated with another series of chemicals. The processed film is then projected back in the way described in the previous section. Film comes in different types, based on the width of the filmstrip. These are known as the different **gauges** of film:

- **8mm** is the smallest size and was traditionally used for home movies or for artistic filmmaking;
- **16mm** is still used in an educational context, and was formerly popular for documentary and television production;

Figure 2.8   *Leaving the Lumière Factory*, Louis Lumière, 1895

- **35mm** is the professional standard for feature-film production;
- **70mm** is a large-gauge format that is sometimes used to produce film with a particularly clear and detailed image;
- **Imax** is a specialized large-gauge format, creating the most detailed and large-scale image. It is screened in Imax cinemas equipped with the right types of projector and screen.

With video, the process starts at the same place: light enters the camera through the lens. Thus, working with video involves understanding the same principles as film in relation to exposure and the use of the lens. Next, a computer chip converts the light into electrical impulses that are recorded as digital signals on the videotape or hard disk inside the camera. Here there is a series of computer chips known as **CCDs** (older **analogue** cameras used **tubes**). A camera can work with either one or three CCDs. One CCD converts all colours of the spectrum of light into a digital signal, whereas a higher-quality three-CCD camera converts the light into three basic colour groups: red, green and blue. Unlike film, video needs no processing so you can see the image as you shoot it. Video is cheaper to create and requires less technical expertise; at its simplest video can be shot by anyone who has the necessary equipment. The high-end video equipment used by professionals, does, however, require skills and training and can be both expensive and complex to operate. Digital video is very versatile in the many ways in which it is viewed. It can be projected on video projectors, or converted to film and projected that way, it can be watched on television, burned to **DVD**, uploaded and downloaded onto a computer, viewed on the internet or transmitted over a mobile phone.

Like film, video has been available in different formats, with a wide variety changing over the years, some becoming obsolete as higher-quality formats have taken over. Videotape was introduced in the 1950s, as an experimental form of the 1940s development of television. The earliest videotape was two inches wide (known as **two-inch quad**), placed on open reels rather than in an enclosed cassette, and because of its relative expense it was used mainly by television professionals in studio settings. It wasn't until the introduction of portable video decks such as the Sony **Portapak** in 1965 that video became technologically sophisticated enough to be used outside the studio. In 1971 Sony introduced the **Umatic** format, the first cassette-based videotape. Umatic tape was a portable and accessible type of video. It became popular for electronic news gathering (**ENG**) and accessible to video artists. The development of videotape over the following years featured an increase in accessibility, making video media available to different communities. In Chapter 5 we will touch on how video was adopted by artists as well as by political activists who employed video as a tool to disseminate their messages. In the late 1970s video became commercially available to the home user with the introduction of the **VHS** format by JVC and the **Betamax** format by Sony. Both of these formats fought for the market share, with VHS finally dominating as it was able to increase the recording length of the tape. Part of video's complex history, emerging from an international growth of television, gave rise to three distinct technical systems of television playback within the regions of the world. These systems are based on the number of **frames per second (fps)** and how the playback functions scan the image onto a television monitor. In North America the system is **NTSC** (approximately 30 fps), in most of Europe the system is **PAL** (25 fps) and in France, Russia and much of Africa the system is **SECAM** (25 fps).

Analogue video dominated from the 1960s until the mid-1990s, when a variety of **digital video (DV)** formats became more common. Early digital technology was introduced in the 1980s, but was expensive, experimental and restricted to professional use. The introduction of DV tapes in 1995, and the cheaper, more readily available **MiniDV** format, standardized the digital-video format. These formats produce a higher-quality image at a cheaper price, and have levelled the market between professional and consumer products and productions. Today there is an increasing switchover to **high definition** (**HD**) video and television and a move to hard-disk storage and away from tape-based formats. HD is being increasingly used in professional situations where film once predominated and hard-disk storage simplifies the editing process.

Video has a separate history and trajectory from the development of film, and it is important to understand where the differences and convergences lie. Video allows for a greater freedom as it is a cheaper medium, requiring less-specialized technical knowledge to operate. It also provides immediate results and doesn't involve a processing laboratory. Videotape also allows for longer periods of shooting to occur; most tapes run for an hour rather than the four minutes of a **Super 8** reel or the ten minutes of a 400-foot reel of 16mm. This changes the way camera operators think about shooting. With film, more planning and discipline is needed; with video, it is easier to experiment and let the camera run without as much care and thought to execution. Film is expensive and mistakes are costly, whereas videotape can run continuously at little expense and mistakes can be taped over. This allows taping to occur over longer stretches of time and the possibility of continuous surveillance. Although video is a less expensive format than film, it is constantly changing and upgrading, so that the cameras and tapes in use now will be replaced by more sophisticated models in the next year or so. Thus, keeping up to date with video requires an ongoing investment in technology. Finally, as video is an electronic medium, it quickly became easy to affect the image with a manipulation of the digital signal. As video editing developed, video effects, often distinct from the types of special effects used in film, were included in even the most basic systems. With video editing, **dissolves** and **fades** could be achieved by this basic system, whereas film editing required a laboratory.

To continue with our discussion of the basics of film and video technology, let's look at the area of animation. The process of creating animated films most clearly illustrates the principles of how still images become movement.

Animation

Although all films are based on the same principle of intermittent motion, it is perhaps the filmmaker working within the tradition of animation, who is most conscious of how still images are turned into motion. The term 'animation' covers a variety of styles, but they are all linked by the process of taking the inanimate (from drawn film and clay figures to computer-generated art) and making it move. As we saw earlier, the **flipbook** is a primitive example of animation: a series of individual drawings combined to create moving images. Animated film takes this a step further; the still images are filmed in a sequence, and then projected back. But animation is not limited to drawn art, the same procedure can be used to move different types of objects; figure animation can bring to life things such as traditional puppet theatre or set everyday objects in motion. Further, animation covers a wide range of styles and practices. Although you may be familiar with the styles of Pixar, Disney or Ghibli, you will see from the following examples that animation can use many different experimental and alternative techniques.

One of the reasons for these different styles is the mode of production; animators range from individual artists working at home, to large studio productions with thousands of workers.

Animation can be created from the simplest of materials, given the right combination of artistic dedication and time. On the other hand, many animated features involve the participation of very large crews of experts and investment in expensive equipment. This variety of practices makes animation an exciting field of practice and study. In the discussion that follows, we will look at some basic principles and examine particular styles, from cameraless through traditional **cel** and figure, to state-of-the-art computer animation.

Cameraless animation

Cameraless animation is a style of filmmaking that is accomplished by drawing directly onto the film itself. With this technique, the filmmaker takes **clear leader** – a strip of clear plastic film that is usually used at the beginning and end of a reel – and draws or paints directly onto it. When projected back, the film appears as animated and often has an intensely artistic feel. A good example of an animation specialist who worked with the cameraless style was Norman McLaren. His film *Begone Dull Care* was made in Canada in 1949 by painting the images onto the strip of clear film. The film used no photographic process at all, projecting the light and colour of a painting. The process of creating a film like this is intense. Every frame is painted individually and, remember, it takes twenty-four frames to make up a second of finished film. In addition, all the elements of the painted film are synchronized to the music, which also takes careful planning and execution. The filmmaker's intention is to combine the arts of painting and music into a film that is literally a painting moving through time. (Another example of cameraless animation by the experimental filmmaker, Stan Brakhage, is discussed in Chapter 5.) As we progress from cameraless animation we can see how painting and drawing, and the photographic process, combine to create the classics of traditional animation.

Cel animation

Today we are all familiar with computer animation from films like *Finding Nemo* and *Up* (2009). Yet, this innovation is a fairly recent development in animation history. It is only since the mid-1990s that mainstream, feature-length, computer-animated films have been made. Even today, computer animation stands as only one technique in a variety of styles that are still used. In a later section we will examine computer animation more closely and see how it is a development from the principles and artistry of traditional animation. The term 'traditional animation' generally refers to a drawn cartoon style. The most prominent and well-known examples of this are the films of the Disney Studio. In the 1930s and 1940s, the Disney Studio, under its founder Walt Disney, institutionalized a classical style of animation backed by the power of the studio system and steeped in the industrial practices of Hollywood (discussed in Chapter 1). Classical Disney animation is created through a complex process that uses a clear division of labour and relies on a financial system that can support expensive equipment and experimentation with new technologies.

As we have seen, animation is created through the combination of still images projected as motion. To better understand how this works, let's break the animation process down into its simplest steps.

- First, the artist creates a series of drawn images tracing some movement incrementally between each drawing, similar to a flipbook;

Figure 2.9   Norman McClaren working on *Fiddle-de-dee*

- Second, the camera sequentially captures a **frame** or a series of frames of each of the images;
- When the film is projected back, the drawn figures appear to move.

This basic idea can be demonstrated by an early example of an animated film. One of the first artists to experiment with making still images into motion pictures was Winsor McCay. In 1914 he produced the short *Gertie the Dinosaur*, which was a simple, line-drawn animation; the principal figures move – Gertie and the other creatures she fights – while the background remains still. This film was created by the artist drawing these individual pictures, each charting a slightly different position in the sequence. This technique of animation is known as **line animation**, and is a style that has been adopted by other independent animators ever since. This form of animation is the type you are most likely to try as a beginner: although it is time-consuming it is relatively simple and can be executed with minimal equipment, but can also produce excellent results. In the more complex films of the classical Disney style, line animation is known as a **pencil test** and is a stage in a longer process. Animators preparing a complex **cel-animated** film will first produce drawings to serve as guidelines for the fully colourized images.

Cel animation developed as a labour-saving method. Rather than having to draw and redraw all elements of each area, the animated images are divided into different levels representing background and foreground elements. Cels are clear sheets of acetate on which images are drawn (originally they were made out of **celluloid**, the origin of their name). They are lit from below and the

Figure 2.10   *Gertie the Dinosaur*, Winsor McCay, 1914

camera is placed above to capture the images. Each cel can contain a different set of images that are layered one on top of the other. For example, in the animated feature *Bambi* (1942), a cel would be created for the background forest, and another layer for the main figure of the deer Bambi in front. As Bambi moves, only the top layer of the cel need be changed for the next frame in the sequence. Thus, parts of the background that are not moving at any given moment can use the same cel with changes made to the cel on the top. This is just a starting point in a complex system, however, as there is often more movement involved. For example, as Bambi walks through the forest, the background also changes. So there are two levels of action occurring: Bambi is walking and the background appears to be passing. In order to accomplish this, the animator would have the background-image cel on a roll that would be shifted to the side every frame, at the same time as the front cel is changed.

During the late 1930s when *Bambi* was in production, the Disney Studio developed a technique to enhance the visual style of its animation. This is the use of the **multi-plane camera**, which allows for creating and shooting backgrounds to give them a three-dimensional appearance. The background is divided onto several planes each painted onto separate cels placed on glass. These cels can then be moved towards, and away from the camera at different intervals, giving the background image an appearance of depth. If you watch the opening scene of *Bambi*, you can see this process in action, as the camera appears to move through the forest.

Aside from the time-consuming and complex work of preparing and animating cels, animators also have a couple of challenges and techniques they need to master in order to create satisfactory work. The first of these is calculating and reproducing movement, and the second is synchronizing speech to the animated cels. Part of the animator's job is to understand how the drawn images will translate into motion. If the difference between one image and the next is too great, the movement will not appear smooth and the figure's motion will be jerky. But the difference of movement also governs the speed of the figure's action. Thus, if the change is too small, the movement may be too slow. Another factor in movement is how many frames of the film are taken: too many frames will appear slow and too few will speed up the movement more than is necessary. Animation is a careful art that requires repeated calculations and testing to produce the desired effect. Another challenge for animators is to create convincing facial movement that coordinates with the patterns of the character's speech. In the process of producing animation, the actors generally pre-record the dialogue from the script and the animators synchronize the movement of the mouth to the sound. Many animators compare the process of animating their characters to acting. In a sense this is true, as they have to reproduce convincing facial movements and make the animation clearly

Figure 2.11   Disney multi-plane camera used in the production of *Bambi*, 1942

coordinate with the way in which the actors have read their lines. In facing and overcoming the challenges of animation, the creators of *Bambi* produced a complex film that combines the movement and actions of animals with the caricature and impersonation of aspects of humans, in particular speech and facial expression. This film relies on **anthropomorphism**, the imitation of human characteristics by animals in the story. The very expressiveness of the animals could not have been accomplished as effectively with live-action film techniques.

Bambi also uses **Expressionistic** techniques. This means that the aim of the style is not to reproduce the natural world but to explore and represent the emotional world of the characters.

Figure 2.12   *Bambi*, David Hand, 1942

The misty fantastical backgrounds are not painted in a **realistic** style, but evoke the feeling of the romanticized environment of the forest. One particular scene shows the expression of the emotional action rather than realistic representation. In the spring, when Bambi is a young, growing deer he fights another deer over the doe Feline. As Bambi starts the fight, the colour and light of the scene shifts to high-contrast bright red, emphasizing the emotions of the characters rather than the action. This is effectively done and highlights the artistic, painterly nature of the film.

Figure animation

Three-dimensional figures can be animated in the same way as two-dimensional drawings. Artists involved in figure animation create their figures, shoot a small number of frames, then move the characters slightly, shoot the same number of frames and repeat the cycle. This process is known as **stop motion**. Like other forms of animation, it is a time-consuming process, moving a few frames many times to reach the necessary twenty-four to create a second of film. As these animation techniques can make anything move, the possibilities are endless, with household objects and a video camera with single-frame operation, figure animation can be incorporated into a basic student project. While some animation relies on making simple everyday objects move, more complex styles can create complete narrative worlds. Let's look at two specific examples of three-dimensional animation: puppet animation and **claymation**.

In this context, a puppet is a freestanding three-dimensional figure that can be placed in a variety of positions. A puppet is constructed by first building an **armature**, which is a metal

Figure 2.13 *The Corpse Bride*, Tim Burton, 2005

skeletal form with movable body joints. The armature is then covered with a material, for example, **foam latex**, which produces the body's shape, finally, it is costumed. An example of puppet animation is *The Corpse Bride* (2005). In *The Corpse Bride* the armature is a carefully articulated metal body with ball joints in the neck for full movement and hinges for the knees and ankles. The armature is then covered in moulded foam latex, coloured and costumed in fabric. It took a full three years to create the puppets for this film from their conception to the final completed product, ready to be animated. The puppeteers also made multiple copies for different scenes.

One of the challenges of the design of these specific puppets was their shape, as the characters are tall and thin with small feet. This makes it difficult to create an armature that would support the weight while giving the character a full range of movement. Another challenge is to create puppets with a full range of facial expressions and a method of changing those expressions easily and accurately throughout the process of filming. In an interview with Ron Barbagallo, puppet-maker Graham Maiden describes how this was done by creating a series of gears within the heads of each puppet.

> We managed to get a gearing system the size of a small orange and have it accessible through the back of the head. Paddles and strings with fixing points within the skin were attached to the gearing system. This allowed us to manipulate the puppet's expressions. The puppet of

Victoria, for example, has a hole in her bow in her hair and also in her ears, as does Corpse Bride and Victor. You access the gearing system with an Allen key and turn the gears that open and close her mouth, that way they can make her smile or pout. The heads also have paddles in them to make the eyebrow raise or fall so they can either look surprised, angry or serious. (Barbagallo, 2005)

Following the building of the armature and the features of the puppet, the next stage is to create a costume that will cover the figures. As with the other parts of the puppet, the costumes need to be able to both move incrementally and hold their shape while the camera films each frame. This proved particularly difficult for the character of the Corpse Bride as her flowing wedding dress and veil blows in the breeze. To design and animate this puppet, the makers had to work with wired fabric that would allow the veil to move and create mechanisms that would reproduce the action of the wind on the fabric. All of these elements combined must also maintain **continuity** between the different versions of the characters used for various scenes.

As they are freestanding, three-dimensional beings, puppets can suggest a strong sense of character. The puppet designers and the animators work together to give the characters the appearance of life. Similarly, as they are not characters with the limitations of human appearance they can more easily take on aspects of caricature such as exaggerated features and expressions. Puppet characters are intrinsically non-naturalistic and their external appearances can represent their internal states of mind. For example, in *The Corpse Bride* the characters are easily identifiable by shape and distinct in their characteristics. Their appearance represents their role in the story and their thoughts. This style works for the fantasy genre of the film. The world of *The Corpse Bride* shows a vision of life after death and creates a fantastic world of the dead that is more lively and colourful than the drab world of the living.

Another form of figure animation is known as clay animation, which is generally just contracted to the term claymation. This is the creation of animated figures out of a malleable substance, rarely actual clay, more frequently plasticine. This is a synthetic material that can be modelled into different shapes and is more flexible than clay. This allows the animators to make small, subtle changes to the plasticine figures during the process of animation. The works of animation artists at the Aardman studios, responsible for the feature *Wallace and Gromit in The Curse of the Were-Rabbit* (2005) is one of the most popular examples of claymation. Using plasticine figures, the filmmakers are able to create an entire world of characters.

Like the puppets of *The Corpse Bride*, these claymation characters are built over an armature, although in this case a simpler wire frame as the plasticine is more easily manipulated than the foam latex of the puppets. The plasticine figures perhaps appear less slick and polished than the puppets, but this suits the comic genre, in contrast to the fantasy world of *The Corpse Bride*. Yet, as with the puppets, the plasticine figures are three-dimensional

Figure 2.14   *Wallace and Gromit in The Curse of the Were-Rabbit*, Nick Park and Steve Box, 2005

and exhibit a strong sense of character; Wallace and Gromit are easily identifiable and can carry the story across a number of films and a variety of situations. On the one hand, the style is more naturalistic than *The Corpse Bride*, the human characters are believable everyday people, but on the other hand, the humour is a broad physical manipulation of what is possible with live-action filmmaking.

Wallace and Gromit in The Curse of the Were-Rabbit has similar anthropomorphic characteristics to *Bambi*. The human characters carry the story forward, but the animals, without any dialogue, show a variety of emotions and are placed in different situations for dramatic effect. Although they are not principal characters, the rabbits have facial expressions that give them identities and show them to be individuals. The character of the dog, Gromit, is important in the story and he is animated in a more complex style than the rabbits. Not only does Gromit not speak, he also appears not to have a mouth. Gromit's silence is contrasted with the volubility of Wallace (Peter Sallis) who has a distinct vocal style and memorable catchphrases. Gromit's character is created through his physical presence, how he is animated. He communicates through movement and facial expression. In particular, the subtle movements of his eyebrows give the impression of what he is thinking and feeling at any given moment and how he is reacting to what is happening around him.

Computer animation

Computer animation works on the same principles of intermittent motion as traditional and stop motion, but the difference is in how the image is created: generated on a computer rather than painted or sculpted. Computer animation can be an expensive and sophisticated business, the high-quality images needed to produce a feature film require large amounts of computer memory and storage. The process is also very time-consuming as the computer can take hours to render any given effect or change in the image. For all its complications, computer animation is an exciting area as the technology is constantly growing and changing, allowing for more interesting work and expanding creativity.

In film today, you can see three distinct uses of computer animation:

- First, traditional animation is now assisted by computers, making for a hybrid style that capitalizes on the best of both traditional and computer techniques;
- Second, there is an increasing number of animated features that are created entirely on the computer;
- Third, there is the growing use of **CGI** (computer-generated images) that are incorporated as special effects into live-action feature films.

We will briefly look at each of these areas in turn.

Computers are used within traditional animation to speed up the process and to allow for additional effects. For example, computer imaging can create and fill in backgrounds or simulate parts of the animated figure's movements. This allows for more complex use of space and three-dimensionality than traditional techniques. The Disney feature, *Tarzan* (1999), is a good example of the combination of computer techniques with the traditional drawn style. It uses the software program **Deep Canvas** to create the three-dimensional background that Tarzan moves through in the jungle. In a sense, it is an advanced digital version of Disney's old fashioned multi-plane camera discussed earlier. Unlike the three-dimensional scenes in *Bambi*, these environments are complex and the characters can move through the space with fluidity. The animators create a three-dimensional space blocked out with the shapes of the trees. The animator makes a rough version of the character's movement, which is then painted by artists aided by the computer. When the process is complete, Tarzan slides down and around the trees of the jungle, which appear as a fully three-dimensional world. If you compare this scene with the opening of *Bambi*, you can see how far computer-aided technology has changed the three-dimensionality of animation.

Figure 2.15   *Tarzan*, Chris Buck and Kevin Lima, 1999

Computer animation can assist traditional animation, but it is also a technique in its own right. Since the mid-1990s, with such films as *Toy Story* (1995), feature films have been made entirely on computer. This technique involves executing the design of the animated figures entirely through graphics programs and then animating their movement. Animation programs take the figures and mark them with a variety of points that are then manipulated to create the different movements. *Finding Nemo* is a fully computer-animated film that tells the story of a lost fish, and his father's search for him. Like many of the other animation features we have discussed, this film creates a story world that would not be possible in live-action filmmaking. The underwater world can come to life and the fish characters can take on human emotions and actions. The creation of these characters is a lengthy process. First, they are designed by artists who copy their shape and general appearance from actual fish. Then, they are given human characteristics and features, so that they can talk and show recognizable facial expressions and emotional states not associated with fish. Part of the process of design involves sculpted models that can be used to explore the characters' three-dimensional shapes. They are then sketched into computer graphic form where they can be animated for movement.

The background environment is a vital element of this film. Using three-dimensional animation techniques the fish can swim through the underwater world. In addition, the background graphics are given the texture and movement of the water and the subtle shading and colouring of the light as it permeates the sea from above. The computer programs allow for the creation of this complex world more freely than would be possible with traditional animation techniques and that would be impossible in live-action filmmaking.

Techniques of computer animation are also the basis of CGI, the incorporation of computer-generated images into a live-action film. Computer effects have been used since the 1970s, but in the last ten years they have

Figure 2.16   *Finding Nemo*, Andrew Stanton and Lee Unkrich, 2003

Figure 2.17 Andy Serkis as Gollum in *The Lord of the Rings: The Two Towers*, Peter Jackson, 2002

become more common. Now, technology can create sophisticated effects, which are constantly being improved and techniques which were once prohibitively expensive are now employed widely across different types of film and television. *The Lord of the Rings: The Two Towers* (2002), for example, uses CGI characters with convincing results. In particular, Gollum is an example of a CGI character created through a combination of techniques. First, the film is shot in a conventional live-action manner, with the actor Andy Serkis performing the role of Gollum. He is dressed in a plain bodysuit that covers him completely. This means that while shooting he can interact with the other actors on the set, creating more convincing performances. The shot footage of the actor in the scene is known as an **animation reference**. It serves to guide the animators as they build the CGI character. When the film is transferred to computer, the actor can be removed from the image and the CGI character constructed over him. The film also employs a technique known as **motion capture**. This is when an actor performs the role of the character with **motion points** on their face and costume. The image is then recorded using video cameras at all different angles. The actor's movements are then captured onto the computer and can be utilized to help create convincing movement for the CGI character. Ultimately, it is the combination of the shot footage, the animation reference and the motion-capture movements of the actor, that create the complexity of the CGI Gollum as he interacts with the other characters on the screen.

Summary and key questions

Understanding some of the basic principles of film and video production is the first stage in an appreciation of the art of cinema. Before you continue on to explore the styles and techniques of filmmaking, check your comprehension of some of these core concepts.

- What is intermittent motion and how does it work?
- What elements of the camera obscura are models for a working film camera?
- What are the distinctive attributes of film, video and digital technology?

Animation techniques produce a variety of effects in a film. When looking at an animated film you need to ask what type of techniques were used in its creation. You also need to ask if these techniques effectively convey the atmosphere the film is trying to create. When planning to make an animated project, you also need to make informed choices about the styles and techniques you wish to adopt.

- What type of animation technique is being used in a film you are studying? Or, what type of animation technique do you want to employ in a project that you are working on?
  - o Cameraless
  - o Cel
  - o Figure
  - o Computer
- How are these techniques effective in communicating the story?
- Could they be as effectively created through other means?

Want to learn more?

Think about this ...

How did they do that? Examining animation techniques

Objective: To analyze and evaluate examples of the art of animation.

Think about some of your favourite animation films. What techniques do they use – are they cameraless, figure, cel or computer animation? Do you have a preference for a particular style? What about that style do you find effective? Does the style of animation suit the subject or the story? Can you imagine the film made in a different style? How would that change the nature of the film?

Try this ...

Camera obscura

> Objective: To explore the operating principles of a camera and a projector.
> You will need: A room that can be darkened completely and a white sheet of cardboard for a screen.

If you have the necessary conditions to darken a room completely, you can follow the instructions at the start of this chapter and create your own camera obscura. Can you get the image from outside to successfully project onto your screen?

Flipbook animation

> Objective: To experiment with the principles of animation.
> You will need: A small, unruled pad of white paper and pencils.

For this exercise it is best to start on the last page of the note pad and do the last drawing, then as you progress the previous drawing will be visible through the paper and can guide you in creating the next image in the sequence. Use this experiment to explore motion and perception. Make the changes in the images incremental, but noticeable. Through this exercise you will be able to study motion and how small changes can affect how the image appears to move. You will also learn just how labour-intensive the process of animation can be.

Basic figure animation

> Objective: To experiment with the techniques of animation.
> You will need: A film or video camera, one with single-frame advance would be best.

Using the concepts studied in the chapter, try your hand at animation techniques, making an inanimate object move. Set the object in the location you want to use, place the camera on a tripod, advance it by a few frames at a time (if your camera does not have this option try turning the record button on and off quickly), then move the object slightly and repeat the process. From this you should learn a lot about the complexities of animation.

Further reading

Understanding film and video technology is an important prerequisite to using it effectively or to critically analyzing film. A good introduction to some of the ideas that prefigure the development of film and video technology is Laurent Mannoni's *The Great Art of Light and Shadow*. Also interesting for a theoretical perspective on film technology is Jacques Aumont's *The Image*. For further information on the technological aspects of film, see Edward Pincus and Steven Ascher, *The*

Filmmaker's Handbook and for video technology, see Gerald Millerson and Jim Owens, *The Video Production Handbook* or Robert Musburger, *Single Camera Video Production*. As with all technically based texts, these should be read critically, with an awareness of the conventions that they consider.

As the chapter suggests, animation is an area of film practice with a long history. There are numerous good introductory guides to animation techniques, for example, Kit Laybourne, *The Animation Book* or Mary Murphy, *Get Started in Animation*. There is also a growing field of scholarship in animation studies. Important in this area is Paul Wells, *Re-imagining Animation*, Maureen Furness, *The Animation Bible* or Jayne Pilling, *A Reader in Animation Studies*. For a critical take on the work of the Disney Studio, see Eric Smoodin, *Disney Discourse* or Eleanor Byrne and Martin McQuillan, *Deconstructing Disney*.

Films studied in this chapter

Bambi 1942 David Hand (director)
Begone Dull Care 1949 Norman McLaren (director)
The Corpse Bride 2005 Tim Burton (director)
Finding Nemo 2003 Andrew Stanton and Lee Unkrich (directors)
Fred Ott's Sneeze 1894 William L. K. Dickson (director)
Gertie the Dinosaur 1914 Winsor McCay (director)
Leaving the Lumière Factory 1895 Louis Lumière (director)
The Lord of the Rings: The Two Towers 2002 Peter Jackson (director)
Tarzan 1999 Chris Buck and Kevin Lima (directors)
Toy Story 1995 John Lasseter (director)
Up (2009) Peter Docter and Bob Peterson (directors)
Wallace and Gromit in The Curse of the Were-Rabbit 2005 Nick Park and Steve Box (directors)

Other examples to explore

Animation is a wide and varying area of study. Any of the classic animations from the Disney Studio make interesting additional viewing, as do the recent films made with computer-based techniques. In addition to the examples described in this chapter Japanese animation is important. Of particular interest is the work of the Ghibli studio, such as *Spirited Away* (2001 Hayao Miyazaki director) or *Princess Mononoke* (1997 Hayao Miyazaki director). A more experimental strand of animation comes from the National Film Board of Canada which often produces interesting short animations that challenge conventional techniques and expectations. More information about this work can be found on their website: www.nfb.ca.

PART II

Film Form

Narrative Film

Learning objectives

After completing this chapter, you will be able to:

- Analyze the structure of a narrative;
- Apply the concepts of narrative structure to the development of a short script;
- Render a visual representation of a short narrative in the form of a storyboard;
- Apply the basic concepts of narrative theory to the analysis of a film.

Telling stories

Stories are vital to how people communicate. Not only do we watch them for entertainment in movies and on television or read them in books, many of the ways we receive information about the world is through a narrative form. We listen to and tell stories in our daily life; when you go for a weekend to visit family or friends, you describe what is going on in your life by telling them stories and, in turn, listen to the stories that they tell you. Stories are so much part of our daily life that we take them for granted, and we are not always aware how they can be carefully structured through the process of screenwriting. Yet, even as we tell the short stories of our lives to our friends, we add structures: a beginning, middle and end, connecting unconnected events to make patterns, exaggerating certain moments to heighten the drama, and leaving out details we think are irrelevant.

This chapter explores how stories are created through the conventions of fiction films. In the first section we will examine the way that stories are structured, moving on to consider how a writer works to bring their vision to the screen. Then, we will explore some of the elements of the story: how stories move through time and the role of the narrator, the person or persons who are telling the story. While working with the conventions of narrative theory we will keep in mind a critical-practice approach to narrative form. This involves understanding and critiquing the conventions and structures of narrative practice and exploring alternative storytelling styles.

Narrative structure

Many writers of stories acknowledge a very simple and basic structure for their work: a story has a beginning, a middle and an end. Thinking about narrative this way has a long tradition; the Greek philosopher Aristotle introduced this idea in his *Poetics* in the third century BC. Similarly, the twentieth-century narrative theorist Tzvetan Todorov describes a plot structure which is divided into three states:

> The minimal complete plot consists in the passage from one equilibrium to another. An 'ideal' narrative begins with a stable situation which is disturbed by some power or force. There results a state of disequilibrium; by action of a force directed in the opposite direction, the equilibrium is re-established; the second equilibrium is similar to the first but the two are never identical. (Todorov, 1977: 111)

Todorov's idea can be applied to fiction film: at the start things are in a stable situation (equilibrium); in the course of the film something disrupts this stability, producing the second phase of the plot (disequilibrium); finally, the action of the film resolves the conflict and brings us to the third state (new equilibrium).

Equilibrium » (disruption) » Disequilibrium » (resolution) » New equilibrium

For a screenwriter, this structure can be a way to start to develop a script. The principles can also be applied when analyzing examples; this is how it would relate to *The Lord of the Rings* trilogy (2001–3):

- Frodo (Elijah Wood) lives happily in the Shire: equilibrium;
- He inherits the Ring, which is discovered to be a manifestation of the evil Lord Sauron: disruption;
- He runs from the Shire on many adventures, as the chaos of war ensues: disequilibrium;
- The war reaches a climax as Frodo faces Mount Doom: resolution;
- Middle Earth is returned to peace, but Frodo has to leave: new equilibrium.

From the idea of the three-part structure there has developed a convention in the writing of a narrative script, called the **three-act structure**. This structuring device is taught in many books on screenwriting and you can analyze fiction films by applying this method. The three-act structure elaborates on the basic beginning, middle, ending idea, with certain types of action expected at certain points in the story. Some screenwriting manuals, such as Syd Field's *The Screenplay*, have even broken this down so far as to suggest page lengths for each section of a script. They also suggest that certain types of action should occur within each act and at the break of each act. This is the way a conventional screenwriter draws us into the world of a film, by using structure and form to create expectations of action and then fulfilling or undermining those expectations.

Let's first look at the basic three-act structure, before exploring some of its limitations and some possible alternatives. From this basic concept, we can see how far to apply this generalization to the process of screenwriting, before it becomes a restricting and reductive formula.

The three-act structure

Act 1

In the first act of a three-act film a number of different things happen that set up the story and prepare us for what is to come. First, we are introduced to the main characters, as well as the location or setting in which the characters live or start their journeys. Act 1 also initiates the principal conflict. This is achieved through an action or a character that is the agent of change: described as a **catalyst**. Act 1 sets the scene, but also has to fill in any back-story or information that the audience might need, in order to understand what is to follow; this is known as the **exposition**. Writers and filmmakers are often very clever in concealing the exposition within a character or situation, so that the audience does not see it for what it is, but only experiences it as part of the development of the narrative. Some films, however, consciously point to the existence of the exposition. For example, *Austin Powers: International Man of Mystery* utilizes a character named Basil Exposition (Michael York) whose name is a play on his function within the story. He arrives to elaborate the story's exposition and explain action and events that happened before the point where the film starts.

Act 2

Act 2 is the longest act and constitutes the main bulk of the film, a series of actions that escalate the conflicts, occasionally offering false resolutions, leading up to the third act; this part of the story is known as **rising action**.

Act 3

Act 3 brings us to the **climax** of a story, the point where the conflicts are brought to a head. The climax often shows some changes in the film's techniques; the pacing of a film increases, through quicker editing, shorter shots and scenes, or through faster-paced **cues** in the music. This creates a heightened pitch of excitement in the film. Finally, after the climax, the story reaches a conclusion and the conflicts are resolved, or sometimes left unresolved. This post-climax moment of resolution is called the **denouement**.

So, in summary the three-act structure can be broken down as follows:

- Act 1 introduces the characters, sets the scene and initiates the principal conflict;
- Act 2 is the longest act, with events and character development that lead us towards the third act;
- Act 3 brings us to the climax of the story, the pacing of a film often increases and finally after the climax, the story reaches a conclusion and the conflicts are resolved.

Many films using the three-act structure end each act with a decisive moment, or **plot point**, signalling the change in the act. For example, it is frequently the case that a decision is reached at the end of Act 1 that will move the narrative forward. In the trilogy *The Lord of the Rings*, the decision to try to destroy the Ring is a significant turning point that would indicate the end of Act 1. At the end of Act 2, the characters are often in a situation of peril or difficulty, as when Frodo is approaching Mount Doom and the other characters prepare for a hopeless battle.

To continue our discussion of the three-act structure, let's apply it to a specific example: *Stage Beauty* (2004). This film is a period drama set in seventeenth-century England and shows the lives of a group of actors at the time when it first became possible for women to work professionally on the stage.

Act 1

In Act 1 we are introduced to the main characters, and the scene is set. Over the opening credits we get the first example of exposition, as titles tell us that at the start of the story, women's roles on the stage are performed by men. We then meet the two main characters: Ned Kynaston (Billy Crudup) the actor, and his servant Maria (Claire Danes). In the beginning, their situation of equilibrium is that he is a respected performer and that she aspires to act also; in the opening scene she mimics his actions from the wings. Maria then takes the opportunity to act in a version of *Othello* (the play that is Kynaston's speciality) that is being performed in a tavern. This serves as the catalyst for change and conflict, as, when her performance becomes known, King Charles II (Rupert Everett) grants permission for women to act on the stage. The king's announcement is the plot point that signals the end of Act 1.

Act 2

Act 2 develops the conflict between Kynaston and Maria. A series of events leads to a decline in Kynaston's fortunes, while Maria becomes more successful. Kynaston is beaten, loses his job, is abandoned by his lover Buckingham (Ben Chaplin), and cannot persuade the king to allow him to perform women's roles. He is progressively humiliated as the act progresses. Finally, as Act 2 comes to an end Maria admits that she is not a good actor, is replaced on the stage and loses her job. The Act 2 plot point is her decision to look for Kynaston again.

Act 3

In Act 3 the climax and conclusion of the film occur when Maria and Kynaston take on rehearsing for, and performing *Othello*, finally achieving the artistic success that is the goal for both of them. We feel their tension rising through an increase in pace and the film resolves with their joint success.

Characters

In the example of *Stage Beauty*, we see that the two main characters go through a series of conflicts and challenges at different points in the story. A key part of a screenwriter's job is to create, introduce and develop interesting people to populate their film. The growth of the characters is also closely linked to the structure of the story so that the three acts chart their changes over time. Thus, in *Stage Beauty*, both Maria and Kynaston grow as characters, while the story develops. Although Kynaston and Maria both change throughout *Stage Beauty*, theirs is not the only story that is being told in this film. There are also subplots and secondary characters: such as the relationship between the king and his lover Nell (Zoe Tapper). Often as writers are developing scripts they create characters with differing degrees of involvement in the main story. These minor characters sometimes reflect the struggles of the principal characters and also undergo different levels of change during the course of the narrative.

In many conventional narratives, characters can be divided into types. The simplest of these are the 'good guy' and the 'bad guy'. This is popular terminology for a simple concept, that, since stories are based around conflict, there is a **protagonist**: a character representing good in the story; and an **antagonist**: the character representing bad in the story. Narrative theory categorizes the types of character evident in different forms of narrative, who have common functions and structures within stories. For example, the Russian narrative theorist Vladimir Propp studied folk tales and came up with a division of seven types of characters in these classic stories: the hero, the villain, the donor, the dispatcher, the false hero, the helper, the princess (and sometimes her father). Each of these characters is common to many different stories and serves particular functions in the hero's struggle. Other theorists have applied these and other character types to different forms of narrative and found common functions. Certainly stories contain different characters that serve to move the story through its conflicts to its inevitable climax.

One reason why characters become important to the development of a narrative script is because they are one of the means by which we are drawn into a story. We often find ourselves identifying with certain characters: relating to them and understanding their experience by making connections with our own experiences and personality traits. In *Stage Beauty* one may identify with Maria's ambition to break out of her assigned place in the social order and become an actor. The story itself even comments on the process of identification. When Kynaston is at one of his lowest points he appeals to the king, who invites him to prove that he can perform a male role. When he fails, the king (who had lived many years in exile) comments on Kynaston's exile from the stage: 'Exile is a dreadful thing for one who knows his rightful place.' In this way, we see one character identify with the struggles of another, in the same way that an audience member might identify with a character.

One way to ensure that we identify with a particular character is by being shown their motivations. The character's motivations can be their goals within the course of the story. For example, Frodo's goal to destroy the Ring of Power in *The Lord of the Rings* motivates his actions as a character as well as advancing the story. Motivations and goals can also come from a character's internal conflicts and emotions. For example, Kynaston in *Stage Beauty* is motivated by the desire to produce the perfect death scene and Maria is motivated by her desire to become an actor.

Narrative structure in **Star Wars**

To conclude this discussion of narrative structure, let's look at a well-known example that follows these conventions. The *Star Wars* trilogy tells a classic story of the fight between good and evil, with character types that are common across many storytelling traditions. Both the trilogy cumulatively, and each of the films individually, follow the three-act structure. Let's look at the structure of the first film *Star Wars*, then at how the films in the trilogy combine to create another three-act narrative.

First, Luke Skywalker (Mark Hamill) meets the droids who are carrying the secret plans to fight the Empire. He then encounters Obi-Wan Kenobi (Alec Guinness), and together they all embark on an adventure, collecting Han Solo (Harrison Ford) on the way, rescuing Princess Leia (Carrie Fisher), joining the Alliance and destroying the Empire's Death Star. This is the plot summary of

Figure 3.1   *Star Wars*, George Lucas, 1977

Figure 3.2   *Star Wars*, George Lucas, 1977

Figure 3.3   *Star Wars*, George Lucas, 1977

Star Wars in two sentences – obviously omitting many of the nuances of the actual film. However we can fit this film neatly into a three-act structure:

- Act 1 – Luke finds the droids, meets Obi-Wan, hears the Princess's message and finds his family killed. The droids are catalysts to Luke's story and Obi-Wan provides a lot of the exposition.
- Act 2 – Luke and Obi-Wan set off to help the princess. In the rising action we have their adventures escaping Tatooine, encountering the Death Star and finally joining the Alliance. As Act 2 ends, Luke's adventures are rising to a crisis plot point: Obi-Wan has been killed and Han is abandoning the fight.
- Act 3 – Reaches the climax which is the lengthy battle between the forces of the Empire and rebel Alliance. Luke fights to the end with the climactic destruction of the Death Star. The denouement resolves and concludes with Luke and Han honoured by the Alliance.

The next level in which the three-act structure works in *Star Wars* is evident if we expand our analysis to the first three films together. Thus, although each film contains an individual story, with a clear structure, all three films, when put together, also represent a completely structured narrative. (Much as a long-form television narrative does from episode to episode over the course of a series.) When we view *Star Wars* in this way we can see each film as a clear example of each act. So:

- In Act 1, *Star Wars*, Luke meets the Alliance and gets bound up in their adventures;
- Act 2, *The Empire Strikes Back* (1980) continues with Luke fighting with the rebels against the Empire. As Act 2 these adventures take a couple of different turns: Luke's visit to Yoda, and

Han and Leia escaping to Bespin. In this act, we are also introduced to new twists and turns in the story: Han's relationship with Leia and Luke's relationship with Darth Vader (David Prowse). The film then ends with a classic Act 2 crisis plot point with the capture of Han, and Luke's defeat in his fight with Darth Vader;

- Act 3, *Return of the Jedi* (1983), includes the climactic battle between the two forces, which resolves with victory for the Alliance.

Star Wars also shows us the conventional use of character types. The forces of good and the forces of evil are clearly delineated in the characters; Luke is the hero, Darth Vader is the villain. Propp's breakdown is applicable here as there are a number of characters serving the various roles in Luke's quest. The common character types are not evident in this example, but it is interesting to compare the types in this film to the similar ones that appear in *The Lord of the Rings*. There is a remarkable commonality between the groups of heroes and helpers in these stories: Luke = Frodo, Obi-Wan = Gandalf, Han Solo = Aragon, two droids = two supporting hobbits, etc. Obviously, there are differences in the characters, but the similarities point to the existence of these underlying types.

Alternatives to the three-act structure

The three-act structure has been criticized from a number of different perspectives. Even those working with fairly conventional narrative film, find the structural restrictions promoted by writers such as Syd Field, too constricting and limiting. Although this model can be a good place to start, when taken to its extreme, the three-act structure is formulaic and restrictive, rather than creative. However, although not strictly following the three acts, the basic premise of three parts to a story can be found in films with even the most unusual structures. Thus, a film like *Memento* (2000), for example, is very innovative in the presentation of its story, using the short-term memory loss of its main character to motivate an unusual reverse structure to the **plot**. The structure has certain scenes shot in colour moving backwards in time and other scenes in black and white moving forward chronologically, until both timelines converge. Yet, even a film with this level of structural novelty, still works in three parts. It starts by setting up its premise, a mystery to be solved (Act 1), slowly revealing clues to the central character, Leonard (Guy Pearce) and his relationships to the other characters; an antagonist is revealed in Teddy (Joe Pantoliano) (Act 2). It continues with the central mystery slowly unravelling and it ends with a climactic confrontation and a resolution (of sorts) with final revelations about Leonard's past (Act 3). Even with this complex plot structure, the underlying arc of action can still be seen.

Beyond the criticism of the three-act structure as a restriction to creativity, there are also grounds for ideological critiques of this model. One of the aspects of this style is the way it develops individual characters with fairly simple psychologies and motivations. Conventional narrative structure leads the viewer to identify with the struggles of the individual against the adversity that is the source of the story's conflict. These characters are presented with clear motivations and goals to pursued and the narrative brings them through certain patterns of development and growth that are then drawn together in the final climax. Not only does this characterization simplify human thoughts, emotions and motivations, it isolates the individual from the societal and cultural forces that would add a more complex worldview. A number of filmmaking traditions have worked to critique or complicate the simple identification with an individual in a film. In

Chapter 12, we will explore three examples that present different kinds of characterization. The Soviet filmmaker Sergei Eisenstein broke with the expectations of character in his films by using a communal or group hero. Rather than having the audience identify with one specific individual, Eisenstein's films use the actions of a collective group of people, embodying the ideas drawn from the Communist revolution. We will see how this is a reflection of the context in which Eisenstein's work developed. In Chapter 12 we will also explore the example of Jean-Luc Godard's French New Wave film *Breathless* (1960). This film features a protagonist whose motivations and actions remain largely inexplicable, without the simplifying conventions of classical narrative. Finally, in Chapter 12 we will also study *Memories of Underdevelopment* (1968), a Cuban film directed by Tomás Gutiérrez Alea, which features an anti-hero designed to disrupt the audience's processes of identification.

Another ideological critique of conventional narrative structure relates to the nature of the ending or concluding part of the film. Returning to Aristotle, *Poetics* introduces the idea of **catharsis**, the emotional release that accompanies the ending or resolution of a tragedy. When a film reaches a climax which is **cathartic**, there is a release of emotion accompanying the resolution of the conflicts developed in the course of the story. The resolution of conflicts and the return to a stable equilibrium can undermine the possibility of grounding the conflicts of the story in the political conflicts within society and culture. The process of catharsis in art is ultimately passive and takes the passivity of the audience a step further; the viewer's inaction moves beyond the experience of watching, into a political inaction in the face of social problems or injustices, giving the sense that these too, like the conflicts of the narrative, are resolvable without active participation. It is for this reason that filmmakers critical of conventional narrative structures work to disrupt the resolution of a film by deliberately avoiding the restoration of equilibrium and leaving the stories open-ended or unresolved. We will touch on some examples of this again in Chapter 12.

Finally, grounded in traditional ideas from the Greek theatre, conventional three-act narratives are open to the criticism that they emerge from a particular cultural context, rather than embodying a universal ideal. Thus, filmmaking traditions such as **Third Cinema** (examined in Chapter 12) produce films that present stories in different ways. Thus, a film such as the Senegalese classic *Touki Bouki* (1973) uses a structure without the conventional connections: some actions are not clearly explained and the timeline of events moves around without explanation. The characters' motivations are also not clarified in conventional ways. The structure of the narrative is open-ended, without the expected resolution of key elements of the story. Instead there is a sense of circularity to this film as it begins and ends on an image of a boy riding an ox, which is symbolically rather than directly related to the rest of the story. This film uses a West African frame of reference, and a visual symbolism not tied to the classical conventions of European or American cinema. Therefore it is sometimes difficult viewing for an audience with expectations drawn from conventional practice, as it is challenged to relate to the story in new and unexpected ways.

As we continue to study narrative films, it is important to be aware of the alternatives to this basic convention, and in the next section we will look at screenwriting with an awareness that structural conventions are a good basis from which to develop the techniques of storytelling, but can be explored, experimented with, subverted or abandoned completely in the process of developing a script.

Developing a script

With both the model of the three-act structure and the alternative experimentations with form in mind, let's briefly consider how to develop a script. A three-act structure and the ideas of conflict development and resolution are a good basic foundation when working on a script, but they are only part of the process. Even before defining a script's structure, it is necessary to come up with an idea for what your script will be about. Many writers draw on personal experience for their stories, and others are inspired by ideas from other media or art practices. For example, genre conventions can be used in a short script in interesting ways that comment on or subvert conventional expectations. After the initial stage of idea development, a scriptwriter will produce a **plot outline** – presenting all the scenes in a film in the order in which they will appear, and the main action in each scene. A **scene** in scriptwriting terms is defined as any action or dialogue that occurs in a specific location. Thus, a change in location requires a change of scene. Simultaneously with the development of the outline, the writer prepares **character profiles**: brief descriptions of each character, their role in the narrative and any pertinent back-story information and aspects of their psychological make-up. Scripts go through many stages of writing and rewriting. The first milestone is the completion of a **reading script**. A reading script gives a full idea of the story, with the location of each scene, dialogue and description, but not any directorial decisions on how the material is to be shot. The next phase is the **shooting script**, which includes these directorial elements: **camera position**, **camera angle** and movement.

There are many manuals on screenwriting to refer to for more detailed information on the presentation of a script (some are mentioned in the last section of this chapter). When embarking on a scriptwriting project it is worth researching further into the conventions and expectation of the form. It is important to present a script in a correct and consistent fashion, and there is software which assists with this, as well as technical guidelines in these manuals. In addition to further research, an important consideration when developing a script is the process of seeking feedback and response throughout the different phases of writing and rewriting. When you are writing, ask other people to read the script and give you input on how the writing works. As the ultimate goal of a script is to be performed, a reading of the script will allow you to hear the dialogue spoken out loud, and to get a sense of how it sounds.

There are three elements in the layout of a reading script (although these elements are common in all phases of the writing process). The first element is the **scene headings**. These can be drawn from the outline and show the scene's location, whether interior (INT) or exterior (EXT) and time of day. They should be capitalized. For example, 'COFFEE SHOP. INT. DAY'. The second element is the description. This is often hard to write, but key to the development of the visual storytelling: a script can be written with no dialogue if the descriptive storytelling is good. The description should be written in the present tense and action-oriented, introducing the characters and explaining what they are doing at any given moment of the story. Description should be concise and visually strong and relate what will be seen on the screen, rather than abstract ideas or the internal thoughts of the characters. The trick of good description is to demonstrate the character's internal state through the visual action. The final element of the script is the dialogue. This element of writing can be tricky also, as it needs to be written in a way that is lively and engaging, but is still convincing when spoken aloud.

When working with a script, a director will visualize how the elements of description and dialogue are to be realized on screen. This involves developing a storyboard from the written material. First, the director will divide each scene of the script into shots, using the different camera positions, angles and movement as storytelling devices. The storyboard is the first part of the process of the **cinematography**: a visual version of the script with all the shots drawn and presented to give a complete sense of how the scene will look when filmed. Scripting and story-boarding are the first part of the filmmaking process; in Part II we will then see how the techniques of filmmaking are used to bring the script and the characters to life, and how all elements of filmmaking add to the possibilities of what appears on screen. Before we continue with this, however, there are some other important elements to consider when exploring narrative film, the differences between story and plot, the use of time in narrative and the role of the narrator.

Story and plot

In the previous section we suggested that the first part of the scripting process is the development of a plot outline. But what is this idea of plot, and how does it differ from the story of a film? This distinction is important to screenwriting as well as being a key concept from the related area of narrative theory. To summarize:

- **Story** is a sequence of events presented in chronological order. These events are usually joined by causal links, one action or decision leading to another action or event in the story. The story includes many elements that are not directly seen within the course of a film, but are implied through the action and dialogue.
- **Plot** is the way in which a story is told. Quite often fiction films do not tell their stories in chronological order. The story elements are told out of order, shifting in time, with different characters relating different elements of the tale. How a story unfolds is known as the plot.

To clarify these distinctions, let's explore the difference between the story and the plot of the **melodrama** *Letter from an Unknown Woman* (1948). This film is about Lisa (Joan Fontaine) and her long-standing, unrequited love for the pianist Stefan (Louis Jourdan). Most of the film is told in **flashback** as Stefan reads a letter from Lisa. Lisa's letter explains to Stefan the history of their relationship from her perspective; her childhood infatuation, their brief affair, the birth of their child, her marriage to another man, and finally, her tragic death and the death of their child. The shifts in time make the plot fairly complex.

The story ranges from Lisa's early childhood to the duel that is about to take place when the film ends. Not everything that is part of the story is shown in the film. For example, at one point Lisa tells Stefan about her childhood with her father. This part of the story is not part of the plot, since we never see the action of Lisa with her father, but it becomes important background to Lisa's story. We are also never shown what occurs between the time that Stefan Jr is born, and the time Lisa is married to Johann Stauffer (Marcel Journet). With Lisa's comment in **voice over**, 'There are times during those years I prefer not to remember', the viewers can fill in this part of the story with their own imagination. Likewise, the film ends before the duel between Stefan and Johann. Yet it is part of the story, as we can predict, with some degree of certainty, that it will take place.

A lot of stories refer to actions that happened before the actual plot begins. Narrative theorists use the Latin term ***in media res*** to describe this factor. This term means 'in the middle of the action' and refers to the fact that stories are ongoing and often rely on information about what occurred before the plot itself begins. The plot of *Letter from an Unknown Woman* is more complex than the story, since it moves backwards and forwards in time. But it is also simpler to analyze, since it consists of all the scenes that we see when we watch the film. The film is structured around four flashbacks that each present a distinct phase of Lisa's life:

1   Childhood;
2   Her years in Linz;
3   Her youth and affair with Stefan;
4   Her marriage to Johann, her last encounters with Stefan and her death.

The narrative of the present also shows the growth, change and development of Stefan as he reads the letter, from his initial interest to his emotional response when he finally remembers Lisa. This is the plot, and it is the presentation of all the scenes in the order in which the viewer experiences them.

In preparing and developing a script, a writer will work with both the story and the plot. To write the whole film well, all the actions of the story, even the ones not included, will be in the writer's mind. Likewise, during the process, the writer will have a plot outline to work from, presenting all the events in the order in which they will appear in the final film.

Letter from an Unknown Woman reveals some of the important techniques of narrative story-telling that we will develop in this section and the next:

• The film moves between two separate timeframes; the present of Stefan to the past that Lisa is telling. This use of flashback is an example of how film narratives often manipulate and reorder time in their storytelling.
• The story is told by the main character, whose voice returns at key points to move the narrative action along. This is an example of the use of a **narrator** in the storytelling process.
• Finally, in this visual narrative, it is also important to see how the different elements of film-making technique tell the story.

Before we continue to discuss narrative time and the role of the narrator, there is one other concept we need to introduce: the world of the narrative.

The world of the narrative

Let's revisit the end of the last flashback in *Letter from an Unknown Woman*. When Stefan finishes reading his letter, he looks up and is apparently emotionally distressed. This scene is accompanied by music. A string orchestra plays a plaintive and tense melody that accentuates the emotion of the scene. Where is that music coming from? Is there an orchestra hidden in the back of the room? Of course not, music from outside the world of the story is a common convention in film (which we will discuss further in Chapter 10). What it does point to, however, is another important distinction when talking about a narrative film. Most of the elements that we experience when watching *Letter from an Unknown Woman* are part of the fictional world of the film. The characters, their dress and mannerisms, the setting, their dialogue, even the music we hear as we see Stefan play the piano, are all part of the life of Lisa and Stefan in Vienna in the early 1900s. The whole fictional world of a film is called the **diegesis**. Therefore all the elements that go to construct that world are known as **diegetic** elements.

The burst of music that accompanies Stefan's emotional reaction is **non-diegetic**: it comes from outside the fictional world. There are a few other small non-diegetic elements that occur in the film other than the music that returns throughout. For example, the opening shot is accompanied by the title 'Vienna about 1900'. This title is not seen or read by any of the characters, it is a non-diegetic commentary for the audience. All fiction films construct a diegetic world, but are mostly also accompanied by elements and techniques of storytelling that exist outside that world, but provide context and commentary on the action occurring in the story.

Narrative time

Letter from an Unknown Woman tells the story of Lisa and Stefan's relationship as it continues over a number of years. We see Lisa from her teenage years, through her youth, until she is the mother of a ten-year-old child. This timeframe, with absences throughout, is presented within an eighty-nine-minute film. There is also the time of the plot present here: it takes the few hours from the time Stefan comes home to the time he leaves to go to the duel. Thus, in *Letter from an Unknown Woman* the three levels of time would lay out like this:

- The story time is spread out over a number of years;
- The plot time is a few hours and;
- The **running time** is eighty-nine minutes.

From this, it is evident that most films operate with multiple levels of time. In Chapter 9 we will examine how editing is used to fit the story time into the running time. In the section that follows, we will examine how shifts in time bring together the story and the plot.

Shifts in time

If we understand the plot to follow a different structure from the story, we can see how movement between different timeframes can be an important device in structuring a narrative:

- A shift in time to a period earlier in a story, is known as a **flashback**;
- A shift to a period later in time is known as a **flashforward**.

These are common devices in structuring films, allowing the plot to move through time non-chronologically. So what is the purpose of a shift in the temporal order? And why would a writer choose to include flashbacks or flashforwards when structuring a narrative? To answer these questions, let's look at some examples of films that use flashbacks and see what function they serve, and how effective they can be as storytelling devices.

A flashback structure is often a key feature of specific genres of films, which use the shift in narrative time as a typical plot device. In particular, crime dramas utilize the flashback as part of the way they structure a narrative of investigation. The 'investigative' use of the flashback is a common feature of the detective genre and is particularly popular in **film noir**. An excellent example of classic film noir that is structured through flashbacks is *Mildred Pierce* (1945). This film starts with a murder. In the course of the police investigation the main character, Mildred (Joan Crawford), is brought to the police station and interviewed about the case. As she tells the story we see it in flashback. The film is then structured around her story, occasionally returning to the present of the story to provide the twists and turns of the investigation.

In other examples, flashbacks serve different functions. Flashbacks can be used to link the story to the personal experiences of an individual character. For example *Little Big Man* (1970) is framed by the narration of the main character, Jack (Dustin Hoffman). At the start of the film, 121-year-old Jack is being interviewed by a young researcher who is interested in the 'way of life of the Indian'. As Jack starts to tell his life story the film flashes back 110 years. As the film progresses we get a **revisionist** version of the Western myth, one that, through the character of Jack, gives us the Battle of Little Big Horn from the perspective of a character who is sympathetic to the Native Americans. This subverts many of the expectations of the Western genre, whose narrative is traditionally biased towards the white settlers. The framing structure that situates the whole story as a flashback is key to how the film works. The film invokes the idea that this is an eyewitness account to the events of history. We can therefore feel that there is some level of subjective experience behind the story that is being told, especially since it is presented as an alternative to traditional historical representations of these events.

The idea that the flashback can recount subjective memories of individual characters can be instrumental in certain films. A well-known example of this is the Japanese film *Rashomon* (1950). In this film, several witnesses to a murder all recount their versions of the story, each of which is different. The film comments on the subjective nature of memory on our understanding of the past. We never know which of the stories to believe, or whether, in fact, we can believe them all to be the relative truth from each character's perspective.

Flashforwards are less common in the continuing narrative structure; of course when a flashback is over, the return to the present time of the film could be considered a flashforward. However, it is less frequent to interrupt the flow of a story with information that has not yet occurred. One example of a film that utilizes flashforwards is *Easy Rider* (1969). In this film there are brief shots that introduce action from a future point in the narrative flow. In this instance, the flashforwards serve as premonitions, evoke the idea of drug-induced hallucinations, but also foreground the constructed nature of the narrative.

It is also interesting to note how a shift in time is introduced into a film. As the above examples show, it is common for a flashback to be accompanied by a **transitional editing device**. *Little Big Man* and *Mildred Pierce* introduce their flashbacks with dissolves (one image replacing the other slowly). At another point in *Mildred Pierce*, the plot returns to the present with a device that appears to be a fast **pan** of the camera. In *Letter from an Unknown Woman* the time shifts are signalled by the image going slowly out of focus on the first shot, and coming back into focus on the second shot. These transitions are conventional markers that the audience understands, as they occur repeatedly in different films and help to keep the viewer from being confused about where or when particular action takes place.

A less conventional, although extremely effective, use of flashback occurs in Ingmar Bergman's *Wild Strawberries* (1957). This film tells the story of an elderly doctor, Isak (Victor Sjöström), taking a journey to receive an honorary degree. As he drives through the Swedish countryside he reflects

Figure 3.4   *Wild Strawberries*, Ingmar Bergman, 1957

on his past life and interacts with his travelling companions: his daughter-in-law (Ingrid Thulin) and three hitchhikers. Early in the film he stops at the house where he spent his childhood summers with his family. In this sequence we see a number of scenes from his earlier life. This is not a conventional use of the flashback, however, and instead of the scenes being isolated from the present, Isak remains, as an older man still in the scene while the action goes on around him.

The flashback is introduced with Isak's voice over as he says: 'the clear reality of day gave way to the still clearer images of memory which rose before my eyes with all the force of reality'. As he looks at the boarded-up house, it dissolves into the house of the past, alive and in use. Then we see him, still an old man, trying to talk to his cousin (Bibi Andersson) as she appeared in the past. She does not see or acknowledge him and the scene plays out between her and Isak's brother while he watches. As the sequence continues, he enters the house and observes his family eat lunch and celebrate his uncle's birthday. He is clearly in the scene, but the characters around him don't see him.

This is an unconventional, but very effective, flashback. Like some of the examples we have discussed already, this is a very subjective memory, taking the viewer into Isak's mind and perspective on the story. To add to the complexity of the scene, it is unclear what the flashback represents. It is not fully Isak's memory, as he was not present on the original occasion. He is watching a moment that was important in his life, when his cousin Sara chose his brother over him as a romantic partner. Yet he never witnessed this. Is this his imagination or is this his memory? The film leaves this moment ambiguous and this is part of why it works so well.

As the examples above show us, flashbacks often revolve around a scene where a character recounts something from the past, the action then follows the story that they tell. This act of storytelling is known as **narration**, and throughout the next section we will discuss this process and the effects it has on the storytelling of a film.

Narration

Star Wars has an amusing and self-conscious storytelling scene. In *Return of the Jedi*, Han, Leia and the two droids are on a mission to lower the shields on the planet Endor, to allow the rebels to break in and fight the imperial troops. On Endor they encounter the Ewoks: a group of teddybear-like creatures that live in a civilization without technology. When they meet the heroes, they mistake C3PO (Anthony Daniels) for a god. After they have made their peace with the Ewoks, and before both groups re-enter the battle, there is a scene of storytelling. C3PO is in a hut surrounded by the Ewoks recounting the adventures of the group up until this point. He is speaking in Ewok and there are no subtitles to accompany the images. His narration occasionally includes bursts of sound effects as he imitates lightsabres and lasergun fire. We follow the story, which we have already seen in the film, by C3PO's use of the characters' names in conjunction with the sound effects. This scene is an example of a traditional storytelling context where the events are related verbally by an individual. This kind of storytelling dates from a time before the printing press made written accounts available, or technology gave us film and television. We still recreate these experiences with campfire stories; one person talking and many people listening.

Film is a long way from this method of traditional storytelling, where the whole story is recounted through the voice and actions of the individual speaker. In film, we get the story in many different ways: camerawork, lighting, mise-en-scène, sound, music and editing. Between the development of the traditional oral storyteller and the film form as storyteller, there are other ways of recounting stories; two key forms are written fiction and theatre. Both of these have a very long history, far longer than the history of film. Film's method of storytelling is often influenced by these other forms. Equally, critics writing about film often compare the filmic storytelling methods to those of written fiction and theatre.

Written fiction is an evolution of the traditional storytelling form. Here, the author writes and the reader reads, but the direct contact is no longer there, and instead becomes a function of the written text, the 'voice' of the author is a technique of the writer. In theatre, the action unfolds on the stage as the audience watches. This is not so much a process of narration as it is of imitation. Yet there are moments when narration plays a role in theatre. Sometimes, a character in a play breaks the illusion of the scene and talks to the audience directly, serving the function of a traditional storyteller or narrator.

In film there are also moments when we are aware of the presence of a narrator – in the form of a voice over or written text, relating part of the narrative. In this section we will introduce the idea of the filmic narrator, and look at some examples.

The narrator as a character

The first basic distinction is between types of narrators in films; the **character narrator** tells us the story from the position of a character within it, whereas the **non-character narrator** tells the story from outside. *Letter from an Unknown Woman* has a character narrator. Lisa's character tells us her story as Stefan reads. We learn at the beginning of her voice over that she is already dead when this part of the action takes place. Perhaps this could take some of the suspense away from the story, but it actually turns the suspense around so that we are left asking who she is, and how she died. As a character in the film we get extra information about what she is thinking and feeling about the action of the story and the other characters.

A good example of a non-character narrator is in Orson Welles's *The Magnificent Ambersons* (1942). This film follows a family through the changes in society that accompany the foundation and growth of the automobile industry. As the film starts, we hear Orson Welles's voice over describing the time and place in which the story is set. The voice over sets the scene, while we watch the world of the story as it is explained. The narrator provides the **exposition**. The voice-over narrator in this film never appears as a character. He remains outside the world of the film. *The Magnificent Ambersons* is a literary adaptation, based on the novel by Booth Tarkington. The voice in this film reminds us of the literary narrator that we might encounter when reading the book.

The narrator in the plot

Orson Welles's voice over is the first thing we hear in this film and, at the end, he introduces the credits. This type of voice over can be said to frame the story. Another distinction between narrators in films is whether their narration is a framing device in the film or whether it occurs within the larger context of the plot. If we look at another example of a film narrator we can see the difference. In *Mildred Pierce* the character of Mildred tells the story that leads up to the murder that is being investigated. She is seated in the police station recounting her story when we see it unfold in flashback. This is an example of an **embedded narrator**; her story is framed by the other parts of the film that are not narrated by a character.

Thus we see the distinction:

- a **frame narrator** who starts and ends the story (*The Magnificent Ambersons*) – containing it like a picture frame;
- an **embedded narrator** who appears after the story has started and tells only part of it (*Mildred Pierce*).

Since so much of the film shown to us is beyond the narrator's control, we are often left wondering how much any narrator actually knows about the story that they are telling. A narrator who has access to all information about a story is known as an **omniscient** narrator. Often the voice over in a documentary is omniscient. The non-character narrator in *The Magnificent Ambersons* is aware of everything all the characters do, how they feel, as well as possessing knowledge about their future, and the larger cultural context in which they live. However, other narrators tell us parts of a story when they do not necessarily know all there is to know. These narrators are said to be **restricted** in their narration.

In *Mildred Pierce*, although Mildred appears to recount the whole story, in actual fact she was not present at some of the scenes she is supposed to be describing. For example, the relationship between Monte (Zachary Scott) and Veda (Ann Blyth) is vital to the story and we see it unfold in a number of scenes where Mildred is not present. When they first meet at the restaurant and flirt and dance, Mildred does not see any of their interaction until late in the evening. Similarly, Veda's birthday party near the climax of the film involves interaction between Veda and Monte while Mildred is at a business meeting elsewhere. This inconsistency in the knowledge of the narrator is important, as the relationship between Veda and Monte, and Mildred's ignorance of it, is key to the investigative plot and the motivation for the murder. Although logically we know that she cannot have access to all the story information that we see, we still accept her narration as a guide, and are equally aware that the visuals, dialogue and music give us the majority of narrative information.

Reliable and unreliable narrators

Narrators have a privileged position in relation to the audience of a film: they talk to us and we follow the story from their perspective. But there are other ways in which the story is enacted, which sometimes make us question the version they are telling. In other words, unlike the storyteller who stands in front of us, or the words in the book that we are reading; in film we get story information from a number of different sources, in addition to the narrator. We see the images, we hear the dialogue spoken between characters, and we are even given narrative information through the music cues. Sometimes, then, we have ways of telling that the information that is given to us by the narrator is not necessarily accurate. This phenomenon is known as **unreliable narration**.

Unreliable narrators appear in fictional writing as well as in film. Sometimes in a novel, we are left with questions about how to interpret the information given to us through the narrative voice. Earlier we discussed the film *Little Big Man* as an example of a film structured by a flashback, with the character of Jack framing the story of his involvement with the Cheyenne and the Battle of Little Big Horn. We also discussed how the film is in the genre of the revisionist Western that gives more weight to the point of view of the Native Americans' than is usual in Classical Hollywood. However, the film also plays with the reliability of the narrator as source of information about these historical subjects. In the course of his adventures, Jack meets and gets involved with a lot of different people and witnesses several important historic events.

In the first part of Jack's flashback, he lives with the Cheyenne. In a fight with a group of white soldiers he identifies himself as white and is returned to the white community. He is then adopted by a preacher (Thayer David) and his wife (Faye Dunaway), where he stays until he discovers the infidelity and hypocrisy of the unfaithful wife. Jack's travels then lead him to be involved with a confidence man (Martin Balsam) who pretends to be a doctor and sells fake snake-oil cures. These two episodes are important as an early clue to Jack's reliability as a narrator. The film accentuates the parts of the Western myth that introduce and foreground stories and actions that are based in lies and deceit. The confidence man of the Old West is someone who makes a living through pretence. In one scene we see Jack fake a miracle cure. His participation in this activity allows the audience to doubt the veracity of the stories he is telling. This doubt is increased by the fact that Jack claims to be involved in so many of the well-known events of the time. In another of Jack's adventures, he makes friends with the gunfighter Wild Bill Hickok (Jeff Corey), later witnessing the famous gunfight when Wild Bill is killed.

Questions about the reliability of Jack as a narrator in *Little Big Man* are key to the film's themes as a revisionist Western. In the opening scene the historian interviewing Jack calls into question the official history of the West and the identification with the white settlers against the Native Americans. The revisionist Western interrogates the **ideological** basis of the retelling of the past, questioning the reliability of the narrative of conventional histories. If we don't believe the stories we have been told in the history books, can we believe the ramblings of an old snake-oil seller? It is in this ambiguity that the interest of the film lies; it calls into question all the ways in which we react to history and stories about the past. Maybe Jack's story is the true one after all. Or maybe there are still other versions to be told.

The *Little Big Man* example shows us the possibility of an unreliable narrative voice. There is another level in which reliability works, however, and that is the question of whether the images we are seeing are to be believed. There is a famous example of a flashback in *Stage Fright* (1950). Near the beginning of the film the character Johnnie (Richard Todd) visits his friend Eve (Jane Wyman), the film's heroine, and asks her to help him escape the law. He recounts the story of how Charlotte (Marlene Dietrich), the woman he is having an affair with, visited him wearing a bloody dress and told him about the accidental death of Charlotte's husband. Charlotte then asked him to go to her home and get a clean dress for her. She changes and leaves the dress with him so that he will destroy it.

Figure 3.5   *Little Big Man*, Arthur Penn, 1970

As an audience, we see the incident unfold and therefore believe it to have happened. Later in the film we find out that the story that Johnnie told Eve is actually false, designed to cover up his involvement in the murder, and to blackmail Charlotte with the dress. This example of unreliability is not just on the level of spoken narration, but also evident in the flashback of images shown. This film is well known for this flashback because it is uncommon to employ this device in such a way, causing audience confusion.

The narration of cinematic techniques

There is a common metaphor used when talking about film, which is to speak of the camera as the narrator. The camera shows us what to look at, directs our attention and frames the image in the many interesting ways which we will discuss in Chapter 6. But there is more to the storytelling of a film than just the view of the camera. All the elements that appear in front of the camera also work to relay the story to us; lighting, costume and set design all work to tell us the story: these are elements we will discuss in Chapters 6 and 7. In *Mildred Pierce*, when Mildred enters the beach house for the climactic final scene, the music engenders a sense of foreboding, working as a form of emotional narration, giving us a premonition of the danger of the scene. Sound and music are discussed in Chapters 8 and 10 as functions of narration. Finally, all the ways that the shots are put together create another level of narration, linking different scenes and making connections for the viewer. Editing as a narrational/storytelling device is covered in Chapter 9. Thus, although the voice of a narrator in a film is present to guide us through their **point of view**, it is important to realize that this only works in conjunction with all the storytelling techniques of the cinematic style.

Summary and key questions

Narrative is very important when understanding how films work. If you are either writing a script yourself, or analyzing one that already exists, these are the questions to keep in mind about narrative form and structure.

- Does the film use a three-act structure?
  - Where do the different acts begin and end?
  - What action occurs in each act?
- Does the film use an alternative structure?
  - How do these structures function?
- What is the story of the film? What is the plot of the film? How do they differ?
- How does the film move through time?
  - Are there flashbacks or flashforwards?
- Is there a narrator in the film?
  - How does the narration function?

Want to learn more?

Think about this ...

Narrative structure

Objective: To analyze the structure of a narrative.

Pick a fictional film that you have seen recently and consider how it might break down into the three-act structure. Where are the plot points? What part of the film is the climax? How does the structure relate to the characters' development?

Narrative analysis

Objective: To apply the basic concepts of narrative theory to the analysis of a film.

Using any film that you have seen, compare the structure of the story to the structure of the plot. How do they differ? Is the plot structure effective in communicating the story? How does the film structure time? What forms of narration does it use?

Try this ...

Short script

Objective: To apply the concepts of narrative structure to the development of a short script. You will need: This is a written exercise. Additional screenwriting software will help you format your script correctly.

Develop a short three- to four-page script with simple characters and a basic story. Be aware of the elements of structure discussed in the chapter and try giving the script a beginning, middle and end. Work through the process of outline and character development to produce a reading script.

Visual storytelling

Objective: To render a visual presentation of a short narrative in the form of a storyboard. You will need: A storyboard sheet (plain paper with 3:4 or 16:9 boxes) and a pencil.

Using the storyboard sheets, develop a short visual narrative. You should try to tell the story visually in twelve simple illustrations. Try to avoid any gaps or to rely on written explanations. Don't worry about the quality of your drawing: concentrate on communicating the story.

Further reading

There is quite a large field of writing on both narrative theory and the practice of screenwriting. As we saw in the chapter, narrative theory starts with the ideas discussed by Aristotle in *Poetics*. Also important is Tzvetan Todorov, *The Poetics of Prose* and classic character types are presented in Vladimir Propp, *The Morphology of the Folk Tale*. As a field of study, narrative theory is quite broad; a good basic introduction is Shlomith Rimon-Kenan, *Narrative Fiction* or Gérard Genette, *Narrative Discourse*. Seymour Chatman, *Coming to Terms* is more specifically about film. For an updated view of classic storytelling conventions see Kristin Thompson, *Storytelling in the New Hollywood*. There are a variety of screenwriting texts available; one classic, although somewhat dogmatic example is Syd Field, *The Screenplay*. Robert McKee's *Story* is also a good starting point. More recent texts question the dogmas of the three-act structure, such as Ken Dancyger and Jeff Rush, *Alternative Scriptwriting* and Linda Aronson, *Screenwriting Updated*. Steven Maras integrates theory and practice in his *Screenwriting: History, Theory and Practice* and Jane Bradley's *Screenwriting 101* focuses on practical creative-writing exercises to help develop an effective script. When moving from written script to visualization on the screen, guides to storyboarding include John Hart, *The Art of the Storyboard* or the initial sections of a book on directing such as Steven Katz, *Film Directing Shot by Shot*. The specifics of narration are often written about and debated within narrative theory; David Bordwell's *Narration in the Fiction Film* is a good place to start with these debates. Avrom Fleishman also studies a variety of forms of narration in *Narrated Films*.

Films studied in this chapter

Austin Powers: International Man of Mystery 1997 Jay Roach (director) Mike Myers (writer)

Breathless 1960 Jean-Luc Godard (director) Jean-Luc Godard (writer)

Easy Rider 1969 Dennis Hopper (director) Peter Fonda, Dennis Hopper and Terry Southern (writers)

The Empire Strikes Back 1980 Irvin Kershner (director) Leigh Brackett and Lawrence Kasdan (writers)

Letter from an Unknown Woman 1948 Max Ophüls (director) Howard Koch (writer)

Little Big Man 1970 Arthur Penn (director) Calder Willingham (writer)

The Lord of the Rings: The Fellowship of the Ring 2001 Peter Jackson (director) Fran Walsh, Philippa Boyens and Peter Jackson (writers)

The Lord of the Rings: The Two Towers 2002 Peter Jackson (director) Fran Walsh, Philippa Boyens, Steven Sinclair and Peter Jackson (writers)

The Lord of the Rings: The Return of the King 2003 Peter Jackson (director) Fran Walsh, Philippa Boyens and Peter Jackson (writers)

The Magnificent Ambersons 1942 Orson Welles (director) Orson Welles (writer)

Memento 2000 Christopher Nolan (director) Christopher Nolan (writer)

Memories of Underdevelopment 1968 Tomás Gutiérrez Alea (director) Edmundo Desnoes (writer)

Mildred Pierce 1945 Michael Curtiz (director) Ranald MacDougall (writer)

Rashomon 1950 Akira Kurosawa (director) Akira Kurosawa and Shinobu Hashimoto (writers)

Return of the Jedi 1983 Richard Marquand (director) Lawrence Kasdan and George Lucas (writers)

Stage Beauty 2004 Richard Eyre (director) Jeffrey Hatcher (writer)

Stage Fright 1950 Alfred Hitchcock (director) Whitfield Cook (writer)

Star Wars 1977 George Lucas (director) George Lucas (writer)

Touki Bouki 1973 Djribil Diop Mambéty (director) Djribil Diop Mambéty (writer)

Wild Strawberries 1957 Ingmar Bergman (director) Ingmar Bergman (writer)

Other examples to explore

Many classic and contemporary films use the structural style discussed in this chapter. A classic film such as *Citizen Kane* (1941 Orson Welles director) is a good example as it is innovative in its plot structure, but still maintains many features of conventional storytelling. With the ideas of narrative structure in mind it is useful to view many different types of films to discover when these models fit and when other narrative structures are in place. View examples of French New Wave style, such as François Truffaut, *400 Blows* (1959) or *Jules and Jim* (1962), or Jean-Luc Godard, *Vivre sa vie* (1962) or *Weekend* (1967). As we saw in this chapter, West African cinema often demonstrates innovative storytelling techniques. See for example the work of Ousmane Sembene, *Ceddo* (1977) and *Mooladé* (2004), as well as Djibril Diop Mambéty, *Hyenas* (1992).

Documentary Film

> ## Learning objectives
>
> After completing this chapter, you will be able to:
>
> - Explore ways of structuring a documentary;
> - Analyze how documentaries address their audiences;
> - Experiment with the use of testimonies, interviews and encounters;
> - Consider the use of visual and aural evidence.

Critical practice: documentary

When a filmmaker chooses to work in the documentary mode, they establish a particular relationship to their audience and can use the medium of film to explore an issue, inspire the viewer to act on the information they learn or become more informed about and engaged with the topic. As mentioned in Chapter 1, documentary is produced and consumed in a variety of ways from the cinematic productions and releases of popular filmmakers such as Michael Moore, to the small, independently produced and distributed internet productions. In this chapter I want to think of the broadest definition of documentary while questioning both how to analyze and how to create documentary using a critical-practice approach.

The basic definition of documentary is that it is a film founded in fact, but this does not encompass the full diversity of documentary style. The form is difficult to define because of this diversity. Documentary practitioners have their own sense of what a documentary entails and viewers likewise have particular expectations about the form. Often it is these expectations of what a documentary is that define how we view them and how we react to the material presented. Ultimately, one of the great potentials of documentary is its wide range of techniques and the fact that it can experiment with its own form and incorporate different viewpoints and aesthetic styles. In this chapter, while looking at the effects of different documentary techniques, we will consider the gamut of documentary style in order to engage with its full potential.

The term 'documentary' originates in the 1930s with critical practitioner John Grierson, who first used the word to describe the work of American ethnographic filmmaker Robert Flaherty. Grierson went on to become an important influence in the development of film as a medium for disseminating information. He worked as a producer of documentaries for various state-sponsored organizations in Britain in the 1930s, before moving on to be one of the founders of the National Film Board of Canada. Grierson defined documentary film as 'the creative treatment of actuality' (Grierson, 1966: 147). Underlying Grierson's definition is a belief in the social or political functions of the documentary form. Both Grierson's theory and practice accentuated the idea that documentary had a role to play in public life, informing the audience and guiding social policy and civic responsibility. Not all documentaries are made according to Grierson's ideal, but it points to documentary's specific public-information relationship with the audience. In some ways, audience expectations define a documentary. Documentary in both its form and its expectations has evolved since the time of Grierson and it now encompasses a wide range of styles that blur the stylistic boundaries in various ways, such as: incorporating elements of fictional reconstruction; integrating **avant-garde** and experimental techniques; or intersecting with the popular entertainment forms of factual or 'reality' TV.

Grierson's definition also avoids the term 'reality'. Perhaps, this is because 'reality' is hard to define. We often evaluate films and other artwork according to how 'realistic' they are yet 'reality' is different for everyone who experiences it. Realism in filmmaking terms must always be seen as a style: filmic techniques used to give the audience the feeling of immediacy and unmediated access to what happened. Thus, any definition would lead us to expect that documentaries will deal with subject matter based in experience, yet they acknowledge that experience is interpreted creatively through the methods of the filmmaking process. Likewise there is a common-sense assumption, that many students of documentary adopt, that these are films to be analyzed or produced using the criteria of objectivity or lack of bias. Many styles of documentary, such as the **Direct Cinema** movement of the 1960s, sought to use cinematic tools to create observational documentaries as free from bias as possible. Yet, as we will see, the very nature of cinematic language and apparatus makes this task impossible. Often, the success of a documentary lies exactly in the way in which it uses this language as a rhetorical tool, to argue a point or present an opinion on the topic it is addressing.

With these thoughts about documentary in mind, approaching its critical practice requires thinking analytically about the form. Documentaries are as tied to **ideology** as any other form of representation and part of the ideological functioning of the documentary is its assumed relationship to reality and to objectivity. Thus a critical-practice approach questions the assumptions regarding how documentaries are viewed and evaluated, seeing them as part of a system of representation, rather than as an unmediated relationship with the 'truth'.

Many students when they start to learn the styles and techniques of documentary practice adopt a conventional approach to the style: using interviews or voice over to introduce and structure the topic, and illustrative material to visually support what is being discussed. A critical-practice approach to documentary involves applying the theoretical ideas on documentary to create a practice that is aware of its own status as documentary and which engages critically with debates in ethics as well as representational issues. Critical-practice productions also push the boundaries of the form, challenging these expectations and moving beyond the conventions of the informational format of the illustrated interview, to explore different forms and engage creatively and critically with practice.

If working outside of conventions, how do we approach the creation of a documentary on any given topic? As we look at some of the techniques of non-fiction filmmaking, let's think of the questions we might want to ask ourselves as we go through the process of creating or analyzing a critical-practice documentary:

- How does the documentary structure the material?
- How does the documentary address its audience?
- How does the documentary use participant testimonies?
- How does the documentary marshal different forms of visual and aural evidence?
  Let's start by considering different forms of documentary structure.

Structure

When deciding how to make a documentary, a film- or videomaker generally approaches the subject with a particular style in mind. One of the elements of that style is the film's structure: a series of specific and defined choices that guide the viewer through the material presented in the film. Even critical-practice documentaries that experiment with conventional style use their structures with an increased awareness, rather than being formless or abandoning structure entirely.

Although documentaries don't always rely on a story structure as clearly as the fiction films we discussed in Chapter 3, narrative is still used in documentary. As viewers, we react to stories, relate to characters and are moved by the struggles of individuals. Therefore, the narrative approach to documentary can be very effective and appropriate. Stories in a documentary can help a film to achieve other goals: to inform or educate the audience, to change their opinions, argue a point of view or inspire them to action. Therefore, the narrative structure often works in combination with other structures. In this section we will examine three general types of structure that can be seen in documentary film; rhetorical, observational and lyrical.

Rhetorical structure

Documentary films often argue a position or develop an opinion, rather than just tell a story or present factual information. Even those that appear not to show a bias towards a particular perspective are still guided and informed by a point of view and concealing this perspective is in itself a tactic of the rhetoric of the film. When they are deciding what to include and what to exclude, documentary filmmakers express their views about a subject. This opinion can form the underlying structure of a documentary; therefore giving the documentary a rhetorical, or argument-based, structure.

During the 1930s, rhetorical form and style developed as part of a movement of documentary filmmaking that started in Britain under the guidance of John Grierson, but ultimately influenced the international institutionalization of the form. These documentaries were strongly tied to educational and social movements for reform. As such, their rhetorical strategies are fairly transparent; their point of view is clearly, almost simplistically, argued. A good example of a rhetorical documentary from this era is *Housing Problems* (1935). This film presents the problem of slum housing and then offers a solution, in the form of the building of improved public accommodation. The structure of this film is simple, it presents the problem with the voice over beginning: 'This film is going to introduce you to some of the concerns.' Then a local politician, functioning as an expert on the topic, explains the issue of poor housing in general terms. The next section gives four slum residents the opportunity to recount their experiences of living in the slums. These testimonies mostly take the form of stories, as each individual describes an incident with vermin or the dangers of bad construction. The solution is introduced in the form of

Figure 4.1 *Housing Problems*, Edgar Anstey and Arthur Elton, 1935

a new housing project, which is described by the omniscient voice over, while the image shows, first model versions of the new housing, then some of the new buildings. The film ends with three witness accounts – two residents and a caretaker – who testify to the improved conditions of the new housing. The structure here is very simple: problem > solution. Both the problem and the solution are supported by evidence in the form of visuals, interviews and voice-over information. A more complex form of a rhetorical documentary would perhaps present different solutions to the problem, and review many sides of the debate. The problem could also be presented with more complexity and the reasons for the poor housing explored in more depth. The rhetorical structure, however, is an appropriate choice for presenting this subject.

Contemporary documentaries also rely heavily on rhetorical structures. *Super Size Me* (2004) makes an argument that eating too often at the fast-food chain McDonald's can be bad for your health. As the film unfolds, the story of director Morgan Spurlock's experiences with this diet builds a case that eating food from McDonald's is unhealthy, as the viewer is led to evaluate the negative effects that the food has on the filmmaker's physical condition. Here, Spurlock's first-person voice provides a different strategy from the more detached third person voice over of *Housing Problems* for introducing the rhetoric of the film. In addition, while following Spurlock's personal struggle with fast food and his health, *Super Size Me* also presents information about diet and nutrition in US society in general. Among other topics, he deals with food in schools; he visits lunchrooms and looks at the eating habits of teenagers, and the policies schools adopt towards providing food for their students. At one point he also interviews a fan of McDonald's who eats Big Macs daily without appearing to suffer the negative effects that Spurlock shows. This amusing interview functions like a counter-argument (although not a very persuasive one) to Spurlock's position against McDonald's. With statistical information, historical background and responses from nutritionists, he builds an engaging case for the problem with the fast-food diet. He also entertains the viewer, making the argument more palatable. This rhetorical structure is more subtle than the previous example from the 1930s, as it allows the viewers more space to draw their own conclusions from the information presented to them.

Observational documentary

Some documentaries are structured to appear to merely observe some element of life as it unfolds. This style of filmmaking was particularly popular in certain periods of history, such as the 1960s, when a combination of factors led to a movement of documentary known as **cinéma vérité** in France or Direct Cinema in the US. These films reacted against the overly didactic and controlling practices of earlier rhetorical documentaries. Direct Cinema filmmakers believed in creating films that just showed a slice of life occurring in front of the camera, with little or no intervention from the filmmaker, such as interviews or reconstructions. *Salesman* (1968) is an example of Direct Cinema. It uses observational techniques to show the life of Bible salesmen as they attempt to do business door-to-door in different communities. The camera, and with it the audience, appear just to be watching the salesmen's lives unfold. The narrative is minimal, with no conflict or excitement of action. Through the style of this documentary, the viewers are given the chance to observe this group of people about their daily business.

One of the limitations of the observational style is actually that sense of realism itself. Observational documentaries show life unfolding, but this in itself is deceptive. Many filmmaking techniques are used in these documentaries to shape the films and create certain meanings or ideas. With the cinematography, the camera operator selects and frames an image, always choosing which information to include, and which to leave out. At the same time, the documentary's action is influenced by the presence of a film crew, changing how people might act or react to a given situation. Finally, in the process of editing, the selection of which shots and what information is included, and how it is structured together, functions to interpret the information presented. This is also accomplished by how scenes are placed next to each other, and when a scene begins or ends. Thus, although the observational style may appear more realistic, this appearance underlies a level of manipulation that a filmmaker can use to create meaning.

Lyrical documentary

A lyrical documentary is a form of documentary that presents its subject in a poetic manner rather than an argumentative or story-based style. Lyrical documentaries employ association, abstraction and other experimental techniques to create a feeling about a particular subject. Just as poetry functions differently than prose in written work, poetic or lyrical documentary style uses different cinematic language to express its ideas. The documentary *The Song of Ceylon* (1934) is an example of a lyrical documentary that presents its subject through abstraction and association. The film was sponsored by the Ceylon Tea Board and offers a portrait of the country and its traditions. Unlike its Hindu neighbour, India, the majority religion of Ceylon is Buddhism. At the time this film was made, Ceylon was a colony of the British Empire, and did not gain its independence until 1948, when it became known as Sri Lanka. *The Song of Ceylon* was made by the British documentary filmmaker Basil Wright, as part of the same movement that produced *Housing Problems*. This film, however, is a clear departure from the conventional rhetorical style, using a more abstract form to establish a mood and convey a series of emotions. It is ambiguous in its meaning; it does not directly argue for a public policy towards the British colonial occupation, nor does it give a tourist travelogue account, nor a sales pitch for tea. Instead it presents us with moments in the life and religious practices of the Ceylonese people. In many ways it uses observational techniques, showing the life of the people as it unfolds. It departs from this style in its utilization of other techniques such as the **voice over**, which is more commonly associated with the rhetorical form. What marks this work out as a lyrical documentary, however, is the inclusion of aesthetic elements more for their own sake than for the information that they develop.

The film is divided into four parts:

- The first part 'The Buddha' deals with the history and the religious practices of the Ceylonese.
- The second part is the most conventional in its documentary approach as it provides information about the cultivation of agriculture and the everyday life of the people.

Figure 4.2   *The Song of Ceylon*, Basil Wright, 1934

- The third part 'Voices of Commerce' uses a more lyrical approach. Rather than produce an informational document about the effects of colonialism, commercialism and trade on the traditional culture of the people of Ceylon, the filmmaker chose to contrast a series of images of Ceylonese culture with the culture of international trade. These images are accompanied by a **counterpoint** soundtrack of the international and colonial workers and their telecommunications systems.
- Part four, 'The Apparel of a God' returns to the opening sequence, showing the Ceylonese religious culture, with accompanying music, **sound effects** and a fragmented voice over evoking the beliefs being illustrated.

This style allows viewers to make their own inferences about the relationships between these images and these sounds. The juxtapositions between the visuals and the sound evoke emotional reactions in the viewer which can affect the conclusions they reach about the subject. The lyrical documentary is often more abstract in its approach, leaving its meanings more open to the interpretation of the viewer.

When creating a documentary film, the structure is key in conveying information clearly to the viewers. This decision on structure then guides a filmmaker to incorporate certain elements and combine them in such a way as to create the desired effect. Different structures have different processes. With a rhetorical documentary, for instance, there is more likely to be some form of scripted direct address, preplanned interview questions, onscreen presentation or voice-over narration. Observational practice is more often structured in production and postproduction. As the name suggests, the production involves observing a situation with a camera, with fewer preconceptions from the planning phase. In these cases, much of the structure of the documentary is then created in postproduction, as the editing is used to shape the shot footage, to find connections and to create a meaningful work. The approach taken for a lyrical documentary can vary, sometimes scripted and preplanned and sometimes structured through the shooting or editing of the material. The structure that a documentary-maker utilizes is also dependent on the subject. The form should be appropriate to the content and to the effect that the filmmaker is trying to produce.

The way in which the film employs its techniques to address the viewer is known as the film's **mode of address**. With rhetorical documentaries, for example, it is common to address the audience with the intention to inform them, or to persuade them of a particular perspective. This is different from narrative films that mainly focus on telling a story. For this reason documentaries use certain techniques, such as a speaker directly addressing the camera, or a voice over giving information, far more commonly than do fiction films.

Modes of address

In documentary film, the filmmaker is often talking to us, telling us about things that have happened, arguing rhetorically about various subjects or making associations between different events and people. The way documentary films talk to their audience to achieve these various aims is known as the mode of address. As a basic division, there are two modes: **direct address** and **indirect address**. Most documentary films combine direct and indirect address, although some use indirect address only. Direct address refers to those times when somebody on screen directly talks to the camera and gives information to the audience.

Direct address

In contemporary film it is not unknown for an actor to break the illusion of a scene and look directly at the camera and the viewer. This practice has a long history, drawing on the soliloquy of classical theatre; Hamlet and Macbeth stopped in the action of their dramas to express their fears and hopes to the audience. It is not common for a fiction film to use this convention, but it is more common to have a voice-over narrator telling us parts of a fictional story. Fictional examples of direct address change the relationship between characters on screen and members of the audience, by speaking to them and acknowledging their presence. Direct address is a common feature of many types of documentary, as we see in the television news, when the presenter looks directly towards the camera and addresses the audience from a position of authority. It is this association between direct address and authority that gives power to the speaker's voice: we listen to what they are saying and believe in it.

Another form of direct address is voice over, when you hear a voice on the soundtrack speaking over images. When this voice stems from an authoritarian source, it can be described as an omniscient narrator, or sometimes in casual circumstances as the 'voice of God'. Voice over is an **offscreen** version of direct address, but, as the voice comes from a source that is not seen, it establishes less of a personal connection. The voice therefore becomes more of a disembodied narrator, speaking from a position of power outside (or even above) the world of the images. The effect the voice over has on the audience can be related to the type of voice that we hear. For example, convention often suggests that a man's voice has more authority than a woman's voice. Filmmakers therefore, sometimes select a man to do the voice over in particular situations. Similarly, a woman's voice is sometimes used for subject matter that might be more sensitive. Traditional uses of voice over give the audience certain expectations and reactions to the information. Likewise accents and dialects can subtly influence how a viewer interprets the information presented. This is part of the way that ideology functions in how we respond to a documentary and, as with other conventions should be questioned, critiqued and undermined in a critical-practice documentary.

Titles are another form of direct address, giving information about the subject. Like the other forms of direct address, titles talk directly to the audience and can range from simple information written on screen, identifying things such as time, place or interviewee's name and role, to more complex titles incorporating facts and statistics. Direct-address titles can be creatively included, such as those in the 1968 Argentinian film, *Hour of the Furnaces*. In this film, titles appear to emerge out of the screen towards the audience in time to the rhythm of the background music, consisting of quotations on neo-colonialism from various writers and political figures. The titles are a central part of the address of this film, as well as giving background context, they add to the visual strength of the film and are designed to inspire the audience to action.

There are two primary effects of direct address. First, by acknowledging the presence of the camera, direct address breaks the illusion that what is going on in front of the camera is happening regardless of the camera. This effect is important in a documentary, as the filmmakers may not want to maintain the illusion of an unmediated world. Instead, the goal is to engage the audience openly in the topic under discussion. This helps to persuade the viewer that the information or opinion expressed in the documentary is true and accurate. The second effect of direct address is to remove any sense that there is any mediation between the subject and the audience. In other words, when direct address is present, the person speaking wants the power implied by directly talking to the viewer.

In summary, let's see how direct address works in a particular example. In *Super Size Me*, Morgan Spurlock talks directly to the audience. From the beginning of the film, Spurlock is heard in voice over telling the audience information about trends in weight in the US and relating these to the popularity of fast food. This narration is personalized as he compares the fast-food diet to memories of his childhood, when his mother cooked dinner every day. The tone of Spurlock's voice is conversational, encouraging the audience to listen to him, but not alienating them with a cold delivery. The effect of this narration is to engage with the topic on a personal level, and introduce himself as an individual who will guide the viewer.

At the end of the opening sequence, Spurlock is on the screen standing on the street, directly addressing the audience and setting up the premise for the film: his thirty-day experiment with a McDonald's diet. At this moment, as he is talking to us, introducing himself and the rest of the film, his tone is casual and his presence personalizes the address. He is conscious of the camera, which allows him to present his argument and tell his story directly. His first-person direct address also gives the sense that he is in control, as you can see if you compare this sequence to the camera to the interviews with the other people you see later in the documentary. In the following sequence Spurlock visits three doctors. While the doctors perform their medical check-ups, they interact with Spurlock, but ignore the camera. Mostly, Spurlock talks to the doctors, but occasionally makes a side comment to the camera, and with it, to the audience. For example, after the general practitioner has performed a rectal exam, we hear him say 'I like to be more thorough than that.' Then we see Spurlock directly addressing the camera with the comment 'I like doctors to be thorough.' The effect of this moment of direct address is to confirm Spurlock's privileged relationship to the audience. He has the control in this situation, and it is clearly his opinions and perspective that we are given.

Indirect address

Indirect address is a common way of structuring interviews in a documentary. This is when an interviewee appears to talk to someone **off screen** rather than directly to the camera. Here the information is aimed at the audience, but is, in a way, translated and mediated through the person of the interviewer, whether they appear on screen or are implied by the interviewee's gaze. When the interviewer is not seen the effect is more casual than a direct-address approach as the person speaking appears just to be relating accounts of their experiences, unaware of the camera. This type of address, however, acknowledges the filmmaker's function to mediate between the speaker and the audience. Even if we neither see nor hear the person the interviewees are speaking to, we infer their presence and the interview subject does not have that power to talk directly to us; they talk through the unseen interviewer.

The interview is just one of the techniques with which documentaries address us indirectly. In some documentaries, the action taking place around the camera is a method of indirect address. For example, in Direct Cinema films, the action just occurs on screen without the presence of an interviewer or voice over. *Salesman*, for example, follows the life of Paul, a door-to-door Bible salesman, and his co-workers and customers. There are no moments of direct address and no interviews, the action just appears to happen in front of us. In one scene Paul is at work trying to sell a Bible to a client; neither of the subjects acknowledges the presence of the camera in any way. Unlike a conventional interview, Paul and his client are not telling a story or making a rhetorical point, they are just going about their business. Is there any mode of address here at all? In this most indirect way, the filmmakers are addressing us, by showing us the workings of Paul's business. They are making a point about the commercialization of religion, the dreariness of life as a travelling salesman and how manipulative human nature can prove under the pressure to sell.

The way documentary filmmakers address their audience is important to how they communicate their message. When working in the documentary style, choosing a mode of address occurs early in the process as it defines how the filmmaker interacts with the participants during production. Thus, selecting mode of address is part of the preproduction of a documentary. Direct address is suited to a first-person approach, with the central presenter performing the role of guide to the subject. This requires scripting, to plan what is said in this presentation of information. Direct address in the form of a voice over is often more formal, but equally requires a script that will structure the film as well as relate the information through the narration. This narration is often developed during the course of production and in response to interviews and other material collected. Indirect address appears more unmediated, with a stronger focus on the content. In choosing this style the documentary-maker approaches the content through the participants, either with planned interviews – scripted in the form of questions – or through observational techniques.

As the documentary maker moves from preproduction to production, one of the key questions is how participants are to be included, whether through interviewers or other forms of interaction and engagement. This is the issue we will turn to next.

Documentary's participants

Interviews are often an integral part of a documentary as well as fundamental to its mode of address. In this section we are going to think about the presentation of information through the documentary's participants more broadly than the conventional interview, deploying the ideas of testimony, encounters and first-person voice as ways in which documentary can be a collaborative practice. Testimonies include traditional interviews, but also stretch beyond this to encourage creative thinking about the presence of participants in documentary. Participant testimony allows us to explore the ways in which many people involved in documentary, both on the screen as well as behind the camera, are active in how a film makes meaning.

Interviews and encounters

It is a common practice, and it is often where the student filmmaker starts, to construct a documentary from interviews with participants, shot in medium **close-up**, framed slightly off-centre, looking off screen, located in a home or work location (depending on the topic), talking about the subject at hand. These interviews are known as **talking heads** and are such a standard practice that many critics find this style so conventional that it runs the risk of being dull. This traditional interview, however, has a place in documentary practice. Its effectiveness is often dependent on different things: what the participant is talking about, how interesting and charismatic they are as a speaker, how the interview is lit and shot, and how it is edited and contextualized into the rest of the film.

Throughout the history of the documentary form, the interview has served different purposes, as far back as the 1930s, when *Housing Problems* made innovative use of interviews. Although watching this film from a contemporary perspective, the interviews seem artificial and the participants uncomfortable, it nevertheless shows the potential to shift the address of the documentary. In *Housing Problems*, the working-class individuals and families living in slum conditions are given the opportunity to recount their experiences and be heard by the audience. This sense of empowerment that the documentary interview offers is one of the strongest arguments in its favour. The feeling of authenticity is increased by the participation of people with different perspectives and experiences, making interviews important to certain documentary traditions. For example, feminist documentary practice in the 1970s included interviews as part of the process of 'consciousness-raising': giving voice to people and issues that were often overlooked by mainstream representations. In this tradition, the interview is part of the documentary's strategy to allow the participants to tell their own stories and relate their experiences to the audience.

In contrast to this view, it is important to realize that the empowerment offered by the documentary interview is only partial, as the filmmaker retains primary control of the shooting situation. The directorial choices include the questions that are asked of any participant and the power of an interview often lies in the interviewer's skill to set the agenda, lead the discussion and guide the responses. Of equal importance is the way in which an interview is edited, which can position the participant as the filmmaker chooses through the selection of responses, the order in which they are presented, and the supporting material that accompanies or surrounds the speaker. The filmmaker retains the ultimate power of the image. Some documentary conventions include the participants more actively than traditional interviews, using collaborative authorship in such forms as participant video diaries, or feedback and discussion between participants about the material included.

Despite the ongoing debate about the status of the interview subject's role as a participant, conventional interview documentaries can be very effective. An example of this is in Spike Lee's 2006 *When the Levees Broke*, which is an account of Hurricane Katrina and its aftermath. Lee relies heavily on people who experienced the hurricane firsthand to retell the story and to explain the impact it had on them and the events that they witnessed. The film is effective partly due to the range of interviews, demonstrating how this catastrophe affected many different people in various ways. Given the hurricane's impact on people's lives, this is an appropriate method of approaching this topic. The testimony of these witnesses adds to the authenticity of the film; these are the people who really suffered this disaster.

The conventional seated talking head is only one form of interview; other styles can include an action-oriented interview, with the participant demonstrating something or being involved with an event or discussion with other participants. For example, in *Super Size Me*, Spurlock talks to a head cook in a high school about how they prepare the school lunches. In the interview she walks around the school kitchen showing Spurlock the pre-packaged food that she is sent from the government which she only has to reheat. In this location, she can lift the boxes of spaghetti sauce to illustrate the point she is making, thus engaging the viewer visually as well as descriptively with the issue at hand.

Similarly, a form of testimony that stretches beyond a conventional interview is what I would call an encounter, a meeting between participants, or between filmmaker and participant that accentuates the conflict or debate within a documentary. A good example of an encounter is in *Heir to an Execution* (2004), which is created from the perspective of Ivy Meeropol, the granddaughter of Ethel and Julius Rosenberg, a couple who were executed in the US in the 1950s for conspiracy to commit espionage. The Rosenberg case was a key historical moment in the Cold War and their

Figure 4.3   *Heir to an Execution*, Ivy Meeropol, 2004

execution an indicator of the depth of anti-Communist popular political sentiment in the US at the time. Despite the historical importance of the Rosenbergs' execution, Meeropol's documentary charts a highly personal and emotional journey into her family's past. At one stage she tries to contact and talk to members of her extended family who all lost touch after the execution, most of whom were trying to hide their connection to the Rosenbergs. Few family members agree to talk to her, but one does, and she visits a cousin in California. Because of Meeropol's involvement in the story, the moment is quite emotional in a manner not typical of a detached interviewer–participant question-and-answer interview. Their conversation is more of a dialogue than an interview, appropriate for two family members who meet due to the circumstances of the film that is being made. The moment's emotional resonance is unexpected, lending the encounter a greater sense of authenticity.

First-person voice

Some types of documentary media use the presence of an onscreen reporter to present information or to interview the subject. *Super Size Me*, for example, works around Spurlock's presence in the film, his voice speaks in the 'I' form and his experiences with fast food guide the viewer through the story and the argument. Other filmmakers incorporate a first-person style to explore various subjects, many related to their own identity and experience. The first-person voice works in an interesting way in *Heir to an Execution*. Here the filmmaker, Ivy Meeropol, is investigating the legacy of her family history. Her presence in the documentary gives a specific focus to the story; she is not the passive observer of events, but an active participant in the story. She does not claim objectivity about the subject, but instead makes her personal involvement part of the approach she takes to the subject; she reacts emotionally rather than dispassionately to the information she unearths. We see her perspective, and through her point of view we get a personal response to a historical subject. This is a particularly appropriate approach as she directly links her personal and familial struggle with her grandparents' trial and execution, which has been represented differently in historical documents. She witnesses this in one memorable scene, when she and her adopted brother visit a museum display about her grandparents and the central conflict between the official and the personal history is made clear.

Evidence

Although some documentaries preference informational content over visual style, it is important to realize that documentaries can be so much more than illustrated lectures, and their visual and aural aesthetics fully engaging experiences. Thus, as we move through the process of creating a documentary, we can see how important it is to work with the visual style and material available. After choosing a topic, deciding on the appropriate structure and mode of address, based on this decision, the documentary maker will then start to construct the work from the various components, such as interviews, encounters or observational footage. Rhetorical documentaries, in particular, also involve other elements that are drawn from a filmmaker's research and incorporated into the film. These elements can be known by different names. Some filmmakers use the term **B-Roll** for the additional footage that is used to link interviews or illustrate aspects of the voice over. This term originates from film editing, and describes a situation when one set of images is on one reel and another set on a second (or B) reel. For the discussion that follows, I want to look at B-roll and other elements of the construction of a documentary as a form of evidence, evidence that is brought forward to illustrate a point or support an argument. Yet in using the term 'evidence', I also mean it in the broad sense to refer to all the visual and aural components that filmmakers use to support the opinions expressed in their documentary. It is also important to consider sound as part of the construction of a documentary's evidence.

Visual evidence

There are a number of types of visual evidence. Let's break them down into three broad categories:

1   Current evidence, which includes any visual evidence collected at the time of the production of the film;
2   Archival evidence, which includes images created in the past which can be incorporated into the documentary;
3   Constructed evidence, which includes anything created or recreated by the filmmaker to support the goal of the documentary.

Current evidence

Current evidence includes the testimonies, interviews and encounters described in the previous section. Filmmakers can also gather other forms of evidence from the contemporary setting. Current evidence can be as basic as the observational style, recording things as they happen, as with the earlier example of *Salesman*. Or in *Super Size Me*, we see Morgan Spurlock going about his business at work and at home, while living on the McDonald's diet. In a memorable scene, he is in a car eating a super-sized meal which the camera shows until he is finally sick. This moment unfolding is particularly strong visual evidence for his rhetorical case against the fast-food diet as it provokes an emotional response in the viewer.

Many documentaries use graphics as a form of evidence. This can include title screens with statistical information, or maps and graphs that demonstrate something about the subject of the documentary. In *Super Size Me*, for example, there are a number of sequences that give statistical information accompanied by maps, charts and animated diagrams. In one instance, as Morgan Spurlock is travelling through Texas researching the effects of a McDonald's diet on health, he states 'out of the top fifteen fattest cities in America, Texas has five'. This information is accompanied by an animated map showing the cities he mentions.

Another form of current evidence can involve revisiting the location of an incident that is being recounted in the documentary. These moments can work in a similar manner to the encounters between different people that are part of a film's testimony. For example, in a key scene from *When the Levees Broke*, the crew returns to the location of devastation with a family who has lost their home. The sequence starts in the car as they drive towards the house, speculating on what they will find there. When they arrive, their reactions are captured by the camera. As they move through their home, their emotions are clear and the space is a powerful form of visual evidence of the extent of the devastation. This moment accentuates the sense of loss caused by the hurricane, as the viewer shares the feelings of the family looking over the wreckage.

Heir to an Execution uses locations of past events particularly effectively. Throughout the film, Meeropol visits a number of locations that invoke the history of the story that she is telling. In one particular scene she goes with her father and uncle to the apartment where they lived as boys with their parents. This scene allows for the participants to recount part of their story, in particular for her father Michael to recall the emotional memory of when his father was arrested. The scene links the present location, now the home of a different family, to the past, through old photographs and film footage of the arrest. At one point, the filmmaker poses in the kitchen in the same manner as her grandmother did in a photograph taken fifty years earlier. This moment combines the past and present through the location and accentuates the theme of the family living with the difficult memories of what happened to the Rosenbergs.

Archival evidence

As this scene in *Heir to an Execution* shows, filmmakers directing documentaries about the past, and working to reconstruct historical events, depend as much on archives and research, as do historians writing history books. Archival evidence can include **footage** (filmed images shot at the time being documented) as well as documents, photographs or audio recordings.

A film that relies heavily on archival images is the 2004 documentary *The American Experience: The Murder of Emmett Till*. This film tells the story of the murder of a fourteen-year-old African-American boy from Chicago who was visiting his family in Mississippi in the summer of 1955. The Emmett Till case was of particular importance in the history of the US Civil Rights movement, spurring many people to political action against the system of racial segregation. The documentary recounts Emmett Till's encounter with a woman in a store, his subsequent murder, the reaction that followed and the trial in which the accused murderers were acquitted by an all-white jury in the context of heightened racial tension. Depending on archival footage to construct much of its story, the film shows images of Chicago, of the train that accompanies the narrator's description of Emmett's trip, the South, of the town of Money, of the Bryant store Emmett visited, the river, the funeral and the trial. This is probably only a small part of the footage that the filmmakers had at their disposal. Other news crews would have covered this event, and there are undoubtedly many images of Chicago, Mississippi and the Tallahatchie River that could have been used as well. One skill required of a team of documentary-makers is that of editing – collecting, sorting through, selecting and combining all the possible images to effectively tell a story.

Part of the archival footage used in this example includes the interview with Mose Wright, Till's uncle who was no longer alive when the film was made. This interview was clearly shot at the time and is used in conjunction with the current interviews and the voice over to tell the story and reconstruct the events. Again this is just one possibility available to the filmmakers, but it is an important piece of evidence. The eye-witness account of Mose Wright, given through direct address, describing the abduction of his nephew, adds much weight to the retelling of the story. In addition, the interviews with Till's mother tell us a lot about the political climate at the time of the trial, much of what is elicited is a result of how the interview is conducted. The way in which the white reporters question this grieving mother ('How could you possibly think you could be a help ...?') shows a level of disrespect that verifies the accusations of southern racism that the narrator has emphasized.

Naturally there are significant moments in the story for which no footage exists. We rely heavily on the graphic accounts of the witnesses to understand what took place in the Bryant store.

Figure 4.4   *Heir to an Execution*, Ivy Meeropol, 2004

Figure 4.5   *Heir to an Execution*, Ivy Meeropol, 2004

The film uses photographs to fill in other gaps. The images of prior lynchings are graphic reminders of the contemporary culture. The before-and-after photographs of Emmett Till also vividly and emotionally portray what is at stake in this story, and underscore both the violence and the tragedy involved. There is also the important moment of Mose Wright's accusation at the trial, which is described by the witnesses and supported by an unclear yet graphic photograph of Wright pointing across the courtroom.

The final form of archival evidence is the written account. All historians, as well as historical-documentarymakers, rely on the evidence of documents and written accounts to construct, support and verify their stories. Images of such documents or accounts can add to the visual evidence of a documentary. In addition to being used as a visual source, these written accounts can develop the background information provided by the narrator. In *Heir to an Execution* the filmmaker's journey to discover more about her family's past involves her revealing her process of archival research. The camera follows as she enters the National Archives to look at the official documents of her grandparents' case. She shows, and discusses her reactions to the different parts of the evidence contained in the archives. Here we get a sense of the importance of these documents to the construction of the history she is telling. But we also get more from this scene as the history comes alive through her emotional reaction to the information she encounters. In another scene we watch as Michael Meeropol talks to his daughter who is holding the camera, as they examine the contents of a bank vault, containing documents and letters that further explicate the story of the family's loss. We see close-ups of letters as Michael shows them to Ivy. These personal letters and mementoes are a contrast to the official government documents that introduce evidence of the Rosenbergs' potential involvement in espionage. The two sources – the official record and the personal family record – are both part of the same history reflected from different perspectives.

Figure 4.6 *Heir to an Execution*, Ivy Meeropol, 2004

Figure 4.7   *Heir to an Execution*, Ivy Meeropol, 2004

Constructed evidence

The third form of visual evidence is event re-enactment or the reconstruction of locations. These retellings are dramatised, and can be used in a supporting role within a documentary. This can be controversial, as in the example from the documentary series *Mighty Times*, the Academy Award-winning short, *The Children's March* (2004). The directors chose to show events that occurred in the past by re-enacting certain key scenes. *The Children's March* tells the story of a 1963 Civil Rights protest by children and young students in Birmingham, Alabama. The re-enactments are carefully constructed to look like material shot during the time the film is set. They are then combined with archive images and conventional documentary techniques. This film caused some controversy over its use of these re-enactments because it is not clear which parts of the film are original and which parts are recreated. This blurring of the distinctions between fiction and fact calls into question the film's status as a documentary. Another filmmaker, Jon Else, reviewed the film for accuracy and summarized its controversial status as a documentary:

> The question with this film … comes from the fact that the … real archive footage and the very skilfully dramatized archive footage are seamlessly woven together so the audience has no way of knowing whether a particular shot, say of police commissioner Bull Connor, is the real Bull Connor or an actor. (Else, 2005)

However, the film employs actors to illustrate the events of the past and the re-enactments are scripted and performed. These reconstructions are incorporated into the film, contextualized by voice-over narration and original footage. Yet despite its use of supposedly non-documentary elements, this film is considered a documentary as it deals with an actual event primarily through use of conventional documentary techniques. Re-enactments are frequently considered an acceptable part of documentary style that can be utilized in creative and interesting ways.

Aural evidence

As well as the visual evidence that we have just discussed, documentaries also employ sound in different ways as evidence. Sound adds emotional weight to the subject matter being portrayed. The sound can include what was recorded at the same time as the images, such as the interview with Mose Wright in *The Murder of Emmett Till*. It can also include the voices of the people being interviewed, while the images are shown. There are also sound effects from particular locations, for example, the opening shot of *The Murder of Emmett Till* shows us the Tallahatchie River and we hear a combination of sounds, including sound effects that fit with the location, such as birds and crickets. Finally, there is the music, which contributes to the authenticity of the scene as it comes from the time period depicted. The music also increases the emotional effect, as we listen to a melancholy gospel track during Emmett Till's funeral.

Summary and key questions

The creation of meaning in a documentary is in part a function of the selection, structuring and presentation of the material. When preparing to create or to analyze a documentary these are some of the questions that might guide you to a deeper understanding of the form.

- How is the documentary structured?
- What modes of address are used to talk to the audience?
- What kinds of testimony are included?
- How does the documentary incorporate evidence?

Want to learn more?

Think about this ...

Mode of address

Objective: To analyze how documentaries address their audiences.

Thinking about a variety of documentaries that you have seen, categorize them according to how they address their audience. Which documentaries use direct address? Which use indirect address? How do the different styles work with or complement their subject matter?

Try this ...

Gathering testimony

> Objective: To experiment with the use of testimonies, interviews and encounters.
> You will need: You can use a video camera or just do a practice interview.

Choose someone you know to interview and decide on a specific topic. Practise interview techniques: asking questions that will encourage full answers, listening, drawing out responses from your subject. Which kinds of questions work best to elicit the kinds of answers you need? How do you structure the interview to ensure the best results? Think about how the interview is presented visually. How will you frame the subject? What background or location will you use?

Adding evidence

> Objective: Consider the use of documentary visual and aural evidence.
> You will need: You can use a video camera or just do a preplanning exercise.

Using the interview above, explore the different types of visual and aural evidence that you might bring in to complement the interview. What B-Roll might illustrate what the participant is discussing? What additional soundtrack elements would also support the visual scheme?

Further reading

A number of books on the practice of making documentaries provide good overviews about how to approach this. Michael Rabiger's *Directing the Documentary* is a good place to start, covering the whole process from conception to completion. Alan Rosenthal's *Writing, Producing and Directing Documentary Film and Video* is also useful with particularly strong sections on scripting and preproduction. Ilsa Barbash and Lucien Taylor's *Cross-Cultural Filmmaking* is geared towards ethnographic documentary, but the general advice is applicable to other styles of practice. There are several theorists writing on documentary; of particular interest is Bill Nichols's *Introduction to Documentary*, which covers many important aspects and deals in detail with the definitions and styles of documentary practice. He also includes a full discussion of mode of address in *Blurred Boundaries*. A more theoretical approach is considered in Michael Renov's *The Subject of Documentary*. Another good overview is to be found in Michael Chanan's *The Politics of Documentary* and Stella Bruzzi's *New Documentary* covers recent trends and developments in the style. The critical-practice writings of John Grierson can be found in the volume edited by Forsyth Hardy, *Grierson on Documentary*.

Films studied in this chapter

The American Experience: The Murder of Emmett Till 2004 Stanley Nelson (director)
Heir to an Execution 2004 Ivy Meeropol (director)

Hour of the Furnaces 1968 Fernando Solanas and Octavio Getino (directors)
Housing Problems 1935 Edgar Anstey and Arthur Elton (directors)
Mighty Times: The Children's March 2004 Robert Houston (director)
Salesman 1968 Charles Maysles, Albert Maysles and Charlotte Zwerin (directors)
The Song of Ceylon 1934 Basil Wright (director)
Super Size Me 2004 Morgan Spurlock (director)
When the Levees Broke 2006 Spike Lee (director)

Other examples to explore

There is a plethora of documentary styles to view that can inspire ideas for creative practice or further analysis. It is interesting to consider classical rhetorical documentaries such as the work of the British movement of the 1930s and 1940s, *Night Mail* (1936 Harry Watt and Basil Wright directors)*, Coal Face* (1935 Alberto Cavalcanti director) or *Listen to Britain* (1942 Humphrey Jennings and Stewart McAllister directors), or the American documentaries of Pare Lorentz, *The River* (1938) or *The Plow That Broke the Plains* (1936). Other examples of Direct Cinema or the observational style include *Primary* (1960 Robert Drew director), *Gimme Shelter* (1970 Albert Maysles, Charles Maysles and Charlotte Zwerin directors) or *Titicut Follies* (1967 Robert Wiseman director). For interesting uses of interviews, see the work of Errol Morris, particularly *The Fog of War* (2003) or for his use of reconstructions, *The Thin Blue Line* (1988). Interesting first-person filmmakers' films include Nick Broomfield, *Kurt and Courtney* (1998) and *Tracking Down Maggie* (1994), Ross McElwee, *Sherman's March* (1986) and Jonathan Caouette, *Tarnation* (2003). For a film that stages its testimonies as **reflexive** encounters see Jean Rouch and Edgar Morin's *Chronicle of a Summer* (1960).

Experimental Film

What is experimental film?

The first time you come across examples of experimental film practice you might find yourself a bit confused. What does the filmmaker intend by it? Why is there no plot or action? Where are all the elements that you are used to in fiction film? Unlike narrative film or documentary, there is often no story to follow, nor any information to understand. In place of all these things that we expect, an experimental film can offer many other pleasures or insights. Experimental films emerge from a different tradition than conventional feature films or documentaries, they are grounded in the practices of fine art and are best understood in the context of modern and contemporary art. Thus, it is important to understand this context in order to appreciate these types of film. An experimental film can take different forms. It can be purely abstract, a play of colours and visuals; it can be personal in nature (images and thoughts drawn from the artist's life and experience); or it can be stylistically formal or reflexive, including items that are often considered 'mistakes' in a narrative film – scratches, marks on the film or title cards.

It is difficult to do more than briefly summarize some key points about experimental film in the context of an introductory film book, for a couple of reasons. First, you may not have the same frame of reference for experimental films as you do for other types of film; you are more likely to have seen a variety of narrative and documentary films. Additionally, it is equally hard because experimental film is such a large and diverse area of production and incorporates so many ideas, styles and influences. Nevertheless, let's start by considering some general points about experimental film, in order to understand better what it entails.

Experimental film is a general term for a brand of filmmaking practice that is different from, or alternative to, the more mainstream traditions of narrative and documentary. Other terms have also been used to describe this third branch of film art. These include **avant-garde** film, which is a French phrase that translates as 'advance guard' and encompasses many artistic practices – painting, sculpture, installation, performance art – but, of course, includes filmmaking. This military metaphor suggests that avant-garde artists are leading the charge to discover and deploy new, innovative and cutting-edge techniques and ideas in their practice. Other terms have come to the fore in different periods. For example, **Expanded Cinema** was a phrase introduced by Gene Youngblood in the 1970s when shifts in technology led to the growth of experimental practice beyond the medium of film, so that video and other screen media were considered as part of the potential Expanded Cinematic image. Another phrase currently in vogue among experimental media artists is **artist film and video**. This phrase is wider and more all-embracing than previous terms, referring to any film or video artist working in the fine-art tradition. In this chapter, however, I have used the more traditional term 'experimental film' to link this strand of practice to critical-practice methodology and to encourage the experimentation with practice, and the search for and exploration of diverse methods of expression. The chapter will include, however, some ideas drawn from the field of video art and concludes with an examination of some of the specific issues addressed by video and new media practice.

In general, experimental media is considered to be the work of artists, individuals or groups of individuals, who are outside the commercial film industry. These artists' frame of reference is primarily the art world and their work is influenced by other art practices and often screened in that context: in art galleries, art-house cinemas, film festivals, among groups of enthusiasts and via the internet. The second frame of reference for experimental film is popular media such as other films, or television, and the result often critiques or questions these other forms. Thus, it is important that these films are made outside the commercial film industry as this allows them to serve as a commentary on or criticism of the mainstream.

So, what do we as viewers experience when we watch this type of film? Experimental films don't fit into the structures of commercial consumption, and therefore, they are not constrained to follow any standard expectations of length; many are shorter than feature-length narratives and some, such as Andy Warhol's film *Empire* (1964), are much longer. In contemporary video art an audiovisual project can be continuous and ongoing. When we go to see experimental film we have our expectations challenged, we watch films that make us think and ask questions about (among other things) the nature of the film medium itself, the role of film within society and culture and the status of film as art. Experimental films can also address philosophical questions about different subjects – identity, meaning, psychological processes and experience – and how these are interpreted through film.

One feature of experimental film is that it is often designed to be viewed actively, thought about and experienced completely, rather than purely watched for enjoyment. This directly links experimental practice to the concept of critical practice that we introduced in Chapter 1. Experimental practice is a critical practice on many fundamental levels, as it engages with ideas of form and structure, and is often used to comment on or subvert dominant traditions. Experimental film is a potential source of inspiration for the work and thinking of a critical practitioner. Once you have actively viewed a number of examples of this type of art, you will see that the 'experiments' that are being made in visual style and personal expression are applicable to a variety of situations. This practice is influential within the filmmaking world as many unconventional techniques were first developed by experimental artists and then appropriated by mainstream filmmakers. In addition, experimental film is a fundamental influence on the areas of advertising and music video. Much of the imagery and many of the editing techniques used in television ads and music videos are inspired by the work of experimental filmmakers. You too can draw inspiration as well as a deeper cultural understanding from the work of experimental media artists.

What follows is a brief introduction to the world of experimental film. First, we will go back to its origins during the silent era, when the first group of modern artists started using film as part of the early traditions of modern art. We will then briefly explore two other eras and tendencies in later experimental film: personal filmmaking and the structuralist/materialist tradition. We will conclude the chapter with a look at Expanded Cinema: video art and the growth of new media. This is by no means an exhaustive account of experimental film and video practice. There are many other movements and styles but this chapter should provide a flavour of some of the debates and tendencies that will serve to inspire further engagement with the critical-practice of experimental film.

Film and modern art: the first avant-garde

Cinema was introduced in the latter part of the nineteenth century, with the first Lumière and Edison shorts in 1893–5, coinciding with the beginnings of a shift in the world of art. This time was one of major global upheaval, particularly in the areas of science and industrial development; advances in technology changed the way that the world and society were perceived. Changes were taking place in the arts also that reflected this different worldview and the increased importance of technology. This era in arts and literature is known as **modernism**. Modernism incorporated different views of art; formally, the artworks were not so grounded in classical realism, and thematically they expressed an interest in technology and a celebration of the mechanical age. In addition to the themes of science, technology and industry, modernism also grappled with the effect that new technologies had on culture.

This period saw the introduction of experimental or avant-garde film, integral to the early experiments in cinema. In order to truly understand and appreciate experimental film, we have to examine the context in which it arises, the practices of modern art. Thus, before we study specific examples of experimental film, let's look at the context and themes of modern art at the start of the twentieth century to see how these themes are reflected in the work of early experimental filmmakers.

Context and themes of modern art

Modern art is an expansive term that embraces many cultures, art forms, movements, styles and periods. Thus, any summary of its main ideas will have to be a simplification. Yet there are important features of the late nineteenth- and early twentieth-century culture that affect the images, concepts and progress of film as modern art. These themes are taken up in the work of different artists of the movements of the early twentieth century and include the changing world of technology, the mechanized violence of World War I and Freud's theories of psychoanalysis.

In contemporary society we almost take for granted how fast technology changes, with one format for watching or making videos quickly replacing another. At the end of the nineteenth century there were also great advances in technology. We cannot imagine the world without many of the things that were developed at this time: recorded sound, radio waves, powered flight and the motor car. Cinema was one of these inventions, occurring shortly after the invention of the phonograph, and around the same time as the first experiments in radio transmissions. Many of these changes significantly affected the way people lived and how they saw the world. For example, the development of the Ford motor car (1893) altered the nature of transportation, and in doing so, affected the appearance and geography of the city. Modern art responded to these technological changes in numerous ways. For one thing, since the arrival of photography, painters no longer sought to represent images with complete accuracy; the photograph could do that. Classical realism as a painting style became less important with the arrival of the pre-modernist movement of Impressionism.

Another important invention of the 1880s was the machine gun. This particular piece of technology mechanized war, and in 1914, with the beginning of World War I and large-scale industrialized warfare across many countries, modern art evolved in reaction to these horrors. Many artists experienced the mechanized action of the war at first hand and their work reflected this trauma. The movements of Dadaism and Surrealism, for example, were both strong reactions to the war.

Surrealism in particular was also influenced by a major intellectual upheaval caused by the work of Sigmund Freud in psychoanalysis. Freud published his *Studies in Hysteria* in 1895. This volume introduced the notion of the 'unconscious' into popular thought. This is the idea that there is a part of our brain outside of our awareness and control. It was a seminal idea at the time and much of later psychology depends on this insight. It also proved a powerful inspiration to artists, that they could explore the ideas and images emerging from their dreams and try to tap into the psychological processes of the unconscious.

With these three broad themes in mind, let's look at the some of the different early modern art movements. Modern art progressed when different schools or groups of artists working in a similar style explored an idea or made a statement associated with a particular approach to art. Some early experimental films were made by various artists working within particular movements. In the following section, we will examine examples of this, in order to place the work of avant-garde filmmakers into its proper context.

Cubism and Ballet mécanique *(1924)*

One of the earliest movements of modern art was **Cubism**, usually associated with the work of two painters, Pablo Picasso and Georges Braque. The key element that distinguishes paintings of the Cubist movement is their use of geometric shapes and disjointed representations of form that tend towards abstraction. In 1910, the French painter Fernand Léger joined the Cubist movement. His work moved away from the origins of Braque and Picasso, as his subjects were often mechanical objects or his human models painted to look mechanical – transposing flesh into machine. Léger's work continued throughout World War I. He had fought in the trenches in France, experiencing first hand the mechanization of war, and witnessing the fruitless waste and violence that resulted from war. His combining of body and machine reflects that experience, ambiguously imagining the machine as saviour and destroyer of humanity. Léger explained his choice of machine technology as subject in a letter written in 1922:

> I like the forms necessitated by modern industry and I use them; a smelting furnace will have thousands of coloured reflections both more subtle and more solid than a supposedly classical

subject. I consider that a machine gun or the breech of a 75 is more worth painting than four apples on a table or a Saint Cloud landscape. (Léger cited in Stern, 2004)

Although primarily a painter, Léger worked with American filmmaker Dudley Murphy and together they were responsible for an important early example of experimental film: *Ballet mécanique*. *Ballet mécanique* is an exploration of the art of the machine age. The title expresses Léger's desire to mechanize the art form of ballet, a tradition grounded in the aesthetics and graceful movement of the human form. *Ballet mécanique* was made at a moment in the development of film as art when artists working in other media began to be interested in the potential of film, not to entertain nor tell stories, but as a form of visual expression. Thus, the images in the film have been chosen for their aesthetic qualities and do not fulfil any storytelling function. Stylistic choices have been made to ensure that the images of the film work together: the abstraction of images through various camera angles and positions, the emphasis on movement within the frame, the repetition of images and the rhythmic juxtaposition of shots. The camera is often placed so close to an object that the viewer cannot tell what the object is. Near the beginning of the film there are a series of disjointed discs that move around the screen. These images were created by saucepan lids, appearing fragmented through the use of mirrors. At other points, a woman's mouth is shown in close-up, repeatedly smiling. This image separates the mouth from the woman herself and makes it abstract; the interest is in the visual form rather than the whole person.

In addition to the placement of the camera, the elements in front of the camera are constantly shifting. There is a woman on a swing whose movement back and forth is repeated.

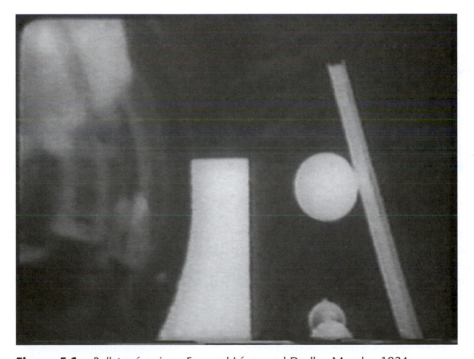

Figure 5.1   *Ballet mécanique*, Fernand Léger and Dudley Murphy, 1924

Figure 5.2   *Ballet mécanique*, Fernand Léger and Dudley Murphy, 1924

These movements are the pieces that combine in the creation of the mechanical ballet. When we watch ballet, or any form of dance for that matter, we take pleasure in the kinetic physicality of the dancers. We enjoy watching dance for the aesthetic of bodies in motion, just as in this film we watch all the objects, people and parts of people in movement together.

The editing juxtaposes a variety of images which are related to each other through their visual similarity: how they move, and how the shapes and forms of the images look similar or different when placed next to each other. This is accentuated in the shots that are repeated. For example, near the end of the film a woman walks up a flight of stairs carrying a bundle. Through repetition this image becomes more an abstract study in motion than a representation of the woman herself. Dudley Murphy described why they used this particular repetition:

> I saw an old washerwoman climbing a flight of stone stairs. When she reached the top, she was tired and made a futile gesture. The scene in itself was banal, but by printing it 20 times and connecting the end of the scene with the beginning of her climb, it expressed the futility of life because she never got there. This scene in the editing followed a very intricate piece of shiny machinery, somehow correlated in movement and rhythm to that of hers. (Murphy cited in Freeman, 1996: 21)

All these techniques work together to create a film that is an abstract study in movement and form. Rather than telling a story, the filmmakers have used film aesthetically to look at the world, the people and objects around them, as visual points within a moving canvas.

Léger's interest in film demonstrates the cross-fertilization taking place between the different branches of art in the early part of the century. Léger was one of several visual artists who experimented with the new medium of film and used it to explore the boundaries of art. Other painters and photographers who also worked in film in this era included Man Ray, Marcel Duchamp and Salvador Dali. Next, we will look more closely at Dali's collaboration with the filmmaker Luis Buñuel.

Surrealism and Un Chien andalou (1929)

Surrealism is one of many and varied movements of modern art of the early part of the twentieth century. Partly through the reputation of the later work of Salvador Dali, it is one of the more popular movements of modern art. Dating from the beginning of the 1920s, surrealism was a reaction to the earlier work of the Cubists, such as Léger. Surrealists were not as interested in technology, being far more influenced by the growth of psychology and the changing views about the nature of the human mind. Understanding surrealist art requires you to look at the images as representations of a dreamlike state or an embodiment of the unconscious. It is not a classical art that imitates nature but a form that brings forth imagined scenes of fantasy and desire.

Un Chien andalou was made by Dali, in collaboration with Luis Buñuel. Although both artists were Spanish, the film was produced in France as part of a growing European experimental film culture. It follows the principles of Surrealism, dealing with the unconscious and with the realm of fantasy and desire. It also exhibits a fascination with the human body in all its corporeal functions. The images and symbols of surrealist art often represent repressed desires and try to shock their viewers. Buñuel describes the surrealist process of selecting images to include in the film:

> Our only rule was very simple: no idea or image that might lend itself to a rational explanation of any kind would be accepted. We had to open all the doors to the irrational and keep only those images that surprised us, without trying to explain why. (Buñuel, 1983: 103)

Un Chien andalou opens with the image of a man taking a razor blade and cutting a woman's eye. Just as he takes the blade to the eye, the image changes to a cloud crossing the moon – visually echoing the eye and the blade. There is an element of shock value in this film; this moment is unsettling in its bizarre violence. Although the images in this film are not connected by conventional narrative structures, their creators were using the film to express their social and political ideas. The shock was designed to have a particular effect on the audience, to shake them out of their state of complacency. Buñuel explains:

> All of us were supporters of a certain concept of revolution, and although the surrealists didn't consider themselves terrorists, they were constantly fighting a society they despised. Scandal was a potent agent of revelation, capable of exposing such social crimes as the exploitation of one man by another, colonialist imperialism, religious tyranny – in sum, all the secret and odious underpinnings of a system that had to be destroyed. The real purpose of surrealism was not to create a new literary, artistic, or even philosophical movement, but to explode the social order, to transform life itself. (Buñuel, 1983: 107)

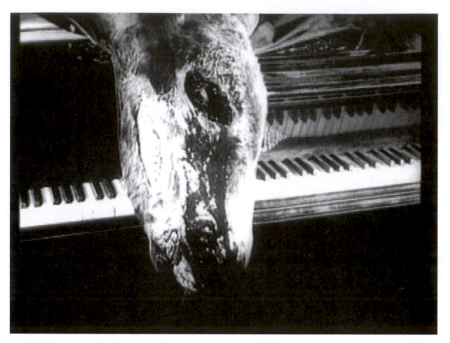

Figure 5.3   *Un Chien andalou*, Luis Buñuel, 1929

Figure 5.4   *Un Chien andalou*, Luis Buñuel, 1929

This theme of scandal is evident in a later section of the film, in a scene showing a man aggressively pursuing a woman who cowers in the corner. The man then stops and picks up a rope harness and, still pulling towards the woman, drags first a piano with two dead cows on it, which then turns into two priests. In this short scene, several elements of the unconscious dream and fantasy are evident, as well as the filmmaker's political perspective. The man's desire and his pursuit of the woman are held back by these grotesque dreamlike animal corpses. The metamorphosis into the priests shows the representatives of religious belief, who control and repress the man's sexual desire. It is a moment of shock value that is surprising and grotesque. This shock value is linked to Buñuel's attempt to use scandal to provoke the viewers. Yet it is also strangely amusing. Surrealist style often harnessed the power of humour as part of its aesthetic strategy.

Early experimental film, from the first wave, laid the groundwork for an alternative use of film that challenged the conventions of narrative and documentary practice. The experimental tradition then developed further from the 1940s onwards, with movements growing in different parts of the world. In the next sections we will briefly summarize some of the moments, movements and themes of experimental practice and envision how they serve as examples of an engaged form of critical practice.

Personal film

Following the period of 1920s avant-garde film, the next experimental movement occurred in the 1940s in the US, beginning with the important film *Meshes of the Afternoon* made in 1943 by Maya Deren and Alexander Hammid, a husband-and-wife team. Deren had experimented in different areas of the arts, writing poetry and doing research into dance, and Hammid had worked in film as a cameraman and had also made short avant-garde films. In the 1940s fewer experimental films were made. Maya Deren was a key figure at this time, as was Kenneth Anger, a filmmaker whose career spans several decades, beginning in 1947. What characterized the filmmaking practice of this era is its personal nature. From this period on, one important strand of experimental film is personal filmmaking; there is an exploration of identity and individual experience that characterizes these early works.

These experiments in personal experience are in many ways an opposition to the industrial practices of Hollywood and mainstream cinema. As discussed in Chapter 1, mainstream cinema is structured by a factory approach to film which includes a clear division of labour between people engaged in the different tasks required to make a film. Furthermore, Hollywood depends on the marketplace, which has no place for the experimental filmmaking about personal experience characterized by Deren, Anger and their successors. Outside the mainstream, many of the early experimental filmmakers chose to explore identities that were themselves not part of conventional society's expectations. Thus there is the combination in Kenneth Anger's work, of images from 1940s gay subculture and intertextual references to the pagan religion of the Golden Dawn. Similarly, Deren's early work shows her interest in the complex role of women and her later work is influenced by her interest in Haitian voodoo rituals. This material was not used by the conventional cinema of the time, except that voodoo might form a backdrop for a Hollywood horror fantasy. The personal experimental film made it possible to explore subcultural identities outside mainstream representation.

Figure 5.5 *Meshes of the Afternoon*, Maya Deren and Alexander Hammid, 1943

This brand of personal filmmaking was a departure from the early experiments of the first wave of the European avant-garde. Although there is a relationship between the experimental filmmakers and artists working in other media, there is not such a direct connection between these films and contemporary art movements. Deren was more influenced by dance, music and ritual than by painting or sculpture, and Anger was influenced by the glamour of Hollywood and his films parodied popular cultural icons.

Meshes of the Afternoon *(1943)*

The first time you view this film it might seem confusing, because of its unconventional structure, but it is a film that you can watch many times to come to a deeper appreciation of its style. The film does not depend on a traditional storyline but instead gives the impression of a dream, and the feeling of poetry rather than prose. It is actually carefully structured, and if you watch it more than once you can see how it works. It starts with the very graphic shot of a flower being placed on the ground, then we follow a woman as she enters a house, moves around, then sits in a chair. We see a close-up of her eye closing and then there is a visual transitional effect, which brings us into her subjective dream world. We then see similar actions repeated as different versions of the same woman come into the house. After the final woman comes in, there is a confrontation between the three versions of the woman and the third woman brandishes a knife threateningly at the sleeping original. She then wakes to see a man's face and it appears as if the film has reached its end. However, after she attacks the man we then go back to the man's arrival to find the woman in the chair dead.

The film uses a variety of visual techniques to explore an uncomfortable and threatening dream state. As each version of the woman enters the house, different camera techniques reveal her movements – the first woman is never shown fully but the camera assumes her point of view and we see what she sees as she moves around the house. After the second woman enters the house, she is seen going up the stairs in **slow motion**, and as she comes down, the camera moves around as she performs dance-like movements. As the third woman ascends the stairs, the camera sways around conveying a sense of disorientation. As she descends, she is shown via a series of **jump cuts** (edits that move her position around the frame). These techniques are part of the film's experiment to represent the very personal experience of a dreamlike state. The disorientation of the scenes of violence is also increased by an edited sequence that moves through time and space; as the woman with the knife approaches the sleeping woman we see a series of shots, linked graphically, of her walking across different spaces. Deren explains this four-step sequence through the different spaces:

> What I meant when I planned that four-stride sequence was that you have to come a long way – from the very beginning of time – to kill yourself, like the first life emerging from the primeval waters. Now, I don't think it gets all that across – it's a real big idea if you start thinking about it, and it happens so quickly that all you get is a suggestion of a strange kind of distance traversed. (Deren, 1965: 30)

Part of the power of the film lies in the uncomfortable experience of the woman's view of her home, which contains a series of everyday objects that are depicted in such a way that they create a feeling of foreboding. For example, the key seems to have its own volition, falling away from one woman, emerging from the mouth of another and transforming into the knife. Other objects – the phone and the record player – seem to move and operate on their own. The mirror and the flower are also foregrounded; endowed with a significance similar to the character's action. Deren has suggested as much: 'Part of the achievement of this film consists in the manner in which cinematic techniques are employed to give a malevolent vitality to inanimate objects' (Deren, 1965: 1).

The film is very important in the history of experimental filmmaking in showing the power of personal vision and the level of significance that can be given to the experiences of the individual filmmaker.

Stan Brakhage

Stan Brakhage is another key experimental filmmaker, who started working in the 1950s and continued to be one of the major voices of experimental film until his death in 2002. Brakhage's films are very personal, foregrounding his vision of the world. Mostly he worked alone, shooting the images himself, editing and manipulating the film by painting or scratching on the frame. His shooting style generally favours a **handheld** approach as this conveys the idea of a **subjective** camera, a style following what the camera sees.

Brakhage's films were mostly abstract in nature and are strongly influenced by the artistic movement of **Abstract Expressionism**. Like Abstract Expressionist paintings, some of Brakhage's films do not represent identifiable objects or people. Instead it is the play of light and colour on the screen that makes up the majority of the film. For example, one of Brakhage's best-known

Figure 5.6
Mothlight, Stan
Brakhage, 1963

works is *Mothlight* (1963), created from insects pasted onto a strip of **clear leader**. This is an example of a film made without a camera as the objects are placed on the film itself rather than represented through photographic means. The patterns made when the light strikes the film create the beauty of the film. Part of the fascination comes from the contrast between the aversion one might feel towards the body parts of dead insects and their transformation into a film of such beauty. Beyond the aesthetics of the film, there are the filmmaker's personal reflections on the nature of the moths' self-destructive attraction towards the light that often kills them. The film is a suggestion of the shared character of that tragedy in the attraction for a light that can also be destructive.

Structuralist/materialist film

From the early days of modernism, one strong tendency has been to break the illusion created by an image or an art object, by focusing on the material that goes into its construction. Experimental filmmakers have taken up this question as central to their work by exploring the film itself rather than the subject or content. An extension of this is the process of considering what the defining characteristic of an art form is, what makes film different from painting, for example. Then it is these specific characteristics that are celebrated in the work. This major movement or tendency in experimental film is known as **structuralism** or **materialism**. This is the fascination that some filmmakers have with the physical elements that go into the making of a film. Structuralist filmmakers have explored the specific nature of the material of film, calling attention to the apparatus itself, and allowing the viewer to reflect on the nature of the medium. These films are 'materialist' films, as their subject matter is the material that goes into their creation, rather than the images that are represented in the film.

A famous example of a materialist film is a short made by George Landow (aka Owen Land) in 1966 and called *Film in Which There Appear Edge Lettering, Sprocket Holes, Dirt Particles, Etc.* This film represents a perfect, if extreme, version of a structuralist/materialist film. The film shows a short colour-test strip with a girl's face and a colour chart. The content of the film is minimal as it is not important. The film has been created to show aspects usually considered to be distractions or mistakes; dirt, sprocket holes (that allow the film to move) and edge lettering (a guide put on the edge of a strip of film to help editors do their work). Watching the film then gives you a heightened awareness that it is a film and that these physical factors are involved in its creation.

Figure 5.7   *Film in Which There Appear Edge Lettering, Sprocket Holes, Dirt Particles, Etc.*, George Landow, 1966

Expanded Cinema: video art and the blurring of the boundaries

An extension of the work of the experimental filmmakers occurred with the development of **video art** in the late 1960s. Video developed at a different time than film and its introduction into the world of art saw it incorporated as a tool at the service of the artist as well as a medium of specialization. There are many video artists who work in video alone, but it is equally the case that video is part of a palette of tools used by artists, which can include film, performance, sculptural elements and digital new media. Like experimental film, video art is a large field, with many different aspects and tendencies. Here we will only look at some of the broadest elements of the work of video artists with some representative examples. Broadly speaking, video art has been concerned with several issues, including:

- Video as a critique of television and the media;
- How video interacts with other art forms, particularly **installation** and **performance art**;
- How video functions as a readily available technology for exploring identities outside mainstream representation;
- How video relates to the development of new media technologies and forms of distribution, such as the internet and mobile phones.

Critique of television and the media

The relationship between video and television is a complex one. On the one hand, they are inextricably linked; video images are the substance that constitutes television. On the other hand, video art deploys that technology for radically different aims. An early trend in video art takes on television and positions the video artist as the alternative to television, critiquing the electronic media from the position of an outside observer. Television is a large commercial industry with a corporate structure to match, providing a saturation of information and images. Video artists on the other hand are active individuals empowered by their access to video technology, offering alternative uses of television and using the same technologies to illuminate the inconsistencies of the media. Part of this process involves highlighting the one-sided nature of television and intervening to alter this. Television is made to be passively consumed by the viewer; we watch but don't respond. Video artists often seek to incorporate their responses to television into the work, to see their jobs as including themselves in the process and democratizing the media. Therefore there is a focus on interactivity, a place in the media where the audience can take an active part in the communication.

An excellent example of an early video artwork that illustrates this tendency is the short *The Eternal Frame* (1976). In this video, a group of performers dress in costume and re-enact the Kennedy assassination in Dallas. The video, and the re-enactment it contains, serves as a critique of how the news media fetishize a piece of footage such as the twenty-two-second home movie of the assassination shot by the bystander Abraham Zapruder. *The Eternal Frame* replays the performance thereby commenting on the way television repeats an image so frequently that it becomes forever linked in the viewer's mind with the event. Likewise, the video also engages with the question of the passivity of the television audience by actively incorporating responses from the viewers of both the performance and the video; the closing sequence includes reactions, some very negative, to a screening of the work. In many ways, the audience is an integral part of the meaning-making and the interpretation of the events.

Video and performance

The Eternal Frame, as well as representing a video-art critique of the power of television news, also involves another important strand in the development of video art. As the actors re-enact the Kennedy assassination they are participating in another art form, that of performance art. The video documents their preparation for the performance, then the re-enactment of the assassination, which we see repeated from different angles shot with different types of camera. At one moment in the tape, an actor playing the role of a security guard speaks to the person with the camera, in a parody of an interview. Both the actor and the interviewer become confused about where the interview happens in the timeline of events. When the actor speaks about having failed to protect Kennedy, the interviewer tells him to pretend that it hasn't happened yet, breaking the illusion of the scene. The video is conscious of its use of performance. Unlike a narrative, the performers want the viewer to be aware that they are performing and to view the video with detachment and amusement rather than get caught up in the fiction.

The response of the audience is integral to the effect of the video; we see and hear different people on the street as they react to what they have seen. This is a key feature of performance art, breaking down the barriers between the audience and the performer. In many ways, this aspect of the video has a documentary feel to it; we see the reactions of the spectators and they relate their reactions in an interview set-up. Yet, since the video has made us so aware of the performance of the actors, we view the interviews differently than we would if this were a conventional documentary. There is a sense of surprise that the people on the street take the re-enactment seriously, rather than view it with the knowledge that the viewer of the videotape has.

Performance in video art also takes other forms. It is a development from the art movement of **Abstract Expressionism** and the work of Jackson Pollock. Pollock's style of work was to spill paint onto the canvas. His method of working was documented in photographs and, in a sense, became part of the work itself, his painting became a performative act. Contemporary performance artists have extended this interest by including the artist's physical presence in the work of art itself. Performance art and video art have become closely linked beyond the use of video to document performance. Video is not consigned to a simple documentary function in the work of performance artists, it is a key medium for the expression of the performative act. The important video artist Nam June Paik has combined video, music, performance and sculpture to create his work. In his collaboration with the cellist Charlotte Moorman he created the 'TV Cello', which, when played, would create image feedback on the monitors that made up the cello's body. The video then became part of the performance, with monitors on the cello in a sense replacing the conventional instrument.

Video installation

The example of the 'TV Cello' brings up another function of video art, its relationship to the three-dimensional object of the television and its position within space. Video artists have often seen the sculptural potential of video and the object of the television, the monitor and the screen in relation to the image. This takes us into the area of contemporary art known as installation. On one level, video installation has been an extension of the critique of television and the media; the object of the television set itself and its position in the home has become a sculptural element. A television is a three-dimensional object that brings two-dimensional images into the home. It is also a piece of furniture. Many artists have incorporated television screens and sets into their installations and sculptures. For example, Nam June Paik's installation 'TV Chair' epitomizes this perception of television as furniture, using it as an element within a sculptural space.

For installation artists, the context in which the video is viewed is as important as the images and sounds themselves are. What does this mean for the audience? Video installation art is

Figure 5.8 'TV Cello', Nam June Paik, 1971

not merely viewed, it is experienced. As you enter an art-gallery space to see an installation you are not just passively watching, you are going into the art and often it is the presence of the audience that completes or makes the installation work. Many installations are interactive; for example, people moving around the gallery can themselves become projected into the work. Alternatively, sometimes the viewer sets off a sensor that sets part of the work into motion. An example of such a type of interactive video installation is *Tall Ships* (1992) created by Gary Hill. This work takes place in a darkened room with small patches of light on the walls. As the viewer approaches these lights, they trip a sensor and they see that the light patches are projected images of people who then appear to move towards them, looking back at them as if expecting a response. Moving through the gallery starts different video portraits moving and one can study the facial expressions and observe the subtle performances of the people represented. This installation demonstrates the power of video as an interactive medium that can create an environment, a complete sensory art space.

Available media

For many years film and video were exclusive arts, the cost of creating and disseminating work meant they were only available to those with access to money and resources. Even now, mainstream filmmaking is expensive, with millions of dollars invested in feature-film production. Video became an important tool in changing this perception of the media, as its advent and relative inexpense allowed people to create their own images. An important strand of video art celebrates video as a medium that allows people without the commercial resources to have access to the power to make their own media.

An important example of cheaply available video technology was created in the late 1980s by the toy manufacturer Fisher-Price. It introduced a cheap video camera called the **Pixelvision** camera that recorded low-quality video images onto an audio cassette. The Pixelvision camera became popular with artists who liked the grainy quality of the images it produced. This invention represented the first very low-cost video apparatus which allowed more people than ever access to media-making technology. One artist in particular who took advantage of this opportunity was Sadie Benning, whose work from the late 1980s, when she was in her teens, shows the potential of the accessibility of the media to capture perspectives from different sources than previously. Her early work shows a teenager in her room expressing her concerns about life, her alienation from her peers and her sexuality. The videos take the form of diaries, where she enters her thoughts and feelings. *If Every Girl Had a Diary* (1990), like most of her other early short videos, is entirely set in her bedroom and uses a lot of close-up and **extreme close-up** shots. The style is personal and the combination of the low-resolution images and the simply recorded soundtrack conveys a sense of intimacy. The objects in her space are abstracted as we see canted angles of a cat and close-ups of parts of her own face as she talks about her life and feelings.

New media

In the twenty-first century, video art is part of the growing information society and culture. Our ideas of cinema and television have fundamentally changed as images and sounds are readily available to us from a variety of sources: the internet, webcams, mobile phones and palm computers. Digital video is a technology that has saturated culture and it is not now the sole privilege of those with access to the corporate world of television. We can now broadcast our own image on the internet to a large audience. Interactivity is common; we can log on and talk back, rather than be passive viewers. The internet is now a space to show and to view video art. It is a key part of the growth of media as a means of personal expression. Not only does it not take a whole production company to make a film, it does not take a cinema to show it. Video art is part of this trend in new media, the growing potential of the web to disseminate digital images and sounds, that is the logical extension of the previous experiments by film and video artists.

Summary and key questions

Experimental film and the related area of video art are both exciting forms of media practice. When you are viewing or analyzing an artist's moving-image work, it is important to consider its structure and style as well as its context of creation. When working to create an experimental work, you should consider these elements as carefully as you would any other type of practice.

- Does the film or video show influence of a particular artistic style or movement?
- How does the film or video deal with issues of form and structure?
- What is the visual style and technique of the film or video?
- How does the film or video engage with critical practice? What ideas does it explore?

Want to learn more?

Think about this ...

Researching experimental film

Objective: To explore the relationship between experimental film and modern art.

Look up the work of an artist working in film or video who also works in another medium. How does their film or video practice show the influence of other arts? What is the relationship between film and the other medium in which the artist works?

Try this ...

Programming experimental film

Objective: To appreciate the variety of forms of experimental film and video art.
You will need: A pen and paper.

Design a programme of experimental films that might show in a film club or public-screening event. You can base your selection on a movement or period or select the films thematically. How would you introduce these films to a potential new audience?

Defamiliarization and abstraction

Objective: To experiment with the creative potential of experimental practice.
You will need: A video camera.

Use this exercise to explore the visual qualities of either an object, a person or an environment. Shoot your subjects so that they are shown in an unfamiliar way, using the camera to make the subject strange. Try to find ways of approaching them that will explore shapes and forms in an abstract way. Do not be anchored to conventional representation.

Creating an experimental film or video

Objective: To explore the themes and styles of different experimental film and video art movements.
You will need: A camera and basic editing facilities.

Try making an experimental project that follows the thematic interests of one of the movements of experimental film: a film that reflects the ideas of a movement of modern art, a reflexive film that foregrounds the apparatus of its production or a film that expresses some element of personal experience.

Further reading

Experimental film is a wide and varied area and there are many different books that you could turn to for further information. An interesting edited collection on the early period of the first avant-garde is Rudolf E. Kuenzli, *Dada and Surrealist Film*. Good general overviews of experimental film include P. Adams Sitney, *Visionary Film*, William Charles Wees, *Light Moving in Time*, Gene Youngblood, *Expanded Cinema* and A. L. Rees, *A History of Experimental Film and Video*. For an appreciation of the critical-practice approach to experimental film, see the written work of the important filmmakers of the different eras, such as Stan Brakhage, *Film at Wit's End*, Malcolm LeGrice, *Experimental Cinema in the Digital Age* or Nicky Hamlyn, *Film Art Phenomena*.

There are a number of good resources on video art, in particular see Michael Rush, *Video Art*, Julia Knight, *Diverse Practices*, Michael Renov and Erika Suderburg, *Resolutions* and Doug Hall and Sally Jo Fifer, *Illuminating Video*.

Films studied in this chapter

Ballet mécanique 1924 Fernand Léger and Dudley Murphy
Un Chien andalou 1929 Luis Buñuel
Empire 1964 Andy Warhol
The Eternal Frame 1976 T. R. Uthco and Ant Farm
Film in Which There Appear Edge Lettering, Sprocket Holes, Dirt Particles, Etc. 1966 George Landow
(aka Owen Land)

If Every Girl Had a Diary 1990 Sadie Benning
Meshes of the Afternoon 1943 Maya Deren and Alexander Hammid
Mothlight 1963 Stan Brakhage
Tall Ships 1992 Gary Hill

Other examples to explore

There are many examples of experimental film. Early avant-garde films by artists include Marcel Duchamp, *Anemic Cinema* (1926), René Clair, *Entr'acte* (1924), Germaine Dullac, *The Seashell and the Clergyman* (1928) and Man Ray, *L'Étoile de mer* (1928). Other classic experimental works include Kenneth Anger, *Fireworks* (1947) and *Scorpio Rising* (1964), Bruce Conner, *A Movie* (1958) and Derek Jarman, *The Last of England* (1987). More contemporary experimental film practices include Nina Danino, *Temenos* (1998). Important video artists include Bill Viola, Nam June Paik, Bruce Nauman, Steve McQueen and Cecelia Condit. Accessing experimental film and video art is sometimes difficult, but has been greatly enhanced by certain online resources; look in particular at UBUWeb.com.

PART III

Techniques of Film

6

Cinematography

Learning objectives

After completing this chapter, you will be able to:

- Recognize the effects of different types and styles of lighting;
- Experiment with the uses of camera angles, positions and movement;
- Analyze composition within a frame.

Introducing cinematography

In Chapter 3 we introduced the idea of narration, the way that the story of a film is told. We concluded that chapter with the acknowledgement that a film uses a complex set of techniques to tell its story to the audience. These techniques are part of the language of film; it is their combination that communicates the film's message. Here, we will see how cinematography is one of the key components of this language. When we look closely at the structures of filmmaking, we realize that our emotional reactions to a film are a response to the decisions of the filmmakers. Cinematography is one creative area that filmmakers consciously control to ensure that the film has a certain effect. Cinematography helps induce the reactions we have to films by producing visuals that are appealing, tense, spectacular, dynamic or involving.

In Chapter 1 we also learned about the process of filmmaking. Cinematography is a key part of the production phase of that process. In a narrative feature film, the cinematographer is an important member of the crew. She or he supervises the placement of the lighting, how the scenes are going to be captured on film, and has creative input into all the visual elements. Working on the cinematographer's team are the **camera operator** and **camera assistants**. The camera operator runs the camera during the actual shooting of a scene and the assistants load film and help with operations when more than one person is needed.

In addition, the cinematographer works closely with the director and the production designer, both of whom also influence the final image.

- The **director** manages all aspects of a production and particularly supervises the movement and actions of the actors. In order to do this, the director works closely with the cinematographer to decide on the most effective composition.
- The production designer is responsible for elements of design: the sets, props and costumes. Working closely with the production designer, the cinematographer decides what is included in the frame and how the different aspects of design are incorporated into the image.

Many times when shooting a first film, beginning filmmakers are most excited to get their hands on a camera. This can seem the most appealing tool of the filmmaking process. So let's 'get our hands on the camera', and start our study of film techniques with cinematography, and all the parts of a cinematographer's job, including:

- The functions of the camera itself;
- The lighting;
- The position and angle of the camera;
- The composition of the frame;
- Camera movement.

The camera

To understand cinematography, first and foremost we have to understand the workings of film and video cameras. Let's continue by examining four key technical features of a camera:

- Speed of motion. The camera can reproduce action at a normal speed, or use **fast motion** or **slow motion**;
- Types of lens. **Telephoto**, **normal** or **wide angle**;
- **Focus**. This controls which parts of the image appear clear and sharp;
- **Exposure**. This controls how much light reaches the film and therefore how light or dark the image appears.

These are basic principles that cinematographers and camera operators understand. Through their control of these operations, they are able to produce a variety of cinematographic effects.

Speed of motion

In Chapter 1 we learned about intermittent motion. When we watch a film we are actually watching a series of still images that our eye perceives as motion. These individual images move through the film camera at a standard speed: 24 frames per second (fps). (Video cameras produce images at different frames per second: 25 for PAL and SECAM and 30 for NTSC.) This reproduces action normally, allowing the figures to move as they would do off screen.

- **Fast motion** is created when a film is shot at a slower speed – for example, 12 fps – and then projected back at normal speed; the image appears to speed up.

- **Slow motion** is created when the film is shot at a higher speed – say, 48 fps – and then projected back at normal speed; the image appears to slow down.

With video, slow and fast motion are produced through digital video effects in editing.

As we watch a film at normal speed, we are not aware of the camera's reproduction of motion. In other words, it does not draw attention to itself as a cinematic technique. When slow motion and fast motion are used, however, we become aware that a technique has altered our perception of reality. Motion effects manipulate time, condensing a shot or scene into a shorter period (fast motion) or lengthening it out, giving more time to the moment (slow motion).

One of the common advantages of slow motion is that, through extending time, it accentuates the emotion of a scene. For example, in *American Beauty* (1999) the main character, Lester Burnham (Kevin Spacey), fantasizes about his daughter's friend Angela (Mena Suvari) during a cheerleading performance. The fantasy scene is presented in slow motion both to differentiate the world of Lester's fantasy from the normal everyday world, and to highlight his feelings of desire. The slow motion, therefore, works with the other techniques of the scene – the repeated action in the editing, the use of colour and the shifts in mise-en-scène – to give the viewer access to Lester's experience of watching Angela.

Conversely, fast motion evokes time passing quickly which can effectively communicate different sensations to the audience. For example, we can watch a flower open in an instant, although we know this takes hours to complete. Contracting time this way is an effect that is very apparent to the audience, making the viewer aware of the work done by the camera to produce the image. As with slow motion, fast motion can be used to express a character's state of mind, imitating the feelings or experiences of a character as they encounter life at a fast pace. An example of this technique occurs in the film *Requiem for a Dream* (2000), which explores the addictive habits of a group of characters. One of the characters, Sara (Ellen Burstyn), has started to use amphetamines to lose weight. After her first dose the following scene is in fast motion, representing her mental and physical state. The scene consists of a single shot. The camera slowly moves through her apartment as she does housework in fast motion, contracting hours of time into thirty seconds. The effect gives us the sense that this woman is experiencing her life in an unnatural way as a result of her diet pills.

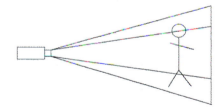

Lenses

Situated at the front of the main body, the lens is an important part of any camera. It is where the camera admits light and focuses it onto the film or videotape. There are three types of lens which show different perspectives on the subject that they shoot. The different lenses alter the apparent distances between the camera and the subject. They also change the perspective between these different objects.

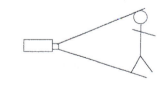

Figure 6.1 Wide-angle and telephoto lens

Figure 6.2   Focal length: telephoto lens

Figure 6.3   Focal length: wide-angle lens

- A **normal lens** shows action in a perspective closest to that of human perception. In other words with a normal lens, the relationships between the objects on the screen appear as they would if we were watching the scene from a given distance with human vision.
- In contrast, a **wide-angle lens** will give the fullest possible view of a scene, as the lens opens to the widest possible angle. In doing so, the wide-angle lens compresses a large field of view into a frame, extending the apparent distance between objects composed in depth.
- With a **telephoto lens**, the viewer appears to be closer to the subject than the camera actually is. With the telephoto lens the distances between objects appear unnaturally close.

Figures 6.2 and 6.3 illustrate the differences between a shot with a telephoto lens and one with a wide angle. The first shot uses a telephoto lens. It was taken at a distance from the character. Here the space between the standing figure and the building in the background is contracted and we see less of the building. The second shot uses a wide-angle lens and the camera is considerably closer to the subject. Although the figure is a similar size in the frame, the background building appears further away and more of it is visible. It is important to realize the effects of different lens types as this greatly changes how the image shows characters in relation to their background.

A lens that moves between these different positions is known as a **zoom lens**. A zoom movement can shift from telephoto to wide in the course of a single shot. We will discuss the use of zooms later in this chapter.

Focus

Focus refers to the area of an image that is sharp and clear, and is set by adjusting a ring on the camera lens. The focus guides our attention to what to look at in the frame. For example, it is most common for a person who is speaking to be in focus. If, however, the background area is in focus, while the subject in the foreground is not, we are guided to look at the background. This technique could imitate the character's attention; the focus allows us to see what they are looking at within the frame.

Sometimes only the subject is in focus. Sometimes, much more, if not all, of the image is focused clearly. The measure of how much of the image in front of and behind the subject is in focus is known as **depth of field**.

- With a shallow depth of field, only a small part of the frame is in focus.
- With a greater depth of field, more of the image is in focus.

When using a shallow depth of field, it is possible to shift the focus within the frame from one point to another during the course of the shot. This technique is known as a **rack focus**. It is a subtle guide, prompting us to move our attention from one area of the frame to another.

Exposure

Film or video images are created when light hits a light-sensitive material. Patterns of light and dark are recorded through a chemical reaction on the photosensitive film. The film is then treated with other chemicals in a laboratory to create the image. With digital video, the information is coded electronically into a digital signal which is decoded in the process of playback. Both of these processes require the camera to receive and control a certain amount of light to produce the necessary result. The camera lens admits the light through a small **rotating shutter** at the point where the lens meets the main camera body. This shutter rotates every frame to allow a certain amount of light through a small hole, known as the **iris**. How much light comes through the iris depends on two things: how long the iris is open (the **shutter speed**) and how wide the iris opens (the **aperture**). Since the shutter speed is standardized according to the frames per second, exposure is mostly controlled through the aperture. Aperture is measured in **F-stops**. These are a fixed set of numbers that is the same with any type of camera.

Setting the exposure before shooting enables the filmmaker to create the kind of image they want.

- When too much light reaches the film and an area of the image is too bright it is known as **over-exposure**.
- If too little light reaches the film it is known as **under-exposure**.

Both over-exposed and under-exposed shots lose detail. Consistent exposure is also important for editing. Cutting between shots with varying exposure levels can be distracting. Although over-exposure and under-exposure are often considered 'mistakes' (you may have experienced them with your own amateur photography), they can both be used for aesthetic purposes to produce high-contrast effects of light and dark.

With a basic understanding of the functions of a camera, let's now consider the other key element required for film to be created: light.

Lighting

Light is one of the principal raw materials of the filmmaking process. When light is brought into contact with the film stock the image is created. Even if we are not aware of the techniques of lighting when watching a film, its effects are felt in the way it establishes the drama and mood. In the process of a developing a scene, the filmmaker can choose different ways for light to enter the shot. The style of lighting is often dependent on the location. One basic distinction is between **exterior light** and **interior light**, whether the scene is being shot outdoors or indoors. Since most of what we will discuss in this section relates to indoor lighting, before we continue, let's briefly look at the conventions of outdoor lighting.

Exterior light

The approach to outdoor lighting depends on the time of day, the time of year and the weather conditions. Roughly, there are three times of day producing different qualities of light. Daylight is the brightest time, but depends on the weather conditions. Clouds affect the brightness and the quality of the light. Night-time produces varying light depending on the cycles of the moon and the proximity of artificial light sources. In between the brightness of daytime and the darkness of night are the periods of sunrise and sunset. This time is known in film lighting terms as **magic hour** or **golden hour** as the light at this time is soft and has a golden colour tone. Filmmakers have exploited the evocativeness of this time of day to add to the mood of a film. The film *Days* *of Heaven* (1978) is well known for its use of 'magic-hour' light. The cinematographer, Nestor Almendros shot the film entirely during sunrise and sunset, to enhance the scenes with the beautiful, evocative colour that comes with that time of day.

Although shooting in daylight provides cinematographers with bright enough conditions for exposure, it does not always give them the necessary level of control over the light. In high-budget films, lighting units are brought into a scene to add a significant amount of additional lighting. Even smaller lighting units can provide additional accents. Also, other equipment can be used to change the quality of the light, reflect the sunlight into areas of shadow, or block bright shafts of light from entering the lens.

Available light

Although many professional productions utilize extra lights and equipment, both outside and inside, one way to shoot is just to use the light that already exists in a location. This is known as **available light**. Certain films are more likely to employ this technique than others. Documentary films are often shot with available light, as are low-budget and student films and it is also effective when trying to create a naturalistic style. However, it is important to realize that even when using lighting with no extra units, you can manipulate the available light by altering the position of the actors or subjects in relation to the light source. Sometimes filmmakers place different objects so that they block light from different areas, or screens to change the way that a light source appears. Filmmakers use available light most successfully when they understand all the different principles of light.

Although available light is occasionally used, it is more common for lights to be brought in specially to illuminate the scene and to ensure correct **exposure**.

Properties of light

To begin the process of developing a lighting scheme, or to understand lighting in order to analyze its use in a scene, it is important to understand the different properties of light: **intensity**, quality, **colour temperature** and direction.

Intensity

The **intensity** of a light relates to how bright it is. Brightness is a function of the light source. For example, a midday sun produces the brightest conditions. With interior light, the intensity depends largely on the wattage of the lamp. The intensity of light in a scene can also be increased by bringing in more light sources and it is altered when something comes between the light source and the subject. This can be effectively used to convey narrative information in a scene. For example, there is a scene in *The Magnificent Ambersons* when the character of Isabel (Dolores Costello) is terminally ill; in fact this is the last shot in which she is seen in the film. While she is speaking to her son (Tim Holt), someone else in the room lets down the curtain to shut out some of the light. The scene darkens with the shadow of the curtain crossing the characters' faces. Logically we understand that the light has been blocked by the curtain to create this effect. But we can also see its use as symbolic in articulating an important moment in the story – if literally the sunlight is blocked, figuratively it is Isabel's light and life that is fading.

Quality

As light emanates from a source it can appear as either **hard light** or **soft light**. This quality is related to how the light waves travel from the source to the subject; with hard light, the light waves travel directly and with soft light, indirectly. The best example of a hard light is the noonday sun on a clear day. If you stand in this light you will notice how hard light creates sharp shadows and often produces a harsh effect. This harsh effect can be used for dramatic purposes as the shadows can sharpen the contours of a subject. It is also easier to direct hard light and to control it, so that it focuses in a particular direction. Soft light is created either when something comes between

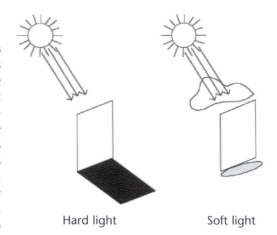

Hard light   Soft light

Figure 6.4   Hard and soft light

the source and subject and scatters the light waves so that they hit the subject from different directions, or when light is bounced off a reflective surface onto the subject. Soft light is also known as **diffused** light, as the object between the source and the subject is said to 'diffuse' the light waves. The most extreme example of diffused light is sunlight on a cloudy day. The clouds diffuse the light so that the sunlight does not hit a subject directly. Heavily clouded daylight is the softest form of light and it produces no visible shadows. Lighting designers have a special type of material called '**diffusion**' which they put in front of lights to create a softer light. There are degrees of hardness or softness of a light as it hits a subject. This depends on how strongly it is diffused. As the light waves are hitting the subject from different directions it is less easy to control soft light. You can place a card in front of a hard light source and the light will be cut off from a particular area of a scene. If you place the same card in front of a soft light, some of the rays of light will bend around and light the area of the scene that you are trying to darken. It is also important to remember that, as diffusion is something that comes between the light source and the subject, soft lights give a lower intensity for the same amount of wattage.

So how do cinematographers and lighting designers use hard and soft light? Hard light produces a harsh appearance accentuating the lines and shadows on a character's face. It is often used for dramatic situations as it increases the starkness of an image. Soft light reduces the shadows on a subject and is more pleasing on an actor's face. Since soft light gives less contrast it can also have a bland effect as it is even across the surface; it can lack character. Lighting designers employ a combination of hard and soft light in any shot or scene. For example, in the classic Western *Stagecoach*, a scene between two characters, Doc Boone (Thomas Mitchell) and Dallas (Claire Trevor), uses both hard and soft light. The primary light source on the close-up of the man is a hard light, whereas the primary source on the woman's close-up is softer. You can see how the woman is evenly lit with no shadows on her face and with her shadow on the back wall much less defined than his. The shadows on the man's face are much clearer and more notice-able. He is in the darker, harsher light which makes his face seem more chiselled and dramatic, and, even though they are in the same space, she appears brighter, softer and more evenly lit. This illustrates one of the conventions of lighting in Classical Hollywood Cinema. Soft light is used to illuminate the woman's features and give her a more gentle appearance. This lighting style also covers lines and dips in the face to make women appear soft or smooth. The man, on the other hand, is given rougher and more dramatic contours and outlines on his face. These lighting choices can be seen as ideological, reinforcing ideas we have about the relative appearances of men and women: women as soft, flawless and to be looked at, and men as dramatic and active.

Colour temperature

If you have ever been sitting at home with the curtains open and with daylight the main light source in the room, but there is still a light or lamp on, you may notice that the lamp appears to have an orange colour. Similarly, on a morning when you have the lights on, and only a little daylight peeps around the corner of the curtain, you may notice a slight blue tinge to the light coming from outside. You see these different colours because the relationship of different lighting sources to their position on the electromagnetic spectrum affects the way in which we perceive their colour. This is known as **colour temperature**.

On film cameras, colour-temperature filters can be used to balance one light so that it appears in line with the other sources. On a video camera, colour temperature is adjusted through the **white-balance** function; setting the white balance tells the camera how to perceive white and then the other elements of the spectrum are balanced accordingly.

Figure 6.5   *Stagecoach*, John Ford, 1939

Figure 6.6 *Stagecoach*, John Ford, 1939

Direction

The direction from which the principal light source comes affects the way the light appears in a scene. In Figures 6.7 to 6.9, you see a small sculpted figure lit from different directions. Here you can see how much the position of the light alters the image. When the light is placed in front of a subject it lights the whole figure evenly. This lighting position is often described as 'flat'. Although the whole figure is equally lit, it is at the sacrifice of any contours that are provided by the shadows. There is no sense of dynamism or drama with front lighting. A light placed to the side of a figure (either 90° as you see in Figure 6.8, or at any other angle) creates a more dramatic image. The shadows from the side light produce a sense of drama. A **back light**, when used on its own, creates a silhouette. As you can see in Figure 6.9, the back light outlines the subjects with a thin line of illumination. Back lights are also effective in separating the foreground from the background and create an appearance of depth.

Figure 6.7 Front light

Figure 6.8   Side light

Figure 6.9   Back light

A light can be placed anywhere in a scene, but each choice has a different effect. For example, light coming from above often brightens the hair and the top of the head, lending an angelic quality to the image. Conversely, if you have ever told horror stories to your friends with a flashlight held under your chin, you will know the effect of a light source coming from below. Lighting from below produces shadows that go up the face and create an eerie look. This type of lighting is often used in horror films.

The conventions of three-point lighting

One of the basic conventions of lighting in narrative cinema is the **three-point lighting** system. Three-point lighting is not just a formula to follow in a lighting by numbers exercise; each of the light positions and characteristics serves a specific function in order to create the total effect. These functions are also important to understand, as they can be used in different design situations. The three-point system is illustrated in Figure 6.10.

The first of the three lights in the three-point set-up is the **key light**. The key light is defined as the primary source of illumination for a scene. It is brighter than the other lights. The position of the key light also has an important effect on how the lighting of a scene works. The light can come from the direction of the **logical light source**: the area of the frame from which we imagine the light is emanating. In other words, if we see an image where the key light comes mainly from one side, we assume that there

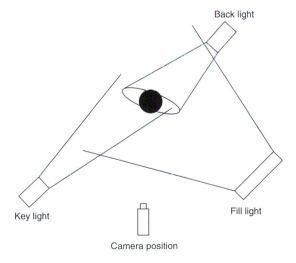

Figure 6.10   Three-point lighting

is a light source on that side, either a window or a lamp. Often the key light is placed high to avoid having shadows from the subject visible on the background area.

When you place one light on a subject, coming primarily from a particular direction, it will produce lighting on one side of the subject's face while the other side will be left in shadow. The **fill light** is used to fill in the shadows on the other side of the subject from the key light. It is placed at eye level or higher, near the camera on the opposite side of the key light. The fill light is almost always a soft light. Since the function of the fill light is to fill in shadows and not to give the impression of an evenly lit subject, which will have no character and no depth, the fill light should be of a lower intensity than the key light.

The **back light** serves to separate the subject from the background and to give the image the perception of depth. It is placed on the opposite side of the key light and also up high to reduce extra shadows and to be out of the frame of the shot. It is aimed at the subject's head and shoulders. The intensity is dependent on the colour of the subject's hair and clothing, but is usually somewhere around half the intensity of the key light.

This lighting pattern has become standard because it produces a certain effect that is predictable from one use to another. With a good three-point lighting set-up, a character is lit to be visible, with the dynamism of side lighting, and separation from the background provided by the back light. However, this is not the only style of lighting and many cinematographers make other creative choices that use the principles of light in dynamic and interesting ways.

Cinematographers use a formula to measure the varying intensity of the key and fill lights. This is known as the **key-to-fill ratio**. It is calculated by comparing the intensity of the fill light to the key and fill light combined. This allows the cinematographer to get an accurate sense of how the lighting of a scene will appear.

- When the key-to-fill ratio favours the key light, with a less intense fill, this is known (paradoxically) as **low-key lighting**;
- When the fill is closer in intensity to the key light it is known as **high-key lighting**.

High-key lighting is common in comedy and melodrama. With evenly lit scenes these types of film evoke brightness. The opposite effect is achieved by the high contrast and heavy shadows of low-key lighting, adding to the dramatic tension of a scene. Low-key lighting is particularly associated with **film noir**, as well as being used for suspense and dramatic thrillers.

An example of the use of light: Mildred Pierce

The Classical Hollywood style of film noir yields particularly good examples of conscious lighting. Let's look at one particular example, the 1945 film *Mildred Pierce*. Pam Cook in her essay, 'Duplicity in *Mildred Pierce*', examines this example, pointing to the way lighting (along with other techniques) is used to support the ideology of the film, which serves to repress women's place and discourse in society in favour of a return to the **patriarchal** order. She identifies a split between the present and past of the film in the style; the present is in the male-defined world of film noir with its low-key lighting conventions and the past is defined by the high-key conventions of the melodrama and its association with women's space. Thus, the film starts in a conventional film noir manner with a murder and a police investigation. During the investigation Mildred tells the police about the events that led up to the murder. Much of the rest of the film is then presented in flashback. The film demonstrates an initial contrast between the film noir style of the present and the melodramatic style of the past, which starts with the break-up of Mildred's marriage to her first husband. This past uses lighting and other elements of design, which are in line with the conventions of melodrama. The Classical Hollywood genre of melodrama deals with family and home life and often features women characters dealing with a family crisis. Melodramatic lighting is more high key, evenly lit, with softer light sources. Film noir is a genre of crime and investigation. In this genre the setting is more likely to feature public spaces than the private spaces of the home. The more high-contrast, low-key lighting accompanies these dramatic situations.

Towards the end of the film, there is a familial love triangle when Mildred discovers her teenage daughter, Veda (Ann Blyth), kissing her second husband, Monte (Zachary Scott). This scene ultimately leads to Monte's murder. The lighting is low-key, hard light that intensifies the dramatic nature of the scene. In the first shot, Mildred comes down the stairs into the family's beach house. She is seen in silhouette, but then moves into the light where she reacts to what she sees in front of her. The reaction of the actress Joan Crawford is accentuated by her movement out of the shadows. As she becomes visible to the audience, she appears startled; this is increased by the fact that she was obscured by shadow only a few seconds before. The next shot then reveals what she is looking at, as we see Veda and Monte kissing. The lighting in this shot imitates what we have just seen as they are initially in partial silhouette, then they move into the light.

This scene is shot in a classic film noir style. There is low-key lighting, with heavy contrast between the bright and dark areas, clearly defined shadows, even across the woman's face. The

Figure 6.11   *Mildred Pierce*, Michael Curtiz, 1945

noir lighting style increases the dramatic tension and the characters' movements in and out of the light mirrors their relationships, as desires and betrayals are first covered up and then revealed. As Veda and Monte move from silhouette to light, their deception and treachery is revealed to Mildred and to the audience.

As this last shot continues, Veda confronts her mother, claiming that Monte wants to divorce Mildred and marry her. Here the lighting works with the other elements of the scene to accentuate the contrast between Veda and her mother. Veda's bright dress reflects the harsh light and increases her character's appearance of hardness. Veda is portrayed throughout as a callous and selfish girl. Here, she is caught in her worst act and is shown in harsh and unflattering light that makes her dress seem almost metallic. In the next shot Mildred, in close-up, moves forward, so that the light on her is less intense and softer, while maintaining the same close-up composition within the frame. Although this is a very subtle move, Mildred's confrontation with Veda places her in a softer light and removes the shadow from across her face. The lighting is flattering and conforms to her role here as the victim, stressing the audience's identification with her emotional state.

Having considered the principles of the camera and lighting as a basis for understanding cinematography, let's continue with an examination of the placement of the camera and the use of the frame.

The frame

What we see on the cinema screen exists within the limits of the frame. The frame is a powerful concept in the creation of art, and the words 'frame' or 'framing' can themselves have multiple meanings. On one level, a frame is an object, part of a traditional painting. From simple wooden to intricately gilded, frames add to the value, as well as the aesthetics, of the picture inside. Even the curtains in the cinema and the box of a television set work to frame the image although we generally ignore them while concentrating on the content within. A less concrete definition of 'frame' refers to the process of selecting the elements that will appear in an image, out of the infinite possibilities of a scene. Thus, the frame is the border between the image and imagined world outside and around it. The process of framing is therefore, in the simplest definition, a process of selection. The cinematographer chooses what to include and what to exclude. Yet, as we will see, framing the film image is not a simple process.

The frame can contain an intense and complex variety of meanings, as well as creating a sense of narrative space beyond its borders. In this section we will review some of the ways in which the frame is constructed, how elements are placed within it and the meaning constructed around it.

Aspect ratio

The image we see on a film or television screen has a certain height and width. These dimensions are known as the **aspect ratio**. Although there have been a wide variety of aspect ratios used over time, here are the most common:

- **Academy ratio** is the name given to the aspect ratio which measures 1.33 to 1 (or 3 to 4). This is the size of some older television sets and also most films made before 1950. It gets its name from the Academy of Motion Picture Arts and Sciences which standardized this ratio in 1932.

- There are also a number of **widescreen** aspect ratios. Most contemporary feature films use a process called **masking**, where the image is shot in academy ratio and then partially blocked off during projection to produce an aspect ratio of 1.85:1. This ratio approximates the widescreen ratio of 16:9, which is now predominant for television sets and films.
- There is also a less common technique of producing widescreen that compresses the image during shooting into academy ratio. Then the image is projected through a special lens known as an **anamorphic** lens which expands the image to the desired width. The anamorphic widescreen technique produces an aspect ratio of 2.35:1.

When a film is transferred to video or DVD and is reduced from a widescreen format to academy ratio it is done through a technique known as **pan and scan**. This involves having the image effectively reshot and re-edited from the larger widescreen version. It often produces unsatisfactory results as the reshooting process can be awkward and ineffective.

Aspect ratio affects the way in which the compositional components work within the frame. For example, a 3:4 ratio lends itself well to the use of a close-up, as the square shape isolates the face of the subject, making it the central focus of the image, with less room for background elements. A 16:9 ratio would place that same close-up of the face within the context of more of the background. Widescreen formats reproduce wider compositions and landscapes better than they do close-ups. This, of course, does not mean that widescreen work should avoid close-ups and academy ratio should avoid landscape composition, but each format has different compositional strengths.

Camera positions and angles

In Chapter 3 we learned that the camera functions as one of the 'narrators' of a film. Working with the dialogue, voice over, music and editing, the camera guides us through the story; it gives us clues about which elements are important, engages us with the emotions of the characters and directs our attention. The position or angle of the camera on the action is one of the ways in which this narration occurs. The director and cinematographer choose how to place the camera to best capture the action of a shot or scene. To fully understand the role played by the camera in a film, it is important to identify the different camera positions. From this point, we can then begin to interpret how camera placement creates meaning and how you can use it in your own creative work.

The distance of the camera from the subject is significant. This determines what elements will appear in the frame and their relative size. The distance of the camera to the subject is combined with the types of lens (wide angle, normal or telephoto) to produce the size, position and perspective of everything in the frame.

If we imagine that we are framing a series of shots of people, these are the terms used for the different shots achieved by the camera positions.

- When the camera frames only part of the face (an eye) or a detail of the body (a hand or fingers) this is known as an **extreme close-up** (ECU).
- When the camera is close to the subject and showing only the face, this is known as a **close-up** (CU).
- A fuller shot that catches the subject from the waist up is described as a **medium shot** (MS).

- A **medium long shot** (MLS) covers the subject from nearly full body length, from the knees up.
- A **long shot** (LS) covers a full figure of an individual but can also include a group shot of more than one person.
- An **extreme long shot** (ELS) includes larger group shots and landscapes.

Camera position can alter how we perceive the way in which characters are positioned in a scene. A long shot shows characters in their setting and in relation to each other. This helps us to see any interaction between the characters. Alternatively, a close-up of a face can draw us into the emotion of a single character as we watch the changes in their expression. Therefore, close-ups are used to bring the audience into the story, by enabling them to identify with the characters. The expression on a character's face tells us what they are thinking, so that we can empathize with what they are feeling. Thus, if an emotional scene cuts from close-ups of two characters to either a medium shot or a long shot, we are drawn away from the individual's face and given emotional distance. The long shot can alienate us from the characters by showing less of their facial expression at a time of intense emotion. Early film theorist Bela Balazs identified the close-up as one of the specific artistic qualities of film. He compares film to theatre, which keeps the audience at a specific distance from the action on the stage. For Balazs, the close-up is how a film can bring us into the workings of the human mind:

> Good close-ups are lyrical; it is the heart, not the eye, that has perceived them. Close-ups are often dramatic revelations of what is really happening under the surface of appearances. You may see a medium shot of someone sitting and conducting a conversation with icy calm. The close-up will show trembling fingers nervously fumbling a small object – sign of an internal storm. (Balazs, 1970: 56)

Just as the close-up focuses on the face, long shots are used to show us the importance of the setting of a film. The Western genre is a good example of this as it often depends on the widescreen, long-shot vistas of the landscape of the West. In most Westerns, the location is as important as a character within the story. The choice of shot in this context is also part of the conventions of the genre, a camera position that works with other elements as part of the visual vocabulary and style of the Western.

In addition, the choice of camera position can also carry a level of meaning above and beyond its narrative function. As with the example of the Western, camera position acquires added meaning through repeated use over a number of films. In the examples we have been looking at, the camera position shows different amounts of the character's body. Thus, just as close-ups can draw the audience into the emotions expressed on a face, an extreme close-up can show, for example, a character's hand furtively concealing an object. Yet close-ups and extreme close-ups can have a different effect when showing parts of the human body. Close-ups isolate part of a person from the rest of their body. When the camera frames certain body parts in this way it can have the effect of objectifying them. **Objectification** is the process of turning a person into an object. A close-up of a face implies a character's emotion or thoughts which helps us to see them as a thinking individual. In comparison, the close-up of a woman's breasts, for example, only shows that body part without relating it to the character as an individual. Part of the way in which people are objectified is through showing their bodies as passive. In the example above, the extreme close-up of the hand concealing the object is doing something active in the story. An objectified extreme close-up would show part of a person that is not doing anything vital in the story, but is merely there to be looked at. Camera position is only one way in which certain characters are objectified. We will return to the concept in Chapter 11 to explore the different levels on which this works.

Along with the camera position, the camera angle is a significant aesthetic factor contributing to the overall impression of a shot.

- An **eye-level shot** places the subject and viewer on the same plane.
- A **low-angle** shot places the subject above the camera and gives the viewer the impression that the subject is looking down on them.
- A **high-angle** shot places the camera above the subject, giving the viewer the feeling that they are looking down on the subject.
- A **bird's-eye angle** is a less frequently used camera angle which comes from directly above a scene and gives the audience the sensation of being outside and above the action.
- A **Dutch angle** (or canted angle) refers to images shot at an angle that is not straight on, but, for example, placed diagonally from one side or another. These types of shots are often disconcerting and are used for, among other things, the point of view of characters who are drunk or fighting.

Let's illustrate how a variety of camera angles can be used effectively in a scene. The film *Far from Heaven* (2002) tells the story of the break-up of a couple's marriage in the 1950s when the husband, Frank (Dennis Quaid), explores his gay identity. In an early scene, Frank goes out at night. As he leaves a cinema, he follows two men into a gay bar. The brief scene which shows him going down the street to the bar uses a variety of camera angles. As he exits the cinema we see him from a high angle, placing him within his environment and keeping the audience at a distance. We then have an eye-level shot from behind, following his gaze as he watches the men go down the street. He follows them around the corner and we cut to a canted angle looking down at him (almost as if from the position of a surveillance camera). This angle comments on his slight discomfort in exploring a new experience. The next shot is a low angle from behind as the men enter the bar. The low angle does not give his perspective, but shows his hand with a cigarette dominating the foreground. We return to the canted shot as he moves towards the door and the last shot is a high-angle, canted shot showing him enter the bar. The use of different angles represents Frank's mind as he experiments with a lifestyle that is new to him.

The camera and point of view

Camera position and angle are often used to show what a character sees in a scene. When the camera is used this way, it is known as a **point-of-view** shot. Point of view is important in the construction of a story. The camera, as we have seen, is a form of narrator, and therefore when the camera takes on the position of a given character in a shot or scene, the camera is narrating from that character's point of view. When a certain character's perspectives are privileged, it affects the way the story is told. The viewer interprets the actions of the characters from this perspective. And, importantly, point-of-view shots guide the viewer to identify with the character whose point of view we are following. This becomes important in how we understand a film's meaning.

Figure 6.12 *Notorious*, Alfred Hitchcock, 1946

An early scene from the film *Notorious* (1946) uses point-of-view shots very effectively. This Hitchcock film tells the story of Alicia (Ingrid Bergman) who is the American daughter of a Nazi and is recruited to spy on a group of Nazis in Rio de Janeiro. In this scene Alicia has woken with a hangover. We see a Dutch angle from her point of view as she watches the American agent Devlin (Cary Grant) enter the room and talk to her. The use of her point of view here gives the scene four separate levels of meaning. First, the camera approximates what Alicia might logically see of Devlin from lying in that position on the bed. We see the character of Devlin as Alicia sees him. On a second level, this point-of-view shot represents Alicia's physical state as canted and disoriented; she has a hangover. But the camera also narrates a third level of meaning. It expresses her mental distress at the situation in life in which she finds herself; her father has just been jailed as a traitor and her own life is in a state of turmoil. Alicia has lost control of her life and in many ways fallen under the manipulative power of Devlin. This scene exaggerates Devlin's power by placing him diagonally above Alicia and increasing her sense of disorientation and powerlessness. The audience is led to feel that disorientation through the use of the Dutch-angle, point-of-view shot and thus is drawn towards her character and identifies with her.

There is also a fourth level of meaning to this scene. The Dutch angle expresses more than Alicia's position, physical state and state of mind; it depicts a fundamental stage in her character development. In some ways it represents a moral judgement on Alicia's actions up to this point in the story. In the early part of the film Alicia has behaved in a manner that is unacceptable to the moral standards of Classical Hollywood Cinema. She is a party girl who drinks too much and entertains a number of men in her home. The story unfolds with her suffering and sacrificing herself for both her patriotic duty and her love of Devlin. It is only through her suffering that she will be able to find redemption at the end. This scene gives us her point of view, physically, mentally but also morally; the Dutch angle reveals her moral disorientation. Devlin stands above her because he is the figure of male authority, who, throughout the narrative, will punish, redeem, reward and ultimately liberate her.

It is useful to compare this scene to a similar scene at the end of the film when Alicia is again lying in a bed, disoriented and unwell. This time her illness results from poison given to her by her Nazi husband, Sebastian (Claude Rains). Although she is physically in a similar position and probably equally mentally disoriented, we are not expected to condemn her for her moral failings. Thus, the scene is shot in a far more conventional manner. It follows the point of view of Devlin as he enters the room looking for Alicia. Then it cuts to a shot from Alicia's point of view as she sees him approach. The scene in the bedroom finishes without any more point-of-view shots. Unlike the earlier scene, we identify more with Devlin. Alicia's one point-of-view shot is very telling, however; we see Devlin approach in a medium shot from a slightly low angle, motivated by her position on the bed. The shot is straight on and not canted as in the earlier scene, despite the fact that she is in much the same physical position. Alicia has changed. Her self-sacrificing actions have redeemed her morally and her physical condition is not the result of her own actions. Devlin has also changed from a character whose function is to punish her, to the man who has come to rescue her. Therefore she sees straight and is seen straight on.

The ideological use of the camera

As this example from *Notorious* demonstrates, camera point of view can enhance the storytelling process and help develop the characters. Camera position and angle are part of the visual language of cinema and are important as devices of narration. This discussion also shows how these elements can relate to the ideological meaning of the film. For example, Alicia's point of view gives a moral perspective on the actions of her character. This moral judgement derives from a set of beliefs about the role of women in 1940s society. We have to understand the moral double standard that condemns and punishes Alicia's sexuality in order to understand why she must be redeemed. As we saw in Chapter 1, the set of beliefs or ideas held by a society, such as the role of women in the 1940s, is referred to as a society's ideology. Thus, in studying the meanings of a film, we analyze the film ideologically, and in doing so, understand more about the society from which the film evolves.

There are many ways in which the camera serves an ideological function in constructing meaning. How the camera is positioned and angled can have a direct relation to the ideology. As we have seen, point of view helps us identify with particular characters. While this affects the meaning of an individual film, ideological meaning is also created through the repeated use of certain techniques over a number of films, for example, a genre can be associated with certain camera techniques. This repetition of technique develops an ideological perspective over a group of films. For example, Westerns feature camera positions that reinforce a particular ideology about this time and location in American history. Westerns privilege the point of view of the white settlers over the native inhabitants. This is accomplished through camera placement which shows certain characters positively while leaving others alienated.

To explore how ideology works in a Western, let's take a look at the chase scene from *Stagecoach*. In *Stagecoach*, a socially mixed group of white people are travelling from one Western town to another, outrunning the threat of an attack by Apaches. At the heart of the film is the interaction between the diverse group of white settlers travelling in the coach. We get to know and identify with the various characters in the group. Towards the end of the film, there is a climactic scene; the stagecoach is attacked by a group of Apaches led by Geronimo. The camera is positioned to show a variety of long shots, medium shots and close-ups. Yet all the closer shots are reserved for the white occupants of the stagecoach. The Apaches are primarily seen in long shots and in groups. This scene alternates between the characters in and on top of the stagecoach and longer shots of the Apaches attacking. The close-ups of the defenders mean that we experience the action from their perspective; the Apaches attack in long shot, and we are expected to see them only as a threat. As Ella Shohat and Robert Stam explain this 'The point-of-view conventions consistently favor the Euro-American protagonists; they are centred in the frame, their desires drive the narrative; the camera pans, tracks, and cranes to accompany their regard' (Shohat and Stam, 1994: 120).

A series of close-ups bring us into the emotional drama unfolding inside the stagecoach. First, Dallas looks down at Mrs Mallory's baby. Then there is an extreme close-up **reverse shot** of the newborn. Immediately following, Hatfield (John Carradine) looks down at his gun followed by an extreme close-up of the gun with the single remaining bullet. We return to Hatfield, then there is a cut to a close-up of Mrs Mallory praying as Hatfield's gun appears on the left of the screen. This short sequence uses the combination of close-ups and extreme close-ups to draw us into the drama of the occupants of the stagecoach, expressing the emotions and fears of the group: the woman's desire to protect the child and the man's fear of the woman's capture.

In contrast, there are only two brief close-ups of the Apaches before the action of the battle begins. We see the stagecoach travelling across the desert in an extreme long shot from a high angle. Then, the camera pans across to the right to show a group of Apaches on the ridge. This shot is followed by two close-ups and a group medium shot as the Apaches look down on the stagecoach. A return to the opening long shot of the stagecoach concludes this sequence. The camera placement in this sequence combines with other techniques, particularly the music and design, to create the meaning.

Unlike the close-ups inside the stagecoach which draw us into the drama of the characters, these shots are of two Apaches who do not speak. They are not represented fully as subjective

Figure 6.13 *Stagecoach*, John Ford, 1939

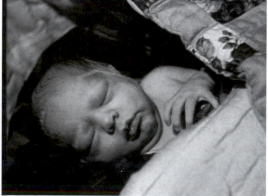

Figure 6.14 *Stagecoach*, John Ford, 1939

people at all, but only shown to us as a threat to the stagecoach. We never see these two men again. The camera narrates a story in which it is of no concern whether these men live or die, except for the fact that their death means safety for the occupants of the stagecoach. There is no identification in these close-ups; we are not invited into these men's lives as we are with the characters in the stagecoach. Once the action begins, they will be relegated to long shots and compositional choices which assure that they are only seen at a distance attacking the stagecoach. They are a danger to the white characters who are our figures of identification.

This scene demonstrates the ideological use of the camera to produce a racial process of viewing. The white settlers are the people the viewer is allowed to get to know through the course of the narrative. We identify with them and we are interested in their dramas, we hope for happy resolutions to their problems and enjoy the interaction among them: laughing at the antics of the drunken doctor, feeling pity at Hatfield's death, cheering on Ringo (John Wayne) in his search for revenge and sharing Dallas's redemption through her love for Ringo. These characters become part of the civilizing process of establishing a white community in the West. The generic nature of the storytelling presents twists and turns in the plot that we all understand. The Apaches, on the other hand, are represented as a murderous threat to the white community. They are a force bent on the destruction of everything that the narrative has presented to us as good and interesting. Their threat helps to unify the characters of the white community, but that unity is only maintained through the destruction of the Apaches. *Stagecoach* represents part of the ideology of the Western in justifying the process of violent colonization. The Apaches are represented as strangers, alien to their own land, as the white settlers are presented as having a legitimate claim to it.

Stagecoach is not an isolated example of this ideology but it is a good illustration of some of the elements that are typical of the Western's ideological deployment of the camera. If we compare this example to other Westerns, for example, *The Searchers* (discussed in the next section), we see that this process of the camera's ideological identification with the white settlers and alienation from the Native American inhabitants is a common generic characteristic.

Now we have studied the way the camera is placed in order to capture the action of a scene, let's turn our attention to how the visual elements are situated within the frame.

Figure 6.15   *Stagecoach*, John Ford, 1939

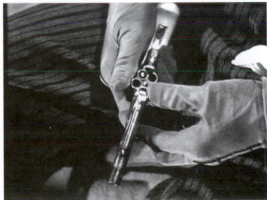

Figure 6.16   *Stagecoach*, John Ford, 1939

Composition within the frame

Another important part of the cinematographer's job is to decide how different elements are placed within the frame. Choices in composition are vital across the arts; painters, photographers and other artists also make decisions about what to include and what to exclude in creating artistic images. Composition requires a complex series of decisions to visualize three-dimensional space onto a two-dimensional screen. Composition for film and video also has to take into consideration movement; motion-picture compositions are constantly changing.

The position of visual elements

One of the first decisions a cinematographer faces when composing an image for film or video is where to place the key elements in the scene. Often with beginner filmmakers, the impulse is to place the subject square in the centre of the frame. This makes some instinctive sense; it is a powerful position which draws the viewer's attention. Yet the centre of the frame is a position that is not necessarily optimal for all situations. Placing the subject in a different part of the frame can create dynamic tensions and exciting plays of force in the image.

When composing images for various forms of media, artists (consciously or not) frequently use a convention of composition known as the **rule of thirds**. This 'rule', like all other conventions, has to be understood as a guideline only. It is based on research into visual perception in the arts. Yet it is, as always, important to understand why this convention is common so that you can recognize how different filmmakers have used or broken it for different effects.

If you look at Figure 6.17, you will see a frame in academy ratio divided by four lines. The lines section the frame vertically and horizontally into threes, producing nine areas of the frame of the same size and shape. This division of the screen is used by cinematographers to compose elements in the frame. The positions of the lines, known as **thirds lines**, are graphically strong. Placing the principal elements of a frame on these lines produces effective compositions. The points where the lines intersect are of particular graphic weight. The framing of an interview subject in a documentary is a very good basic example of the use of the rule of thirds.

If you imagine the grid placed over the interview subject in Figure 6.18 you will see how it follows the rule of thirds. The subject is framed with his eyes on the upper horizontal thirds line and his body on the right vertical thirds line. Had his head been higher in the frame than the upper third line, the top of the head would be lost beyond the top of the frame. Had he been positioned lower, for example, with his face centred in the frame, the extra space around his head would make him appear smaller in the frame, diminishing his importance and giving more graphic weight to the background. This area between the top of the frame and the top of the head is known as **headroom**. It is carefully balanced to provide the desired effect, placing the subject in relation to the top of the frame. Too much or too little headroom would not be as effective; either he would appear to diminish in the frame or the top of his head would be cut off.

You will notice that he is turned and looking towards camera left, as if talking to an offscreen interviewer. There is extra screen space in the direction in which he is looking. The space to his left is known as **look space**. This is an important part of the use of the thirds line; the extra

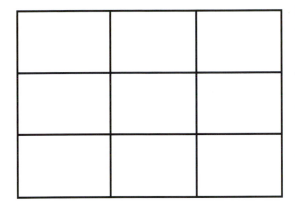

Figure 6.17   Rule of thirds

Figure 6.18   Rule of thirds

space implies the interaction with the person off screen and indicates the direction of his gaze. If he had been looking the other way, the edge of the frame would have obscured the direction of his look, making it appear claustrophobic and cutting off his interaction with offscreen space.

Closure

In Figure 6.18, the viewer is primarily focusing on the man's head as he is speaking. Yet the image also includes his neck, shoulders and upper arms. These other body parts provide the viewer with an important sense of what else exists outside the borders of the frame: in this case, the rest of the person. Human perception often fills in visual information from a series of elements, mentally completing the picture. Thus, the arms, neck and shoulders are enough to give us the sense of the body that continues below the edge of the frame. To better illustrate this point look at Figure 6.19. Do you see a triangle? Your perception fills in the missing lines between the dots to create a triangle from only the points at its intersections. The same is true of the still; the clues to the rest of the subject's body are enough for us to get a sense of the whole person. Therefore, we are not distracted or confused if we see only part of the person. The image gives us enough visual information to realize that the rest of person is there.

Figure 6.20 shows a cropped version of the shot in Figure 6.18. This illustrates the lack of mental closure (as well as the lack of look space and headroom). In this image, we have moved into a tighter close-up of the subject. Unfortunately in doing so we have cut off all clues to the continuation of his body. However, we still impose mental closure on the subject, by perceiving the head in isolation, as a simple circular shape. This is a slightly uncomfortable and distracting composition as it gives the sense of a disembodied head separated from the

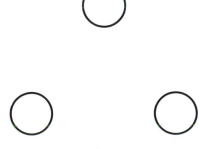

Figure 6.19   Closure

Figure 6.20   Closure

rest of the person. We are not given enough visual information to complete the mental picture of a whole person, and this missing information means the image has a different effect.

Balance

In the example we have been studying, the subject is placed to the right of the screen and is facing left, as if interacting with a person off screen. The look space is to his left and the direction of his eyes balances the composition. Had the subject been framed to the right, facing forward and looking directly into the camera, the composition would not have been as well balanced; the space to his left would have appeared empty. The balance of this composition is created by the interaction of the subject with the different elements, both on screen and off screen. Thus, compositions often position subjects to the right or left of the centre of the frame, but balance the frame through interaction with elements on the other side. This produces images that are dynamic and interesting, as they create the sense that the space of the frame is only part of the world of the film and that there is action continuing beyond the edges of the image. This is a form of balanced composition that is created asymmetrically.

Again, if we see a similar frame, but with the subject facing forward looking directly into the camera but now framed in the centre, the resulting composition would be balanced symmetrically. Although such compositions do not convey the sense of dynamism or action of an asymmetrically balanced image, they do offer a strong compositional force. Balanced symmetrical compositions give the impression of an ordered world or of a situation of rest and peace. They can also be combined with other elements of composition to suggest a form of stationary force that is stagnant or limited.

For example, Figure 6.21 shows such a composition from *American Beauty*. In this image the main character, Lester Burnham is low down and in the middle of the frame. There is almost as much headroom as the space he occupies himself. This renders the impression that he is small in the frame, dwarfed by his surroundings, which are very plain, grey and rather dull-looking. This coincides with the moment in the film where Lester is being told by his boss that he has to justify his job. It is early in the film and an illustration of Lester's belief that he is a loser, not in control of his life.

Balance can be created symmetrically or asymmetrically, and from that position used to suggest these different effects. Another compositional choice is the use of an unbalanced composition: one that accentuates the sense of tension or stress within an image. Unbalanced composition can:

Figure 6.21   *American Beauty*, Sam Mendes, 1999

- Be similar to a **Dutch angle**, evoking a sense of the world out of order;
- Occur at a point in the movement towards a balanced composition;
- Need resolution; we look for something to fill in the empty spaces and return the elements to a balanced position within the frame;
- Place elements close to the edge of the frame. In this case the edge of the frame acts as a graphic force pulling the figure out of the frame.

Lines

Compositional frames often feature strong lines that draw our attention in a horizontal, vertical or diagonal direction. Horizontal compositions are often flat spaces, for example, a landscape with a straight horizon. A horizontal composition, similar to a balanced one, gives the impression of rest and stability; after all, a human figure composed horizontally would be lying down. Vertical compositions, on the other hand, lead the eye up and down the frame and often interrupt whatever horizontal lines may be present. This lends a sense of dynamism to the image. Vertical lines can be imposing, like the height of a building as it towers above us.

Diagonal lines are also used compositionally for a given effect. When a diagonal line represents the horizon it is part of the effect of a Dutch angle; the horizon is canted. A camera position that accentuates the diagonal line of an element that we associate with being vertical, such as a building perhaps, also has a similar effect. Diagonal lines also appear in compositions independent of

Dutch angles and can be used to direct our attention to a certain part of a frame. Diagonal lines can also recede into the distance, suggesting depth perspective.

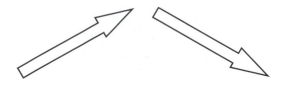

Figure 6.22 Directional lines

One important thing to note about diagonal lines however is how they are positioned across a screen. Culturally, we are trained to move our eyes from left to right across the screen as we do when we read a page of text. Thus when we see diagonal lines, we also read them from left to right. Look at Figure 6.22. Reading from left to right, the left line appears to be going up and the right line appears to be coming down. This method of perception can be used in diagonal compositions. For example, someone walking uphill from left to right will appear to be having an easier time than someone walking uphill from right to left.

Drawing attention to parts of the frame

Compositional choices draw our attention to specific parts of the frame. This can be done in different ways;

- Through the arrangement of shapes and design elements;
- Through the use of colour or light;
- Through the use of focus and the depth of field;
- Through movement.

The position, shape, design and movement of visual elements, guide where we look in the frame. The layout of the different components in the frame draws our attention. For example, our eyes are often most strongly drawn towards human figures in long-shot compositions; we look towards the people first. Likewise, in medium shots, our eyes are drawn to the face and in close-ups we are often drawn to look at the eyes, as this is how we interact with people when we are talking to them.

The lines of composition that we discussed earlier can also function to draw the attention of the viewer to a certain part of the frame. In other words, compositional lines can point towards an element in the frame and draw our eyes along that line to a certain point. In Figure 6.23 from the 1920 German Expressionist film *The Cabinet of Dr. Caligari*, the character in the shot is located centrally and low in the frame. Yet the lines of the set bring our eyes down towards him as the focus of the shot. Secondarily, those same lines point up towards the window that is small and partially out of frame. If the composition of this shot were different we might have ignored the small window. In this case, however, the strong compositional lines bring our eyes up from the seated figure of the prisoner to the impossibly high and small window. All these compositional choices work to accentuate his position as a trapped man.

There are many other means by which a film can direct our attention from one part of the frame to another. Bright, contrasting colours or patches of light can achieve this. Similarly, we tend to look at the area of the image that is most clearly in focus. If a composition has a shallow depth of field it is even more likely that we will look at the part of the frame that is clear and crisp.

Figure 6.23 *The Cabinet of Dr. Caligari*, Robert Wiene, 1920

Composing in depth

An important consideration when composing images for film or video is to realize that one is working in three-dimensional space. Composition therefore takes into consideration where each component is placed, not just in the two-dimensional field across the frame, but also through depth in space. Watching a film we see two dimensions as three; it is through the visual clues of perspective that we get a sense of the depth of the frame. These clues indicate to the audience the relative positions of elements through space, by using compositions that accentuate the different planes of the image, positioning elements in foreground, mid-ground and background. It is often important for the artist composing the frame to use all the possibilities of space to avoid creating scenes that are purely flat and one-dimensional.

One of the most obvious ways of composing a frame for the perception of depth is through the relative size of elements in the frame. Background items appear smaller in the frame than the larger items in the foreground. Compositional choices that place elements on the different planes of foreground, mid-ground and background use the relative size of these components to increase the sense of depth. For example, in Figure 6.24 from *Citizen Kane*, the relative size of the objects on the different compositional planes accentuates the sense of depth in the space. The bottle and glass in the foreground appear unnaturally large – as big as the background characters themselves. In the mid-ground the main character of the scene is also dominated by the foreground elements. This character has just attempted suicide. In the foreground is the bottle of pills, and in the background her husband has broken down the door.

Figure 6.24   *Citizen Kane*, Orson Welles, 1941

Frame within the frame

Although, in general, the aspect ratio is consistent throughout a film (once we start watching a film in widescreen, it is pretty much going to stay that way), there is a technique of composition that can alter the way in which the frame shape can be perceived within a shot, by using compositional and graphic elements to create a frame within a frame. Internal framing can appear to change the shape of the screen, accentuating vertical, horizontal or diagonal lines. This technique can be utilized in various ways for many different effects. Frames within frames can be used in the composition of shots to isolate a character and visually comment on their situation, environment or personality.

For example, the 1956 Western *The Searchers* employs frame-within-frame techniques as part of its method of exploring the film's themes of the relationship of the home to the rest of the world. They are also used to develop the audience's understanding of the characters at different points within the story. As the film starts, we see a woman opening the door to a Western farmhouse. She then exits and watches a man riding towards the house. In the opening seconds of the shot she is framed by the dark of the door and in silhouette with the background outside clear and imposing, as she exits the home. The camera tracks out with her through the door frame to follow her as she looks out on the arriving character. Such frame-within-frame compositions appear throughout this film. Thus, the opening scene is mirrored in the ending which uses a similar composition, giving the film a sense of **closure** and formal completion.

In the closing shot Ethan (John Wayne) and Marty (Jeffrey Hunter) – the 'searchers' of the title

– have returned with Debbie (Natalie Wood), who had been abducted by the Comanches when she was a young girl. She is taken from Ethan by another woman, who brings her through the door into the house. The camera **tracks** back into the house to again use the door as an internal frame. Other characters follow through the door. Ethan is then left isolated in the doorway as he turns his back on the house and walks away. The door finally closes, ending the film.

This framing device at the beginning and end of the film comments on both the character of Ethan and the development of the narrative. It also suggests an ideological interpretation of the process of the white characters' colonization of the wilderness. Ethan is the character who represents the spirit of rugged, masculine individualism that initiated the colonization of the West. After the arrival of the families and the homesteaders, the individualist, male gunfighter of the old West gets displaced to make way for the centrality of the home and the security of the domestic space. Ethan's role in this process is over by the end of the film. Thus, he is visually isolated outside the domestic space; there is no place for him in the newly civilized and reintegrated community. It is the narration of the camera, as it isolates him in the internal frame of the doorway, that restates this theme.

The composition of offscreen space

In our earlier discussion of framing, we saw how the rule of thirds often relies on interaction with elements external to the frame to balance the composition. The subject in the frame is looking at something/someone beyond the edges of the frame. We talk about this phenomenon as **offscreen space**. But it is important to realize that the interaction between onscreen and offscreen space is vital to how the camera narrates the action. Sometimes when a novice filmmaker, or even a more experienced one, is going through the stages of framing a shot, they consider using the edges of the frame only to exclude certain elements. In conventional narrative cinema, the cinematographer frames out the crew and edges of the set. Yet when we are watching a narrative film and involved in the pleasure of the action, we don't think that anything lies beyond the edges of the frame except a continuation of the fictional world of the film.

Filmmakers can often use the framing techniques discussed above to perpetuate this illusion and to give the viewer the sense that the elements in the frame are interacting with the world of offscreen space. In composing a shot then, a filmmaker has the potential to use the frame creatively to allow the viewer further access to the fictional world. Offscreen space works with all the other techniques of filmmaking; the composition of the frame and the movement of the camera combine with the interaction of aspects of design, the editing and the sound to give the illusion of the world beyond. We will return to these important elements in subsequent chapters to develop a sense of how cinematic techniques combine for this purpose.

To conclude this discussion of cinematography we will look at camera movement and consider the visual world of the frame in motion.

Movement

So far we have studied framing by applying the principles of composition to a stationary frame, principles that can relate to painting and photography as well as film. But it is important to realize how framing changes when we add movement. Movement distinguishes film from other art forms. Film is dynamic compared to painting and photography because of the creative potential of movement. Movement on the screen can take different forms:

- Movement of the camera;
- Movement within the frame – for example, how the characters move during a shot;
- Movement between the shots, in the process of editing.

The last two types of movement will be dealt with in subsequent chapters, but to complete our discussion of cinematography we need to consider how camera movement functions. In this section we will analyze some of the different effects that can be accomplished through mobile framing. Camera movement falls into different categories. These are very general distinctions, as a camera in motion often uses more than one type of movement simultaneously. It is still useful, however, to break down the different types of movement to better understand how they work, both separately and in combination. The first distinction in relation to movement is based on how the movement is created, either through:

- Optical movement: the zoom function on the camera;
- Movement of the camera itself.

Camera movement can then be categorized based on how the camera itself is moved. Here there are three basic distinctions:

- Movement of the camera placed on a tripod;
- Movement of the camera on a vehicle;
- Movement of camera operator with the camera.

So, let's discuss each of these types of movement in turn.

Zoom movement

As we learned earlier in this chapter, during a zoom movement, the camera itself does not actually move. Yet, when the zoom lens changes from telephoto to normal to wide angle it creates the illusion of movement within the frame. The appearance of motion is created by changing the angle of view within the lens, so that items in the frame change, appearing closer or further away. You may also remember that a change in lens involves a shift in the perspective. Thus a close-up created by a telephoto lens and a close-up created by the camera's proximity to the subject look distinctly different. As an extension of this, a zoom involves a shift in perspective as well as a change in the size of the objects on the screen. Because of this shift in perspective, a zoom gives a different sensation to the audience than the movement of the camera towards or away from the subject. A zoom in, for example, brings the action towards the viewer, giving the sense that the scene is moving closer. In contrast, when the camera itself moves into the scene it gives the audience the sense that it too, along with the camera, is moving towards the action. Therefore, filmmakers use zooms and camera movements for different effects.

The effect of a zoom can be accentuated by the speed at which it is executed. Fast zooms are obvious and draw attention to the camera and can be used for dramatic purposes, consciously bringing the image quickly towards the viewer. In contrast, a slow zoom is less obvious to an audience, as it subtly shifts perspective. For example, documentary films use slow zooms during interviews, when the interviewee begins to talk about personal or emotional subjects. The zoom brings the speaker closer to the audience at a moment of emotion, and at a point where it would be difficult to move the camera. Through the zoom, the audience is drawn subtly into the subject's emotion.

It is also important to note how a zoom is executed. A zoom is made smooth and less visible by a technique called **tapering**. To do this, the camera operator starts the movement slowly, reaches the desired speed, then slows down again before stopping. This makes the beginning and end of the movement less abrupt and noticeable, the zoom therefore looks smooth and professional. However, as with most techniques, zooms can be consciously rough and bumpy, so that the audience becomes aware of the technique.

Zooms are often used in combination with other camera movements. For example, we learned earlier in this chapter how filmmakers frequently frame the principal element of interest, such as the subject's face, above the centre of the frame. In this case, if the camera zooms in on the character's face, the camera will need to move up slightly (a tilt movement, which we will discuss in the next section) as the zoom continues, in order to keep the subject's face in the frame. A zoom with a tilt is a common and fairly simple combination camera movement.

Types of camera movement

Tripod movement

There are two types of movement that are based on moving a camera from a fixed or locked position on a tripod. With tripod movement the camera pivots from a stationary position, giving the feeling of looking around, but not moving around.

- A **pan** moves the camera horizontally across the action of a scene;
- A **tilt** moves the camera vertically, up and down the action.

There are a number of different situations when a cinematographer might choose to pan or tilt. First, pans and tilts are used to make adjustments in framing when characters or objects move within the frame, or enter and exit the frame. As a scene unfolds, and characters move through the frame, small changes are needed to follow the action; this is known as **reframing** and it is done so that the principles of composition are maintained. For example, if a shot is framed using the rule of thirds and a character moves towards the centre line, the camera might pan slightly to reframe the character on the thirds line. Pans can also follow action across the screen; as a character enters a scene the camera pans with them across the space. A principle similar to **look space** is at work here. The character is often given space to move across the frame. **Lead room** follows the character a little bit ahead of the action so the character is given room to move through the frame. Pans and tilts can also reveal a surprise by moving to show something that was previously off screen. For example, in the chase scene from *Stagecoach* the pan reveals the Apaches watching from the ridge. In combination with the other techniques of framing and the music, this movement is used to create the element of surprise and threat.

Vehicle movement

A lot of camera movement is created by placing the camera on some type of vehicle, such as those designed for the particular purpose of moving a camera, or other types; cars, boats or helicopters can be used as well as the professional cranes and dollies. The movement of the camera can imitate the experience of being in, or on, a specific type of vehicle. There are many ways vehicles can move a camera, but let's look at a representative example. Car chases can be shot in different ways. The smooth camera movements of professional cranes and dollies can shoot long shots of the high-speed action from outside any of the cars involved. However, choosing to place the camera inside one of the cars can produce interesting and effective vehicle movement. The opening scene of *Amores Perros* (2000) features a car chase, with the camera placed inside one of the cars so that the action of the scene comes from that perspective. The scene starts with the view from the window of the moving car as the road quickly crosses the screen. The next shot is from within the car followed by a sequence of shots alternating between the characters in the car and views of the street seen from inside the car. The car's own movement, rather than helicopter or crane shots from outside, brings the viewer into the chase with the two characters being pursued. We are brought to identify with them and to experience the chaos and fear of the car chase from their perspective.

In contrast to shooting from a moving car, a **dolly** is one of the principal types of vehicle designed specifically for camera movement. Dollies can take various forms, from simple wheel attachments for a tripod, to complex machinery with hydraulic **cranes** and lifting mechanisms. As these particular tools are frequently fairly expensive, this type of vehicle movement is associated with professional production. Dolly movements are fluid and give the impression that the camera controls the space and can move around without making the audience overly conscious of the movement. A camera can be moved on a dolly in three different ways:

- Moving in towards the scene – known as a dolly shot;
- Moving sideways across the scene – known as a **tracking shot**;
- Or circling around a scene.

A dolly shot moves the camera closer into a scene; effectively bringing the viewer into the action. A tracking shot can be used to pass through a space, observing the different parts of action occurring in that space, or following a character as they pass through. Circling camera movements are more self-conscious and can be somewhat disorienting to the viewer. Yet they also give the sense of the control of the space of the film, seeing the action from all sides.

Just as dollies and tracks move on a horizontal plane, a crane moves on a vertical axis, bringing the camera up and above the action. Cranes are often combined with dollies so that movement can be both horizontal and vertical at the same time. The crane shot is also fluid and professional-looking, evoking a sense of the camera's freedom to move around the space, yet without calling attention to the camera's presence. Crane movements can also take a position that is not available to any of the characters in the scene; conveying the impression that an omniscient camera is narrating the scene. A crane shot can show the action within a larger context so that it is seen as a small incident in a larger world or a small incident representative of a larger world.

For example, the opening scene of the 1958 Orson Welles film *Touch of Evil*, is a famous example of an extremely **long take** with an extensive use of dolly and crane movement. At the beginning of this scene someone places a bomb in the trunk of a car. The shot then cranes out over a wider space, as the car enters and exits the scene, before finally blowing up. The opening medium shot gives us information about what will occur in the scene and the crane movement then creates suspense as we see the car within the larger context of the action.

Operator movement

The job of a camera operator can be an exciting and arduous one. This is especially the case when a scene calls for operator movement. In this case the operator has a lot of power and control over how the final image appears. Novice filmmakers using operator movement quickly learn that it is a skill that requires work and practice. There are two different ways that an operator can move the camera, either on a **Steadicam** or handheld.

A Steadicam is a camera mount that attaches to the operator's body, moving the camera's centre of gravity away from the operator. Thus, when the operator moves with the camera, the movement is fluid, without the distinctive jolts that occur with handheld camerawork. In many ways, Steadicam movement is a combination of vehicle movement and operator movement as the person serves as the vehicle to create steady moving shots, allowing for the mobility of a hand-held situation with the fluidity of a vehicle movement. A well-executed Steadicam shot can move through a space without calling attention to itself, but still allow the viewer to feel the motion and be brought more closely into the world of the film.

An example of excellent Steadicam operation is the 2003 film *Russian Ark*. In *Russian Ark*, the camera moves through the space of the Hermitage Museum in St Petersburg in one single eighty-nine-minute take, where all the drama takes place and the camera catches it without any edit points. The Steadicam makes this film possible, moving with the action through the space. Cinematographer Tilman Büttner, had the very hard job of running the camera for the entire film attached to the Steadicam arm.

Handheld camera movement contrasts with Steadicam operation. Handheld movements are often unsteady and shaky and can be associated with amateur practice. Non-professional camera operators often use handheld techniques and with lack of experience, the result is often a camera movement that appears to be looking around, seeking out the areas of action to capture. This style of handheld movement is often imitated by filmmakers wanting to give their work the impression of roughness, or a style that is not predetermined.

Handheld movement, when used in combination with a zoom or telephoto lens, accentuates the shakiness of the camera. In the telephoto position, the movement is exaggerated and the image in the frame appears to shake more significantly than it does in a wide-angle position. Many non-professional operators who do not understand this principle will use handheld zoom movements and create a very shaky form of camera operation that is often hard to control and difficult for viewers to watch. The combination of zoom movement with handheld operation, then, is used for particular effect to intensify the experience of a chaotic moving camera.

Handheld shots are often used as one of the conventions of point of view. As we learned earlier in this chapter, the camera is often positioned so that its perspective imitates that of a particular character within a scene. This camera position can be combined with the handheld movement of the camera to simulate the movement of the character through the scene. As this technique conceals the character in motion, it can give the point of view of an attacker in a

Figure 6.25   Tilman Büttner operating a Steadicam for *Russian Ark*, Aleksandr Sokurov, 2003

horror or suspense film. In this case, we see from their point of view, but do not know who they are.

Handheld shots are also common in documentary production where they are used out of necessity to capture a moment of action as it occurs rather than action that is constructed or reconstructed for the camera. Documentary camera operators are often faced with the task of shooting unpredictable action taking place around them, a situation over which they have no control. A handheld camera is often the best for this as the operator can move through the action and capture the moments as they arise. Documentary operators are more likely to use a handheld zoom movement to capture action that is occurring at a distance if they are unable to approach. They are often very skilled at complex handheld work, following what is happening, while maintaining framing to best show that action.

It is due to the prevalence of handheld operation in documentary that this type of camera movement is associated in the minds of filmmakers and viewers with a realist aesthetic. Fiction filmmakers who wish to give their work the impression of realism (of action occurring in front of the camera, rather than for the camera) use handheld work as one of their principal techniques. Handheld camera operation establishes a sense of immediacy, that the action is right there, captured by the camera and drawing the audience into the world of the film. These movements can be chaotic, combining the jerky, less polished or controlled movement of the camera with the unpredictable movement of the people in the scene. This can even reach the point where participants in the action bump into the operator, adding to the movement of the camera, or attempt to cover the camera lens to stop the operator from shooting.

As this suggests, handheld camerawork can be very self-conscious; the presence of the camera, and the operator, is more strongly apparent than in the smooth and illusionistic practices of vehicle movement, or even a Steadicam. There is a level of reflexivity in the use of handheld operation as the viewer is likely to become aware of the presence of the camera. A film using handheld work can consciously acknowledge and foreground the camera, breaking the illusion of the world of the film. Documentary practices often do not hide the presence of the camera and in many instances ensure that the viewer is aware of the filmmaking process. This is distinct from the style of Classical Hollywood narrative, which is to create illusion, making the fictional world of the film autonomous and concealing all consciousness of the production of the film and the elements and techniques that go into its creation. The roughness of handheld work, its association with realism and documentary on the one hand and amateur cinematography on the other, can make this aesthetic choice a self-conscious rejection of illusionistic practices.

Summary and key questions

When you are preparing to analyze a scene from a film you need to review the cinematography and ask how the lighting and camera operation communicate visually. Beyond simply identifying these techniques it is important to question how they work to tell the story and make meaning within the film. Similarly, when you are preparing to shoot a creative visual project, these decisions become crucial – how can you best use the camera to communicate the ideas and vision of your work?

To conclude this chapter, let's review the elements of cinematography:

- How are the technical components of the camera used?
    - Is there slow or fast motion in the scene?
    - How is the focus used to draw attention?
    - What effect does the choice of lens have?
- What is the lighting style?
    - Does the scene use interior or exterior light?
    - What direction does the light come from?
    - Does the scene use a conventional three-point lighting set-up or a different one?
    - Is the lighting style high key or low key?
- How does the framing of the image illustrate the themes of the film?
    - What aspect ratio does the film use?
    - How does the choice of camera positions and angles draw you into the characters and the story?
- How do the elements of composition work in the scene?
    - How are the visual elements placed in the frame?
    - Do the compositions use the rule of thirds?
    - Are the compositions balanced or unbalanced?
    - How does the composition draw attention to different areas of the frame?
    - Does the scene use depth composition?
    - Is there a frame within a frame?
    - How do these different visual elements work to elucidate the narrative?

- What types of camera movement are there in the scene and how do they work?
    - o Does the scene use a zoom movement? How is it used?
    - o How are pans and tilts used in the scene?
    - o Does the scene use dolly, track or crane movements?
    - o Is there a Steadicam shot?
    - o Does the scene use handheld camerawork?
    - o How does the choice of camera movement work with the other elements of cinematography?

Want to learn more?

Think about this ...

Composition choices

Objective: To analyze composition within a frame.

View a film that you enjoy and observe the compositional choices. Occasionally, pause the image to study the composition in the frame. How often does the framing use the rule of thirds? When is the centre of the frame used? How do these compositional choices relate to the development of the narrative?

Try this ...

Observing light

Objective: To recognize the effects of different types and styles of lighting.
You will need: Some basic lighting units (household lamps or flashlights will do) and a large sheet of white card.

The key to this exercise is observation. Use whatever lights you have and experiment with different qualities, positions and combinations to explore how light can work. Try using reflected soft light. See what effect you get when you move the main light source. What can you learn about light from these practical experiments?

Storytelling through composition

Objective: To experiment with the uses of camera angles, positions and movement.
You will need: You can use a variety of tools to do this exercise. You can compose your shot by drawing on a storyboard sheet, or with a still camera or a video camera.

Without using any dialogue, compose a shot to illustrate one of the following moments in a scene:

- A student in class has a 'crush' on a classmate. Compose a shot that can show this to the audience, while also showing that the classmate does not know.
- A student discovers that a classmate has copied his homework and now they are both in trouble. Compose a shot that illustrates their conflict when they meet again in class.

Use this exercise to really explore the storytelling possibilities of the camera as a tool. How can you use composition and movement to communicate the gist of the story?

Further reading

All areas of cinematography are much studied and written about. For a first-rate examination of some of the conventions of framing and composition techniques, read Herbert Zettl's *Sight, Sound, Motion*. Other practical guides to cinematography can be found in Kris Malkiewicz, *Cinematography*, Blain Brown, *Cinematography: Theory and Practice* and Joseph V. Mascelli, *The Five Cs of Cinematography*. Collections of interviews and discussions with cinematographers include Dennis Schaefer and Larry Salvato, *Masters of Light* and Benjamin Bergery, *Reflections*. Studies of lighting include Ross Lowell, *Matters of Light and Depth* and Kris Malkiewicz, *Film Lighting*. For theoretical discussions of lighting, see Richard Dyer 'The Light of the World', in *White* and Jean-Pierre Geuens, 'Lighting', in *Film Production Theory*.

Films studied in this chapter

American Beauty 1999 Sam Mendes (director) Conrad L. Hall (cinematographer)
Amores Perros 2000 Alejandro González Iñárritu (director) Rodrigo Prieto (cinematographer)
The Cabinet of Dr. Caligari 1920 Robert Wiene (director) Willy Hameister (cinematographer)
Citizen Kane 1941 Orson Welles (director) Gregg Toland (cinematographer)
Days of Heaven 1978 Terrence Malick (director) Nestor Almendros (cinematographer)
Far from Heaven 2002 Todd Haynes (director) Edward Lachman (cinematographer)
The Magnificent Ambersons 1942 Orson Welles (director) Stanley Cortez (cinematographer)
Mildred Pierce 1945 Michael Curtiz (director) Ernest Haller (cinematographer)
Notorious 1946 Alfred Hitchcock (director) Ted Tetzlaff (cinematographer)
Requiem for a Dream 2000 Darren Aronofsky (director) Matthew Libatique (cinematographer)
Russian Ark 2003 Aleksandr Sokurov (director) Tilman Büttner (cinematographer)
The Searchers 1956 John Ford (director) Winton C. Hoch (cinematographer)
Stagecoach 1939 John Ford (director) Bert Glennon (cinematographer)
Touch of Evil 1958 Orson Welles (director) Russell Metty (cinematographer)

Other examples to explore

Almost any film can be studied for the effects of cinematography, exploring what works well and what is not as successful. A good introductory guide to cinematography is the documentary *Visions in Light* (1992 Arnold Glassman and Todd McCarthy directors). Studying the work of well-known cinematographers is also helpful, for example, Gregg Toland, *The Grapes of Wrath* (1940 John Ford director), Haskell Wexler, *One Flew over the Cuckoo's Nest* (1975 Milos Forman director), Laszlo Kovacs, *Easy Rider* (1969 Dennis Hopper director), Sven Nykvist, *The Seventh Seal* (1966 Ingmar Bergman director), Vittorio Storaro, *The Conformist* (1970 Bernardo Bertolucci director) or Ellen Kuras, *Eternal Sunshine of the Spotless Mind* (2003 Michel Gondry director).

Mise-en-Scène

Learning objectives

After completing this chapter, you will be able to:

- Explore the different elements of design in a film;
- Analyze the mise-en-scène in a film;
- Experiment with how a narrative scene is staged.

What is mise-en-scène?

'**Mise-en-scène**' is a French phrase that translates as 'putting into the scene'. The term originated in relation to the staging of a play, and refers to everything that was put on the stage for a scene. When translated into the production of a film, the mise-en-scène includes most of the things that exist both in the theatre and in the cinema, including the design of the sets, costume, make-up and props. There are important differences between the mise-en-scène of a stage play and that of a film. For example, in a theatre the action takes place on the stage and the illusion of the location is created by the set. In film, the action is frequently shot on location, allowing more freedom and possibility. Another difference is that in a theatrical context lighting is considered part of the mise-en-scène of the stage. In filmmaking, lighting is key to exposure, and is supervised by the cinematographer. Therefore, it is part of the cinematography and we studied it in the previous chapter. If we define the mise-en-scène of a film as all the things that are happening within the frame, the other important element is the **staging**: the placing and movement of the performers on the screen. This chapter looks at these aspects of mise-en-scène. First, we will look at aspects of the design: setting, costume, make-up and props. Then, we will study staging: the placement and movement of the actors in the frame.

Within the production of a film, the mise-en-scène is the responsibility of several different members of the crew. Design is supervised by the production designer, who is responsible for the overall visual look of a film. Working with the production designer are the **costume designer**, the **set designer**, the location manager (responsible for securing locations for shooting) and the **art director** (who assists the production designer in the day-to-day operations of the art crew). The staging, position and movement of the actors is the responsibility of the director, working with **assistant directors**.

The elements of design

It is quite common for a novice filmmaker to pay little attention to the elements of design. They might choose a location because it is easily available to them, make use of the props that are already there, have the performers use whatever clothing they have on and use no make-up at all. However, it is important to realize the incredible possibilities of design and maximize the creative potential of everything that goes in front of the camera. The elements of design do not accidentally appear in the frame; in most narrative films they are carefully selected and placed to interact with all other cinematic elements, to support the storytelling and the development of the characters.

Design decisions are not made for convenience, but to communicate important narrative information and can be analyzed on a number of levels:

- Logically: the design follows the sense of the narrative and choices are made to reflect the time period and circumstances being represented;
- For storytelling purposes: the elements of design also say something about the characters or the development of the story.
- Thematically: the themes of a film are also articulated through the design.
- Aesthetically: the selections are made to produce the most pleasing, dynamic or interesting compositions.
- Ideologically: the choice of design elements can also reflect ideas and beliefs about a society beyond the meanings contained in the film. We will explore a number of ideological uses of mise-en-scène in the sections that follow.

Setting

The setting of a film refers to where the action takes place and this is vital to establishing the tone and visual style. Where a film is shot is more than just the backdrop for the action, it is an integral part of the world of the film. For example, *O Brother, Where Art Thou?* (2000) is set in the southern part of the US. The geographical location, with the mangrove forest and swamps, is fundamental to the look of the film and as important as the action. Changing the location would completely change the meaning of the story and would turn it into a very different film. Settings can also be a function of a particular genre. For example, films in the Western genre typically have similar settings. The American West is the defining feature of the Western genre: the desert, the violent frontier town, the cattle range and the wide-open expanses of the West.

When shooting a film, the filmmakers decide whether to work on location or on a set.

Figure 7.1 *O Brother, Where Art Thou?*, Joel Coen and Ethan Coen, 2000

Shooting on location involves finding a place that suits the action of the scene and taking the cast and crew to that place for production. In contrast, a film can be shot on a set, an area built specifically for that film. These choices have different effects on audiences and can have ideological consequences. Let's review both of these options of settings for a film.

Studio sets

In Chapter 1, we saw how one of the features of Classical Hollywood cinema was the development of the studio system. This system consolidated major Hollywood production into eight companies. As the name 'studio system' suggests, filmmaking took place in studios. This gave Classical Hollywood style a strong dependence on the use of built sets. The tradition of the Hollywood backlot dates from the 1920s when elaborate sets were created to imitate numerous different locations. The practice of shooting films on built sets has continued, with varying popularity, since its early development in the silent period.

One reason for the choice of a set over a pre-existing location is that is allows for more flexibility in staging the action of the film. The fast-motion scene from *Requiem for a Dream*, mentioned in Chapter 6, is shot in a space that was built specifically for the film. Thus, the camera can be placed to observe the action from the position of the missing fourth wall. The fast-motion scene with the **tracking shot** would not have been possible in a real apartment location. A created set also allows for a freer use of fantasy or non-naturalistic filmmaking. The classic German horror film *The Cabinet of Dr. Caligari* is also staged on a set designed and built by designers Walter

Figure 7.2   *The Cabinet of Dr. Caligari*, Robert Wiene, 1920

Reimann, Walter Röhrig and Hermann Warm, which is one of the hallmarks of this innovative film. The film was influenced by the artistic movement of Expressionism, a practice that explored internal, psychological states by projecting them onto the environment around them. This set includes elaborately painted backgrounds, with a décor that is consistent to the overall vision of the Expressionistic space.

Although some studio sets are built indoors, many film sets are constructed outside. These external sets combine elements of the internal studio with the outdoor setting of location shooting. For example, for *The Lord of the Rings: The Fellowship of the Ring*, a set was constructed outside to create the village of Hobbiton in the fantasy world of Middle Earth. After selecting the outdoor area, the designers went to work bringing in all the components of the set, positioning the house fronts, windows and doors and giving the ground and lawns their trim, cut appearance.

An excellent example of a constructed set is in the film *Black Narcissus*, shot in Britain in 1947. This film tells the story of a group of nuns living in the mountains of India. The location is a palace in the mountains. Every part of this location was constructed in a studio; the mountain palace was created through the combination of miniatures, painted backdrops and studio sets. Even by the standards of today's special effects, *Black Narcissus* is an excellent example of the techniques of studio shooting and it was all done without the help of modern computer technology. However, the choice to use the studio rather than the actual location lends the film more of an air of fantasy than you get with a film shot on location. This film has even been described as surrealistic in its use of a set that is so artificial yet so evocative of, not so much a real place, as a westerner's fantasy about life in the exotic mountains of the east. The filmmakers managed to create the illusion of a place that they probably didn't know first hand, imagining what it might be like, rather than drawing from experience.

On location

Since the term mise-en-scène originated to describe theatrical practice, it is useful to compare how the elements of design function between the two different art forms. When staging a play, the setting has to be created through the use of a set; carefully chosen items are placed on the stage to simulate the effect of that locale. In film, however, it is possible to take the camera and the actors out on location to any place where the film might be set and shoot the action there. The selection of locations for film production is vital to the success of the film, and often the locations are key to the visual style.

The choice to shoot on location can be more than just a convenience. For example, at key moments in the history of film, filmmakers have chosen to use a location outside the studio setting for aesthetic reasons or to make a political statement in breaking with the artificiality of studio shooting. In these cases, studios were seen to be restrictive: an indication of the excess and limited fantasy nature of studio-based films. The use of actual locations then marks an increase in realism, a return of a film to its source of inspiration among the people rather than the construction of fantasy for escapist wish-fulfilment.

An example of such a movement in cinema history is the period known as **Italian neo-realism**. This movement occurred immediately following World War II and was influential in the subsequent development of film style. The 1945 film *Rome Open City* is a quintessential example of the neo-realist style. The film is set in Rome towards the end of the war and the director's aesthetic choices all increase the sense of realism. In addition to shooting on location, the film

Figure 7.3   *Rome Open City*, Roberto Rossellini, 1945

uses non-professional actors and long takes, a style more common to documentaries. The choice of location shooting convinces the viewer to believe in the realism of the issues that face the people actually living in war-torn Rome, rather than offering a constructed fantasy about these experiences.

Costume design

What can we tell about a person from the clothes that they wear? We can make many assumptions based on clothing. Clothes can tell us about a person's social status, whether they are rich or poor. People also dress differently for different occasions, formal wear for parties or special events, business suits for one type of work and overalls for another. In the world of film, what people wear is more than just clothing, it is 'costume'. We have all heard of a '**costume drama**'. This term is often synonymous with **period drama**, a dramatic film set in the past and often requiring the design and construction of elaborate clothing, appropriate to the era in which the film is set. Yet, all films require some degree of design and development to clothe the actors in costumes which illustrate important aspects of their characters.

Costume and authenticity

Frequently in period dramas the costumes are based on careful research and thorough historical knowledge. This is done to ensure that the fabric, style and cut of the costume is authentic to the period represented. The film *Gosford Park* (2001), for example, is set in 1930s England. It tells the

Figure 7.4   *Gosford Park*, Robert Altman, 2001

story of a group of aristocrats spending a weekend hunting together. The story is told from the perspective of both the wealthy living in the mansion, and their servants who must do all the work to maintain their employer's lifestyle. All the costumes have to be consistent with that time period. In this film you do not see any clothing style that was developed after this time and thorough planning goes into making all the appropriate costume choices.

Costume designers study the historical development of clothing styles, researching the correct costume for the time. For example, artificial fibres, such as polyester or rayon, were not developed until the mid-twentieth century. These fibres have a different appearance from natural fibres. A designer who is attempting to achieve the maximum authenticity for a nineteenth-century period drama would choose natural fibres (cotton, silk, wool or linen).

As well as being authentic to the time in which a film is set, costumes need to be appropriate to the characters who wear them and situations in which they find themselves. They vary according to social status or employment, and depend on a character's role in society. It would be an illogical costume choice to have a postman delivering the mail dressed in a tuxedo, unless for surrealist or comic effect. Although many designers strive for authenticity, it is not the goal of all. Sometimes a film uses an eclectic style that is not exactly suited to one period or another. Fantasy and science-fiction films in particular do not usually base their design choices on a specific time in history. In the epic film series *The Lord of the Rings*, for example, the design choices draw on different historical sources, but cannot be placed in any specific era of history. Thus, some of the warriors are dressed in a style inspired by Anglo-Saxon historical designs, while others follow one inspired by medieval knights.

Narrative and thematic uses of costume

Costumes are made to be appropriate to the characters and the time period in which a film is set, but they also serve to tell us something about the characters who wear them. In other words, it is not enough to say that a particular costume is the kind of costume that a character of a certain time period or narrative situation would wear. The process of analyzing or designing costumes involves more serious consideration of all the implications of costume choice, including how it influences the development of a particular character.

A common saying in the world of filmmaking is the phrase 'Show. Don't tell.' This means a costume designer's challenge is to create costumes that communicate fundamental elements of a character's personality. What a character wears, and how they appear on screen, can tell us as much about them as almost any other technique of filmmaking. Actors also have a strong relationship with their costume as it can help them to develop their characters. Taking on a particular clothing style can enable an actor to understand a character better and to project their characteristics to an audience. In addition, period costume often involves a contemporary actor having to learn a new way of moving. For example, the intricacies of dress in the nineteenth century change the body shape and movement of an actor through corsets, hooped skirts and large hats and headdresses for women and frock coats, tails and cravats for men. Wearing these items can give an actor a deeper appreciation of the context in which their character lives and aid understanding of aspects of their personality.

One further way in which costumes are used to illustrate aspects of character is through contrast. Costumes differentiate between characters and groups of characters as a method of shorthand for exploring different aspects of personality. In *Gosford Park*, the contrasts between different groups of characters are very important to the development of the story. The first contrast is between the servants and the privileged class of landowners; in fact, this is one of the fundamental themes of the film. Much of the action and conflict of the story arises from the differences between the rich people and their servants. A principal way in which these two groups are distinguished from each other is through their costuming. The servants are dressed in uniforms, whereas their employers are dressed as they choose. All the servants' costumes are in black or white; they are rough-textured with few fancy or elaborate elements. In contrast, the character of Lady Sylvia (Kristin Scott Thomas), for example, wears dresses that have textured material which is sheer, sleek, form-fitting and elegant, for show rather than work. Even within the ranks of the servants there are differences in status represented by the types of uniform worn. The servants who work upstairs are formally dressed compared to the rough clothes of those who work in the kitchen. The distinctions of character through dress exist within the upper-class characters as well as the servants. The variations of dress are even cause for comment among the characters. In particular, the character of Mabel Nesbitt (Claudie Blakley) is of a lower class and position in life than the other weekend guests. Mabel is a middle-class wife, married to a poor but aristocratic young man. Her clothing is not as fine as that of the other rich women; she wears a simple string of pearls rather than the elaborate jewellery of the other guests. The contrast between her costume and Lady Sylvia's is used to illustrate the differences in their characters and stations in life, and is even the source of comment among the servant characters.

Throughout *Gosford Park*, costumes also reflect their use. Thus, the servants wear costumes designed for the particular type of work that they do and the upper-class characters wear different clothes for different activities. In the scenes where the characters are going shooting, they wear specific clothes for this. One guest, the American, Mr Wiseman (Bob Balaban), is not used to the conventions of the English shooting party and is dressed differently, in a fur coat, unlike the plain country dress of the others. At other points in the story, the cast wears different costumes for dinner, riding or lounging around during the day. Thus, costume is used to create depth of character and meaning, show the differences between characters, and thematically explore those differences.

Costumes can change over the course of a film to say something about the development of an individual. Changing costumes can be a visual indication of shifts in a character's perspective or outlook on life. This is very clearly illustrated in the Classical Hollywood melodrama *Now, Voyager* (1942). In this film, the protagonist Charlotte Vale (Bette Davis) undergoes a series of changes. In the beginning, Charlotte is under the control of her domineering mother, who is keeping her at home and repressing all of her attempts to lead an independent life. Early on, Charlotte is put into the care of the psychiatrist Dr Jaquith (Claude Rains), who undertakes her treatment. Charlotte's change is shown through a combination of cinematic techniques; the use of the camera, lighting, music and editing all combine to present her differently. However, it is the elements of mise-en-scène (costume, hair and make-up) that are the strongest indicators of Charlotte's new approach to life. As the repressed daughter, her appearance is dowdy; she wears an unflattering, loose-fitting dress and make-up that accentuates heavy eyebrows. The new Charlotte is more conventionally presented in a glamorous Hollywood style: a sheer, close-fitting costume with an elegant hat. Although the story is telling us that the differences are psychological, a shift in her personality, her emotions and her outlook, what we see are physical changes and changes in costume.

Aesthetic use of costumes

In addition to the important role in the development of character and story, the costumes also work with other aspects of the design to produce the overall effect or ambience of a film. For example, in *Batman Returns* (1992), the costumes match the visual scheme of the film, which emphasizes a monotone, dark world. Throughout the mise-en-scène, there is a predominance of dark, cool colours, with a strong focus on greys and blues. In contrast, the French musical *The Umbrellas of Cherbourg* (1964) uses a visual scheme based on lighter, pastel colours. These mise-en-scène choices are significant in establishing the tone of the film, which is a romance that looks at the sentimental attachment of two young people experiencing their first love. In a parody of gender conventions, the heroine's home features warm colours like pink and red in the décor, whereas in the hero's home the cooler colours of blue and green predominate. These design choices are not made for purposes of realism, but to set an aesthetic tone for the film that creates a mood of youthful sentimentality that works with the film's themes.

Ideological use of costume

In Chapter 1, we were introduced to the concept of ideology. We learned that a society's set of beliefs can be reflected in a film through the choices of techniques such as camera angles and positions. This process also works through a film's mise-en-scène. When we analyze a film, we can see how the choices of costume reflect that film's ideological stance. Let's look at an example from *Batman Returns*. This is a superhero film from the early 1990s in which the costumes are consciously non-naturalistic, instead being used to project a fantasy of beauty and power. *Batman Returns* demonstrates a creative and consistent mise-en-scène. The costume choices articulate important differences between the characters and particularly work with the film's commentary on the relationships between men and women and on gender stereotypes.

Batman Returns is the second in a series of films following Batman's adventures as he fights various villains with superhuman powers. In the second film we are introduced to the character of Catwoman (Michelle Pfeiffer), a secretary called Selina Kyle who survives a deadly fall to discover she has the nine lives of a cat. She takes on many of the characteristics of a cat, dresses in a provocative costume and prowls the streets at night, getting into fights. Catwoman's character is introduced as a type of commentary on the limited role of women in society; she is frustrated and overlooked in her job and a victim of the scheming of her boss. When she transforms into Catwoman, she is able to assert her rights and discover her power. As Catwoman she becomes the antagonist to Batman (Michael Keaton), while out of costume Selina develops a romance with Batman's *alter ego*, Bruce Wayne.

As Batman and Catwoman, the characters' costumes enhance particular physical attributes. Catwoman wears a shiny, form-fitting bodysuit that accentuates her shape. It has visible seams that outline her body and she carries a whip. She wears stiletto heels and has metal claw-like nail extensions. Her costume could bring to mind fantasies of fetishism or pornography. The costume focuses more on Catwoman's sexuality than her power as a fighter. Batman's costume contrasts with Catwoman's in many ways. They are both similar in that they are black and non-naturalistic.

Figure 7.5 *Batman Returns*, Tim Burton, 1992

Batman wears what appears to be a rubber suit, much of which is concealed by a large cloak. Under the cloak, the chest of his costume is contoured to simulate a muscular physique. Unlike Catwoman's costume, these 'muscles' are a feature of the suit rather than the form-fitting costume showing his actual body. On the whole, Batman's costume covers more than it reveals. What we do see of Batman's costume focuses on giving the illusion of contoured muscles. This plays into gender stereotypes that associate men with strength and activity and women with passivity and display. Catwoman is costumed as a stereotypical woman to be looked at for her sexual attributes. Batman is costumed to accentuate his male attributes of power and strength, as fighter and hero.

Although the costuming decisions in this film are based on these **stereotypes**, there is also an overt commentary on the gender roles of these two characters and a questioning of the ideology that underlies society's sexism. Batman's costumes reflect his power, which is mainly a function of his wealth and position in society. He has the money and resources to clothe himself in perfect, powerful clothing. In contrast, Catwoman's power is inherent. Like her costume, she is self-made and an ambiguous villain. Bruce Wayne's wealth has given him the ability to become Batman. He is a superhero whose fighting, flying and driving capabilities come from technology: his car, his costume and all his gadgets. Catwoman has a supernatural power associated with her assumption of the characteristics of a cat, a natural rather than technological power. Catwoman becomes a hero/villain through her own initiative, inspired by her experiences of the sexism of her boss, Max Schreck (Christopher Walken). In one early scene she is shown making her own costume with a sewing machine from various bits and pieces in her apartment.

The costumes are integral to our understanding of these elements of character. In one scene, Selina and Bruce are together, watching television in Bruce's mansion. A news report comes on of trouble in town and they both leave to go there, neither knowing what the other is doing. Batman goes to his cave and selects from a number of well-kept, pristine costumes. All is ready for him in his aristocratic mansion. Selina transforms into Catwoman while driving her car. She pulls her home-made costume out of her bag with her teeth while she is driving. She looks rough and ill prepared.

These contrasts underline the role of costume in illustrating the difference in power between these characters. It is clear in the film that power is related to gender and that Catwoman/Selina is a disempowered character using her own abilities to try to find justice as a woman. Bruce is a powerful yet sensitive man, who we assume, uses his position for good. Thus the costumes give us a mixed message about gender and power. The woman is dressed to be looked at, rather than to fight effectively. She is also stereotypically associated with nature and with a cute, furry domestic animal, whereas Batman is associated with a threatening, nocturnal and mysterious flying mammal. The man is a powerful, muscular fighter associated with the intellectual power of technology. Yet in showing how both characters access this power, the film highlights some of the ideological assumptions of a sexist culture.

Make-up

If costume design works to help an actor construct a character in a film, make-up, as it is applied to an actor's actual body, is an even more intimate method of creating a role and drawing the audience into the world of the character. Make-up is applied to film performers for many different reasons. We will talk about six different categories of make-up:

- Basic;
- Character;
- Glamour;
- Physical states;
- Special effects;
- Expressionism.

Even characters that do not appear to be made up often use light basic powder in order to appear at their best in front of the camera or to counter the effects of being placed under harsh or bright lighting conditions. This coat of clear powder reduces the appearance of 'shine' on a person's face, which can be distracting to the viewer and unflattering to the subject. Make-up can also be used to show various aspects of character or to change an actor's appearance to accentuate different features of their character. In the film *The Hours* (2002), for example, the actor Nicole Kidman played the role of Virginia Woolf. As Woolf was a real person, there are images of what she looks like. To create the character of Woolf, Kidman was given an artificial nose to transform her appearance.

A certain style of make-up is utilized to ensure a performer looks their best. We will call this style glamour make-up. Glamour make-up creates an ideal of beauty and perfection that is characteristic of popular Hollywood cinema. Outside the world of film production this style is evident in the 'how-to' guides in popular magazines and 'make over' television shows. It is primarily associated with women and accentuates certain features, while downplaying others. The glamour style evens out the texture and shape of the face, often lightening the eyes by shaping the eyebrows, highlighting the lashes and shading the eyelids. Colour is also applied to make the lips appear fuller, and powder accentuates the cheekbones and de-emphasizes the nose. Bette Davis in *Now, Voyager* is an example of a character made up in the glamorous style of that time period. You will remember how this film features a transformation of Davis's character Charlotte from a proverbial 'ugly duckling' into the conventional glamorous woman. When we see Charlotte reborn, the make-up even the tones on her face and accentuate her eyes and cheekbones.

Figure 7.6 *The Hours*, Stephen Daldry, 2002

Make-up can be used to express different types of physical states. For example, a bottled spray can be applied to the body or face of someone running to simulate sweat. Similarly, make-up can accentuate the emotions of a character who is tired or ill. In *Black Narcissus*, one of the nuns, Sister Ruth (Kathleen Byron),

camera positions for a simple scene between two characters staged in continuity. Continuity staging greatly affects the production phase of a film as the scene is shot repeatedly from the different camera positions, using multiple takes. This is where the first definition of continuity comes into play, as everything has to be recreated exactly the same for each different camera position; any changes will be noticed on screen. This also requires the actors to reproduce their performances in exactly the same way for multiple takes, both in dialogue and movement. Yet many more creative decisions are made during postproduction, as the editor selects the best takes from among the shots, and combines the different camera positions for maximum effect. In the production of a film, each shot is repeated as the camera is moved to the different positions. This allows each shot to be composed most effectively and lighting altered for aesthetic purposes, though still within continuity.

Alternatives to continuity staging

Films can also use an alternative construction of space that does not solely shoot the action of a scene from multiple angles and then construct the scene through editing. Scenes made up of one continuous long take, for example, use staging in a fundamentally different manner. For example, *Russian Ark*, is an eighty-nine-minute film all made in one long take. Such a filmmaking feat requires a break with the conventional expectations of staging for continuity or coverage. All the action is presented in one long continuous flow and the camera, mounted on a Steadicam, moves in and out of the action to give us a variety of shot positions from long shot to close-ups. This requires that the actors move in different patterns; instead of being positioned for the camera to catch the action from preset positions multiple times, often the scene plays out in front of the

Figure 7.10   *Russian Ark*, Aleksandr Sokurov, 2003

camera while the camera moves around the scene. The actors also move around the camera as the scene unfolds, at times stepping out of the way as the camera passes. One of the unusual elements of how this is staged is that some of the characters acknowledge the presence of the camera and interact with it. A voice is heard, speaking from the position of the camera as if it was a character. This example is a very unusual, but very effective use of creative staging.

Performance as an element of mise-en-scène

Often we judge a film on the performance of the actors. We are so attuned to this that amateur acting stands out clearly. Student filmmakers also struggle to ensure believable performances in their work. Yet we often identify 'bad acting' when we may not have the language to express what makes it bad, nor the ability to understand how it could be made better. As we watch a narrative film, and get caught up in the action on screen, what we see appears to just happen so that we are often unaware of the amount or kind of work that goes into creating a screen performance and often, because it looks effortless, student filmmakers think that anyone can do it. In this section we will examine screen performance in such a way as to make it possible for you to see some of what the actor and director do in creating a film performance, and how the actors and director work to bring the script and the characters to life. In preparing a film role, actors create whole personae for their characters, often transforming their physical appearance and voice. Actors use many techniques to embody the characters they represent, sometimes even gaining or losing weight. They may also undertake voice training to give them the tools and techniques to use their vocal range or change the tone of their voice or assume a particular accent.

Another point to remember when considering acting is how a screen performance is defined by cinematic techniques. A screen performance can be greatly enhanced by how an actor is lit, where the camera is positioned, what music and sound accompany the scene, and how the scene is edited.

Acting styles

As critics, we often evaluate performances against standards of realism. When we come out of the cinema, we praise or condemn a performance by saying that it was realistic or unrealistic. Yet, as we have seen before, 'reality' is a subjective response. What seems realistic at one time, and in one circumstance, may seem artificial to another type of audience. Therefore, an accurate reproduction of reality is hard to define in many contexts. For example, who can assess the reality of the representation of the characters of Middle Earth in *The Lord of the Rings*, when we know that no such place exists and there are no real 'hobbits' to imitate? It is therefore more appropriate to examine how a performance works in relationship to the goals and choices of the film. We can then assess whether a performance is consistent with the overall aesthetic of the film.

Although we judge acting by the criteria of realism, some performance styles aspire to goals other than to reproduce action in a purely realistic manner. The choice of performance style relates to how the director and actors interpret the text. Realism is one such choice; it is an acting style that attempts to draw as little attention as possible to its own status as a performance. In other words, a realistic performance maintains the illusion of the fictional world of the film, encouraging the viewer to believe in the character's situation.

At the other end of the spectrum, there is a type of performance that gives the viewer the sense that the actor knows and is consciously aware of the fact that they are performing. We call this a **stylized performance**. Some people criticize musicals because bursting into fully orchestrated song when you feel like it does not happen in 'real life'. Again, the goal of an actor in a musical is not to deliver a realistic performance but a stylized one. The singing and dancing routines of a musical show a consciousness of performance and, on some levels, an awareness of the presence of an audience. Thus, acting styles can also be a function of the genre or type of film.

Rather than look at acting styles purely as a set of discrete categories, it would be useful to consider them on a continuum. Realism and stylization do not exist as absolutes as a script can be interpreted in many ways, on a scale between these two poles. '**Heightened realism**' is a style between realism and stylization that retains a realistic core, but adopts some consciously stylized features.

How an actor develops a performance

Separate from the acting style chosen to interpret a script is the way in which the individual actor prepares for a role. This is a function of actor training and what process the actor uses to embody a character. However, it is important to realize that in analyzing a film, the viewer won't necessarily be able to identify which approach or method the actor is using to achieve the necessary effect. Two broad distinctions exist as approaches to acting, between an internal or psychological method, and an external, physical approach.

An internal, psychological approach encourages the actor to explore the emotional world of a character. This often means investigating the character's motivation and connecting to what they are feeling. This approach developed over the course of the twentieth century and uses such techniques as **emotional memory**. This is when an actor recalls an event from their own experience that inspired similar emotions to the ones that the character is feeling and uses the recalled emotions as fuel for the performance. An early proponent of this style was Konstantin Stanislavsky who worked in Moscow in the early part of the twentieth century. This was a time when great strides were made in the field of psychology, including the work of Sigmund Freud. Stanislavsky's approach applied these new psychological concepts to the development of performance. Stanislavsky's system also linked the approach to performing to the style of performance; the internal acting technique is commonly associated with realism. Stanislavsky was developing these techniques around the same time as narrative film was being developed. Therefore, there is a connection throughout the twentieth century between the internal approach to acting and screen performance. The acting style developed by Stanislavsky and his followers, in particular the American Lee Strasberg, is described as **Method acting**.

External or physical approaches to acting have a longer history. Stage performances historically were developed through the codified use of certain gestures and forms. A **presentational** style of acting was the norm for many years, focusing on presenting the performance to the audience rather than creating the illusion of a closed world of the story. Presentational performances appear stylized to those watching, who may be more used to the conventions of the realistic Method acting. The presentational tradition influenced early film; many examples from 1895–1905 used a style that was theatrically presentational rather than realistic, for example Georges Méliès's *A Trip to the Moon* (1902). Here the actors are facing the camera (in **direct address**), consciously aware of, and presenting their performance to, the audience.

Figure 7.11   *A Trip to the Moon*, Georges Méliès, 1902

Performance in Stage Beauty

The film *Stage Beauty* foregrounds the process of acting itself and in doing so allows the audience to see some of the techniques that create the artifice of performance. This film is set during the seventeenth century and concentrates on the lives of a group of Shakespearean actors in England. (A full breakdown of the plot is available in Chapter 3). Throughout the film the main character Kynaston performs in a presentational style, based on the classical technique that focused on the external expression of emotional states. You can also observe in his performance style the importance of gesture in projecting an idea of the character's emotions and thoughts. For example, in one scene he asks Maria if she knows the positions of 'feminine subjugation'. He demonstrates in gestures the different positions that are used to express this (ideologically loaded) state of mind. These are highly stylized attitudes, which express heightened emotional states.

Thus Kynaston's acting method is stylized, presentational and uses an external or physical approach to developing a character. The film narrativizes a change in this acting style and the move towards an internal, realistic and representational approach to developing a performance. The film reaches its climax when Maria and Kynaston together prepare, then perform, the roles of Desdemona and Othello, with Kynaston finally performing a male role. The film replays the final scenes of *Othello*, when Othello kills Desdemona because he falsely believes she has been unfaithful to him. As they rehearse, Kynaston prompts Maria, asking her to adopt a realistic rather than a stylized performance. When she assumes a presentational pose in bed, similar to the one

Figure 7.12   *Stage Beauty*, Richard Eyre, 2004

that he would use, he asks her 'Is that how you sleep?' His coaching guides her to perform from memory, rather than to project a stylized ideal.

The change in gender casting signals a move towards increased realism – as cross-gender casting is a form of stylized performance. The techniques and the style of acting that he is using in the final rehearsal illustrate the modern convention of psychological acting, which focuses on the internal emotional state of the character rather than their external outward presentation of it. This final scene shows the two actors performing in an intense style that focuses on the power of the scene and transmits Desdemona's fear and Othello's rage to the audience. This film is not historically accurate; the techniques of internal performance were not developed at the time in which the film is set. This is a conscious choice on the part of the filmmakers to use creative licence with the historical representation of acting styles. It does, however, allow the viewer to consider the film's themes of performance and identity, and to see particular acting styles at work.

Summary and key questions

Many people on a production crew work together to create the overall visual feel of a film. The aspects of design combine with the staging and performance to tell the story and develop the characters. Here are some of the questions you might want to ask about mise-en-scène when preparing to shoot a scene or to analyze an already existing film:

- How does the setting work?
  - Is the scene shot on location or in the studio?
  - How does the setting express elements or themes of the story?
- How do the costumes illustrate aspects of character?
  - Are they used to contrast different characters?
  - Are they used to show a character's development over time?
  - How do the costumes serve thematic or ideological functions?
- How is the make-up used?
  - Is there special-effects make-up?
  - How does the make-up define the characters?
- What props are used?
  - What functions do they serve in the narrative?
  - Are the props used to comment on the themes of film?
- What style of staging does the scene use?
  - Is it staged in a conventional continuity style?
  - Does it use an alternative to the continuity system?
- Can you assess the performance of the actors?
  - Are the performances realist, heightened realist or stylized?

Want to learn more?

Think about this ...

Costuming choices and character

Objective: To explore the different elements of design in a film.

Take the characters from an older film that you have seen (*Stagecoach* works very well) and imagine how you would redesign the costumes for the various characters in an alternative contemporary style. You should use this exercise as a way to think about how the costumes demonstrate character and to see how conventions of clothing change over time. How do your costumes communicate aspects of character?

Try this ...

Staging a scene

Objective: To experiment with how a narrative scene is staged.
You will need: You need to do this exercise in a group and you will need an area of open space. You should also have a pencil and a storyboard sheet to note down the results. If you have a video camera available, you can tape the scene.

> Set up and plan staging decisions for a scene where one character is trying to return something they have stolen or borrowed and they are caught by another character. This scene should have no dialogue. You should decide how the actors move around the space and where the camera is placed in relation to the actors. (If you do not have a camera available you can place a chair where it would be and move the chair to the different camera positions.) Keep in mind all the possibilities for creating tension in the scene through the combination of staging and camera position. You may find out quite quickly how much a director has to think about.

Further reading

There are a number of books that deal with mise-en-scène from different perspectives. A good introduction to the analysis of aspects of mise-en-scène is John Gibbs, *Mise-en-Scène*. Art-design history and aesthetics are covered in Charles Affron and Mirella Jona Affron, *Sets in Motion*. A more practical guide is Robert L. Olson, *Art Direction for Film and Video*. A collection studying some of the ideological effects of costume design is Jane Gaines and Charlotte Herzog, *Fabrications*. Discussions on direction are broad-ranging; for an interesting critique of conventional staging and the practice of coverage, see Jean-Pierre Geuens, 'Staging', in *Film Production Theory*. For more conventional practical guides to directing and staging, see Steven Katz, *Film Directing Shot by Shot* and Michael Rabiger, *Directing*. For a study of Method acting in film, see Richard A. Blum, *American Film Acting* and for more general discussions of performance in film, see the edited collection, Cynthia Baron, Diane Carson and Frank P. Tomasulo, *More than a Method*.

Films studied in the chapter

Batman Returns 1992 Tim Burton (director) Bob Ringwood and Mary E. Vogt (costume designers)

Black Narcissus 1947 Michael Powell and Emeric Pressburger (directors) Alfred Junge (production designer)

The Cabinet of Dr. Caligari 1920 Robert Wiene (director) Walter Reimann, Walter Röhrig and Hermann Warm (production designers)

Gosford Park 2001 Robert Altman (director) Stephen Altman (production designer) Jenny Beavan (costume designer)

The Hours 2002 Stephen Daldry (director) Maria Djurkovic (production designer) Jo Allen (prosthetic make-up designer)

Little Big Man 1970 Arthur Penn (director) Dean Tavoularis (production designer) Dick Smith (make-up artist)

The Lord of the Rings: The Fellowship of the Ring 2001 Peter Jackson (director) Grant Major (production designer)

Now, Voyager 1942 Irving Rapper (director) Orry-Kelly (costume designer)

O Brother, Where Art Thou? 2000 Joel Coen and Ethan Coen (directors) Dennis Gassner (production designer)

Requiem for a Dream 2000 Darren Aronofsky (director) James Chinlund (production designer)

Rome Open City 1945 Roberto Rossellini (director) Rosario Megna (production designer)

Russian Ark 2003 Aleksandr Sokurov (director)

Stage Beauty 2004 Richard Eyre (director)

Stagecoach 1939 John Ford (director) Alexander Toluboff (art director)

A Trip to the Moon 1902 Georges Méliès (director)

The Umbrellas of Cherbourg 1964 Jacques Demy (director) Bernard Evein (production designer) J. Moreau (costume designer)

Other examples to explore

As with cinematography, almost any film can be useful for the study of mise-en-scène. Classical Hollywood films made under the studio system are good examples of films that use the conventions of studio set design whereas post-classical films and European art cinema frequently use interesting location shooting. Costume, make-up and props are often more evident in period dramas such as *Elizabeth* (1998 Shekhar Kapur director) or in films that focus on fashion or design, such as *The Devil Wears Prada* (2006 David Frankel director). Nevertheless, films with a contemporary setting can be equally revealing about how the elements of design communicate character, narrative, thematic and ideological meaning. In viewing films of interest for analyzing acting styles, it is important to see how the conventions of different genres are evident in the performance; musicals such as *Moulin Rouge!* (2001 Baz Luhrmann director) demonstrate more stylized acting than realist dramas such as *Vera Drake* (2004 Mike Leigh director).

8

Sound

Learning objectives

After completing this chapter, you will be able to:

- Develop a soundscape concept on paper;
- Experiment with the creation of sound effects;
- Analyze and evaluate how sound works within a film.

Sound in film

If, as suggested in Chapter 6, novice filmmakers get most excited by the camera when they start a project, equally, they often take the sound for granted. A basic digital video camera is the tool with which many start out. These cameras have a built-in microphone. Listening to the sound as it is recorded requires more work than glancing through the viewfinder; you need to locate and plug in headphones to listen actively to the sound. Do we truly pay as close attention to the sound in a film as we do to the image? Yet the sound is vitally important and can have a strong impact. Through the last two chapters we have begun to build an appreciation of how visuals can make meaning. In this chapter we will continue by adding an awareness of sound to the experience of a film.

Most of the sound you hear when you 'watch' a film, however, would have been created and mixed together later. Thus, sound is an important part of both the production and postproduction processes of a film. During production, the **sound recorder** sets up microphones to record the dialogue in **synchronization** with the image that is being filmed. This involves controlling, not only the recording equipment, but also the environment of the production so that only the sounds that are needed are recorded. Much of the work of the sound team continues through postproduction as the dialogue is often re-recorded, **sound effects** and music added and all the sound mixed together and matched to the image. Music is also part of the overall sound of a film, but it is an interesting area that is governed by its own rules and conventions. We will return to it in Chapter 10 after editing – as it is more frequently part of the postproduction process.

Throughout this chapter we study the effectiveness of sound:

- We will start with some observations about the ways in which sound is perceived, then go on to;
- Break down the different elements of the soundtrack: voice, sound effects, music and **ambience**;
- Introduce the basics of recording sound;
- Study how sound is used in a particular example: 1993 biopic *Thirty Two Short Films about Glenn Gould*;
- Finally, we will look at how sound works within the narrative with an example from the 1988 film, *Distant Voices, Still Lives*.

The circle of sound

All the film techniques discussed so far are experienced through the sense of vision. Sound in film activates a different sense, adding hearing to vision, making the experience of film a more complete and complex sensory experience than merely 'viewing'. If we are simultaneously watching and listening to a film can we truly reduce the experience to 'viewing?' As we experience a film are we 'viewers', or do we perhaps need a more complex and all-embracing term? Perhaps we can call ourselves 'perceivers', at least for the space of this chapter, as we study film sound.

As we activate the sense of hearing we find that our direction of perception changes. Our eyes, placed in the front of the head, see forward: the screen in the cinema is before us, we see in one direction and our vision is framed, as is the cinematic image. Our ears, on the sides of our head, hear sound from all around. Sounds from sources not directly before our eyes enter into our perception; we hear **omnidirectionally**. 'Surround-sound' playback systems remind us that our aural perception is 'surround'; we hear from all different directions: elements we do not see before us, we can hear from behind us.

As sound in cinema is experienced by a different sense of perception, it is in many ways distinct from the image. Sound is created and reproduced separately from the visuals of a film, just as sound recording was developed independently of the growth of the cinema. The advent of the phonograph was unrelated to the development of film technology and recorded sound was only standardized as a part of film production in the late 1920s, after many years of successful and popular silent films. Even after sound was introduced into the filmmaking process, it was created independently of the image, recorded on a separate device from the camera. It is edited separately, although in synchronization, and finally it is **married** to the strip of film in the final stages of postproduction. The married print includes a visual frame, with an **optical soundtrack** to the side. Unlike film, sound for video is recorded at the same time as the image and encoded onto the same video tape. But the **microphone (mic)** on the camera is a discrete entity to the lens; the mic collects sound separately from the image which is then encoded onto a different part of the tape. Sound can be shifted in and out of synch, removed completely or replaced or combined with alternative sounds during editing.

When projected, sound emerges from a separate space than the image in both film and video. The image appears projected on the screen in front of the audience, while the sound comes from speakers that can be placed in a number of different configurations around the room. Even the playback systems available for home viewing or headphones plugged into a television set or a computer monitor offer stereo playback, and surround-sound systems are common at home as well as in the cinema. Unlike cinematography and mise-en-scène, film sound is in all these ways an independent art from the rest of the film and, perhaps for this reason, has been most neglected in the study, and even sometimes in the practice, of film. In this chapter we are going to give sound the full attention it deserves as an integral part of the filmmaking process.

Types of sound

Listening well

Stop reading for a moment and listen to the sounds you hear in the world around you. Jot them down in a notebook.

I am drinking coffee at home in my study and I can hear a world of sound. From the adjacent room, I can hear the quiet music coming from my stereo, from the kitchen I can hear the creaking whir of the extractor fan. Outside my window they are digging up the streets and I can hear the lorries moving and the occasional break of a drill. As I work in my study in the mornings I often programme my mind to ignore the distracting sounds around me. They are part of the background noise of my life that I take for granted and I don't even listen to them. We all go through a psychological process of sound filtering. We listen actively to the sounds in the environment that interest us, and ignore others.

Most of us, at some time, have been at a party where there are many conversations going on simultaneously, with other sounds in the environment – music, eating and drinking noises – all competing to create noise. As listeners we have a selective perceptual process that allows us to shut out certain sounds and focus in on others. If you know anybody who has a hearing impairment and uses a hearing aid, they could relate a different experience. Unlike the human ear, an electronic device, such as a hearing aid or a microphone, does not have the capability to select certain sounds and ignore others.

It is because electronic devices collect sound without the selection process of the brain that artists who design sound for film go through a complex process of creating soundtracks through recording and mixing separate elements. What we hear in a film may appear naturalized, one of the many things we take for granted, but we must realize that it is a careful construction, designed to simulate the sounds experienced in any given location. Initially the sound environment is analyzed, then isolated and recorded separately. The dialogue is often recorded with the images, with the sound effects and music added at a later stage. During editing, the different sounds are synchronized to the image on multiple tracks. This allows the **sound designer** to control the levels, to create a sound environment using the same precision and attention to detail used by other members of the creative team.

At the postproduction stage, the audio is mixed together in a manner appropriate to the playback system. The ultimate goal is to create a soundtrack where specific sounds are brought forward at certain points, to work with the overall structure and form of the film. Music can swell to increase the emotion of a scene; the background sounds rise to the foreground to create a sense of space or to mimic the perception of a character; silence can create suspense when carefully contrasted with the world of sound. For artists interested in sound, all the noises of the environment can demonstrate creative potential. Later in this chapter we will discuss the short film 'Truck Stop' from *Thirty Two Short Films about Glenn Gould*. In this film, as the pianist, Glenn Gould (Colm Feore), sits waiting for his breakfast to arrive, he hears, enjoys and even conducts with his finger a symphony of sound. Studying the soundtrack of a film for the first time will place you in a similar position to Gould as you concentrate on and listen to different sounds.

Now let's continue our exercise. Take your list of sounds and separate them into tracks, as you might do if you were a sound designer recording and editing them into a scene. This example shows a potential soundtrack for the scene of my morning cup of coffee, placed into a four-track paper sound mix.

Track 1	Loudest sounds are of me drinking the coffee: clattering of the cup, drinking noise
Track 2	Continuous music at low level
Track 3	Noises from the exterior, muffled by the building: truck driving along the dirt, the burst of a drill, men's voices
Track 4	Low-level ambient noise of a fan

These are all very plausible audio elements from a scene of a film. Yet in many cases, film soundtracks are simplified so that the audience is not overwhelmed by the complexity of what they are hearing. Thus, through the process of creating the soundtrack, the sound designer makes a selection from all the potential sounds in an environment and gives the audience clues as to which are important; thus, the perceiver's attention is drawn to certain visual elements, as well as the principal sounds.

Where is that sound coming from?

In the example above, if the image is showing us the room where a character is sitting, then the key components in the scene are likely to be in the visible space. Thus, the source of the outside noise would not necessarily be visible in the scene. Sound coming from a source that is not visible on the screen is often described as 'offscreen' sound. Yet, with sound, the onscreen/offscreen division is not that simple. As discussed earlier, the sense of hearing is omnidirectional and sounds themselves are heard and not seen. Thus, sound is never truly 'on screen', but heard through the speaker. Often sound emerges from a source or action that we can see; someone speaks and we hear his or her voice. We hear them, whether we see them or not. Thus it is not the sound itself that is off screen so much as the visual source of the sound. In comparison, when something is off screen, we do not see it, but infer its presence through the interaction with the other visual elements, or through the sound. When a sound is heard, without the source being visible, it is the source that is off screen. It would thus be useful to find a better term than 'offscreen sound' to describe this phenomenon. Film theorist Michel Chion uses the term **'acousmatic'** to refer to sounds where the source is not visible. He draws on an old dictionary definition of acousmatic as 'sound one hears without seeing its source' (Chion, 1999: 18). In our example, the sounds coming from outside the scene are acousmatic, since the source of the sound is beyond the visible frame.

If we combine our recent discussion of the relative position of the perceptions of sound with our knowledge of framing, we know that there are many potential acousmatic sounds in any given shot of a film. In our example, sound is coming from outside, beyond the visual space of the scene. There are also a number of acousmatic sounds that can be significantly closer, from a source that is within the space of the scene, but beyond the edges of the frame. The nearer a shot is to a close-up the more potential that shot has for acousmatic sound. Editing from one shot to another frequently involves the use of sound from offscreen sources. In this way, sound is used to help create the sense of filmic space.

Acousmatic sound can be used effectively to relate to what we see on screen. Sound can create expectations of what will be revealed visually. If, for example, the sound of a door is heard in a scene, when a door is not visible, we are set up to expect a character to enter or exit the room. Acousmatic sound can also work to cheat expectations when visual elements contradict the evidence of the soundtrack. The film *Come and See*, made in Belarus in 1985 and set in World War II, uses acousmatic sound in a very evocative manner. In this film a boy has left his village to join the army. He returns to find that the people of his village have been killed. Before he discovers their bodies he moves around his home, taking food from the fire, obviously unaware of what he is about to discover. The soundtrack gives the first indication to the audience that there is something wrong, as we can hear the sound of flies from an offscreen source as they gather around the pile of bodies outside. The sound effect of the flies raises the audience's expectations, to prepare it for the revelation of the death of the boy's family.

If we now return to the paper soundtrack we are developing for our morning scene, as sound designers it is important to question the significance of all the sounds we plan to include. Taking the example of sound coming from an outside source, unless the work taking place outside is relevant to the story, the form of the film or the subject of the documentary, then it would make sense to eliminate it from this scheme, to focus the aural attention of the viewers on what is occurring inside.

Before we remove Track 3 from our hypothetical film let's consider some of the examples where it would be appropriate to include it:

- Let's imagine that the film is a thriller where the outside space becomes key to a mystery that the character is unravelling. Maybe the workers outside are concealing something that the character may later discover, burying a body, perhaps. In this case the noise outside could be a deliberate subconscious clue to a central aspect of the film.
- Let's imagine that the film is a documentary about the noisy nature of a particular neighbourhood. The subject inside could now be being interviewed, with the background noise outside a key factor, illustrating the topic.
- Finally, if we imagine our film to be an experimental, formal exploration of the environment of home, then the external noise could become a key motif in that exploration.

If we accept that none of these cases hold, and that our use of sound from outside the visible space of the scene will not add to the action, then we can remove Track 3 and allow the soundtrack to focus our attention on the interior world of the scene. Let us use our spare track to expand our scene to include dialogue with another character in the room.

Track 1	The loudest sound is now the dialogue
Track 2	Drinking coffee: clattering of the cup, drinking noise
Track 3	Continuous music at a low level
Track 4	Low-level ambient noise of a fan

Our scene now has all the major components of a film soundtrack. The first track involves dialogue; the human voice is perhaps the most obvious element in a film soundtrack. The second track involves the sounds of specific noises that relate to action in the frame but that do not use the voice directly. These are known as sound effects (often abbreviated to **SFX**) and are added to a soundtrack at a later date, or created specifically for the film. Our third track involves music, a vital part of a soundtrack and one we will return to in Chapter 10. The fourth track in our scheme consists primarily of a very low continuous noise that is characteristic of the room in which we are shooting. This sound is known as an ambient track (sometimes also called an **atmos** track). All rooms, even when very quiet in other ways, have a very low level of sound, a characteristic **room noise**.

Voice

In our new scheme, the voice track of our imaginary scene is now predominant aurally. In most cases, the human voice is a key factor in the soundtrack. Speech carries meaning, develops the plot and articulates aspects of character. The audience often listens to the voice as the bearer of fundamental information within the soundtrack; the dialogue can tell much of the story. We listen to the dialogue to guide us through the plot and as viewers and listeners, we are sometimes uncomfortable when important information is inaudible.

The priority given to the voice is clear in the history of cinema, as early sound films were called 'talkies'. If we compare the idea of a 'talking picture' to the idea of a 'sound picture', we see a different emphasis. It is useful to recognize that silent films were never truly silent – they were accompanied by music and sometimes by spoken commentary. The innovation of the late 1920s was the incorporation of speech synchronized with the visuals. In one of the first sound films, *The Jazz Singer*

Figure 8.1   *The Jazz Singer*, Alan Crosland, 1927

(1927), it was Al Jolson speaking the phrase 'You ain't heard nothing yet', that proved the great novelty, the arrival of synchronized speech to the world of film. Although the sound of a film is never reduced solely to speech, at the same time, voice and speech are key parts of the soundtrack that cannot be underestimated.

In this history, great importance is placed on the ability to synchronize sound to the visuals. You will remember from our earlier discussion that sound is recorded separately from the image. Therefore filmmakers and technicians have developed techniques to ensure that sound and image stay together at all points in a film. Sound and image that go together are known as **synchronous** sound. As with other elements of the soundtrack, synchronicity is something we often take for granted and only become aware of it when it is absent; **out-of-synch** sound is referred to as **asynchronous**. The 1952 musical *Singin' in the Rain* uses asynchronous sound consciously as a commentary on the process of early sound filmmaking. This musical is about a group of actors making the transition from working in silent film to sound

Figure 8.2   *Singin' in the Rain*, Stanley Donen and Gene Kelly, 1952

film. During the première of the first sound film starring two of the main characters, the sound goes out-of-synch. In this scene the woman clearly mouths the words 'no, no, no', while we hear the man's voice say, 'yes, yes, yes'. This is an ironic use of synchronicity for comedic effect.

Although the audience follows the speech of the characters in a film and values the comprehensibility of the voice in the soundtrack, many films obscure the information in the dialogue at certain points. For example, in the melodrama, *Letter from an Unknown Woman* (1948), there is a scene where the main character, Lisa (Joan Fontaine), has been proposed to by Lt Leopold (John Good). She refuses, and they walk back to the outdoor café where his father and her parents are waiting expectantly. As Lisa and Leopold move toward the café, a brass band marches past, and its playing completely obliterates the dialogue. The audience does not hear the dialogue as Leopold speaks briefly to his father and the two men leave the café. After they leave, the band trails off, and then the voices become audible again, as we hear Lisa's parents questioning her about what has just happened. She finishes the scene by summarizing what she said to Leopold: 'I told him that I wasn't free.' This moment in the film is a turning point; it represents the first time that Lisa openly reveals to another character the feelings that she has for the pianist Stefan (Louis Jourdan). Those feelings, and her inability to communicate them, are fundamental to how the narrative in the film is structured and indeed, ultimately, to what the film is about. As we saw in Chapter 3, the plot of *Letter from an Unknown Woman* is structured as a series of flashbacks centred on Lisa's confessional letter to Stefan. The film thus plays thematically with the giving, receiving and (most importantly) the withholding of information. The obscured dialogue in the proposal scene is relatively insignificant and the visual imagery is sufficient to carry the narrative information, but the audience here is implicated in the cycle of information denied. This brief moment in the scene functions to withhold part of the verbal information that would propel the narrative. The marching band music places the audience in a position only moments before held by the parents, as they looked on at a scene without being able to hear it. They have misunderstood the conversation and made assumptions based solely upon what they could see. The obscuring of dialogue may leave viewers wondering whether they, too, will be misled by their expectations.

Speech, as well as being the bearer of information, carries an additional function as an abstract force, an element of listening pleasure independent of the message it conveys. For example, in *Thirty Two Short Films about Glenn Gould*, the film, 'The Idea of North', dramatizes Glenn Gould's production of a radio documentary of the same name. A speaking voice becomes an abstract element interwoven with other voices to create a form of spoken vocal music. The different-sounding voices, with varying pitches, accents and rhythms, create the intensity of the sound-track of this short film.

Sound effects

We are so used to hearing different sounds around us all the time that we are sometimes not even aware of them. This often works in film as well; we listen to a complex soundtrack and just assume that what we hear is part of the natural sound of the scene. Actually, a soundtrack is created by a team of specialists who construct a multilayered aural experience, with sound effects so natural-ized as part of the world of a film that we are sometimes not fully aware of them. Sound effects can be created in the same manner as synchronous dialogue; that is, recorded at the time that the image is shot. Yet since this potentially interferes with the operator's efficient recording of the dialogue, more often the sound effects are added to a production after its completion. This work is done by a specialized professional who creates different sounds either in a studio setting or on location, using many resources. This person is known as a **Foley artist**, named after Jack Foley, an early sound innovator of the 1920s.

Many of us may have seen the stereotypical representation of the work of the Foley artist: clomping coconuts to imitate horse hoofs. In reality, Foley work is actually quite complex. For example, it can be challenging for a Foley artist to produce effects for science-fiction or horror film situations, creating sound for things that have no existing counterparts. For example, what does Spider-Man's web sound like? Foley artist Paul Ottosson describes how he developed this sound for the film *Spider-Man 2* (2004):

> I went to one of the biggest stages they have here on the lot – it's about 300 feet long – and I rigged it up with microphones and I went in with a sling shot and started shooting all these objects past the microphones. I shot everything from pieces of copper piping to coins, hoping to get some sounds that would work for the trail of the web as it goes through the air. (Jackson, 2010)

This is only the first stage of the process as the sounds recorded in this situation are then mixed with other sounds and incorporated into the final film.

Although sound effects are often background noise, sometimes they become foregrounded, when other sounds (voices and music) are absent for various reasons. *Children of a Lesser God*

(1986) is an interesting example of a film where the issue of sound has formal and thematic weight. In this romance, a hearing man, James (William Hurt), develops a relationship with a deaf woman, Sarah (Marlee Matlin), who can only communicate in sign language. The film's point of identification is the hearing character and the communication between the two provides the film with its narrative tension. As the film is fundamentally about the need to communicate through barriers of sound and silence, it invites the viewer to pay closer attention than usual to what is happening with the sound.

As much of the film is signed, James translates the conversations for the audience, speaking back what Sarah is signing. Thus, the dialogue is as important as always in conveying narrative and character information. Yet it is the moments when the voice is absent that the sound effects are brought forward and effects that might otherwise be ignored become noticeable. As the relationship develops, James begins to feel isolated from Sarah's circle of deaf friends. In a party scene halfway through the film, the absence of the expected sounds of conversation and music makes this particularly apparent. In this scene we hear various sounds, the predominant of which is the noise made by the characters conversing in sign language; we hear the tapping and touch of their hands as they sign. The secondary sounds include the consumption of food and drink, the clinking of silverware on china and the swilling of drink. In this scene we sympathize with James, who watches and feels alienated from the interaction going on around him. The quietness of the scene is used for effect, to help us to identify with his character.

Ambience

All rooms, even when very quiet, have a very low level of sound, a characteristic room noise. This translates into film; even in their quietest moments, a sound film is never entirely silent. Novice film and video makers often make the mistake of leaving silence between sounds in their films. These moments of quiet are best achieved by the incorporation of a track of sound known as an ambient track, which gives a low level of sound from the environment of the scene. At the end of a shoot at a particular location, the sound person will record the ambience that can be used by the editor to fill in any quiet moments and to give a consistent background to the scene.

Sound recording

In the first part of the exercise we developed a sound design – a plan of how to create the audio for a scene. This gave us a brief introduction to the process of conceptualizing sound design and a chance to think creatively about the kinds of decisions made by sound designers when preparing the aural part of a film production. Now to take this a step further, we will look at some of the basics of sound recording and mixing before concluding with a discussion of the role of sound in the development of a narrative film. As we have already discovered, creating and recording good sound for video involves a lot more than turning on the onboard camera microphone and hoping for the best. To truly make the most of the possibilities of sound, it is important to understand not only creative practice, but also to have a working knowledge of sound-recording and -mixing equipment.

For all recording situations, the first decision is which microphone to select for the kinds of sound and the specifics of the environment. There are two basic distinctions between microphones; the first relates to the microphone construction and the second to its **pick-up pattern**. There are two types of microphone based on their design and construction. Both have different functions that work optimally for various applications. The **dynamic microphone** is a mechanical device that converts sound-waves into electrical pulses. It is a sturdy microphone, good for outside use as it is not very sensitive to wind and not affected by temperature and humidity. On the whole it is not a very sensitive microphone and does not reproduce the full range of frequencies. The **condenser** microphone uses a capacitor to convert the sound-waves to electrical pulses. It is more sensitive to various sounds, including picking up wind noise when used outside. It is a more delicate microphone than a dynamic, with a greater frequency range and it is battery-operated.

The **pick-up pattern** of a microphone indicates from which direction the microphone receives the best sound. An omnidirectional microphone picks up sound in a circular pattern around where the microphone is placed. If you are recording in a situation where it is not vital to isolate one particular sound or group of sounds this is an appropriate microphone to use. It is useful for collecting ambient sound from around a space. A **cardiod** microphone is named for the heart-shaped appearance of its pick-up pattern. In this case the microphone collects sound best in the area directly to the front. The area behind the microphone, where the camera or recording unit is placed will pick up the least sound. This microphone is best used for dialogue or isolating particular sounds. The **super-cardiod** or **shotgun** microphone isolates even further a specific area or speaker in a scene. This microphone is commonly used for dialogue scenes, often attached to a long pole known as a **boom**.

Specialized types of microphones include the **lavalier** or lapel microphone, which is a small condenser microphone that can be attached to a subject's clothing to record them directly. It is usually fairly directional, collecting sound from just the one subject. Its most common application is the documentary or studio interview, as it is often visible and would be a distracting continuity error if seen on a character in a narrative production. It is, however, a useful microphone to conceal on a set for extra sound recording in awkward situations. Many lavaliers are also radio microphones. These microphones include a transmitter and a receiver which is plugged into the recording device. The microphone transmits sound to the receiver through radio waves, eliminating the need for connecting cables. These microphones are useful in situations where a subject might move away from the recording device.

One major consideration for recording sound is working with synchronized voice in a scene. Most situations have multiple sound components, so if you are recording a scene where speech or dialogue is the principal element, then it is important to record that sound as faithfully and accurately as possible without distraction; background sounds and music can be added later in the editing stage but they cannot be removed. During recording, you need to attempt to eliminate sounds that will muffle or override the voice you are recording. A number of techniques can guarantee this, but the key factor is to monitor the sound effectively, listening as carefully as possible to the sound as it is being recorded. Another consideration is the continuity of the sound you are recording. For example, if you record an interview with music playing in the background, when the time comes to edit that scene, the music will jump around as you cut the shots together from the different parts of the interview. This distracting background sound would be much more easily eliminated in the first place by turning off the music at the source. Working with sound effects is similar to recording voice in that it is best to record the effect isolated from other sounds, then combine the effects that you want in the mixing process.

The location in which you might find yourself recording sound makes a lot of difference to how that sound is recorded. Sound reacts and travels differently in different environments. Problems with recording sound outside can include wind noise and other extraneous sounds that you cannot control. On the other hand, recording inside is affected by the **acoustics** of the surrounding environment. As sound-waves travel around a room, some of them bounce off the walls, floor and ceiling. Thus, the sound heard inside comes both directly from the source and indirectly from the sound-waves reflected from the surrounding surfaces. This is known as **reverberation**. Soft surfaces, such as curtains and carpets, do not reflect sound-waves as effectively as hard surfaces, such as walls and mirrors. Soft surfaces are said to **absorb** sound. Recording in a space with primarily hard surfaces produces increased reverberation and the resultant recording can have a hollow and cavernous feel to it. This can be controlled by inserting soft surfaces around the recording area, such as one sees in many professional recording studios. It is easier to add reverberation to a sound after recording it than it is to eliminate it afterwards, so it is important to minimize the reverberation in a room. If, however, too much sound is absorbed it can give a muffled or dead sound to the recording, as the acoustic properties of reverberation are also part of the sound world that we usually hear. As with every aspect of sound recording, it is vital to strike the right acoustic balance for the situation. Another factor that affects the way in which sound-waves are absorbed is the presence or absence of people in a room. As every actor learning to project their voice knows, it is far harder to be heard in a theatre full of people than it is to be heard during a rehearsal in an empty theatre.

When recording sound, it is crucial to monitor the sounds both by looking at the sound-recording meter and listening attentively through headphones. Watching the sound meter, the recordist makes sure that the sounds recorded remain below zero as those above can be distorted. Sound recorded at a lower level has to be amplified to be audible when played back or mixed which will also raise unwanted background sounds. Higher-quality cameras or sound recorders will allow you to adjust the level of sound recorded. It is often best to test and preset the levels before the start of a scene, as 'riding' or adjusting the levels during shooting can be difficult and cause erratic quality.

Sound mixing

Mixing sound is an important part of the postproduction process and involves editing the sounds as well as the images and coordinating the two together. The sound levels can be mixed to foreground different elements: to draw attention to certain areas of the frame or to suggest activity in the world outside the frame; to accentuate the dialogue or to undermine it; to simulate the point of perception of a character or the perspective of the acoustic environment. Most video-editing software allows for the inclusion of multiple tracks of sound and these can be used effectively to accentuate certain aspects at different times and to balance them so that the requisite sounds are more audible than others. Mixing sound also provides the potential to work with stereo or surround-sound effects to create a three-dimensional audio environment.

One of the reasons why sound levels are adjusted in mixing is to imitate the perspective of a space. Sound can be used in a similar manner to the visuals, to convey a sense of three-dimensionality. Thus, sounds with sources in the background of a scene are often quieter than those with sources visible in the foreground. Sound uses a similar type of perspective shift as visuals and can create perception of depth. This can also be achieved through a manipulation of the acoustic properties of the sound; reverberation lends an added sense of depth to a room and too much sound absorption makes a space seem smaller.

Yet films often abandon the rules of perspective for the sake of narrative clarity. Once you have started paying closer attention to the use of sound in film, you will begin to notice how certain sounds, such as the dialogue of the principal characters, are always louder and clearer than others, despite their relative position within the frame. This is a logical use of sound levels, since, as previously discussed, the dialogue is the main means by which information is aurally transmitted to the audience. It is one of the conventions of narrative cinema that sound from the main dialogue is fully audible regardless of the logic of perspective. The audience accepts this convention as the norm when viewing and listening to scenes where the perspectives have been created for effect. Sound can also be used subjectively, in a similar manner to the point-of-view shot discussed in Chapter 6. In this case, sound is used to imitate the experience of one of the characters and we hear the sound they are listening to through their selective perception. This is discussed in the example of 'Truck Stop' which follows.

Changing the levels of sound can achieve many different effects. The sound editor mixes the audio carefully to focus attention, build suspense, simulate a character's point of perception and to ensure that the dialogue carrying the principal narrative information is clearly audible. To see how the different types of sound work together creatively let's look at an example, the short film 'Truck Stop' from *Thirty Two Short Films about Glenn Gould*.

An example of sound types: 'Truck Stop'

'Truck Stop' is a segment of a longer film, *Thirty Two Short Films about Glenn Gould*, which tells the life story of the Canadian pianist Glenn Gould in an innovative manner through, as the title suggests, thirty-two short films. The structure is inspired by the classical musical piece 'The Goldberg Variations' by J. S. Bach, famously recorded by Gould. The series of short films all work together to tell the whole story of Gould's life. 'Truck Stop' shows Gould going to eat breakfast in a diner. As he sits waiting for his food, he simply listens. This simple structure makes for an engaging exploration of the interactions between all four elements of sound.

After Gould enters the diner, the sound is balanced at first in such a way that none of the background dialogue takes precedence. Then, as the film progresses, after Gould has spoken to the waitress, he starts actively listening to his environment. At this point, the sound shifts to simulate his perspective. Just as we studied the use of visual point-of-view shots in Chapter 6, this film takes on the **aural perspective** of Gould as he uses his selective perception to listen to specific conversations and block out other sounds of the environment.

In a scene such as this one, the ambient track is almost impossible to hear; there are other sounds occurring at the same time that draw attention far more forcefully, but we would probably notice if the ambient track were absent. The music starts out as a central element, but later fades to the background. It is signalled as coming from the radio, with a shift in tone when Gould enters the diner and we see the radio inside. The song gives rhythm and continuity to the scene when we first hear it. When the sound perspective begins to shift, the music fades out entirely. It returns at the end of the film with the other sounds of the diner.

The sequence also includes a carefully orchestrated set of sound effects. You can identify them: voices, plates and cutlery, paper rustling, the chair scraping, footsteps, a cash register, a door opening. These are a few of the components in the sound world of this sequence. If we re-view the image, we can see which of these sounds are synchronized with the image, directly related to what we see on the screen. For example, the noise of the paper is made when Gould places it on the table, the chair scrapes as he pulls it out and the footsteps belong to the approaching waitress. Others are not directly synchronous, so much as atmospheric background sounds. The voices in the sequence start with Gould's exchange with the waitress. This is balanced more quietly than principal dialogue often is in a film; although it is clearer than the surrounding sounds, it is not significantly louder. As the waitress leaves, we hear the voice of the first trucker. As the trucker talks, his voice becomes the focus of the scene and the other sounds fade out. This represents the subjectivity of sound, following Gould's attention and leading the audience to focus on what Gould is listening to rather than what he hears. This imitates the way we perceive sound in the world. If you think back to the exercise at the beginning of this chapter, you will realize that when you stopped reading to listen to the sound environment, you were making a selective choice about what you would hear. Similarly, Gould in this scene is actively listening to the different conversations in the diner. The film ends with a return to a normal sound environment as the music and background effects are more evenly balanced with the voices.

'Truck Stop' is an example of a film that uses its soundtrack consciously and which focuses the perceiver's attention on the sound as an equal partner with the image in creating the scene. Let us continue our discussion of sound by examining more exactly how sound works within a narrative structure to tell the story of a film.

Narrative sound

As one of the key elements in a fiction film, the soundtrack often comments on and interacts with the visuals, in order to develop the narrative. It is a vital storytelling device that can guide us through the narrative, give perception of depth to the space, explore the point of perception of a character, and add to the emotional intensity of a scene. It is therefore important to examine some of the ways in which the soundtrack communicates the story: first, where the sound exists in relation to the world of the narrative, and second, how the sound is positioned in relation to the narrative order.

Sound in the world of the narrative

In 'Truck Stop', all the sound appears to come from the world which Gould inhabits. The film starts with the music over images of the road, and then we see Gould adjusting the car radio, signalling that the music comes from that source. This is then confirmed when the shot is linked to the radio inside the restaurant, indicating that the music also emerges from that location. The voices in the diner are synchronous with the action and all the sound effects are logical parts of the sound world of the diner. As we learned in Chapter 3, elements that exist within the world of the narrative are known as diegetic elements, thus sound that comes from inside the world of the film is known as diegetic sound. 'Truck Stop' is a film that primarily uses diegetic sound.

It is a common practice in film soundtracks to also use sound from outside the fictional space of the film. Music, in particular, often appears to emerge from outside the scene. This is known as non-diegetic sound. The use of non-diegetic sound is such a common convention that the audience accepts it without question and does not look for its source within the film. Non-diegetic music can be used to provide a background and an external emotional commentary on the action of the film without being part of the world of the narrative. Since the element of sound that is most frequently used non-diegetically is the music, we will return to this discussion in Chapter 10.

Sound and the narrative order

In addition to using primarily diegetic sound, 'Truck Stop' also locates all of its sound at the same moment in the narrative as the image. When watching the film we are aware that, not only does that sound occur in that space, it corresponds in time to the visuals. This is a fairly common use of sound in film; image and audio move together through time as the narrative progresses. When sound and image work together at the same point in the narrative time this is known as **simultaneous sound**.

There are examples where sound and image do not exist in the same moment in the narrative order. This is known as **non-simultaneous sound**. There are moments in the development of a story when the narrative is led primarily by the image, as there are moments when the narrative is led primarily by the sound. When a character is relating an event that occurred in the past, and we see images of the event while their voice continues over these images, this is an example of non-simultaneous sound. In this case the sound moves the narrative forward in time, while the images flash back to a previous moment. This is a fairly common way in which sound and image work together in a narrative.

An example of this happens in *The Lord of the Rings: The Two Towers* (2002): the second film of the trilogy. Near the end of the first film the wizard Gandalf (Ian McKellen) falls into a crevasse in the mines of Moria. In the second film he returns reborn and meets up with three of his companions. He recounts for them how he came back from his adventure alive. As his voice continues through the present of the film, we see brief visual flashbacks illustrating the story that he is telling. This non-simultaneous sound is an effective way to explain to the audience and the characters a part of the story that happened previously.

Non-simultaneous sound can also be used in the opposite fashion, when the image continues in the present and we hear sound from a previous moment in the narrative. This type of **sonic flashback** often involves the perspective of a character as they hear in their mind something that occurred at an earlier point in the film. There is a famous example of a sonic flashback at the end of the 1939 melodrama, *Gone with the Wind*. In the last scene the main character, Scarlett O'Hara (Vivien Leigh), has just watched her husband leave and has finally come to the realization that she loves him and wants him back. As she sits on the stairs crying, we hear in the soundtrack her memory of other characters telling her to return home to Tara. These sonic flashbacks allow us access to what is going on in her mind, reminding both Scarlett and the viewer of conversations that occurred at previous points in the story. In this case, the narrative progresses through the

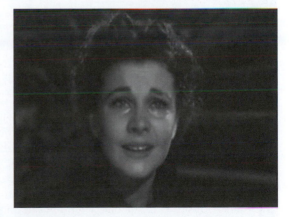

Figure 8.3 *Gone with the Wind*, Victor Fleming, 1939

visuals as the sound returns to an earlier point in time. This lets us know the character's thoughts and motivations as she decides to return home.

Another way in which sound is manipulated in relation to the narrative order is through an editing technique known as a **sound bridge**. This is a sound-editing technique that involves the linking of one scene to another via the continuation of sound; either the sound of the second scene starts before the visuals of the first have ended, or the sound of the first scene continues after the visuals of the second have started. To clarify these points, let's look at an example. *Distant Voices, Still Lives* is a film that uses sound on multiple levels. It shifts position in the narrative order, using sound both simultaneously and non-simultaneously, and it demonstrates examples of both diegetic and non-diegetic sound.

An example of sound in narrative: Distant Voices, Still Lives

Distant Voices, Still Lives uses an unconventional approach to narrative and much of this experimentation is embodied in the soundtrack. The film works to evoke the memories of childhood, looking back to the family relationships that formed the adult characters' experiences. Visually, the film uses sepia-tone colour and a slow evolving pace, combined with an **elliptical narrative** to explore these memories of a past life. Here we will examine the opening sequence (about five minutes' long) to see how the sound is used to express and complement these visual and thematic cues.

Figure 8.4 *Distant Voices, Still Lives*, Terence Davies, 1988

The first thing that happens in this film is the start of the soundtrack as we hear the noise of rain over a black screen, before the title fades in. This is followed by the sound of the radio announcer as the house comes into view. When the image joins the sound of rain we are led to associate that sound with that space – it is raining in the street. This is an example of simultaneous sound; it is part of the scene that we see. As it is also sound that comes from the world of the film, it is diegetic sound. Later in the shot the mother enters and collects the milk bottles. The sounds we hear, like the rain, are simultaneous and diegetic. As the sounds correspond with the actions shown on screen, they are also synchronous. The sound of the radio, however, is different. We don't see a radio on the screen, nor is the speaker in the space outside the house. We understand from the context, however, that the radio exists in the world of the film, probably in the house with the woman. Thus, we recognize this as acousmatic, diegetic sound.

When the woman enters the house and calls up the stairs, the simultaneous, synchronous, diegetic sound continues, but when we hear, but don't see, her children coming down the stairs, the sound is diegetic but non-simultaneous – coming from that space, but at a different time from that which we see. The film doesn't make these temporal relations clear at this point; we are not sure whether what we see occurs before or after what we hear. The choice to have this moment in the film when the audience sees an empty staircase, but hears the voices of the family, is an interesting one. It evokes the feeling that is prevalent throughout the film, which is of memories that can be stirred by being in the location of home. Whether the family is visible or not, they inhabit the space at different times and can be recalled just like the memory that the film is trying to capture.

The next few shots of the film are accompanied by the sound of singing. The first song 'I Get the Blues When It Rains' is sung by an amateur-sounding voice and we learn later in the film that a number of the characters sing. Although it is left ambiguous, it is probably sung by the mother, making it diegetic sound, yet again the temporal relation to the image is not fully clarified. The second song is obviously a professional recording and therefore non-diegetic. The images that go with this song are visual flashbacks to the father's funeral and are accompanied only by the non-diegetic song with no synchronous or simultaneous sound – for example, we do not hear the sound of the car door closing, or any other sound emerging from that time or space. There is a contrast between the singing of the character and the professional singer. Amateur singing is very important in this film as part of the way the community comes together. The opening song foreshadows how important song will be throughout the film.

The image returns from the flashback to the present and there is a moment of synchronous, diegetic sound as the first daughter wishes for her father. The second daughter's reaction is in thought only, therefore diegetic and simultaneous, but not synchronous. Her thoughts then link to a sonic flashback of her father (diegetic, non-simultaneous, asynchronous) and a sound bridge connects this to the scene in the basement. This moment is very important for introducing the characters and their different perceptions and memories of their father. As you hear the second daughter's thoughts you get an added perspective through the use of sound; we hear her think what she would not say to her sister.

This very complex scene illustrates all the various types of uses of sound in narrative and is worth the effort of close study to fully appreciate the complexity of the uses of sound within a narrative context.

Summary and key questions

The choices made in bringing together all the elements of a soundtrack are really important when analyzing or creating a film. Let's remind ourselves of the key questions to ask about the sound in a film:

- What elements of sound are in the scene?
  - o Are there voices, sound effects, music, ambience?
  - o Are the sounds synchronous or asynchronous?
  - o How are the different elements balanced?
  - o Does the sound come from an onscreen source?
- How are the sounds recorded?
  - o Which type of microphone is best for the scene?
  - o What elements of the acoustic environment can be controlled to achieve the desired result?
- How does the sound work within the narrative?
  - o Is the sound simultaneous with the visual action?
  - o Is the sound diegetic or non-diegetic?
- Is the sound effective in communicating information?

Want to learn more?

Think about this ...

Sound in the narrative

Objective: To analyze and evaluate how sound works in a film.

Choose a scene from a film that you enjoy and actively listen to the sound. You may even want to listen to the sound without watching the picture. What types of sound does it use? Which sound effects are synchronous with the action? How do the sounds work within the narrative scheme of the film? Are there examples of sound that come from a different point in the narrative than the image?

Try this ...

Soundboard

Objective: To develop a soundscape concept on paper.
You will need: Storyboard sheets and a pencil.

Using storyboard sheets with extra space for developing the soundtrack, plan a short sequence with simple visuals and at least four tracks of audio. How many different kinds of sound can you work into one sequence?

Creating sound effects

Objective: To experiment with the creation of sound effects.
You will need: For this exercise it is best to use a recording device. A camcorder or a simple tape recorder will do. If you don't have a recording device you can experiment with creating sound effects without recording them.

Try creating and recording different sound effects. It is best to keep a log as sometimes it is hard to identify sounds after you have recorded them. Try out Foley art. Can you make one noise sound like another? Try recording in environments with different acoustics. What do you learn about the complexities of creating sound?

Further reading

When researching the area of sound, one of the best places to start is the website filmsound.org, which includes articles, bibliographies and links to various resources on both the theory and practice of sound. Basic guides to recording sound are Stanley R. Alten, *Audio in Media* and David Lewis Yewdall, *Practical Art of Motion Picture Sound*. Theoretical discussions of sound in film include the work of Michel Chion, in particular, *Audio-Vision*; see also Larry Sider, *Soundscape*, John Belton and Elisabeth Weis, *Film Sound: Theory and Practice* and Rick Altman, *Sound Theory, Sound Practice*.

Films studied in this chapter

Children of a Lesser God 1986 Randa Haines (director) Robert A. Grieve (supervising sound editor)
Come and See 1985 Elem Klimov (director) V. Mors (sound engineer)
Distant Voices, Still Lives 1988 Terence Davies (director) Alex Mackie (supervising sound editor)
Gone with the Wind 1939 Victor Fleming (director) Frank Maher (sound recordist)
The Jazz Singer 1927 Alan Crosland (director)
Letter from an Unknown Woman 1948 Max Ophüls (director) Glenn F. Anderson and Leslie I. Carey (sound)
The Lord of the Rings: The Two Towers 2002 Peter Jackson (director) David Farmer (sound designer)
Singin' in the Rain 1952 Stanley Donen and Gene Kelly (directors) Douglas Shearer (recording supervisor)
Spider-Man 2 2004 Sam Raimi (director) Paul N. J. Ottosson (sound designer)
Thirty Two Short Films about Glenn Gould 1993 François Girard (director) Stuart French (sound mixer) John Douglas Smith (sound editor)

Other examples to explore

One filmmaker whose work stands out for the use of sound is Robert Bresson. Any of his films are interesting to study in this area, but especially *A Man Escaped* (1955). Also of interest is *The Conversation* (1974 Francis Ford Coppola director).

Editing

The final stages

Editing is the last phase of a film's creation when the images that have been shot during production and all the sound that has been recorded, are combined into the final film. The work of the cinematographer and camera assistants, the designers and their teams is done, and the **editors**, sound mixers, **composer** and visual-effects technicians take over. There is some overlap in these processes as reshooting may be required, and the actors remain on call to dub over the originally recorded dialogue. The editor is a crucial member of a film crew who oversees the extensive work of postproduction. As we will see, editing can make a considerable difference to the look and feel of the final film. Editing is a powerful tool in the world of filmmaking and in this chapter, we will explore the final stage of the filmmaking process, the editing of a film:

- First, we will look at the different types of transitions that can be used between shots and the conventions governing their use;
- Then, we will look at how the continuity system works to establish cinematic space;
- We will examine some of the aesthetic decisions that editors make when performing their craft;
- Then, we will consider how editing works to create a sense of time and space;
- Finally, we will touch on the theories of **montage**, first proposed by the Soviet filmmakers of the 1920s, which continue to be a fundamentally influential way of thinking about editing.

Transitions

When the editor joins two shots in the final stages of making a film, they can be cut together using different types of transition. The simplest of these is the **straight cut**, which just involves the two shots placed next to each other without any linking device. Shots, however, can also be joined by a number of transitional edits, including dissolves, fade ins or fade outs, and wipes.

- A **dissolve** replaces one image with another, superimposing the second image as the first fades out.
- A **fade in** brings an image in from a black screen (or occasionally another colour).
- A **fade out** goes from image to black (or another colour).
- **Wipes** come in many different shapes, but they basically take one image and replace it with another through some form of line, pattern or shape.

Wipes are not as common in feature films as the other transitional techniques. With wipes, the second shot crosses the screen to replace the first shot. This can be achieved with either a simple line moving across the screen or one image can replace another using a variety of patterns.

Different transitional edits are used for different purposes. Straight cuts are most common between shots within the same scene where there is no shift in time or space. Dissolves are often used to indicate the passage of time, either between one scene and another or within the same scene. A fade in can also indicate an even longer passage of time. Fade ins start new scenes or sequences and fade outs indicate completion or closure. As well as moving the narrative forward in time, transitional devices can introduce a flashback sequence, a convention popular in Classical Hollywood. Certain types of wipes are often associated with a shift into fantasy or memory. Transitions are part of the basic grammar of editing, the starting point for creating the complex levels of meaning that go into a completed film. In the following section we will discuss the basic structures of editing for narrative film and introduce the conventions of **continuity**, a way to structure narrative space through editing.

The continuity system

Editing for film is a complex art that requires certain choices to fashion the raw material of shot footage and recorded sound into a consistent and coherent whole. At the outset, editors choose a style appropriate to the type of film. Different conventions of linking shots govern narrative and documentary styles. Likewise experimental films, by their very nature, often use a variety of editing styles, trying different techniques in order to explore their effects. Even within a particular type of film, or in one film, more than one editing style can be used effectively.

From early on, narrative filmmaking has favoured one particular style of editing known as the continuity system. As we saw in Chapter 1, the continuity editing system is a convention that developed as a key component of Classical Hollywood cinema. This editing style is used to draw the viewers into the story without consciously reminding them that they are watching a film. In other words, continuity is designed to make the workings of the filmmaking process invisible. In Chapter 7 we learned that continuity starts with decisions made by the director during the production phase. In order for an editor to construct a scene that follows the rules of continuity, the scene has to have been staged and shot that way. This is known as shooting to edit, acknowledging that the director must understand how the editor will assemble the shot **footage**. In the postproduction phase the editor puts the shots together, making certain aesthetic choices. The ultimate goal of the continuity style is to create logical spatial relations between the characters and within the location. Thus, when the audience looks at a scene, it can see the positions of the different characters in relation to each other and their location, and therefore understand the interactions between them.

To demonstrate how continuity editing works, we will start with some basic elements of a scene and examine the options editors face when cutting this scene in a continuity style. In doing this, we can see the rules that govern continuity in operation and pay close attention to why these rules developed and what happens when they are broken. As we progress, we will begin to look at how a scene can be shot and edited with more complexity, in order to fully understand how space is constructed through editing. Let's begin with this very basic and simply shot scene: two people having a conversation. This type of scene is very common in narrative filmmaking and Classical Hollywood has produced many examples, shot and edited in the continuity style. We will use as our example a scene from *Stagecoach* (1939), a love scene between Ringo (John Wayne) and Dallas (Claire Trevor).

Stagecoach, which we also studied for cinematography, is an example of Classical Hollywood cinema. In fact there are other scenes in the film constructed using similar patterns. In this scene, Ringo asks Dallas to escape with him to his ranch.

The scene is shot using three principal camera positions:

- A central position which shows both characters;
- A shot of Ringo from the left side of the scene;
- A shot from the right, showing Dallas.

The scene starts with a long shot as Ringo follows and approaches Dallas; the camera favours his side and she is seen from behind. They are outside in the corral at night, leaning against opposite sides of a fence. This shot is known as an **establishing shot**, as it establishes the setting and the characters. In continuity editing, establishing shots are customarily placed at the start of a scene to show the characters within the setting and to indicate their relative positions in relation to each other. This is important as it orients the audience to the space. When the scene continues, the space is broken down into a medium shot and close-ups. The establishing shot has anchored the audience so that it fully understands where the characters are. So when the scene cuts to the medium shot and close-ups, the relationship between the character on screen and the character off screen remains clear. The second shot is a medium **two-shot** from the central position, bringing us closer into the scene. In this shot we see the two characters; their positions in relation to each other are equally clear and less is shown of the background, focusing our attention on the two main characters.

The subsequent two shots are in a pattern known as **shot/reverse shot**. The first shot shows one character looking in one direction, and the second shot (the reverse shot) shows what they are looking at. In this case it is the other character looking back at them. This can be done with just one character in frame (as it is here), or it can include the second character seen partially from behind, an **over-the-shoulder shot**. We then cut to the reverse shot to see the second character

Figure 9.1   *Stagecoach*, John Ford, 1939

Figure 9.2   *Stagecoach*, John Ford, 1939

Figure 9.3   *Stagecoach*, John Ford, 1939

to whom he is talking. This simple pattern is the basic building block of many dialogue scenes in the continuity system. It establishes the space and the logical positions of the characters within that space.

180° rule

This scene also follows the **180° rule** of continuity editing. In other words, all the camera positions are on one side of the action. Figure 9.4 shows you the camera positions for all the shots in this scene. You will notice that there is a line crossing between the characters and marking the positions in which they are looking at each other. This line is known as the **axis of action** (sometimes also referred to as the '**action line**') and it defines the spatial relations between the characters. The 180° rule keeps the camera on one side of the line, moving to different positions, but not crossing the line to shoot from behind. Why? Let's look at what happens when the camera crosses the axis of action.

In Figure 9.5, the camera has crossed the axis of action. This creates a distracting sense of space for two reasons. First, the background

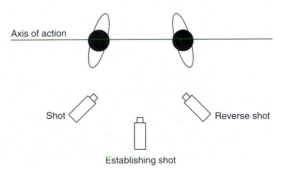

Figure 9.4   180° space

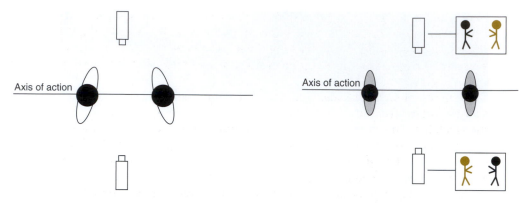

Figure 9.5 Axis of action   **Figure 9.6** 180° space

will have changed and, after being accustomed to viewing one side of the space, the audience is suddenly shown another, without a corresponding shift in context. Second, the characters have now replaced each other in space so that cutting between these two shots makes it appear that the characters are talking to themselves, rather than to each other. This is even clearer when the shot moves to the **shot/reverse shot** position. If we move from one character to another across the line, the characters will appear not to be looking at each other, but staring off into space in the same direction.

To emphasize the point of the 180° rule, imagine that the action in Figure 9.6 is a football game with a team in black playing against a team in green. If there are cameras on both sides of the stadium and the shots cut from one position to another it will appear as if the two teams are playing against themselves, rather than against each other. It will be hard for the audience watching to understand what is happening in the game, or in what direction the players are moving.

Shot selection

From the point where the dialogue starts until they are interrupted, the scene from *Stagecoach* is nearly two minutes long. In that time the camera is placed in basically four positions: the position of the establishing shot, the central position for the two-shot, and the shot and reverse shot positions. In the production phase, the whole scene might well have been shot from each of these positions and the editor would then have four different camera positions to choose from when constructing the scene. This selection is not done randomly, however. The editor constructs the scene so that it can tell the story in the most effective way and enable the audience to empathize with the emotions of the characters. In this scene the shifts from the long shot to the medium shot, and from the medium shot to the close-ups, are used to punctuate or accentuate particular moments of dialogue.

During the establishing shot the conversation is casual, with Ringo expressing his fears for Dallas's safety outside at night; the take is fairly long as they continue to discuss why they are both travelling to Lordsburg. When Ringo tells Dallas that his family were killed, the scene moves into a medium shot; she responds by recounting her own losses. These moments of revelation about the characters' histories remain in medium shot as they are background to the emotional core of the scene that follows. When Ringo starts to talk awkwardly to Dallas about his feelings, the shot moves into a close-up. Close-ups bring the character towards the audience; they are used to draw the viewer into the emotion. In Chapter 6, we learned how the close-up can often be used to enhance emotion and here the close-up gives increased emotional weight to this particular moment.

As Ringo continues telling Dallas about his ranch, the shot cuts to her reacting to what he is saying. It is an important technique when editing; the shot selection does not always show the character who is talking. The editor can include a **reaction shot** to show the character who is not speaking, but reacting to what the other character is saying. In this moment, Dallas's reaction is as important as Ringo's offer, as she listens to him and starts to hope for a better life. The close-up exchange is then quicker as Ringo asks her to go, then the shot cuts back to her telling him that she doesn't know him. At this point, after she has not yet agreed to go, the scene moves back out into the two-shot which pulls the audience out of their emotional world, before Dallas despairingly walks away from Ringo and they are interrupted by Curly (George Bancroft).

30° rule and jump cuts

There is another convention that regulates where the camera is positioned for shots that follow each other. This convention relates to how close the camera can be placed to the position for the previous shot. The **30° rule** suggests that the camera must move at least 30° between two consecutive shots or change lens from wide angle to telephoto. If this does not happen, the two shots will appear too close to each other and will therefore be confusing and disconcerting to the audience; the viewer becomes more aware of the cut. When the camera does not move sufficiently between shots it is known as a **jump cut** and is considered to be a break with the rules of continuity editing.

Of course, many filmmaking styles consistently break continuity conventions for effect. Jump cuts became popular during the late 1950s and early 1960s in a film movement known as the **French New Wave**. This was an important moment in film history when a group of young filmmakers were experimenting with different techniques and themes in film, and breaking with standard conventions such as the continuity system. One of the first New Wave films was *Breathless* (1960) directed by Jean-Luc Godard. This film is well known for its use of jump cuts. (See Chapter 12 for further discussion of the jump cuts in *Breathless*.)

Adding complexity to the scene

As we have seen, the rules of continuity editing work to place characters in relationship to each other and to the space and setting. As always, these 'rules' are a starting point, not an absolute standard. With 180° space, the axis of action functions as a general guideline only. There are three particular ways in which the axis of action can be seen to be fluid and shift within a scene:

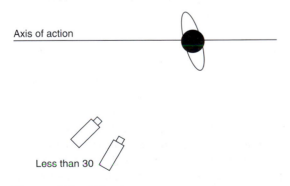

Axis of action

Less than 30

Figure 9.7   30° rule

- Through the movement of the performers on screen;
- Through camera movement;
- Through cutting around the line.

It is very important to realize that the axis of action itself moves with the characters. In a scene where the characters are not seated at a table, but are moving, the axis then assumes different positions relative to where the characters are at any given point in the scene. The characters' movement, action and interaction with each other also establish multiple action lines in any given scene. If, instead of being stationary during their conversation, Dallas and Ringo had been walking, there would have been three action lines: the one between them and one each along the direction in which they moved. The camera could then be placed at different points around the space in relation to the position of the characters and their forward movement. Also, in a conversation between three or more characters there are multiple action lines linking the different characters in the conversation; as in the group scenes in *Stagecoach*.

In addition to the axis of action shifting with the characters' movement, the camera itself can move across the line. When the camera passes two characters, with the action line between them, the viewer also moves around the line with the camera. Therefore there would not be the same disorientation that occurs when there is a straight cut across the line. A cut across the axis of action is most noticeable as a break with continuity when it occurs from positions directly opposite each other. When the camera is placed close to, or on the line, it assumes a neutral position. From this neutral position it is less perceptible as a shift in the scene's spatial relations, to cut across it to another neutral position near the action line on the other side. Thus, the neutral position near the line on one side and a neutral position near the line on the other side can be used to move around the line without confusing the audience's sense of the space or presenting conflicting signals as to the relationship of the characters to each other. As with all film techniques, it is important to remember that these three methods of crossing the action line can be used in combination. For example, a scene can contain moving cameras, following moving performers, using editing that cuts across a neutral angle, on or near the action line.

This scene from *Stagecoach* uses a very common, but fairly simple, camera set-up, and clear, conventional editing techniques. These kinds of scenes appear in many films. However, as can be seen in the multi-character scenes in the stagecoach, there are more complex ways of staging and editing between various characters in motion. These scenes also maintain clear spatial relations so that the audience can understand the positions of the various characters, while the characters and the camera move through the space in more complex patterns.

The ideological significance of continuity editing

It is the very clarity of spatial relations constructed by the continuity system that has left it open to criticism from filmmakers and theorists looking to deconstruct the ideological and stylistic dominance of Classical Hollywood cinema. The continuity system is a cornerstone of Classical style and it is important to understand it in order to critique how it constructs its narrative form. As we saw first in Chapter 1, a key feature of the Classical style is the invisibility of technique, the convention that binds the film spectator into the narrative, concealing the tools of production so that the viewer forgets that they are watching a film. Continuity editing does not call attention to itself as a technique in comparison to the alternative forms of editing such as the Soviet montage style (discussed at the end of this chapter and in Chapter 12). The Soviet style editing is self-conscious, and shows an awareness of technique, allowing the viewer to break with the seamless identification with the story and appreciate the workings of the production.

Continuity editing constructs a particular cinematic space in which the spectator is bound into a specific position in relation to the action of the scene. This is how conventional Classical narrative draws the audience into the world of the film. Thus when, for example, the French New Wave directors break with continuity conventions, they disrupt the audience's place of uncontested identification with the characters. In Chapter 12, we will see how a film such as *Breathless* undermines these conventions and so critiques the ideological effects of the continuity system.

It is important to understand the conventions of continuity when viewing a film, to recognize how the editing makes meaning. It is also useful for the student filmmaker to explore and practise these conventions, to know how these rules can be utilized, abandoned, modified or deconstructed. With our understanding of the principles of continuity editing and its alternatives in mind, we will continue this discussion by considering the techniques that editors use to make their cuts effective in the overall construction of a scene.

The aesthetic techniques of editing

In addition to following or breaking the conventions of narrative editing, editors also make a series of aesthetic choices to ensure that the final film is as effective as possible. In this section we will examine three techniques: **graphic matching**, **cutting on movement**, and the pacing of the editing. In conventional narrative filmmaking, these choices often work in conjunction with the rules of continuity editing. Editing aesthetics support the continuity system; these are decisions that contribute to the invisibility of the editing style. These techniques are also used in alternative-style editing.

Graphic matching

When cutting a sequence of shots together, editors use particular techniques to accentuate different components in the scene. One of these techniques is the graphic match. Graphic matching directs attention by linking shots together that have points of interest in the same part of the frame. If you remember in the discussion of composition in Chapter 6, we studied the importance of placing subjects within the frame to create the strongest effect. In particular, we saw how different elements could be positioned for compositional balance to draw the audience's attention towards certain areas of the frame. This is an important consideration in editing also, as an editor often links different shots through the connection between the compositional features. As we watch a film, our gaze is drawn to a particular area of the frame through the compositional techniques and editing.

For example, when a subject is framed screen right with her eyes at the intersection of the right and upper thirds line, this is the area of the frame where the audience's principal attention will be focused. If, in the cut to the following shot, the attention is shifted to the lower left of the frame it will take the audience a moment to search the new shot to find the area of interest. It is more common, however, for an editor to cut between two shots keeping the area of graphic weight in the same part of the frame, or, alternatively, to draw the audience's attention through movement or composition to a point of interest in the subsequent shot. This creates a sense of graphic continuity, a comfortable sense of connection between shots that is not distracting or disorienting to the viewer.

Occasionally, a graphic match directly replaces one image with another, as the composition and point of interest are placed in the same point in the frame. It is more common, however, for more general principles of graphic continuity to be used. In the scene from *Stagecoach* that we studied for continuity, the shot/reverse shot sequence does not directly replace one character's head, the point of interest in the shot, with the other character's head, but it does keep the attention focused on the same level of the frame and draws the attention across the frame through the use of the character's gaze, maintaining the principles of look space. Thus, both characters have their eyes placed on the upper thirds line, keeping the attention on the same horizontal plane. They are both looking in the direction that would lead the viewer's eyes along the third line to the position in which the other is placed.

The use of the character's gaze to direct the viewer's attention to a part of the screen in the next shot is known as an **eyeline match** and it is one of the conventions of the continuity system, used to establish and maintain consistent spatial relations between shots. Thus we already know from the establishing shot that Dallas and Ringo are standing opposite each other, with their eyes at approximately the same level, looking at each other. Therefore we can follow their eyeline across the screen of each cut to the point of graphic interest.

Cutting on movement

Like **graphic matching**, editors use movement to smooth over cuts between shots. Cutting on movement can be as simple as editing between two shots within a scene where there is a slight hand or body shift at the point of the cut so that the viewer sees the movement and becomes less aware of the edit itself. In the scene from *Stagecoach* not every cut is accompanied by significant action by the characters. This scene is fairly static, it is just two people talking to each other without moving much. At the end of the two-shot before the cut to the close-up on Ringo, Dallas turns partially toward him, and the movement is at the moment of the cut and when the scene cuts to her close-up she is turning again, this time fully towards him. These are good examples of the principle of cutting on movement, as although the movements are fairly subtle, they correspond with the emotion of the scene as Dallas progressively draws closer to Ringo.

In cutting between two shots, the movements made by the actors must be the same from one camera position to the other or the difference will be apparent to the audience. During the shooting phase of a film, an actor performs movements in the same manner for as many camera positions and takes as is necessary. The editor then cuts together the scene, finding the point where the action between the two shots most closely matches. This type of cut on movement is known as **matched action**. Matched action is part of the continuity system that provides links between shots, using movements that are the same from one position to another. Unlike matched action, cutting on movement between different spaces can either go in the same direction or move in opposite directions. Movement in opposite directions adds a sense of conflict to the edit and can be effective in creating stress or tension. Such choices can have different effects on the overall edited sequence. In subtle ways, editing that uses conflicting movement begins to add to the tension of the scene and subtly builds up the suspense. In the final section of this chapter, we will examine the theories of montage, a style of editing that often uses cutting on movement in various ways and in different directions to create tensions and evoke the stress of the action.

Pacing and rhythm

When putting together a scene, an editor makes many different choices. As we saw in the analysis of the love scene from *Stagecoach*, different types of shots are used to underscore the action. Editors choose not only what type of shot to cut to at any given moment, but when to make those edits. Choosing when to cut over a series of shots provides a sense of rhythm and pacing. Pacing is also an important factor in the aesthetics of editing. To start with a basic generalization, fast pacing is associated with action in a scene, and slower pacing with dialogue. Often in a film, the points where the editing pace increases are moments of heightened action or of the intensification of emotion. We take this generalization as a starting point, and, in this section, first discuss how the pacing of the editing affects the structure of a scene, and then of a whole film. Then we will look at how pace can be used to heighten certain types of screen action. It is also useful to consider how some scenes are influenced by other factors. For example, in a scene cut to music, the rhythm, pace and style of the music can affect the editing, as the beats of the music can be used to motivate the cuts.

Pacing within the scene and within the film

How the viewer assimilates the information in any given frame is a function of many criteria, including how complex the image is, how long it has been on the screen and how frequently it is repeated. When there is a cut and the image changes, the viewer then needs to absorb the information in the new shot. In the course of a scene, when a shot returns to a camera position that has been seen before, it takes less time for the viewer to recognize the information in the frame. Therefore, shot length can decrease over the course of a scene, as certain camera positions and compositions are repeated.

In the love scene from *Stagecoach*, the editing follows the pace of the dialogue, cutting from shot to reverse shot on the different lines of the characters, with lengthy reaction shots of Dallas as she listens to Ringo tell her about his ranch. In this way the editing is used to support the vital function of this scene, how the dialogue develops the relationship between the characters. The pace of editing in a scene can often increase to create tension, suspense or build up the action. Frequent cutting keeps the viewer's attention moving from one element to another and adds to a sense of excitement. Slower-paced editing keeps the focus on one subject for longer periods of time, allowing the viewer to pay attention to the dialogue. This gives stronger weight to the characters' thoughts, emotions and interactions.

An interesting example of the pacing of a scene from *Notorious* (1946) is when Alicia (Ingrid Bergman) steals a key from Sebastian's (Claude Rains) ring in order to allow Devlin (Cary Grant) to check the wine cellar for evidence of an illegal Nazi plot. The scene starts with two establishing shots, the first from outside the building and the second of a clock outside the room. Then there is a lengthy shot of Alicia as she approaches the room where the keys are. It then cuts to the reverse shot as she looks into Sebastian's dressing-room. Sebastian is off screen, behind the bathroom door. The next cut shows Alicia looking towards the table, then we have a fairly lengthy take of the camera moving in on the keys, from Alicia's point of view following her attention as she thinks about the keys. She moves forward, keeping an eye on Sebastian, and takes the key. The scene continues with Sebastian exiting the bathroom immediately afterwards and reaching out for Alicia's hands, in one of which she is holding the key. He takes one hand to kiss it and she throws her hand with the key around his neck and embraces him, while passing the key over his back and dropping it to the floor.

This is a suspenseful scene. Will she get the key away without him noticing? The suspense is created through the combination of the all the cinematic techniques:

- The mise-en-scène (particularly Ingrid Bergman's performance);
- The cinematography (with the mobile camera following the action);
- The music and dialogue (Sebastian says 'With you in a minute' at the very moment Alicia is taking the key);
- And, of course, the pacing of the editing.

The editing combines longer takes of certain moments with quicker cuts. The longer moments, as Alicia approaches, as she takes the key, are included among the quicker cuts. These cuts increase the audience's sense that she is taking too long and might get caught. The quicker cuts include the moment when Sebastian first speaks and when he exits the bathroom and approaches. The pacing of this scene then combines fast and slow cutting to underscore the action and to work with the other elements in creating the tension.

The editing pace can gradually increase over the course of a film. In Chapter 3 we studied story structure, noting how, towards the end of a narrative film, there is often the rise to a climax, where the film reaches its most intense point of conflict. Scenes that occur towards the end of a film can be accompanied by an increase in the editing pace. Quite often these later scenes are shorter, and the editing within them is quicker than at the beginning of the film.

Pacing for different types of screen action

At the beginning of this section we started with the generalization that action scenes use quicker-paced editing than dialogue scenes. By comparing an action scene and a dialogue scene from the film *Spider-Man 2* (2004), we will see how far this generalization holds true. Then we will consider examples that do not use these same principles. This will allow us to question how choices in the pace of the editing create different effects, for instance, accentuating certain types of screen action. It is important to realize that the quick cuts of action scenes are often combined with camera and performer movement to increase the intensity of the violence or to add an aura of commotion to chase scenes. In *Spider-Man 2* Spider-Man's *alter ego*, Peter Parker (Tobey Maguire), goes with his aunt (Rosemary Harris) to the bank to ask for a loan. They are interrupted when the villain Doctor Octopus (Alfred Molina) comes in to rob the bank. Peter Parker runs off and returns as Spider-Man to fight his enemy. This sequence illustrates the difference between a dialogue scene and an action scene. In its first part, as Peter and his aunt talk to the loans manager of the bank, there are shots of varying lengths, but very few quick cuts. The length of the takes is motivated by the dialogue. As they are main characters, there are more shots of Peter and his aunt than the manager. This includes reaction shots, when we see their response to the rejection of the loan. The editing moves quite quickly as the scene is not one of vital emotional importance. If you contrast this scene with a later shot/reverse shot dialogue scene between Peter and his love interest, Mary Jane (Kirsten

Figure 9.8 *Spider-Man 2*, Sam Raimi, 2004

Dunst), as they meet in a coffee shop, you will notice that in this case the shots are held longer. Unlike in the bank scene, here the characters are discussing intense emotional issues at the core of the film's love story. This is also accentuated by the use of close-ups. Both these dialogue scenes are paced differently from the action sequences that follow them.

The scene in the bank switches to action with a track back from Peter and his aunt at the table. Then there is a pan across to where Doctor Octopus is breaking into the vault. This is the first instance when the generalization does not hold, as this is a fairly lengthy take. Unlike the static shots of the dialogue at the table, this shot delivers a lot of visual information. The camera locates the villain, then we are shown the special effect of his arms ripping open the vault, and the destruction of the bank as he tosses the debris. It is not only the editing that creates the action of the scene as there is extensive camera movement and movement of various sorts across the screen and the CGI of the limbs. When Doctor Octopus reaches into the vault and grabs the bag of money, the edits get faster. Spider-Man enters the scene and the pacing of the edits moves between slower establishing shots of his arrival to quicker cuts of the fight. There is a long take of Peter's aunt and the loans manager on the floor as she catches him stealing the discarded money. This lengthier take provides a moment of comic relief that is a break in the action. Then Doctor Octopus picks up Spider-Man and he fights to free himself. This moment is the most quickly paced of the scene so far, only holding momentarily on the image of Doctor Octopus trying to squash Spider-Man's face, a moment which serves to accentuate the tension. The following action is also fast paced as Spider-Man frees himself from the grip of his enemy.

One of the reasons that action lends itself to faster-paced editing than dialogue is that there is more movement in the frame. This gives the editor more opportunities to cut on movement; there is a greater potential for matched-action cuts. In this scene you can see this principle at work as the cuts occur in conjunction with the movements in the fight. These editing choices also have

Figure 9.9   *House of Flying Daggers*, Zhang Yimou, 2004

an effect on the viewer; the faster-paced action creates the tension and excitement we feel when we watch this type of sequence.

This film is a good example of fast-paced editing being used for action sequences. Not all film-makers abide by this convention. For example, in *House of Flying Daggers* (2004), there are elaborate fight scenes that are played out differently. This film, by Chinese director Zhang Yimou, tells the story of the assassin Mei (Zhang Ziyi) and her struggles of loyalty. In the first fight sequence, she attempts an assassination and ends up in a sword fight. The fight scene does not use the same fast-cutting techniques, but rather lengthy takes to show the action of the fight so that we can study and appreciate the movements of the performers. The scene also cuts in the specialized stylistic features of martial-arts fight sequences, slow motion and actors fighting while suspended on wires. The effect of these choices is to create a more stylized form of violence that can be beautiful to watch and that is closely akin to the experience of watching a dance.

Editing and the world of the narrative

So far we have seen how the editing choices work within the continuity system, and how editors use particular techniques to produce the most effective cuts within a film. As we continue, it is also important to recognize how the editing of a film can be used to tell the story. In Chapter 3 we studied the concept of narrative time. We saw how a film can present a story by contracting time. In the example of *Letter from an Unknown Woman* (1948) the story takes place over many years, but is contracted into an eighty-nine-minute film. We also saw how this film was structured through shifts in time, flashbacks that take us into the past or flashforwards that bring us back to the present or into the future. This way of storytelling through time is a function of the editing of a film, so with the grammar and techniques of editing in mind, we will now turn to the question of how editing works to tell stories.

The development of narrative editing techniques has an important base in early film history. During the years of **early cinema**, before feature-length films were introduced, the first short films consisted of one shot per scene; editing was not fundamental to the storytelling. These scenes were shot from a camera position similar to the third row of a theatre, with the stationary camera taking the place of the theatrical audience. Not only did the early films emerge from one camera position, they unfolded in real time; the action appeared on screen without the potential to shorten or lengthen the scene. As film developed an artistic style of its own, the shot composition changed, integrating medium shots and close-ups with the long shots of early cinema. The use of various shot compositions required the growth of a grammar of editing that would link sequences together and create a sense of time and space. As editing developed, so did a grammar of scene construction, that allowed shifts in both space and time. In this section we will examine how editing helps to construct the time and space of a story.

Time manipulation through editing

The structure of a conventional narrative film moves through time, generally in a way that is easily comprehensible to the audience. Yet, the narrative is not bound to unfold in a chronological sequence. It is through the editing that we are moved through different points in time in the telling of the story. It is also editing that can shorten time or work with other techniques to lengthen narrative time.

An example of editing expanding time occurs during a fantasy sequence in *American Beauty* (1999), when Lester Burnham (Kevin Spacey) is watching the cheerleader Angela (Mena Suvari) perform, and fantasizing about her undressing. As we saw in Chapter 6, to emphasize the significance of this moment, the film uses a combination of slow-motion cinematography and repeated action to expand time. The shot as she goes to open her shirt is cut so the action recurs several times prolonging the moment from Lester's subjective experience of desire. As well as including shots that repeat actions, cutting away to reaction shots is another method of expanding time through editing. For example, in *The Lord of the Rings: The Return of the King* (2003), there is a scene of suspense when the King of Rohan (Bernard Hill) is deciding whether to go to war in aid of Gondor. We see a reaction shot of the other characters who are awaiting his answer. This scene uses time manipulation through inserted **cutaways** to make a short period of time play out on screen over a longer period.

Similarly, editing is frequently used to compress time into a shorter period, by cutting out unnecessary elements and using shorthand for certain actions we take for granted. Compressing time through editing is known as a **temporal ellipsis**. In *Notorious*, there is a good example of this; in the middle of the film there is a sequence of scenes, which show Alicia first learning of her spying assignment. Since arriving in Rio, Devlin and Alicia have not been working but their romance has been growing. After a romantic scene in Alicia's apartment, Devlin leaves to meet with his superiors. There he learns that Alicia's assignment is to seduce Sebastian to gain access to and information about the Nazi ring. He then returns to have dinner with Alicia and tell her about her assignment. Through the transitions between the scenes, certain parts of the action are left out. Had all the action been shown, the sequence would have been unnecessarily long and quite dull. However, the scenes open and close in such a way that the audience is left in no doubt as to what occurred in the missing time.

At the end of the first scene, Devlin leaves. Alicia has just asked him to bring back a bottle of wine for dinner. The next scene shows Devlin pulling up in a car outside the office building. The short scene ends after he gets out of the car holding the wine. The next scene then dissolves to the wine on the table where he meets his associates. This scene then ends with a shot of the bottle on the table as Devlin has forgotten to take it with him. In the next scene he arrives back at Alicia's apartment.

What is missing here? After the end of the first scene of the sequence, Devlin leaves Alicia's building, buys the wine and drives to the office building. We don't need to see all this action; the scenes close and open with enough information for us to fill in the blanks. Between the scene of Devlin's arrival and the point we join the meeting, he enters the building, goes to the office and is told what Alicia has to do. We join the scene part of the way through the action (*in media res*) as Devlin gets up and shouts, 'She won't do it.' This is the most interesting moment of **ellipsis** as part of the significant narrative action has been omitted. We enter the scene at its explosive point and at the most crucial moment, to witness the effect that the news has on Devlin. By cutting into the scene at this point, the filmmakers have emphasized Devlin's reaction. We can then deduce for ourselves, out of the dialogue and action of previous scenes as well as those that follow, anything we're supposed to know.

The last ellipsis in this sequence omits Devlin's return journey to Alicia's apartment. We cut directly from the wine he left in the office to the point where he enters her home. We see none of the journey, as we did in the last sequence, but we know enough to fill in the missing action. The ellipsis here is used to accentuate the abandoned bottle which represents the end of the romantic interlude for Devlin and Alicia. This example demonstrates a crucial way that editing works to construct the time within a film. It is also used to link different spaces.

Linking spaces

It is common in a film for the action to appear to take place in different locations at the same time; this is known as **parallel editing** or **cross cutting**. The power of cross cutting was recognized during the period of early silent film. The director D. W. Griffith made many films that demonstrate a skilled use of parallel editing and he became well known for this technique. For example, in Griffith's early short, *The Girl and Her Trust* (1912) a railway employee is protecting a box of money from thieves. She locks herself in a room at the railway station, while the thieves attempt to break in to get the key for the payroll safe. From inside she uses the telegraph to summon help. This scene only works if there is parallel editing between:

- The woman in danger;
- And those threatening her;
- And those who will ultimately rescue her.

The action in the three spaces has to be simultaneous, and the audience has to feel that the danger to the woman is imminent and that the rescuers are in a race to reach her. Our understanding of time and space is vital to the effectiveness of cross cutting, and for the scene to create

Figure 9.10 *The Girl and Her Trust*, D. W. Griffith, 1912

Figure 9.11 *The Girl and Her Trust*, D. W. Griffith, 1912

Figure 9.12   *The Girl and Her Trust*, D. W. Griffith, 1912

the necessary tension. This early example shows the basic principles of parallel editing. This style continues to be an important technique in creating suspense in a film. It is frequently used in the climax to escalate tension, suspense and expectation.

A good contemporary example of this occurs in *The Lord of the Rings: The Return of the King*. The climax of the whole trilogy comes at the moment when Frodo must destroy the Ring in the fire of Mount Doom in Mordor. Here he is confronted with his nemesis Gollum. As Frodo and Gollum fight over the ring, the scene cuts to the battle taking place outside the gates of Mordor. This is a similar use of cross cutting to that shown in the Griffith film. The actions in one space depend on the actions in the other, happening at the same time. We have learned throughout *The Lord of the Rings* that everything depends on Frodo destroying the Ring. Thus, cutting to the other scene increases the suspense and tension as the characters' lives are seen to be at stake.

Inserts

Sometimes in a scene, shots are inserted that do not appear to have any temporal or spatial relationship to the action. **Insert** shots, also known as cutaways, are common in documentary style (a type of B-Roll). An insert can be used to illustrate something being mentioned by an interview subject; we move away from the visual, temporal and spatial flow of the interview and see shots relating to what has been said. Inserts in narrative film can take many different forms; there can be a cut to an object within the diegesis of the film, but perhaps in another space or time from the main action. Inserts can shift the viewer out of the time and space of the narrative and into a flashback or flashforward. Another function of inserts is to show the audience the dreams or fantasies of the characters.

An innovative example of the use of a series of insert shots is found in the 1968 Cuban film, *Memories of Underdevelopment*. In one scene, the main character, Sergio (Sergio Corrieri), fantasizes about the young woman, Noemi (Eslinda Núñez), who has come to clean his house. The way that Sergio's fantasy is shown in this scene is through a few short shots, cut quickly in and out of the scene as the main action continues. In the first of Sergio's fantasy shots we see him look in Noemi's direction. In the next shot she enters his bedroom with a broom. Then we see him looking towards her again followed by a brief fantasy shot of him kissing her. We then return to the shot of him sitting at his desk, which gives us the clue that the preceding shot was not part of the real world of the story. His second fantasy follows with two shots, unconnected by continuity. He is on the bed with Noemi, then she is naked on the bed alone. The next shot returns to him at his desk again. Then the narrative continues as Noemi leaves. This is an unusual scene in that the fantasy is introduced with a straight cut; there is no transitional device to indicate the move from the regular flow of narrative time and space. The fantasy sequence is introduced with the shot of Sergio looking at Noemi.

Sergio's fantasy in *Memories of Underdevelopment* appears naturalistic because it does not employ any Expressionistic techniques to indicate that it is a fantasy. As this film uses the techniques of realism (**location shooting**, rough lighting, black-and-white **film stock**), it seems ambiguous about entering the mind of the principal character. (We will explore this further in Chapter 12.) In fact, you can watch this scene and not at first be clear that this is fantasy – it is inserted so naturally into the flow of the action. It is the editing, the straight cuts, short takes and use of cutting on movement that allow this scene to function as fantasy and to integrate it into the film in a way that makes sense.

Montage

The continuity editing style that we have studied so far developed as part of the film language of Classical Hollywood cinema. This system was the dominant method of visual storytelling in Hollywood from the 1920s on. Other models of filmmaking have used different forms and styles of editing. Around the same time that Hollywood consolidated its methods, other filmmakers and theorists were experimenting with different editing styles and theorizing about the importance of a diversity of editing techniques. In the Soviet Union in the 1920s, very important steps were taken towards the understanding and development of editing as part of filmmaking. One of the great innovations of film editing comes from this period and is embodied in the work of a group of filmmakers and theorists that include Kuleshov, Pudovkin and Eisenstein. These theorist-practitioners developed a concept known as montage. To conclude this chapter we will examine some of the work and ideas of the montage theorists as they apply to editing practice, considering how some of their ideas still influence filmmaking today. We will return to examine their theories more closely in Chapter 12.

The term 'montage' has a number of different meanings and can refer to different aspects of editing theory, depending on the context. The word 'montage' means 'editing' in both French and Russian, but when it is used in English it has a more specific meaning. **Montage sequences**, when used in Classical Hollywood style describe a series of shots in which the shots do not maintain spatial and temporal continuity, but link together related images over time or across space. In the context in which it developed in Soviet filmmaking of the 1920s, montage referred to the use of editing as one of the principal meaning-making devices of filmmaking. The montage theorists all had different concepts about how editing should be used, but they each saw it as fundamental to the process of filmmaking.

Eisenstein and the montage of conflict

Montage uses shots out of spatial or temporal order. A leading exponent in this field was Sergei Eisenstein whose most famous example of the montage of conflict is a sequence known as the 'Odessa Steps' from the film, *Battleship Potemkin* (1925). This film recounts incidents in the failed revolution of 1905. In this scene, the Russian authorities attack a group of civilians who are gathered to watch the arrival of the battleship. If this scene were edited using continuity techniques the soldiers and victims would be edited so that they appear on different sides of the screen from each other. It would also use shot selection that moves progressively between shot sizes.

As a montage sequence, however, there are quick cuts, shifts in screen direction, rapid moves between long shots and close-ups and cutting on action that crosses the screen in various directions. As the sequence starts, we see repeated action and throughout not all the action is shown. The sequence uses conflicting movements across the frame. Another feature of montage is evident, which is the movement in space between long shots and close-ups, in such a way as to disturb the audience and stress the conflict. If you think back to the Classical scene from *Stagecoach*, the movement between shots was in stages, from long shot to two-shot to medium close-up. The montage of conflict moves more drastically between these camera positions, accentuating the feeling that this violence is being perpetuated on a large group of people, but affecting each person on an individual level.

Despite its politically radical beginnings, the practice of montage has now significantly infiltrated different areas of media production independent of its original context. Montage is very popular in advertising. It is fairly standard for television ads to use fast edits for a particular effect. It is also a popular approach in music videos, when the editing style can appear driven by the music and beat, with the images shot for effect, rather than following spatial or temporal continuity. Television ads and music-video editing, using montage techniques, have in their turn influenced feature-film production, so that elements of montage are used in certain films: quick cutting, shots using conflicting movements and the abandonment of the practices of clear spatial continuity (180° space).

Summary and key questions

The editing of a film is key in how meaning is created. When analyzing a scene, it is important to look at how the editing brings everything together into a coherent whole. When preparing to shoot or edit a scene, directors and editors keep these questions in mind:

- What transitional devices does the editing use?
    - Does it use cuts, dissolves or wipes?
    - How are the transitional devices used? Do they signal shifts in time or space?

- Does the film use, or break with, the continuity-editing system?
  - o Does it maintain the axis of action?
  - o Does it use the shot/reverse shot pattern?
  - o Are there jump cuts, or does it follow the 30° rule?
- What choices are made in shot selection?
  - o When does the scene move into close-up?
  - o How do the cuts interpret the dialogue?
  - o Does the editing follow the dialogue or does it use reaction shots?
- What aesthetic techniques does the scene use?
  - o Do the edits use graphic matching?
  - o Are the shots cut on movement?
  - o How does the editing give pacing to the scene?
- How does the editing construct the time and space of the narrative?
  - o Are there flashbacks or flashforwards?
  - o Does the editing create a temporal ellipsis or expansion of time?
  - o Is there parallel editing?
- Does the scene use inserts of fantasy or thought?
- Does the scene use montage?

Want to learn more?

Think about this ...

Identifying edits

Objective: To identify the key features of the continuity-editing system and to analyze the aesthetics and rhythm of editing.

For this exercise watch a film that you have seen before. Think about the edits. For one scene, you may want to count every time you see a cut. This makes you more conscious of how often the edits occur. It will also make you aware of the pacing of the film. Identify the different editing techniques: shot/reverse shot patterns; jump cuts; graphic matching; cutting on movement; fast-paced action scenes; montage sequences. How effective is the editing in this scene?

Try this ...

Visual storytelling through editing

Objective: To construct a scene using the continuity editing system.
You will need: A storyboard sheet and pencil.

This is an extension of the exercise in Chapter 3. Using the storyboard sheet, draw a short visual narrative using between twelve and eighteen images. Concentrate on how the editing is used to construct the meaning of the film. How are the shots linked together? Do they follow or break with continuity? Do inserts or close-ups bring us into the action?

Editing sequence

Objective: To construct a scene using the continuity-editing system.
You will need: For this exercise it is best to use a video camera and a basic editing system.

Stage a short scene with two characters in a bar or restaurant, having a conversation. The scene should include the entrance and exit of the bartender or waiter. Try to work on the basic concepts, incorporating a medium two-shot and a shot/reverse shot sequence. Think about when and where in the dialogue it would be appropriate to cut to close-ups for emphasis or to draw the audience in. Concentrate on creating an effective sequence using continuity editing.

Further reading

There are a number of technical books dedicated to the practice of editing for film and video: Karel Reisz and Gavin Millar, *The Technique of Film Editing*, Ken Dancyger, *The Technique of Film and Video Editing* and Karen Pearlman, *Cutting Rhythms*. Conversations with editors about their practice include Walter Murch, *The Conversations* and Gabriella Oldham, *First Cut*. See also the writing of the Soviet montage theorists, in particular, Sergei Eisenstein, *Film Form* and *Film Sense*. See also Jean-Pierre Geuens, 'Editing', in *Film Production Theory*.

The films studied in this chapter

American Beauty 1999 Sam Mendes (director) Tariq Anwar and Christopher Greenbury (editors)
Battleship Potemkin 1925 Sergei Eisenstein (director and editor)
Breathless 1960 Jean-Luc Godard (director) Cécile Decugis and Lila Herman (editors)
The Girl and Her Trust 1912 D. W. Griffith (director)
House of Flying Daggers 2004 Zhang Yimou (director) Long Cheng (editor)
Letter from an Unknown Woman 1948 Max Ophüls (director) Ted J. Kent (editor)
The Lord of the Rings: The Return of the King 2003 Peter Jackson (director) Jamie Selkirk (editor)
Memories of Underdevelopment 1968 Tomás Guttiérez Alea (director) Nelson Rodríguez (editor)
Notorious 1946 Alfred Hitchcock (director) Theron Warth (editor)
Spider-Man 2 2004 Sam Raimi (director) Bob Murawski (editor)
Stagecoach 1939 John Ford (director) Otho Lovering and Dorothy Spencer (editors)

Other examples to explore

To best study editing, it is important to view films that employ a variety of techniques, continuity or its alternatives. Most Classical Hollywood films would demonstrate the continuity conventions and filmmaking from the French New Wave and the Soviet montage style would use different editing styles (see Chapter 12 for further suggestions). Some interesting examples to study for the aesthetics of editing include *Don't Look Now* (1974 Nicolas Roeg director), *Psycho* (1960 Alfred Hitchcock director) and *Moulin Rouge!* (2001 Baz Luhrmann director).

10

Film Music

Learning objectives

After completing this chapter, you will be able to:

- Trace the uses of **musical themes** throughout a film;
- Experiment with the process of choosing and adding music to a project;
- Analyze how music contributes to the meaning of a film.

Listening to a film

Sometimes, when we are watching a film and hear a familiar piece of music, we become aware of it and perhaps listen to it with more attention than we would usually give to accompanying music. At other times, during a suspense or horror film, we hear that 'horror-film music' and are led to expect a certain type of action. These examples show how music heightens our reactions to a scene. Music is so well integrated into a film's structure that it can enhance the experience without drawing attention to itself or stimulate emotion in a viewer who might later be unable to recall anything in particular about the music. Of course there are instances when the music is very memorable. Could you imagine the opening scene of *Jaws* (1975) without composer John Williams's distinctive music track anticipating the shark attack? Or would *Star Wars* (1977) work so well without the same composer's easily recognizable theme tune?

As we saw in Chapter 8, music is a key part of the overall soundtrack of a film. Likewise, in the last chapter we identified editing as a crucial element in postproduction. The addition of music is also part of this last phase of a film's creation. (Later we will touch on the exception that makes this rule.) Although the creative team may have ideas about musical choices from the start of the filmmaking process, the final inclusion of the music is part of postproduction. This is when the music is composed, recorded and mixed in with the other soundtrack elements. The key figure in the creation of the music track is the **composer**, who writes or compiles the musical **score**. Also vital is the **music editor**, whose job is to liaise between the composer and the editing team to integrate the music into the film.

Music in film can draw on a variety of styles and influences, but the final selection ultimately helps define how a film works and the effect it has on the audience. For example, the choice of classical music for a student project, rather than a popular track, is unexpected and could imply many things. It could demonstrate a familiarity with what is considered to be highbrow culture. Similarly, it could indicate the serious nature of the topic, the classical music endowing it with greater significance. Musical styles and periods carry associational meanings for the listener and the choice of a style can lead to a particular interpretation.

Studying film music requires us to become aware of all the music that is heard in a film. We need to train ourselves to hear when music is used and to recognize any associations it might evoke and how it works with the visual storytelling. Thus, we must actively and consciously listen to a film in order to understand what the music does. As part of the process of production of a film or video, the selection or creation of music is an area of some importance, although sometimes taken for granted. This chapter will provide an introduction to the basic concepts of film music and put us in a good position to start recognizing what to listen for in the music of a film.

- First, we will examine how the different musical elements of a film are selected or created;
- Then we will explore the composer's and music editor's jobs within the film's creative team;
- Then we will look at some of the basic methods of adding music to a film;
- We will extend this to discuss the ways music interacts with the film's story, in particular how its melodies and themes are used within the structure of the overall film;
- Next we will consider how music adds to the meaning of a film and how we can ascribe an ideological significance to a film's music;
- The chapter concludes with a discussion of the use of music in the film trilogy *The Lord of the Rings* (2001–3).

Sources of film music

If we think back to the short film 'Truck Stop', which we studied in Chapter 8, we noticed that music served an important function as part of the overall sound of the film. As Glenn Gould drives, he listens to a song on his car radio. The music then continues, with a qualitative difference, from the radio in the truck stop. Some of the audience will recognize this particular piece of music: the 1965 popular song 'Downtown', sung by Petula Clark. This is an example of what is known, in film-music terms, as a track from a **compiled score**. A compiled score uses music and songs from other contexts, not specifically written for the film, but drawn from pre-existing sources. Most of the music in *Thirty Two Short Films about Glenn Gould* comes from different contexts: Petula Clark's song, the classical piano music of Bach and Beethoven, Gould's own compositions, as well as music from other classical composers. This film, therefore, uses a compiled score, one of the two possible sources of film music. This categorization is based on where the music in the film originated. In contrast, *The Lord of the Rings* uses only the music composed specifically for it by Howard Shore. This type of film is described as having a **composed score**.

Composed and compiled music scores have interesting and different histories. For example, Classical Hollywood cinema developed a set of conventions around the use of music, giving primacy to the composed score. The Classical Hollywood score's purpose was to support the visual storytelling of the film, to create emotion, underscore action and work with the rhythm of the editing. This era gave rise to well-respected and prolific film-music composers such as Max Steiner, whose famous scores include *Gone with the Wind* (1939) and *Casablanca* (1942). There is a growing field of study on film music that explores how this type of score works within the representational systems of Classical Hollywood (suggestions for further reading on this topic are in the final section of this chapter). Classical Hollywood scores engage the audience in the world of the film; they create a mood. In a sense, a composed score is self-contained, as it doesn't remind the audience of music they might already be familiar with. In contrast, a compiled score relies on pre-existing music, directly calling upon musical references that the audience will have encountered before seeing the film. These references give compiled scores a different feeling, calling attention to the music of a film, as the audience has a heightened awareness of the songs and associations that may accompany them.

Compiled scores came into prominence towards the end of the era of the Classical Hollywood system, as the strength of the studios waned. Films made in the 1960s such as *Easy Rider* (1969) used popular songs for their compiled score. This film has a memorable sequence early on, when the two main characters ride their motorcycles to the tune of the 1968 song 'Born to Be Wild' by Steppenwolf. This song expresses the characters' experience and communicates their goals and attitudes to the audience. The lyric conveys their state of mind: 'Get your motor running, head out on the highway.' The rhythm matches the scene of driving on the open road. Although in this instance it does not come from inside the world of the film, this is music that these characters would listen to at other times; it is well suited to the action.

Figure 10.1   *Easy Rider*, Dennis Hopper, 1969

Adding music to a film

As a novice student filmmaker, you are most likely to experiment with compiled music for your film. For your first experiences in production, you will probably add pre-existing music to your project to complement the action. If you are lucky, however, you may know (or be) a composer or musician and have the opportunity to work with original music. In order to better understand this process of creating music for a film, let's review how an original piece of music is composed, recorded and edited into a film, before looking at the process of adding music to your own student project.

The music is usually incorporated during the postproduction phase. In the course of the initial editing with a composed score, the music editor goes through the **rough cut** and adds some available, pre-recorded music. This is called a **temp track**. This helps the editors and composer to know what type of music will be placed at different points. The composer then develops the music, while being able to view the partially edited images. During this initial stage, the composer meets with the music editor and the director. This meeting is known as a **spotting session**. Here the team views the rough cut of the film to decide when and where the music should enter, and how it should sound.

The composer then begins to create the score for the film ('score' is the term for the musical 'script'). Composers of music for films have to use a particular approach, unlike that used in other contexts. The music is created in short segments known as **cues**. Each cue covers a period of time or an action within a film and is recorded in isolation from the other cues. This is a very different approach to the composition of a symphony or song that is played continuously. Once the score has been written, it is recorded with the orchestra or whichever instruments are required. During this recording session, the relevant part of the film is screened in the background while the orchestra plays each cue, to closely match the action on the screen.

There is one type of film that differs in the way that music is integrated: the **musical**. With musicals, the composer enters the process during preproduction. Thus, the music can be used during shooting and the action staged to match the existing music. Yet, even in this case, the postproduction is key, as the score is re-recorded and mixed after the production is complete.

Adding music to your own film or video

When you are working on a low-budget or student project, you need to think about how the musicalization process might be adapted to your own context. Although you may not have the budget to hire a professional composer and orchestra or rent a recording studio, the effect music can have on your video is similar to that it might have on a big-budget, large-scale feature, increasing the emotional effect and linking concepts and ideas through association. Thus, it is important to think of music creatively, in tandem with other elements of your production. It is sometimes easy just to edit in a piece of pre-recorded music without thinking the choice through. A good way to develop your skills in music selection is to widen your knowledge of music in general. Listen to a variety of music in different styles, both live and recorded: classical, jazz, popular, world music. Experiencing different types of music gives you many more examples to choose from and an understanding of what effect music can have. It is also worthwhile studying films closely to pay particular attention to how the music works, to gain a deeper knowledge of musical styles and the conventions that govern film music.

Figure 10.2   Recording session for *The Lord of the Rings: The Fellowship of the Ring*, Peter Jackson, 2001

There are times, especially when you are new to film and video practice, when it is advisable to limit the use of music as it can sometimes take over. In particular, be aware that tracks or cues with strong melodies and beats can overwhelm the visuals or narrative. Adding a good track can be an easy way out, giving a structure or emotional coherence to a sequence that is visually weak or poorly edited. An edited sequence should hold up on its own without the benefit of the music track. Poor pre-recorded music can detract from some of the subtleties of the image or visual story-telling. The choice should relate to the image or enhance the storytelling function of your project. One alternative to overpowering music is to focus on other components of the soundtrack, particularly sound effects and the interesting ways in which these can be used musically, exploring their different **rhythms** and timbres. For example, the sound of breathing or a heart beat can be used to add **tempo** to the visuals. As an extension to the musical use of sound effects, instrumental compositions can be more subtle and less intrusive than tracks with lyrics. It is also important to be able to combine music with other soundtrack elements, such as the voice or sound effects. This requires skills in sound editing, balancing the levels of music to the other sounds, but produces a more layered and engaging soundtrack than music alone.

Music can have a strong influence on the effectiveness of the visuals. When editing with music, it is useful to explore the relationship between the sound and image. Part of the rhythm and pacing of editing discussed in Chapter 9 is editing to music; cutting to the beat and using the musical structures to motivate the editing. These choices then guide which point in the process you add the music to the edit. For example, editing to a music track that is already laid down is different from adding music to a scene that has been edited. When making this decision, ask yourself whether the music leads the scene or provides support. Which is paramount? These editing skills are important, but working with music effectively often means moving beyond simply cutting to the beat, to explore the complexities of sound and image relations. It is often effective to select music that works in **counterpoint** to the images, contrasting styles and making juxtapositions that allow for ironic commentary.

Finally, be aware that most pre-recorded music is copyrighted. There are several online sites that provide copyright-free alternatives that are worth exploring. It is also worthwhile considering working with a composer. There are many student composers and musicians who may be interested in gaining such experience. Even if the results of these collaborations are not ideal, the experience of working with a composed score increases vital skills and an understanding of the relationship of music to image.

Music in the world of the narrative

Think back to the music in 'Truck Stop' from Chapter 8. In this example, the song is on the radio. Since the music comes from a source within the world of the story, it is diegetic music. In contrast, the scene from *Easy Rider* uses a pre-existing track, but there is no source for this music in the world of the film. This is an example of non-diegetic music. These are terms and ideas we encountered in relation to narrative in Chapter 3 and sound in Chapter 8. Film scholars and practitioners often develop different terminology to describe similar things. So far we have been using 'diegetic' to describe elements inside and 'non-diegetic' for elements outside the world of the film. Film scholars use these terms to describe how the music relates to the narrative. Film composers, however, use different terms when describing the same concept, terms that more accurately describe what they are doing when composing a film score. For composers, music that appears from a source within the story is known as **source music**. This roughly corresponds to what the scholars would call diegetic. Music that does not have a direct source within the story world is known as **dramatic scoring**. This corresponds to non-diegetic music.

We are aware of the music's source inside or outside the world of the film, and this affects how we respond to it. We know that source music is something the characters create or can hear. With dramatic scoring we know that the music is not something the characters share. Thus, we respond to it as an abstract commentary on the action of the scene. To illustrate this, let's look at an example. Daniele Amfitheatrof's score for *Letter from an Unknown Woman* (1948) uses music both as source music and dramatic scoring, motivated by the fact that one of the main characters, Stefan (Louis Jourdan), is a pianist. Furthermore, the same pieces of music are used in both source and dramatic scoring contexts. The first example of source music in the film is when Stefan is practising and the young Lisa is listening from outside. The music is part of the action in this scene; it is crucial to character development that they both hear and share the music. Lisa's infatuation starts when she hears Stefan playing.

The piece of music he plays in this scene gets repeated in the dramatic scoring throughout the film, producing a different effect. Towards the end of the film, Lisa and Stefan meet for the last time and the music returns as dramatic scoring. The scene is in Stefan's apartment and Lisa is shown in by Stefan's servant. As Stefan enters the room, we hear a string arrangement of the same tune Stefan played earlier. Since the characters do not hear the music, it does not have the same effect on the action as before. The music is emotional commentary, indicating to the audience

Lisa's feelings on seeing Stefan, expressing her internal state. The audience associates the music with Stefan's playing and therefore the dramatic scoring connects us to Lisa's memories.

This example of source music and dramatic scoring works because the association has been established between the two uses of the same piece of music. The repetition of a particular melody is what is known as a musical theme and we will examine this phenomenon in the following section.

Musical themes

In order to serve their specific function in relation to other aspects of a film, musical scores often have a high level of consistency and internal form. A principal method by which the score interacts with the progress of the narrative and the delineation of the characters is through the use of musical themes. A musical theme is a short phrase or **melody** that is repeated during the course of the film. This practice has its origin in the operas, and theories on opera, developed by the German composer, Richard Wagner. Wagner's operas used a technique known as a **leitmotiv**, translated as 'leading theme'. Wagner's leitmotivs are associated with specific characters or actions in an opera's narrative, and through their repetition, they take on a representational function associated with that character or action. This concept translates into the practice of film scoring, as musical themes (leitmotivs) are introduced with different characters or situations, and then repeated when those characters or situations recur. Thus, through association from one use to the next, the music creates an expected reaction.

In the example from *Letter from an Unknown Woman* the musical theme is associated with the relationship between the two principal characters and is heard in scenes when they are together. It is a common practice for romantic films to have a 'love theme'. Leitmotivs can also be connected with individual people, with places or with actions. In the film trilogy, *The Lord of the Rings*, for example, each area of Middle Earth has its own musical theme. These themes vary in style and have contrasting sounds. Throughout the films, as the heroes travel through Middle Earth, the viewer is guided to understand features of the different cultures partly through the changing musical styles.

Classical scores sometimes incorporate melodies from outside sources into the composed score as themes or leitmotivs. In other words, film composers can include tunes or musical phrases from popular or folk songs in their repertoire. This type of musical quotation draws on themes from pre-existing music and can bring particular associations of another context. For example, the score of *Stagecoach* (1939) is made up of musical allusions to well-known folk songs. As a composed score, it has elements of compilation as pre-existing music has been incorporated into original compositions and arranged into a score, which is then recorded specifically to tie in with the film.

In *Stagecoach*, one of these quoted themes is the 1854 song 'I Dream of Jeanie' by Stephen Foster, a composer of popular Southern American folk tunes in the nineteenth century. It is a short musical phrase associated with the relationship of the characters of Hatfield and Mrs Mallory, and is an example of how a theme can work within the narrative to tell part of the story. The theme appears for the first time as the **main title**, as the cue played over the opening-credit sequence. It then occurs three times during the journey as Hatfield engages in acts of chivalry towards Mrs Mallory: when he asks Doc Boone (Thomas Mitchell) to put out the cigar; when he

Figure 10.3   *Stagecoach*, John Ford, 1939

offers her a seat at the table away from Dallas; and when he gives her a drink of water from his silver cup. It returns for the climactic scene in which Hatfield considers shooting Mrs Mallory to save her from capture by the Apaches.

The use of this theme is more complex than that of a conventional love theme, as these characters are not romantically involved. It does, however, express an emotional link between them that is crucial to the story. If you listen closely to when you hear the theme and when you don't, you can tell what that emotion is. The theme does not mark the presence of either of these characters separately. It is not used when Mrs Mallory worries about her husband or talks to Dallas. Nor does it relate to Hatfield as a gambler or killer. It is not even heard during Hatfield's death scene. The theme is directly used to evoke the gallantry of Hatfield, the Southern gentleman, towards Mrs Mallory. This point can be proven by the one occasion the theme occurs when Mrs Mallory is absent. As the male occupants of the stagecoach look around a farm burned down by the Apaches, Hatfield finds the dead body of a woman and covers her with his coat and the theme is played. This action is an extension of his expressions of gallantry towards Mrs Mallory. This is his theme and it evokes his idea of gentlemanly conduct. The theme expresses nostalgia for the romanticized, old-fashioned lifestyle of the South that has been lost after the end of the Civil War.

In describing this use of the Hatfield/Mrs Mallory theme in *Stagecoach*, our analysis has touched on how music functions to evoke meaning for the audience. We will continue this chapter with a discussion of how music creates meaning within the structure of a film.

Music and meaning

For many people studying the arts, it is a widely held belief that music is the most abstract art form, rarely ever directly representing an idea or telling a story. Unlike many forms of visual representation or spoken dialogue, music by itself does not show us an action or a character. How then do we interpret, analyze and seek to understand the music in a film? Is it purely abstract and aesthetic, or does it perhaps have a more tangible effect when combined with the film's visuals? Despite the supposedly abstract nature of music, even on its own terms, isolated from the visuals of a film, music is open to interpretation and analysis. For this, we only need to hear the music and grasp certain concepts, in order to be able to discuss and analyze the reactions it creates. Then we can develop an understanding of how music interacts with the visuals of a film, to support the film's narrative and generate emotions in the viewers.

As we have just seen, musical themes (leitmotivs) are internal references linking together different moments of a film through the use and re-use of a particular phrase or melody. In other words, the audience connects together different elements through a scheme of associations created by the music. In addition to these internal references, there are also external references. Film music has a set of conventions that works from one film to another. Certain types of music can lead the audience to expect a certain type of action or the appearance of a type of character. To illustrate this we need only return to our earlier example of 'horror-film music'. Horror films use conventions that set up our expectations for something scary. These are part of the learned behaviours we have, as an audience, when reacting to music.

A number of factors create these reactions. We will summarize them into four categories:

- **Key**;
- **Tempo** and **rhythm**;
- **Melody** and **harmony**;
- **Instrumentation**.

Key

A musical composition is based in one of two keys, **major** or **minor**. The choice of key affects how the music sounds. On the most basic level, we associate music in a major key with bright, positive emotion, whereas music in a minor key evokes melancholy. It is hard to understand this idea without practical application, so the difference between major and minor is best illustrated by listening to particular examples. As we discussed earlier, the score for *The Lord of the Rings* trilogy contains a series of themes associated with different places and people. If you listen to the Rohan theme, introduced in *The Two Towers* (2002) and used during sequences set in that location, you will hear a good example of a melody played in a minor key. Contrast this with the bright-sounding major key theme associated with the Shire, that you hear at the start of *The Fellowship of the Ring* (2001), and you get a sense of the difference between compositions in major or minor keys.

Tempo and rhythm

The speed or tempo of a musical piece also creates meaning through association. For example, a fast tempo can be used for a chase scene, heightening our involvement and anticipation. We associate running and chasing with an increased heart rate and this reaction is simulated through an increase in the music's pace. A related concept to tempo is **rhythm**. Rhythm is the temporal structure of music, the timing in which different notes are played. When listening, we react strongly to rhythms; as we dance our movements follow these patterns as we physically imitate the musical beat.

Melody and harmony

Music conventionally contains melody. Kathryn Kalinak defines melody 'as an extended series of notes played in an order which is memorable and recognizable as a discrete unit (hummable if you will)'. (5) Melodies can be incorporated into musical themes and used in the system of filmic meaning. Most of the themes that we have discussed so far (the 'love theme' from *Letter from an Unknown Woman* or the Hatfield/Mallory theme from *Stagecoach*) take the form of melodies, easily remembered tunes that link one occurrence of the theme to another. It is also interesting to notice when musical forms are not melodic. Some of us are probably familiar with the very famous 'shower scene' in the 1960 Alfred Hitchcock film *Psycho*. Bernard Herrmann's innovative **score** uses the sounds of a high-pitched violin in a highly non-melodic fashion for this scene. Whereas melody is the sequential use of notes, harmony is created when the notes are played at the same time. A solo singing voice would sing a melody, whereas a choir sings in harmony, with the different voices joining together. Harmonic structures are basic units of music and can give a cue a pleasant and easy sound or can add tension or discomfort based on how the notes are combined.

Figure 10.4   *Psycho*, Alfred Hitchcock, 1960

Instrumentation

The type of instrumentation used in a score also affects how it creates meaning. For example, string instruments sound close in tone and range to human voices and inspire softer emotional reactions. Therefore, string instrumentation is common in melodrama and romance. Brass instruments call to mind the associations of a military or marching band. They are loud and powerful sounds. Therefore, brass is often used for emphasis and suspense. These are broad generalizations about musical instruments; the aforementioned 'shower scene' in *Psycho* uses strings for a very different purpose. However, such generalizations can be used as a starting point to question and interrogate how music functions to create particular emotional reactions.

Let's illustrate the effects of different instrumentation through another example from *The Lord of the Rings*; this time from the third film, *The Return of the King* (2003). The Rohan theme, which we identified earlier, changes its instrumentation throughout the film. It is played as the characters ride towards the city of Edoras, in the centre of Rohan. This is the way the theme is established in *The Return of the King* and it calls to mind the last time we heard it in *The Two Towers*. It is a clear melody played on a stringed instrument, over a simple acoustic background accompaniment. This theme is in keeping with the location of the wooden built city and evocative of the pastoral lifestyle of the people of Edoras. Shortly after this scene, the riders of Rohan are summoned to war in support of their neighbours in Gondor.

Gondor also has a theme, played when the wizard, Gandalf, arrives in their city. This theme is in a major key and played on brass instruments. It is an appropriate sound for the warrior

Figure 10.5   *The Lord of the Rings: The Two Towers*, Peter Jackson, 2002

culture of the people living in the stone city. Early in the film, Gandalf and his hobbit companion, Pippin (Billy Boyd), engineer the lighting of the beacons that will summon Rohan to war. In this sequence the visuals are heightened by judicious use of the musical themes. As the first beacon lights, a musical passage begins to develop that rises in tone creating increased suspense and anticipation as the other fires are lit. The instrumentation is loud brass in the lower registers and strings playing faster sequences in the upper registers. As the fifth beacon is lit, and an aerial shot sweeps over the snow-capped peak, the Gondor theme is picked up by the brass in the lower register. Finally, Aragorn (Viggo Mortensen), one of the characters waiting in Rohan, sees the last beacon lit. With a shift to a different non-melodic suspenseful break in the music, Aragorn runs to the hall and tells the King of Rohan and his followers, that he has seen the beacon. In the moment of suspense when all wait for the king to answer, the music fades out entirely and the sense of anticipation is increased by the silence. When the king finally gives the order, the Rohan theme returns, this time with brass instrumentation and a quicker tempo than previously. This shift from string-solo to group-brass instrumentation is in keeping with the development of the narrative at the moment when the warriors of Rohan are about to enter the conflict. It is as if the brass instrumentation of Gondor has been delivered along with the message.

With the techniques of music in mind we can look further at how music makes meaning across a variety of films.

The ideological significance of film music

Part of the function of music in creating meaning is also ideological; through recurring themes and associations, music can create a response to certain situations. These reactions are, at least in part, culturally constructed, in that they work similarly over a number of different films. The cultural associations are intrinsic to the music itself, as various styles are associated with the cultures from which they arose.

To examine further how music can work ideologically, let's revisit the section of *Stagecoach* that we studied in relation to the use of the camera in Chapter 6. Throughout the film, the presence of the Apaches is indicated by the use of a musical theme, establishing the threat of attack. It is first heard during the main title sequence, in conjunction with several other themes that weave in and out of the narrative. In the opening scene, as the army receives a telegraph about Geronimo, the theme is brought in as a sudden burst of music (known in film music terms as a **stinger**) to represent the threat.

The 'Apache theme' contrasts quite strongly with the leitmotivs that are associated with different characters and express different relationships. For example, the stagecoach itself is accompanied by a melody in a major key that is bright and fast. In contrast, the slow, solemn church-organ music is introduced, with comic embellishments, when the church ladies expel Dallas and the doctor from the town. The 'Apache theme' also contrasts with the melodic romantic theme that always accompanies the relationship between Mrs Mallory and Hatfield, discussed earlier.

The 'Apache theme' has several levels of association. On an initial level, the reference works internally, representing that first moment in the story in each subsequent use. And just as the first use signifies the Apaches as dangerous, every repetition of the theme connotes that idea of danger.

PART IV

Analysis and
Critical Practice

Analysis and Interpretation of Film

Learning objectives

After completing this chapter, you will be able to:

- Critically analyze the use of cinematic techniques;
- Interpret the various levels of meaning and ideas represented in a film;
- Contextualize a film in relation to larger cultural issues;
- Produce a critical reflection on your own work.

Writing about film

In the preceding chapters many of the exercises focused on getting you thinking about the creative choices of filmmakers as they work. The goal of these exercises has been to allow you to think creatively about how a film is made. Writing about film and analyzing it is another way to develop an understanding and appreciation for all aspects of the creative process. The approach we have taken so far has been that of 'critical practice'. As we defined this concept in Chapter 1, critical practice requires you to commit to an engaged form of creative expression, and an active role as both a viewer and a critic. With a critical-practice approach to film, you should be prepared to either try your hand at creative filmmaking, or to apply this knowledge of film techniques to the appreciation of film. Thus, you are now equipped to examine in detail the effectiveness of cinematic techniques through the analysis of specific examples.

   In this chapter we will examine a variety of methods of writing about a film. We will explore examples of written work to see how they exemplify these different approaches:

- To start off with we will consider the different types of writing about film: film reviews, historical research, critical analysis and theoretical interpretation;
- We will then focus more closely on how to write a critical-analysis paper;
- Then we will examine how to apply critical analysis to other forms of interpretation;
- And finally, we will learn how to write a critical reflection on our own creative practice.

Methods of writing about film

Film is written about in many ways: film reviews, star biographies, historical research, etc. When you start to write about a film, you need to be clear about your goals. It is best to consider three separate questions when deciding your method or approach:

- Who will read your writing?
- What exactly are you writing about? (A scene from a film, a whole film, a group of films, or some element of film culture in general);
- Which method or approach do you intend to take? (Examination of a specific technique, film style or a film's place in history).

Ascertaining your readership will help you to make accurate decisions about the style, tone and form your essay should take. The second question deals with the actual topic of your work, and the third, the method you will choose to conduct your research and present your ideas. The following sections introduce the major methods and styles of writing about film, before continuing with an in-depth look at critical analysis, interpretation and writing critically about your own work. These are the approaches that develop the critical-practice methodology applied in earlier chapters.

The film review

The type of film writing that you are most likely to encounter is the film review. Film reviews appear in newspapers or online, on television or on the radio. They are generally written using a combination of description and analysis of technique. The film review is broad and brief and written in a journalistic style, shorter than a critical-analysis essay. A review's purpose is to give an opinion of the value of a film to the reader, so enabling them to decide whether they wish to see it or not. The review will usually include a judgement on whether the film is worth watching. Sometimes writers acknowledge the influence of their own personal taste when reviewing a film. Briefly, these are the usual features of a review. The first three are almost always present and the last two are also frequently included:

- Description of the general plot;
- The reviewer's evaluation of the film's quality;
- The reviewer's recommendation;
- Comparisons with other films of the same style, or by the same director, writer or actors;
- Reference to the style or techniques of the film.

The review relies on subjective personal opinions and the critic is often someone who knows, through experience, a lot about filmmaking practice, although they are not necessarily film-makers themselves. To further explore this type of writing, let's look at an example from the critic Roger Ebert's review of *Eternal Sunshine of the Spotless Mind* (2004):

It's one thing to wash that man right outta your hair, and another to erase him from your mind. 'Eternal Sunshine of the Spotless Mind' imagines a scientific procedure that can obliterate whole fields of memory – so that, for example, Clementine can forget that she ever met Joel, let alone fell in love with him. 'Is there any danger of brain damage?' the inventor of the process is asked. 'Well,' he allows, in his most kindly voice, 'technically speaking, the procedure is brain damage.'

The movie is a labyrinth created by the screenwriter Charlie Kaufman, whose 'Being John Malkovich' and 'Adaptation' were neorealism compared to this. Jim Carrey and Kate Winslet play Joel and Clementine … . That they lose their minds while all about them are keeping theirs is a tribute to their skill; they center their characters so that we can actually care about them even when they're constantly losing track of their own lives …

The movie is a radical example of Maze Cinema, that style in which the story coils back upon itself, redefining everything and then throwing it up in the air and redefining it again. To reconstruct it in chronological order would be cheating, but I will cheat: At some point before the technical beginning of the movie, Joel and Clementine were in love, and their affair ended badly, and Clementine went to Dr Howard Mierzwiak (Tom Wilkinson) at Lacuna Inc., to have Joel erased from her mind.

With this example, we can see how a reviewer might use a particular style of writing and varying levels of analytical engagement:

- Much of the writing is *descriptive*. The first paragraph recounts a critical moment in the story, the introduction of the memory-erasing procedure that provides the principal conflict. The third paragraph summarizes the story, removing it from its plot structure and recounting it in chronological order. The review continues with further description of the story and the characters.
- There is also evidence of *analysis* here. He defines the film as 'Maze Cinema' placing the storytelling techniques in the context of that particular style.
- The review shows less *interpretation* than other levels of analysis. Ebert's comparisons with other Kaufman scripts relate the storytelling structure to his previous work.
- Finally, this quotation from the review shows the process of *evaluation*. He praises the skills of Jim Carrey and Kate Winslet in making their characters appealing despite the complexity of the narrative.

The tone and language Ebert uses is light and engaging, but demonstrates both his knowledge of film and of other aspects of culture. For those in the know, he makes short references to the latter, paraphrasing a song from the musical, *South Pacific* (1958) ('Gonna wash that man right outta my hair') and the poem 'If', by Rudyard Kipling ('If you can keep your head while all about you are losing theirs'). His reference to the post-war Italian movement of neo-realism shows his knowledge of film history. This is critical writing that can relate a film to other types of art and literature.

Historical-research essay

Historical research is a popular form of writing about film and it can take a variety of approaches. Unlike the film review, historical research is not always based on textual analysis. In other words, this type of writing does not necessarily centre around an individual film or a group of films. Historical research can analyze such elements as:

- The technology of film;
- The different types of film audiences;
- The history of exhibition spaces;
- Large movements in film history;
- The political, social or economic factors that affect the development of film.

Some film-history essays do, however, incorporate elements of textual analysis, examining how films emerge from a particular time and place within history. These types of analysis are grounded in the study of the context of a film's production and can follow several approaches. Some work can contrast similar films from different periods of time to test how the context of production alters the stories and themes of a film.

To best understand how historical writing about film works, let's explore an example of this type of research. *Stagecoach* (1939), which we have studied before in relation to style and technique, is a film that can be (and has been) examined from various historical perspectives. For example, Charles J. Maland's article '"Powered by a Ford?": Dudley Nichols, Authorship and Cultural Ethos in *Stagecoach*' is a good example of a historically based analysis of the film.

In this article Maland argues that the screenwriter, Dudley Nichols, makes an important contribution to the film. He suggests a reading of *Stagecoach* with reference to Dudley Nichols's involvement in a particular 1930s political movement: the Popular Front. This was a 1930s leftwing liberal organization linked with anti-fascism; in particular, it opposed Hitler's power in Germany and his international influence. In addition, the Popular Front supported the social-welfare politics associated with President Roosevelt (FDR). Nichols was also involved with the founding of the Screen Writers Guild (SWG), the union that fought for better deals for writers in Hollywood. What does all this have to do with the film *Stagecoach*? Maland elaborates:

> The exposition and early scenes in the screenplay set up a tension between the characters with respectability or upper-class roots – Gatewood, Mrs. Mallory, Hatfield, and the ladies of the Law and Order League … – and the common, unpretentious characters, especially Dallas, Ringo, and Doc Boone … (Maland, 2003: 62)

Maland's historical research reveals that Nichols invented the characters of Gatewood (Berton Churchill) and Boone when adapting the short story 'Stage to Lordsburg' by Ernest Haycox. These two characters in particular show aspects of Nichols's liberal beliefs. Gatewood is the banker who we see stealing money at the start of the film. He 'is obviously designed as a representative of and spokesman for the moneyed interests that FDR opposed'. (62) Maland links Gatewood's actions throughout the film to the Popular Front's notion of the greedy and corrupt, big-business capitalist. In opposition to this, the other character created by Nichols is Doc Boone.

> Although he is judged disreputable by the Tonto respectables, Doc is presented as an altruistic, wise, and compassionate character … . In many ways he serves as a foil to Gatewood throughout the film – if Gatewood functions as entrenched greed and selfish individualism, Doc exhibits kindness and community spirit … . If Gatewood represents the hated economic royalists of the Popular Front era, Doc is the educated but marginalized professional who aligns himself with the common people (and not, incidentally, unlike the successful screenwriter who takes a leadership role in the SWG to fight the recalcitrant studio heads). (Maland, 2003: 67)

The screenplay shows the influence of Nichols's politics by the way the story validates the actions of Doc Boone over Gatewood:

> Both Nichols's screenplay and the final film fully reject Gatewood, the corrupt capitalist ... . On the other hand, the source of good in the film emanates from the marginalized common people, particularly Ringo and Dallas ... . (Maland, 2003: 70)

As historical research, this article exhibits specific goals and methods in constructing its argument:

- It demonstrates an awareness of the film within the context in which it was made, revealing the influence of the 1930s political movement of Popular Front liberalism;
- It examines a specific aspect of the film, in this case the contribution of the screenwriter Dudley Nichols and links Nichols's politics to the themes of the film;
- It relates the analysis of the film to other sources of information about history, examining the political climate at the time.

This last point is important. For effective analysis of a film's place within cultural history, a writer draws on sources other than the film itself. Maland illustrates his point by referring to historical writing about the 1930s as well as political writing from the era. Effective historical research relates the particulars of a film to other evidence about contemporaneous events.

The historical method is interesting as it interacts frequently with other ways of writing about film. Research that is primarily historical in approach also draws on other critical and theoretical methods to support its arguments. Thus, in this article Maland closely analyzes the characters and their role in the film. As we will see below, this article integrates critical analysis with its fundamental basis in historical research.

Critical analysis of film

Writing a critical-analysis essay moves beyond a review, with a more detailed examination of the style used in a film. The techniques studied in earlier chapters are applied to writing about a film, in order to examine a film's form and method of communication. Often this type of analysis is applied to a whole film, but there are other ways in which critical analysis can be used in film writing.

A critical-analysis essay can isolate a single technique and examine how it works throughout the course of a film. Analysis of this sort draws upon an understanding of elements such as the mise-en-scène, sound or cinematography and applies it to the filmic system. For example, at the end of Chapter 10 we traced how music worked within the narrative system of the trilogy, *The Lord of the Rings* (2001–3). This type of analysis refers to the film, but also often relies on an understanding of other art forms and their application to the specific example. In this case, we also drew on an understanding of the conventions that govern music, relating them to the particulars of this film.

It is useful to understand that this type of analysis strongly links the technique under examination with the development of the narrative. Thus, when we discussed the 'Shire theme', we saw how the musical techniques contributed to our overall understanding of the nature of the characters we met in that location. We also saw how this theme was predominant in an early point in the story, the exposition of Act 1, before the characters experienced the danger and war of subsequent acts, which are marked by a different musical style.

A common approach to critical writing is a close textual analysis of an individual scene or sequence in a film. Students who are learning to write about or make a film are often asked to write a **sequence analysis**. This is one way to explore how the elements in a scene come together to create its overall meaning. Unlike the method above that analyzes a single technique, the sequence analysis gives equal attention to the combination of all the aspects of filmmaking and how they work together at a particular point in a film.

Analyzing a scene in isolation only reveals part of what can be said about a film. In this chapter, we will see how a sequence analysis involves relating the techniques, individually and in combination, to how the story is told. An example of this method of critical analysis is evident in Maland's essay on *Stagecoach*. In this quotation, see how Maland relates what occurs in one particular scene to his overall argument about the liberal perspective on social class.

> For example, in one scene invented in the screenplay, the stagecoach arrives at Dry Fork, and the group goes inside to eat a quick meal. The screenplay directions note that 'Dallas is uncertain whether she should sit down, knowing she is not expected to sit with "respectable" people'. The framing of Toland's cinematography and the performances of the characters in two key shots break the group into respectables and social pariahs, criticizing the first and embracing the second … .
>
> 4. MLS of Gatewood glowering, a standing Hatfield looking critically at Dallas, and Mrs. Mallory with eyes down. Hatfield hands Mrs. Mallory a plate …
>
> 10. MS from straight across table, Ringo and Dallas, Ringo says, 'Looks like I got the plague, don't it?'
>
> The hostile reactions of the three respectables immediately brand them as intolerant and petty; Toland's balanced framing helps make those reactions clear. Similarly, his use of camera distance and the depth of the composition show how the respectables separate themselves from the social pariahs. Image, cutting, framing, and performance all blend to realize the screenplay's conception. (Maland, 2003: 71–2)

This critical analysis directly links the techniques of the scene to the narrative and the themes of social division. Here, Maland relies on critical analysis as rhetorical evidence to support his claim about the influence of writer Nichols's liberal political views.

Learning to analyze a film critically can have numerous benefits when both studying and making films.

- As we have seen above, historical research can use critical analysis as evidence to explore the film's period of history.
- Likewise, as we talk about film theory, we will discover that critical analysis is a useful starting point when addressing abstract theoretical questions about film.
- In our work in previous chapters we have used critical analysis as a tool to gain a greater comprehension of filmic techniques. This, in turn, influences how we incorporate these techniques in our own creative work.

Theoretical interpretation of film

In brief, film theory is an attempt to understand how the cinema works as part of the larger culture and society in which we live. Both theorists and filmmakers have asked similar questions, such as: 'What is cinema?' or 'What is film?' With these questions in mind, we can approach the task of writing theoretically about film. Through film theory we ask the larger, general questions about film, rather than focusing our analysis, or critical reaction, on a response to an individual film. These big questions can address several different issues, such as how film:

- Relates to other arts;
- Is placed within a social, political or economic context;
- Relates to questions of art and aesthetics;
- Is viewed and responded to by audiences;
- Is responded to psychologically by viewers;
- Works and communicates as a form of visual language;
- Relates to the identities that it represents.

Sometimes, big questions have led to big answers, grand and complex theories that require close study and knowledge of an advanced and specialized language in order to be understood. Yet, on the other hand, we often already think theoretically about film. We interpret and categorize film based on certain principles and ideas.

For example, when you are going to see a film with a group of friends, you might apply theoretical ideas to your decision-making process. If you decide to go to see an action movie, you apply a genre theory approach to your decision. If you go to see a George Lucas film, because you like other films made by him, you are applying **auteur theory**. Theoretical questions inform how we apply critical analysis to the interpretation of a film. Earlier chapters discussed ideology (the acknowledgement that film style and technique communicates ideas that reflect certain beliefs of society). Ideological analysis is grounded in a theoretical question: how does a film reflect the complexities of the society and culture in which it is created and consumed?

For example, in Chapter 7, we examined the costume choices from the film *Batman Returns* (1992), noting how the costumes reflected particular aspects of the characters who were wearing them. The analysis went beyond this, however, to explore how the costumes could be interpreted as reflecting wider themes in the film related to gender difference. Here, we moved beyond thinking about the stylistic and narrational aspects of the film and raised a theoretical, interpretive question: how does *Batman Returns* reflect, or break with, stereotypical gender roles?

To consider these concepts in more detail, let's look at an example of theoretical writing on film: 'The Woman Who Was Known Too Much' by Tania Modleski, a chapter on the film *Notorious* (1946), from a book that approaches Hitchcock's films from the perspective of feminist theory. Let's see how Modleski relates this film to theoretical ideas. Modleski argues that: 'Alicia is positioned at the outset of the film as object of man's curiosity and voyeurism ...' (1988: 60), referring to the opening scenes when the male reporters follow her from the courtroom and to the early scene when Devlin watches her at her party. She then continues her argument by linking Alicia's role at the beginning of the film to the change she undergoes throughout the narrative:

After setting the woman up as an object of male desire and curiosity, the film proceeds to submit her to a process of purification whereby she is purged of her excess sexuality in order to be rendered fit for her place in the patriarchal order. She is, as the critics say, 'redeemed by love'. Hitchcock accomplishes this purification largely through visual means: in the party sequence, Alicia, photographed in a long shot and standing in a bright, harsh light, is wearing a bold striped blouse with a bared midriff ... and she exudes a kind of animal sexuality that is in keeping with her attire ... . By the end of the film, however, when Alicia is on the verge of dying, she is etherealized and spiritualized until she becomes practically bodiless ... in this later scene Hitchcock shoots entirely in close-up and utilizes low-key backlighting for a kind of halo effect. In the climactic staircase sequence Hitchcock continues to shoot predominantly in close-up, and even when he cuts to a medium or long shot, Alicia's body, draped around Devlin, is entirely obscured by a loose, dark coat draped around it. (Modleski, 1988: 60–1)

In this quotation you can see the application of a theoretical idea to the analysis of a film. First, Modleski introduces the theoretical point she is making, that Alicia's change is a process of 'purification', remaking her into the 'good woman' who fulfils her role within society by conforming to expectations of her gender. Modleski's argument is supported by her use of critical analysis; she specifically scrutinizes the way that the character is dressed and shot throughout the film. This critical analysis of the visuals is then clearly linked to the theoretical point; Alicia changes into a desexualized and romanticized character.

Although writing film theory is accomplished by exploring abstract questions about the nature of film, the critical-analysis work that we are developing can provide a basis for theorizing film. Critical analysis gives us the opportunity to expand a text-based understanding of a film into an interpretation that takes into consideration the ideological forces at work in a film.

In the next two sections, we will expand on the last two areas, working towards combining critical analysis with theoretical interpretation of film. Then we will apply it to critical reflection on writing about your own creative practice. The material covered in previous chapters provides the base from which film writing can be developed. The next section will consolidate the concepts introduced in earlier chapters. Throughout, we will keep in mind the goal of the chapter, which is to use our understanding of film form and technique and apply it to the task of writing about film.

Analyzing a film

In this section we will review what we have learned in previous chapters and apply them to the process of writing a critical-analysis paper. We will focus on close textual analysis: examining a scene from a film in depth and detail, to best relate how the techniques are deployed. This guide is for the analysis of a scene from a narrative film, but it can be adapted for documentary or experimental film.

The need for description

The first stage of preparation when analyzing a scene is to accurately describe the events of the narrative. This description should show a correct understanding of the story and relate what happens to how it is told. Description serves important functions for both the writer and reader of the analytical paper:

- In the early stage of writing about a film, it helps to clarify the writer's understanding of what happens in the story;
- When analyzing a specific scene, it helps the writer relate that scene to the rest of the story;
- Description allows the writer to emphasize certain points that are relevant to the analysis;
- Description also guides the reader who has not seen the film;
- It also reminds the reader who has seen the film of significant moments in the story.

There is a method of writing description known as **thick description**. Borrowed from anthropology, such as the writings of Clifford Geertz, thick description is a tool deployed in ethnographic fieldwork (observations about cultures and societies under study) so that the description includes the context of an observed action, as well as the action itself. This method can be applied to film analysis if analytical, contextual and evaluative elements are incorporated into the process. For example, look at this section from Roger Ebert's review of *Eternal Sunshine of the Spotless Mind*:

As the movie opens, Joel is seized with an inexplicable compulsion to ditch work and take the train to Montauk, and on the train he meets Clementine. For all they know they have never seen each other before, but somehow there's a connection, a distant shadow of déjà vu. During the course of the film, which moves freely, dizzyingly, forward and backward in time, they will each experience fragmentary versions of the relationship they had, might have had, or might be having.

The review describes part of the film's story but the manner in which it is written exhibits elements of analysis and evaluation. The phrase 'freely, dizzyingly, forward and backward in time', adds depth to the description and implies admiration for the storytelling techniques.

It is important to recognize that description is only a small first step in the process of analysis. Your writing about film cannot merely narrate the action of the plot – that is the job of the film itself. Description can be a useful starting point but should be limited to the introduction to your main analysis. Ultimately, it is improbable that you can tell the story as effectively as the filmmakers have done in the film. The goal of your writing should be to move beyond description, to analysis of techniques, thus leading the reader to a deeper understanding of what they or you have seen. When writing an essay, it is wise to start with the description and develop beyond this, remembering to ensure that your description is accurate. Description can be written to accentuate certain points of a story, but a writer should not rewrite the story in order to fit it into a particular analysis.

Identifying the cinematic techniques

After the description when you have a clear understanding of what happens in the scene under analysis, it is necessary to identify the cinematic techniques. Once you have read the earlier chapters, you will be well equipped to do this. Part III in particular, gives you the requisite tools to break down the different elements of a film effectively. You can refer to the summaries of each chapter to guide you on what to look for in a scene. Identify the techniques of:

- Cinematography: How is the camera used? What types of camera movement and framing are there?
- Mise-en-scène: What is the setting or **location**? What costumes are used? How is the scene staged? Where has the director placed the actors? How do they move and interpret the dialogue?
- Sound: What elements are there in the soundtrack: dialogue, SFX, acousmatic sound?
- Editing: Which style of editing is used (continuity, montage)? How does the editing direct the audience's attention to the unfolding action?
- Music: What is added to the scene? How does it function as a storytelling device?

The same scene can be analyzed and interpreted from many perspectives, with the emphasis on particular techniques. For example, in two earlier chapters we examined the chase scene in *Stagecoach*. Chapter 6 introduced this scene in relation to how the camera angles and positions present the film's point of view. The choices ensure that we identify with the characters in the stagecoach and see the Apaches at a distance, as a threat from outside the community. Chapter 10 returned to this scene to examine the music and how certain themes are repeated to create different associations with particular characters and types of action. This analysis demonstrated how the music added to the ideological effect of the camerawork. The techniques have all been used in the same scene. But with an altered emphasis, a writer can highlight how various factors contribute to the overall meaning. In this case, both analyses led to the same interpretation of the ideology but an emphasis on different techniques can lead to different interpretations. To round out the analysis we could include the elements of mise-en-scène, editing and the sound effects to evaluate how effectively the scene makes meaning.

Identifying techniques is a vital step in the analytical process. Next, we must take the analysis further and interpret how the techniques work in relation to the development of the narrative.

Examining how the cinematic techniques tell the story

In Chapter 3 we discussed a film's storytelling as 'the narration of cinematic techniques'. We need to return to this idea and apply it to our analysis, to link the forms we learned about in Part II to the techniques we studied in Part III. Ultimately, these two areas are not only connected but dependent on each other. The cinematic techniques tell the story so you cannot talk about the techniques in isolation without considering how they work within the overall structure of the film. A successful film analysis discusses how the story is told and how the different techniques contribute to this goal.

Let's take an example of how the analysis of a particular technique can be linked to a film's storytelling function. In the article '"Gives Good Face": Mr John and the Power of Hats in Film', Drake Stutesman studies the work of the hat designer Mr John, who worked within the studio system during the Classical period of Hollywood. In arguing for the power of Mr John's hat designs as an element of mise-en-scène, she analyzes a particular example, Marlene Dietrich's hats in *Shanghai Express* (1932).

> For the sake of brevity, one analysis of Marlene Dietrich's hats in *Shanghai Express* gives a good example of John's genius and his cinematic dexterity ... . Only two hats appear in the film; each demonstrate ingenious success at coordinating the hat's multi-purpose ... the *Shanghai Express* story can be summed up in four millinery parts: two hats, no hat, return to hat. The

Figure 11.1   *Shanghai Express*, Josef von Sternberg, 1932

first hat introduces the heroine and hints at what is to come, the second hat shows conflict and the heroine's vulnerability and the third, hatlessness, shows the character in extreme danger, both mortal and romantic. The film's resolution, where the lovers rejoin, returns the heroine to the world of hats, as she resumes her original demeanour.

This is a good example of analysis, making the concrete link between the designer's choice of hats and the character's development within the narrative. In a narrative film, all cinematic techniques are also storytelling devices. They guide the viewer's attention to certain details and illuminate particular moments in the story.

Let's take another example of how cinematic technique is fundamentally linked to the story. In *Notorious*, there is a scene towards the end, when Alicia (Ingrid Bergman) finally realizes that her husband Sebastian (Claude Rains) and his mother (Madame Konstantin) are poisoning her. This is a very good scene for examining technique, as the key narrative information does not come from the dialogue but from the other elements, the visual storytelling, how the dialogue is performed and the music. The scene reveals at least four separate pieces of narrative information that are not directly spoken about:

1   The coffee is poisoned.
2   Alicia realizes that Sebastian knows she is a spy.
3   Alicia realizes that Sebastian and his mother are poisoning her.
4   Alicia reacts to this revelation with fear and tries to escape.

Figure 11.2 *Notorious*, Alfred Hitchcock, 1946

This scene communicates these points so that we clearly understand what is happening at all times. After an establishing shot of the room, Sebastian's mother gives Alicia a cup of coffee. The camera lingers on the cup as the mother carries it across to the table near Alicia. Once she places the cup down, the camera tilts up into a close-up of Alicia. This underlines the significance of the cup in this moment; it represents the plot to poison Alicia. As the scene continues, we see a shot of Alicia with the cup in the foreground; the perspective and mise-en-scène make it appear unnaturally large. This use of **depth composition** highlights the relationship between Alicia and the poison, with the character of Doctor Anderson (Reinhold Schünzel) hovering threateningly above her.

The dialogue conveys little narrative information here. Only twice, when Sebastian interrupts the doctor to stop him revealing any information to Alicia, do we get any indication of his motivation and his real purpose in this scene. After the first of these interruptions, we learn that Alicia is becoming aware that something is wrong. In a close-up shot, without moving her head, she moves her eyes slightly to the side, not quite looking in his direction. The staging of this moment, in combination with Ingrid Bergman's performance, alerts the audience to the fact that she now suspects that her husband knows that she is a spy. The next sequence takes the revelation further, when the doctor picks up the wrong coffee cup and both Sebastian and his mother call out to stop him from drinking it. The combination of shots moving from the close-ups on the cups, to the long shot of the mother and son, leave us in no doubt about what is happening.

The editing effectively reveals the next aspect of the plot, which is Alicia's realization that the others have poisoned her coffee. In a shot/reverse shot sequence she looks first at the cup, then at the mother, then at Sebastian. The first shot of this sequence is accompanied by a musical cue that alerts us to pay attention to Alicia's reactions. In addition, the camera movement accentuates the shots of her adversaries as it tracks in on them. This track gives the audience a sense of where her attention is focused and accentuates the moment when she grasps just how much of a threat they are to her.

This scene (like the hangover scene analyzed in Chapter 6) uses subjective, point-of-view camera angles from Alicia's position. She knows about the plot on her life and gets up to leave the room. We see her point of view when she looks at Sebastian and his mother. The lighting creates a silhouette around them and the image is distorted, conveying what she sees in her poisoned state. Throughout the film we identify with Alicia and these cinematic techniques position her as the focus of the scene. Her reaction to the situation is revealed, her fear, her sense of being trapped and her attempt to escape.

Identifying point of view is vital to the process of examining how cinematic techniques communicate a story. Point of view is a fundamental structuring device in a film showing us:

- Which characters are privileged (as with the POV of the white settlers in the chase scene in *Stagecoach*);
- And when and where the viewer sees what the characters cannot.

These are a few examples of how cinematic techniques tell the story. The key to a successful analysis of a film is linking technique to structure in a way that acknowledges that such choices are not arbitrary, but fundamental to the process of filmmaking.

Evaluating the effectiveness of the storytelling techniques

I would say that this scene in *Notorious* is well executed. If I were writing a theoretical-analysis paper, I might not use those exact words, but something like: 'The scene in *Notorious* when Alicia realizes she is being poisoned demonstrates clever and well-executed use of visual storytelling through camera position and angle, movement, mise-en-scène, editing and music.' The point here is that in my writing I have expressed an opinion about my perception of the quality of the filmmaking. I would only make this statement in relation to analysis that demonstrates it.

Like the film review discussed earlier, your response to a film is partly subjective. Your analysis of a film should include an evaluation of how successful the film is in achieving its artistic goals. This evaluation should be grounded in your own analysis of cinematic techniques. In other words, in making an evaluative judgement, you should apply the principles of rhetorical writing and use your analysis as evidence to back up your opinion. Although this is your response to the film, you need to move beyond the simple assertion of 'I liked it' or 'I didn't like it', to relate your evaluation to your understanding of its use of technique.

Interpreting a film

In the previous section we learned that the process of analyzing a film involves multiple levels, from identifying techniques to relating technique to form and structure. Through this, we develop an understanding of how the techniques are used to tell the story. To produce a truly interesting film-analysis essay, you can go even further than this, by examining how the film form and style can also be interpreted on different levels. Beyond the critical-analysis process outlined above, there are further levels of interpretation that you can apply to a film. As we saw at the start of this chapter, there are several methods of writing about film and in this section we will explore how a film can be interpreted in different ways, drawing on a variety of analytical and theoretical traditions in film studies.

In the first part of Chapter 7 we examined the elements of design, using a method that looked at the different layers of meaning that can be attributed to the creative choices of the designers. To briefly review, we saw that a design choice, such as a prop or costume, can be interpreted as having significance on at least five levels: logical, narrative, aesthetic, thematic and ideological. Here we will expand our analysis to include other cinematic techniques, exploring how they create meaning on similar levels. When studying mise-en-scène, we became aware that designers and directors consciously choose the features that they use to communicate multiple ideas. On the other hand, the critics and theorists of film, interpret how effective these techniques are in communicating different levels of meaning. In applying the analysis techniques that we developed in the last section, we can see how we have already utilized some of these concepts. By identifying the cinematic techniques and examining how they tell the story, we have begun to look at the logical and narrative levels. Similarly, the process of evaluating the effectiveness of the techniques involves incorporating aesthetic judgements about the film. We now move on to the thematic and ideological reading of techniques, which relates to how the film communicates ideas and concepts beyond the narrative level, in relation to the context of the world outside the film.

In order to examine these different levels of meaning, let's introduce another set of terms. Exploring a film's meaning in terms of how it tells the story and communicates narrative information can be described as examining the film's **text**. Analyzing a film's text involves a description of the narrative and the identification of techniques. When we start to interpret the deeper meanings of a film on a thematic level, we explore a film's **subtext**. A subtext is made up of the ideas that we can infer from a text, but that are not necessarily overtly stated. This is the first level of interpretation. Finally, in considering how a film can be examined as a reflection of the ideas and beliefs held by a culture, we study a film's ideology. An ideological reading requires the linking of the analysis of the text and subtext to other contextual or background information.

To illustrate this better, here is an example from a film we have been studying.

- The text of *Notorious* tells us the story of the relationship between Alicia and Devlin, how they develop and grow as characters and about their mission to uncover the Nazi plot of Sebastian and his comrades.
- A subtext of *Notorious* relates to Alicia's narrative of redemption. How she is aligned through her father with the Nazis, how she has behaved outside the moral code of society, how her act of sacrifice in spying for the US proves her loyalty and how she wins the love of Devlin.
- There are many different ways in which you can explore the ideology behind a film such as *Notorious*. Modleski's article, analyzed earlier, is a good example of an ideological analysis. She reads the film through feminist theory to illustrate how Alicia undergoes a narrative of redemption for her 'notorious' behaviour so that she can fulfil the conventional woman's role within a romantic couple, 'her place in the patriarchal order'. (61)

Reading and interpreting a film on these various levels, brings us to an important question about the concept of critical practice. In previous chapters we have considered in depth the role of the creative team and its decision-making processes. So the question is this: What influence do the filmmakers have on the levels of meaning that critics and theorists identify in a film? In many ways this is a rhetorical question. It is very hard to gauge which interpretations of films reflect the filmmakers' intentions. But this leads us to another equally crucial question: How do we assess the validity of a given interpretation of a film if we cannot gauge it by the filmmaker's intent? These questions are vital to another aspect of film interpretation that we will look at in a later section, which is the auteur theory. An auteur analysis would contextualize a film in relation to the intentions of its creators. However, interpretation of film, as with many other arts, sometimes involves seeing meanings that are not fully controlled by the film's creators. The role of ideological analysis in the critical-creative process is to understand the larger function of the work of art in the culture of which it is a part. This larger function cannot always be attributed to the intention of the author.

As we can see from the scheme above, ideology is important in the analysis and interpretation of a film. Throughout the previous chapters we returned to this concept. Up to now we have been working with the following definition of ideology, the system or set of beliefs held by a society. These beliefs are reflected in cultural texts such as films. When analyzing a film you can use an ideological approach and see how those ideas or sets of beliefs are represented in a film.

Ideological analyses can incorporate different forms and perspectives. As we explore different levels of interpretation of meaning, we will look at two specific examples of methods of film interpretation. First, we will use a feminist perspective and second, an analysis of the ideologies of race and nationalism. It is vital to realize that these are just two examples of how to apply analysis and interpretation and that you can use a variety of approaches to investigate the different identities and issues that a film can represent or address.

Interpretation of gender identities

Sometimes we come out of a film feeling uncomfortable about the way certain groups or individuals have been represented. Perhaps they were portrayed negatively or were simply one-dimensional. The issue of representation can concern how characters with certain identities are repeatedly stereotyped in films, and how these stereotypes come to be associated with that identity. This interpretation can be applied to identities such as gender, race, region, class, sexuality or disability.

Feminist critics and theorists have produced crucial work in this area, analyzing and interpreting films to understand how certain ideas about women have entered the belief system of our society. Studying films closely, we can see patterns emerging; women's roles often conform to particular types or stereotypes. Women play a variety of characters in films but these roles often reflect a culture's perception of women in society. Feminist criticism explores the diverse ways in which women are presented in film in order to better understand the ideologies underlying gender.

Feminist film theory and criticism, however, goes further than the study of women's characters and roles within narratives. By drawing on **psychoanalytical** concepts, feminist theorists explore how sexism is coded into a film. In other words, feminist theorists explore how film language (the camera, mise-en-scène, sound, editing and music) can express the ideology of patriarchy, the privileging of men within society. For example, in Chapter 6 we mentioned how the repeated use of particular camera positions can serve an ideological function in representing gender. In the section that follows, we will explore this concept in more depth: looking at the way women are physically represented in film.

Women in film

Feminist criticism has explored the representation of women on at least three separate levels:

- The role of women in the narrative of a film;
- Women's physical appearance through the visual scheme of a film;
- How a film communicates with the ideal spectator.

Women and men play different types of roles in narrative film. A classical distinction is that men are active agents in a narrative and women are passive. For example, in Chapter 3 we saw how narrative theorists define character types across different kinds of stories. One of Vladimir Propp's character types, originating from traditional folk tales, is the 'princess'. The princess is not the 'hero', but the prize that the hero wins. Although gender roles have altered over time, some of these gender stereotypes remain relevant to contemporary film. For example, you can see that these gender roles can apply to even recent films, such as *The Lord of the Rings* trilogy (2001–3). The character of Arwen (Liv Tyler) is the classic fairytale princess, the reward for the hero-king Aragorn after he has undergone trials and won the war. The only narrative purpose she truly serves is to be this reward; she does not participate in the quest or the war in any significant way. She is contrasted with the other main woman character, Eowyn (Miranda Otto) who is more active in the narrative; she participates in one of the major battles and rebels against her assigned role as a woman. But even she acts in support of Aragorn, and it is her unrequited love for him that compels her to fight. In a film series with numerous and varied male characters, there are only three women and their roles are limited in the story, which is mostly about the actions of men.

Without oversimplifying our analysis, we can also say that men and women's physical bodies are represented differently in film. In Chapter 6 we saw how camera position could affect how characters are seen. For example, when a character is shown in close-ups, the audience is led to view them in relation to their physical attributes rather than their mental or emotional capacities. Feminist film theory has examined how women's bodies in particular, are represented through a repeated use of **objectified** close-ups of body parts. Women are fragmented into objects, in shots that do not reveal a full figure or a face. This use of camera position conveys a message that these women can be reduced to parts, rather than being seen as whole people. This can be shown in the example that follows.

The third point raised here is how feminist theory talks about the relationship between the film and the viewer. In an influential essay, 'Visual Pleasure in Narrative Cinema', theorist Laura Mulvey suggests that the way classical film language is constructed, speaks to an implied male viewer. In other words, film language assumes that the ideal viewer is male. Since Mulvey published her essay in the mid-1970s, other critics and theorists have debated the idea of the 'male gaze' and questioned how this works in film. From this assumption, theorists have also questioned how women view film if it's true that film language caters to the male gaze. In the following analysis, we will touch on the way that a film can be addressed to an audience of women, yet still show evidence of the male gaze. [As an interesting aside, Laura Mulvey is a critical-theorist-practitioner. Not only did she write important criticism about the way film language works, she also produced film work (in collaboration with Peter Wollen), such as *Riddles of the Sphinx* (1977) that experimented with her theories and tried to disrupt the pleasure of the male gaze. In the next chapter we will return to this idea when we look at the critical practice of feminist filmmakers.]

Gender in Gentlemen Prefer Blondes

Gentlemen Prefer Blondes (1953) provides a classic example of the ways in which women are commonly represented in film. The film tells the story of two showgirls: Lorelei Lee (Marilyn Monroe) who wants to marry a rich man, and Dorothy Shaw (Jane Russell) who wants to 'marry for love'. At the centre of the film is the strong friendship between the two women, a subplot that threatens to overwhelm the main romantic plot. As a musical, the film combines narrative with spectacle; Monroe and Russell sing and perform at different points to accentuate certain emotional and thematic moments.

Monroe and Russell are set up as sexual display for men; they are objectified. This is evident in their roles as nightclub entertainers and in the frequent scenes where they are objects of male **voyeurism**. In one particular scene, they board a ship to travel to France walking through a group of men who stare, comment and then follow them. This is accompanied by a degree of irony; its comedy lies in the excessive presentation of these classic expectations about women. The film also allows the women to play an active role in the narrative. These are characters in control of their story and in control of the men who are their love interests; in a reverse of conventional expectations, they are the pursuers rather than the pursued. Maureen Turim identifies the split between these two poles in the film:

> … an opposition between the sexual display made of these women (their exploitation as objects within the film's narrative and for the film's appeal) and the women's expressed cynicism and cleverness (the satire in which the objects take on the role of critical subjects). This opposition between 'come on' and 'put down' provides the ambiguity which is essential to the ambience of the sophisticated tease. (Turim, 1990: 103)

The female protagonists provide this film with its ambivalence. However, a more classical example of gender roles is evident in the male and female background choruses that appear in two of the musical numbers.

The film features a famous musical sequence, 'Diamonds Are a Girl's Best Friend'; Marilyn Monroe sings and dances accompanied by a group of men. The song articulates her attitude towards money in a glamorous, amusing and entertaining way. The chorus features both men and women dancers, all dressed in a uniform manner. The men offer their hearts to Lorelei, only to be rejected by her. When they offer her diamonds, she is interested. The women of the chorus start as dancing partners for the men. When Lorelei turns and starts dancing and singing the women disappear and the men dance with Lorelei. The women return briefly and surround her as she sings to them, so it appears as if she is giving them advice on gold-digging.

The other women in the scene are even more interesting; they are featured prominently in the set design as light fixtures. Actual women scantily dressed in a sado-masochistic style are fashioned into the set as part of the chandelier. In this scene these women are objectified to the point where

Figure 11.3   *Gentlemen Prefer Blondes*, Howard Hawks, 1953

they literally become objects. The song's theme, and that of the film in general, revolves around women's exchange value in a capitalist society. Lorelei markets herself as a sexual object to be viewed as a performer, and to be purchased, for the right price, and, finally bought through marriage. The background set accentuates these themes by making a literal visual reference to women as objects and as commodities.

There is also an interesting scene that shows men represented in an objectified manner. One song-and-dance number, 'Is There Anyone Here for Love?', features Jane Russell singing while a group of male Olympic athletes work out around her. This song represents Dorothy's difference from Lorelei. Her solo song is about her search for love and the scene shows her actively and aggressively pursuing men. The men are dressed in flesh-coloured shorts and are shot in an objectified manner, represented purely for their sexual attraction. The men pay little attention to Dorothy and interact more with each other, allowing for a **homoerotic** reading of the scene. Both the male and female background performers in these two scenes are objectified, with one crucial difference. The male characters are active. They are doing something and the camera lingers on their muscular physiques. The women in the chandelier are stationary; they don't do anything and are probably restricted in their movement by the light fixture. This is a key stereotype of gender representation; men are active and women are passive.

Okay, I'm going to throw the proverbial spanner into the works. As an academic film critic writing in the feminist tradition, I can also say, I love this film. And I am not the only feminist critic to make this assertion. Lucie Arbuthnot and Gail Seneca have confronted a similar problem in their article 'Pretext and Text in *Gentlemen Prefer Blondes*':

As feminists, we experience a constant and wearying alienation from the dominant culture. The misogyny of popular art, music, theatrical arts, and film interferes with our pleasure in them … Howard Hawks' *Gentlemen Prefer Blondes* … is clearly a product of the dominant culture. Yet we enjoy the film immensely.

[…]For *Gentlemen Prefer Blondes* presents women who not only resist male objectification, but also cherish deeply their connections with each other. The friendship between two strong women, Monroe and Russell, invites the female viewer to join them, through identification, in valuing other women and ourselves. (Arbuthnot and Seneca, 1990: 112–13)

As feminist film criticism gives us the tools to analyze the sexist representations of the Classical Hollywood system, it also allows us to ask other questions. *Gentlemen Prefer Blondes* classically represents women in a sexist manner, making them appear as sexualized objects. But this happens in a film with a target audience of women. As feminist analysis developed, it opened up debates about how different audiences respond to a film. Feminist theory forces us to question what we enjoy and why. Thus, our interpretation of this film must take into account what it is we enjoy about the way in which the women are portrayed in the narrative. Both Jane Russell and Marilyn Monroe are exciting performers to watch and their friendship in the film is as important as, if not more important than, the conventional romances. This relationship can also be open to a homo-erotic reading. Without ever fully challenging the sexist system in which their characters exist, they appeal to women in the audience because of their resourcefulness, playfulness and the way that they ultimately manipulate the situation to attain their goals.

Here we have seen some of the ways that you can apply a textual analysis to the interpretation of gender identities in film. In doing so, we have focused on a mainstream film made within the Classical Hollywood studio system. Critical-practice filmmakers in the feminist tradition have produced work that has challenged these forms of representation. In the next chapter, we will return to these issues and look at how filmmakers have applied a critical-practice approach to explore issues of gender in their creative work.

The ideologies of race

Just as films can be a reflection of certain ideas about gender relations, they can also demonstrate the construction of different racial, ethnic and national identities. An important area of film analysis and interpretation examines how certain films and film genres reflect ideas about race. We have already touched on this in Chapters 6 and 10 when we examined the ideology underlying the chase scene from *Stagecoach*, and how it represents the white and Native American characters differently.

In analyzing a film through the ideologies of race, it is useful to consider the ways in which other critics and theorists have examined this issue. Theorists have looked at racial representation using a number of different approaches. A key concept in the discussion of racial representation is that of the stereotype. Stereotypes are broad generalized images of given character types. Chapter 3 introduced the idea that characters often exist in types, rather than being individuals and tend to serve a general purpose in the development of the narrative. Later in this section we will discuss *Raiders of the Lost Ark* (1981) which is based around character types that are fairly common across different films; Indiana Jones (Harrison Ford) is a classical male action hero and his companion Marion (Karen Allen) is the female **ingénue**, the love interest/damsel-in-distress. These are common types and audiences for popular mainstream films are used to identifying with characters like these.

Beyond the character type, the stereotype imposes a limited view of a character based on race, class, nationality, disability, sexuality or gender. Stereotypes are complex, but frequently involve negative concepts being attributed to characters in a specific group. Our previous study of the Apaches of *Stagecoach* showed how they were stereotyped as a general threat rather than individualized in any way.

Analyzing race

Theories of racial representation have developed concepts other than the stereotype. For example, the critic James Snead provides a useful model for discussing race and representation in his book

White Screens, Black Images: Hollywood from the Dark Side. He introduces three ways in which characters are defined through race: mythification, marking and omission.

- Mythification is the term for an idea we have already discussed in relation to *Stagecoach*. This is the way that certain racial groups are repeatedly represented over several different films, becoming part of and reinforcing the racial myth. Thus, the lack of close-ups and identification with the Apaches in *Stagecoach* forms part of the racial myth of the Western.

- Marking refers to the process of using aspects of mise-en-scène to clearly indicate a character's racial affiliation. This is a complex concept but basically infers that classical mainstream film uses a visual shorthand to express the characteristics of a race. In Classical Hollywood cinema, marking even went as far as having light-skinned African-American actors wear make-up to appear darker on the screen. An example of marking occurs in *Stagecoach* with the Mexican character, Chris (Chris-Pin Martin), who runs one of the inns where the stagecoach stops. His appearance is particularly dishevelled. His hair is untidy, his clothes don't fit and he speaks in awkward, broken English. His appearance marks him as racially different to the community of the coach. Like the Apaches, whose appearance leaves no doubt about their race, Chris is marked as racially different to the white stagecoach passengers.

- Omission refers to the practice of excluding racial difference in certain narrative situations. For example, in the imagination of Hollywood of 1939, the community in the stagecoach represents a cross-section of American society. Yet they are all white. Westerns have often

Figure 11.4 *Stagecoach*, John Ford, 1939

been criticized for neglecting the historical reality of African-American cowboys or the integration of Mexicans into the society of the time.

In applying this model to *Stagecoach*, we could say that Native Americans are *mythified*; Mexican Americans are *marked*; and African Americans are *omitted*.

Race in Raiders of the Lost Ark

Snead's model is only one way of interpreting racial identity in film, but it includes many of the crucial concepts. Let's apply these ideas to another example of the way mainstream film portrays racial and ethnic difference. *Raiders of the Lost Ark* is a popular adventure story that takes the audience on an exotic and wild journey through many different countries in search of archaeological treasures. It is a useful film to study when examining mainstream Hollywood's perception of Third World cultures. Its protagonist, Indiana Jones, is a conventional action hero. This character's origins are in comic books, earlier serial films and colonial adventure novels (such as H. Rider Haggard's *King Solomon's Mines*). These stories feature similar characteristics and use the same colonial backdrops, with 'exotic' locations and stereotypical 'native' characters. *Raiders of the Lost Ark* becomes part of the process of mythification of these colonial images.

'Indy' is capable of outwitting many opponents; his spirit of adventure and rugged masculinity will always win the day. The film's cinematic style ensures that the audience identifies completely

Figure 11.5   *Raiders of the Lost Ark*, Steven Spielberg, 1981

with his character. Indy travels to several countries, Peru, Nepal and Egypt. So what does *Raiders of the Lost Ark* tell us about Third World cultures? I can think of many answers to this question and none of them complimentary! Here is a summary of the film's underlying assumptions:

- Third World people aren't very clever; one western hero can easily outsmart them.
- Third World people are expendable. It is actually considered funny when they are killed, as with the scene when he shoots the swordsman in the market.
- Third World countries have exotic treasures that can easily be stolen; this is not even considered a crime.
- Third World countries provide a backdrop where American heroes can act out chase scenes and fantasy fights.
- Most Third World countries are the same, with only minor differences in iconography and mise-en-scène. There is an unnerving similarity between the different cultures that Indiana encounters.

These assumptions are all part of the colonial myth, leading the audience to identify with the white male hero and to see all the other characters only in relation to his adventures.

So what is omitted in this narrative? Ella Shohat and Robert Stam interpret this film and its sequels in their book, *Unthinking Eurocentrism*:

> The series assumes an uncontested empire, with no trace of any viable anticolonial opposition … . In the world of Indiana Jones, Third World cultures are synopsized as theme park clichés drawn from the orientalist repertoire: India is all dreamy spirituality, as in the Hegelian account; Shanghai is all gongs and rickshaws. Third World landscapes become the stuff of dreamy adventure. (Shohat and Stam, 1994: 124)

Thus, part of the omission here is the context and culture of the countries represented and in particular, their relationship to the colonizing countries and their struggle against imperial domination.

Using the methods of textual analysis that we have learned, we can look more closely at an individual scene to consider how certain techniques can support this interpretation of the film. In this scene, Indy and his companion Marion, have arrived in Cairo and are attacked in the market by a group of Egyptians working for the Nazis. There is a fight and a chase. We first see the German opponent arrive in the market, flanked by a group of fighters. This shot is accompanied by an ominous musical stinger. Although not in military uniform, these characters are dressed the same, in clothes that quickly evoke the idea of threat. They have a black cloth wrapped around their heads, over white clothing, affording them a disturbing look, making their faces comparatively dark, and concealing their features. Their appearance is evidence of racial marking; their covered faces mark them as anonymous and expendable.

As the scene continues, the group attacks Indy and Marion. The fight is played out as caricature. The music is light, and leads to the action feeling closer to slapstick comedy than real violence. The Egyptian fighters are particularly incompetent and are easily outwitted into stabbing and shooting each other by Indy's slight twists and turns. Marion beats her opponents ineptly with a tray (playing into her gender stereotype as the weak female). These opponents go beyond *Stagecoach*'s Apaches in being expendable, faceless and devalued as people. This stylized fight style is characteristic of the film as a whole. Yet there are differences between the enemies based on race. Indy's European adversaries are more humanized. Although numerous German soldiers are mowed down in the background of later scenes, the featured fights with Germans show them as individualized foes.

Just as in the scene from *Stagecoach*, we can see how the camera position garners sympathy for certain characters. How sympathetic is a close-up of a covered face? In this scene there is only one close-up of an Egyptian pursuing Marion. This close-up of the threatening opponent is even more troubling than the close-ups of the *Stagecoach* Apaches. The camera angle is low and the framing accentuates the character's teeth and the knife in his hand; the image is cartoon-like in its caricature. The character laughs ominously and there is nothing in this image to evoke sympathy or identification. This scene analysis reveals how a film can rely on racist stereotypes and assumptions.

Interpreting a film in this manner can demonstrate how mainstream culture views difference. This understanding can contribute to a critical dialogue about the role of film in culture. Such an awareness of the ideological function of film images can also be an asset for the critical practitioner when approaching the creation of their own work. Analyzing mainstream Hollywood's representation of difference is only one half of the study of the representation of difference. In the next chapter we will revisit this issue when we look at the critical practice of filmmakers from Third World countries.

Relating a film to its context of creation

In studying these two examples of ideological interpretation, we are relying on an understanding of the conventions and belief systems of the world outside the film. Film interpretation should also relate the film to the specific context in which it was made. This means going beyond a simple analysis of the film in terms of its own techniques, to draw on the interrelationship between different films and other aspects of culture. It is useful to remember that films are made by people, who are located in certain countries, under particular social, political and economic conditions. To truly interpret a film and to understand how it reflects ideology, you need to be able to relate that film to its context of production. The following section looks at two methods of achieving this: analyzing the film as the work of its creator (usually the director) – auteurist analysis; and analyzing the film in relation to where and when it was made – a **national-cinema** approach. In addition to these two examples, you can also investigate the film in regard to **genre**.

Auteur analysis

When we think of art, we also often think of artists, painters such as Picasso or writers such as Shakespeare. With film, this question is more complicated as many people are involved in the creation of a film. The 'auteur' theory developed as part of the process of validating film as an art, by associating it with the ideas and expressions of an individual artist. When contextualizing a film in relation to auteur theory, you would study the work of a film's director, looking for connections and similarities between their various films. Often auteur theory was applied to filmmakers working within the commercial world of Classical Hollywood, a system in which marketability was usually seen as taking priority over individual artistry. In using the auteur approach, critics searched for elements of style that distinguished an individual director's work from the rest.

Figure 11.6 *Citizen Kane*, Orson Welles, 1941

For example, Orson Welles has been greatly respected as an artist working within the commercial system of Classical Hollywood. After his first film *Citizen Kane* (1941), Welles did not have the financial support or creative freedom to make the films that he wished. His second film, *The Magnificent Ambersons* (1942), was severely edited by the studio after an unsuccessful preview screening. Yet over the years *Citizen Kane*, which was not a commercial success at the time it was made, came to be considered a great film. This led many writers and critics to look at the work of Welles as an example of the work of an auteur of the cinema, whose artistic genius could rise above the limitations placed on him by financial constraints and studio practices.

Another example of an auteur analysis might investigate the work of a filmmaker such as John Ford (director of *Stagecoach* and *The Searchers*, 1956), tracing connections between the films he directed. For example, in Chapter 6 we looked at the creative use of frame-within-a-frame composition in *The Searchers*. He uses this technique in other films as well, and it is one of the stylistic features that an auteur analyst might use to interpret his work. An analysis of the work of Ford could also examine other elements of his filmmaking style or his focus on particular themes and include:

- His use of certain character types;
- How music communicates narrative information in his films;
- The struggle of the individual against the community;
- The changes brought about by the growth of towns and settlements on the Western frontier.

We can see these last two themes in both *Stagecoach* and *The Searchers*. Both films feature a central conflict between the community dynamic associated with towns and settlements and the individual who lives outside the community's laws. These themes are even more strongly evident in *The Man Who Shot Liberty Valance* (1962) that follows the progress of a town from lawlessness to order, as the territory gains statehood. A comparison between these films would trace the thematic and stylistic continuities in the filmmaker's work.

National cinemas

Ford's films illustrate the fact that the Western genre involves a particularly American style of filmmaking. The colonization of the American West is part of the myth of American culture. Thus, studies of the Western become part of another methodology of film interpretation: the national-cinema approach. Categorizing a film according to the context of its production in a particular country can yield insights into what it is trying to communicate. Critics who study national cinemas must also relate film production to a wider understanding of how national identities are constructed. It is often too easy to assume that the country in which we live has a stable national character. Yet social theorist Benedict Anderson (1983) has used the term 'imagined community' to describe nations, reminding us that our national identity is a construction and not an automatic given fact.

Once national identity has been recognized as a construction, we can begin to understand that film is an element of culture that can be part of that construction of identity. Interestingly, it is often in times of national crisis that film can be most clearly seen to relate to the definition of a national culture. For example, many studies of British film focus on the World War II period as during this time British film began to reflect more of a national identity. Many films of this era represented groups of British people uniting to work across traditional divisions of class and regional background in the common war effort. Laurence Olivier's *Henry V* (1944), adapted from Shakespeare, revisited the time of a successful British martial campaign in continental Europe. Released as Britain and the Allies were preparing for the D-Day invasion of France, it tells the story of a historical battle on French soil in which the English were triumphant against all odds. It is evident that the film relates to the national concerns of Britain at the time.

Indian national cinema in the 1950s affords another interesting reading in this approach. This period followed Indian independence from British imperialism. During this time India was defining itself as a nation state, uniting different language groups and regional identities into the new national identity of India. *Mother India* (1955) relates an allegorical tale about an Indian

Figure 11.7   *Henry V*, Laurence Olivier, 1944

Figure 11.8 *Mother India*, Mehboob Khan, 1955

woman who overcomes numerous obstacles within her village. As the title suggests, the main character signifies the resilience of the new nation of India.

Analyzing your own creative practice

Part of the critical-practice approach to film-making includes being able to think, talk and write about your own creative practice and to apply some of the techniques used to analyze a film to the task of evaluating, interpreting and contextualizing your own work. This section is at the end of this chapter because all the analytical and interpretive tools laid out so far can be brought to bear on the process of self-reflection and evaluation.

Just as there are many ways of writing about film, people have taken various approaches when writing about their creative practice. Filmmakers such as John Boorman in *Money into Light* or Isaac Julien in *Diary of a Young Soul Rebel* have chosen a diary format, with the goal of exploring how their creative process evolves over the course of production. A much more concise form is an artist statement, which often accompanies experimental works of films and videos shown in gallery contexts. An artist statement is often fairly personal and relates the context in which the work can be viewed, introducing some of the thematic concerns that underlie the creative process. Filmmakers often elaborate on their work in interviews or short articles in review magazines, explaining elements of the film, aspects of behind-the-scenes production or part of the context and thinking behind the film. This reflection on practice is also found in DVD commentaries and can combine background commentary with thematic insights. In the following chapter we will look at critical practitioners, such as the Soviet director Sergei Eisenstein, who write theoretically about film as well as exploring their ideas in creative form. It is this last form of writing that is perhaps the most instructive for the critical-practice approach to writing about your work.

A key to producing a successful critically reflective analysis of your creative practice is to apply the principles that you would use when writing about any other type of film as well as the understanding and insight into the techniques that you gain from the process of production. To conclude this chapter, then, let's look at the areas discussed earlier and relate them to writing about your own work. Here I would like to introduce a new concept for the process of writing about film and that is the idea of reflection. Writing about your own work requires a different discipline as you need to reflect on something that is close to you, your own ideas and your expression of creativity.

As with other forms of writing, description should be limited in critical reflection. It is important not to over-describe your work, but to allow it to speak for itself. There is an additional danger here as description includes the narrative of your production process. As the filmmaker you will be quite involved in the story of the creation of your film and the obstacles you had to overcome, the technical accomplishments and the creative inspirations you experienced. However, this narration needs to be treated with caution so as not to overwhelm the analytical and reflective aspects; the analysis and reflection is more engaging and enlightening to the reader and will demonstrate your thought process as a critical practitioner.

Analysis is key to an effective critical reflection, considering all the cinematic techniques – cinematography, mise-en-scène, sound, editing and music – to explore how effective the creative decision-making has been within the final product. Thus, all the critical tools discussed so far can be brought to bear on both the final project and the process of production. In this you can investigate your creative choices and argue for how the style and technique of your work integrates with its themes and content. You should be wary of rationalizing or justifying your work in an attempt to avoid criticism. It is more helpful to welcome and assess the validity of any critical responses as part of the creative dialogue.

With evaluation, one method is to judge the effectiveness of your choices against the criteria you set for yourself. In other words, has your project achieved its goals? It is probable that you are not always the best person to evaluate the effectiveness of your own practice. It is important to seek audience feedback to recognize how different viewers respond to the film.

In the process of creation, you will have engaged in different levels of research, exploring stylistic inspirations as well as aspects of content. The critical reflection is a forum to elaborate on this research and to detail what you learned throughout the creative process. In investigating your research process, it is important to engage with the concepts underlying the choice of both form and content. Finally, it is vital that a successful critical reflection contextualizes your work as part of a larger system of representation. In other words, your own creative practice, like all other media representations functions ideologically. Understanding the ideological implications of your representations may be the hardest aspiration, but it leads to the most successful form of critical practice.

Summary and key questions

This chapter has delineated the different methods and approaches of writing about film. When preparing to analyze a film, you need to consider a series of questions about the type of writing you are undertaking and then address questions about the film itself.

- What type of writing are you trying to accomplish?
  - A review;
  - A historical-research paper;
  - An analytical, interpretive essay;
  - A theoretical paper;
  - A critical reflection on your creative process.
- Have you identified the cinematic techniques used in the film?
- Has your essay related these stylistic techniques to the development of the story or the presentation of the content?

- Has your analysis included an evaluation of the effectiveness of the style and technique?
    - o Is your evaluation supported by your analysis?
- How have you approached interpreting the film?
    - o Are you studying the ideology?
    - o What method are you using: analysis of gender, race, class, sexuality, national identity or disability?
    - o How are you relating the film to the context of its creation?
- Are you writing about your own creative work?
    - o How have you dealt with problems of creative reflection?
    - o Have you analyzed your techniques?
    - o Have you evaluated the effectiveness of your work against the criteria you set for yourself?
    - o Have you placed your production within the context of a system of representation?

Want to learn more?

Think about this ...

Critical analysis

   Objective: To critically analyze the use of cinematic techniques.

Choose a film that you are familiar with and watch it again paying close attention to all the cinematic techniques. Can you identify how they are used to tell the story or express the content?

Try this ...

Ideological frameworks

   Objective: To contextualize a film in relation to larger cultural issues and interpret the various levels of meaning and ideas represented.
   You will need: This is a written exercise.

Using the examples in the chapter as models, try writing an interpretation of a film based on its representation of different identities. Explore how a film deals with one of the following: gender, race, class, sexuality, disability, religion, national or regional identity.

Critique your own work

   Objective: To produce a critical reflection on your own work.
   You will need: This is a written exercise.

Try developing a critical reflection on a piece of your own creative work. Apply the relevant techniques of analysis to your project. Test the work with an audience and gauge their response. Can you contextualize your work within the larger context of representation?

Further reading

There are a couple of good books that guide you through the process of writing specifically about film. See Tim Corrigan, *A Short Guide to Writing about Film*, or John E. Moscowitz, *Critical Approaches to Writing about Film*. For an interesting introduction to how gender roles are visually constructed, see John Berger, *Ways of Seeing* and for examples of engagement with feminist film theory see the edited collections Constance Penley, *Feminism and Film Theory* or Patricia Erens, *Issues in Feminist Film Criticism*. For further discussion of the interpretation of racial identities, see James Snead, *White Screens, Black Images*. To expand your knowledge of film writing, you can explore a variety of sources, such as the journals *Sight and Sound* and *Senses of Cinema*, which mix review-style writing with longer essays. Other journals focus on different types of research. *Screen* and *Camera Obscura* are theoretical and critical; *Cinema Journal* is both critical and historical; and *Film and History* is grounded in historical analysis. *The Journal of Media Practice* is a good place to start to investigate critical-practice writing. See the next chapter for examples of practitioners who also write about their own work.

Films studied in this chapter

Batman Returns 1992 Tim Burton (director)
Citizen Kane 1941 Orson Welles (director)
Eternal Sunshine of the Spotless Mind 2004 Michel Gondry (director)
Gentlemen Prefer Blondes 1953 Howard Hawks (director)
Henry V 1944 Laurence Olivier (director)
The Lord of the Rings 2001–3 Peter Jackson (director)
The Magnificent Ambersons 1942 Orson Welles (director)
The Man Who Shot Liberty Valance 1962 John Ford (director)
Mother India 1955 Mehboob Khan (director)
Notorious 1946 Alfred Hitchcock (director)
Raiders of the Lost Ark 1981 Steven Spielberg (director)
Riddles of the Sphinx 1977 Laura Mulvey and Peter Wollen (directors)
The Searchers 1956 John Ford (director)
Shanghai Express 1932 Josef von Sternberg (director)
Stagecoach 1939 John Ford (director)

Other examples to explore

Critical, theoretical or historical analysis can be applied to any film. The films mentioned in other chapters all provide good examples on which to practise these analytical skills.

Critical Practice in Action

Learning objectives

After completing this chapter, you will be able to:

- Apply the concept of critical practice to the work of specific filmmakers;
- Recognize critical-practice models from different periods of film history;
- Relate the work of critical practitioners to your own creative and critical process.

Critical practitioners

Up to this point we have been engaging with a critical-practice approach to filmmaking. In this chapter, we will see how different filmmakers have integrated this approach into their work by introducing some key critical-practice filmmakers and movements from different points in film history. Critical practitioners come from a variety of filmmaking styles and traditions but can be united through their commitment to integrating practice with theoretical issues and engaging with critical thinking about film. Some of the practitioners we will discuss are critics as well as filmmakers and some incorporate their critical thinking into their art. These are influential filmmakers whose work has inspired creative and critical dialogue.

To understand critical-practice filmmaking better, we will consider examples from the following movements:

- The Soviet montage theorists;
- The filmmakers of the French New Wave;
- The Third Cinema movement;
- Feminist critical practice;
- The New Queer Cinema movement;
- Critical practice in popular 'cult' film.

The integration of theory with practice links these movements and although they use different styles and techniques, they have some general aspects in common.

- Critical-practice films are often stylistically innovative. These filmmakers experiment with technique in order to challenge conventional film language and their films use alternative storytelling, editing, mise-en-scène and camerawork to explore the relationship between film style and thematic content.
- Critical practitioners work to engage their audiences actively so that the viewer is inspired to think and debate the issues raised in the film. In the examples that follow, we will see several of the techniques that filmmakers use to disrupt audience passivity. The filmmakers often want the viewer to participate in a theoretical and critical dialogue with the work.
- One such technique that recurs in the work of critical practitioners is reflexivity. This is the incorporation into the film of an awareness of the filmmaking process. In other words, critical-practice films frequently contain references and allusions to their own process of creation, reminding viewers that they are watching a film. In this way, the viewer is persuaded to think more critically about the filmmaking process.

With these general characteristics in mind, let's examine the work of representative critical practitioners and the contexts in which they produced their work.

The critical practice of the Soviet montage theoriests

We concluded Chapter 9 with an examination of montage as a concept and editing style. We saw how montage theory was a product of a certain time and place: the Soviet Union in the 1920s. The filmmaker-theorists who developed these ideas were excellent models of early critical practice, theorists as well as practitioners. The most well known were Lev Kuleshov, Dziga Vertov, Sergei Eisenstein and Vsevolod Pudovkin. Many of their theories were developed from experiments in practice; their ideas and their films were inextricably linked.

The context of montage

As we saw in Chapter 5, modernism was an important movement in art and culture in the early twentieth century. The Soviet montage theorists were strongly influenced by modernism, in that their experimentation with film concerned the form as well as the content. An understanding of montage becomes easier if we remember that this was the silent era. Montage carried extra visual meaning when dialogue was not an option.

It is useful to consider the context in which montage theories and practices developed. The Soviet montage theorists were working in the period following the Russian Revolution of 1917, which had brought about radical political and social change. Later this movement would reach a crisis point under the repressive regime of Joseph Stalin. But in its early days there was a tremendous sense of optimism and this feeling was manifested in artistic practice. Film in particular was seen as a way to reach a largely illiterate rural population and there was increasing experimentation with its form and its power to express intellectual and social ideas and to inspire change. This desire to use cinema for social change was not limited to the content of the films but also applied to their form.

Montage theory was inspired by a combination of radical political thought and modernist experimental techniques. The Soviet filmmakers rejected the use of film as purely an entertainment medium. The tension and interest in the debates on montage lie in the conflict over the best method of communicating to the widest possible audience. Should film use the seductive techniques of the entertainment style or the radical experimentation of conflicting montage that calls upon the audience to actively engage with the art? This debate was put to an end in the political climate of the Stalinist Soviet Union in 1935 when 'socialist realism' – a conventional realist form of filmmaking – was declared to be the official aesthetic policy of the Soviet Union. At this point, the work of montage theorists was condemned as elitist. Despite this forced end to the movement, the debates around montage and the influences of these theories continue to be very significant in critical thinking about film.

The Kuleshov experiments

A key figure at this time was Lev Kuleshov. Although Kuleshov's films have not garnered the same respect as those of other directors, his theories provided a basis on which those others developed their work. His best-known films are silent: *The Extraordinary Adventures of Mr. West in the Land of the Bolsheviks* (1924) and *By the Law* (1926). They deal with the socialist revolution but with a lighter comic tone than the canonical films of Eisenstein and Pudovkin. Another of Kuleshov's great innovations was founding what is believed by many to be the world's first film school. In this learning environment, he conducted early experiments on the effects of film technique on audiences. Kuleshov shot an image of an actor's face, with a neutral expression and made multiple copies of the same shot. He then edited it together with different shots following, for example, a bowl of soup or a funeral procession. When shown to an audience, viewers believed that the actor's reactions were related to the shot that followed. In other words, when it was shown the sequence with the bowl of soup, the test audience claimed that the actor looked hungry. Conversely when it saw the funeral, it claimed that the actor appeared sad. These experiments affirmed the power of editing to create meaning beyond the individual shot, through the combination of images in conjunction with each other.

The '**Kuleshov effect**' is the term given to this concept. Exact information about Kuleshov's experiments is no longer available as the film and the empirical data collected have been lost and in their place are legends and secondhand accounts. However, the ideas can still be useful for thinking about film editing and for understanding the basic principles of montage. The combination of images can produce meanings beyond that of the individual shots. The theories and practices of montage originate from this. These ideas were then developed in interesting ways by other filmmakers.

Eisenstein and Pudovkin

Montage developed in part out of a debate between two of the principal directors of the era: Sergei Eisenstein and Vsevolod Pudovkin. On the one hand, Eisenstein argued for the radical use of montage editing to create meaning. On the other hand, Pudovkin was more conventional in his approach, arguing for the use of editing in the service of the film's story.

Pudovkin believed that individual shots should be combined to support the overall goal of the film to communicate the story. For him, the individual shots are key. Then these are brought together to construct a coherent whole. Each shot is a link in a chain, or to use another metaphor, a brick in the construction of a wall. This is in line with the conventional uses of editing in classical narrative filmmaking. Pudovkin explains this in his book, *Film Technique*:

The film technician, in order to secure the greatest clarity, emphasis, and vividness, shoots the scene in separate pieces and, joining them and showing them, directs the attention of the spectator to the separate elements, compelling him to see as the attentive observer saw. From the above it is clear the manner in which editing can even work upon the emotions. Imagine to yourself the excited observer of some rapidly developing scene. His agitated glance is thrown rapidly from one spot to another. If we imitate this glance with the camera we get a series of pictures, rapidly alternating pieces, creating a stirring scenario editing-construction. (1959: 42)

Pudovkin's theories can be seen in his films, i.e. as a critical practitioner, his theoretical ideas are demonstrated in practice. In the next section we will look at how these ideas are realized in his film, *The End of St. Petersburg* (1927).

Eisenstein, however, believed that montage should be based on the conflict between shots and between the visual elements within each shot. As he argues:

The shot is by no means an *element* of montage.
The shot is a montage *cell* ... .
By what, then, is montage characterized and, consequently, its cell – the shot?
By collision. By the conflict of two pieces in opposition to each other. By conflict. By collision. (Eisenstein, 1977: 37)

In practice, Pudovkin's filmmaking was more conventional. In contrast, the montage sequences in Eisenstein's films are more radical and innovative and demonstrate a filmmaking style that was challenging to the audience and visually complex. Eisenstein summarizes his debate with Pudovkin in an article 'A Dialectic Approach to Film Form':

To determine the nature of montage is to solve the specific problem of cinema. The earliest conscious film-makers, and our first film theoreticians, regarded montage as a means of description by placing single shots one after the other like building-blocks. The movement within these building-block shots, and the consequent length of the component pieces, was then considered as rhythm.
A completely false concept! ...
According to this definition, shared even by Pudovkin as a theoretician, montage is the means of unrolling an idea with the help of single shots ... . In my opinion, however, montage is an idea that arises from the collision of independent shots –shots even opposite to one another ... (Eisenstein, 1977: 48)

This quotation shows the influence of the Marxist concept of **dialectics** on Eisenstein's thinking. Marx adopted this idea from the philosopher Hegel and Eisenstein develops it as a principle in his theory of montage. This idea is that the conflict of opposing forces will come together to forge a new force. To use Hegel's terms, a thesis and an antithesis combine to create a synthesis, which then becomes the thesis in a continuing cycle. In Marxist thought this basic conflict is reproduced in political struggles; the large sweeps of historical change follow this pattern. Applying this concept to the practice of film editing can lead to interesting results. The juxtaposition of two visual images produces a third, independent meaning that forms the basis for a continuing pattern of development. For example, in the Odessa Steps sequence of *Battleship Potemkin* (1925) (see Chapter 9), when a woman is shot in the eye we do not see the shot, just a cut from the woman's face before the gunshot, to her face after. It is the combination of the two images that creates in the audience's mind the understanding of the action, without ever showing the moment of violence.

For Eisenstein, the conflict between the shots was as important as the content of the shots themselves. He theorized this conflict on a number of levels. Conflict can be produced between different visual elements in the composition, or movement within an individual shot. Thus the principles of framing and composition that we studied in Chapter 6 can be developed to create images that stress conflict and dynamism. This is then extended to the juxtaposition of shots. In practice, Eisenstein's montage sequences often feature rapid cutting, a disruption of temporal or spatial continuity, conflicting movement, often originating from various sources, and an intense sense of rhythm and pacing.

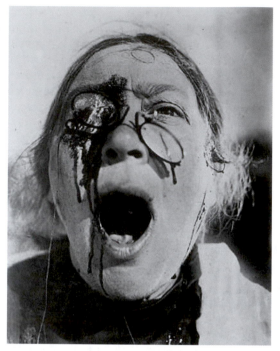

Figure 12.1 *Battleship Potemkin*, Sergei Eisenstein, 1925

Montage in practice: The End of St. Petersburg

In 1927 both Eisenstein and Pudovkin were commissioned to create films to celebrate the tenth anniversary of the Bolshevik Revolution that brought about the birth of the Soviet Union. Eisenstein produced *October*, a significant film, demonstrating complex montage techniques. Pudovkin's film was *The End of St. Petersburg*, a film that clearly integrates montage principles into its filmmaking style. Despite the disagreements in the written debates between Pudovkin and Eisenstein, their styles were sometimes similar, and *The End of St. Petersburg* demonstrates both Pudovkin's, and many of Eisenstein's, ideas in action.

The film is an epic. Its narrative is complex, featuring many characters and large-scale battle scenes. At the start a young man and his mother move from the country to St Petersburg looking for work. He finds employment at a factory where the regular workers are on strike but comes to feel solidarity with his exploited comrades. War is then declared and the story follows the struggles of the soldiers, ending with the Revolution and the founding of Leningrad: this is the 'end of St Petersburg', as the city is renamed after the revolutionary leader Lenin. In choosing to focus on the story of an individual character, who is a representative of the struggles of the workers, Pudovkin differs from Eisenstein. In *October*, Eisenstein chose to represent the group, without singling out an individual protagonist. This is a way in which Pudovkin's work is more conventional narrative-wise than that of Eisenstein.

Early in the film, the main character goes to the factory to try to get his friend released, the friend having been arrested after the hero informed on him. The hero gets in a fight and ends up in the police station where he is beaten. The sequence in which he is knocked down by a police officer demonstrates the complexity and intensity of the montage style. Like the gunshot in Eisenstein's 'Odessa Steps', the actual violence is not shown, but evoked through the combination of shots. The sequence features mainly close-ups, starting, and later returning, to the officer giving instructions. We then see two close-ups of the assailant: his face and his hands as he takes off his gloves in preparation. The five shots that follow intercut between the hero struggling against his attacker, shot from both in front of and behind him, showing his bound hands. In this moment the action on the screen reflects the dynamism of the editing, with effective use made of the practice of cutting on action discussed in Chapter 9. The shots cut just at the moment when the assailant's fist would strike the victim, making the cut feel like the actual point of physical

Figure 12.2 *The End of St. Petersburg,* Vsevolod Pudovkin, 1927

Figure 12.3 *The End of St. Petersburg,* Vsevolod Pudovkin, 1927

Figure 12.4 *The End of St. Petersburg,* Vsevolod Pudovkin, 1927

Figure 12.5 *The End of St. Petersburg,* Vsevolod Pudovkin, 1927

Figure 12.6   *The End of St. Petersburg,*
Vsevolod Pudovkin, 1927

Figure 12.7   *The End of St. Petersburg,*
Vsevolod Pudovkin, 1927

Figure 12.8   *The End of St. Petersburg,*
Vsevolod Pudovkin, 1927

Figure 12.9   *The End of St. Petersburg,*
Vsevolod Pudovkin, 1927

contact. There follows a **medium shot**, showing the attack through the actions of the assailant, ending with the victim on the floor, first in medium shot, then in close-up. The spatial relations remain clear; the main character is identifiable throughout. Yet the fast-paced editing creates a strong sense of violence. The montage adeptly evokes suspense and dramatic tension.

A later sequence shows another principle of montage at work. In the war scenes, Pudovkin recreates moments of epic action, revealing the suffering of Russian soldiers in the violence and destruction of World War I. However, his aim is to show the connection between the destruction caused by war and the profiteering of the city, making the film a direct critique of capitalism. As in the earlier example, we see the effective use of movement within the frame and cutting on movement between the shots. The motion of the crowds and the running soldiers creates a forceful sequence, building in tension and emotionally expressing its political message. The sequence cuts between two spaces that have no spatial, temporal or narrative connection, but have a

Figure 12.10 *The End of St. Petersburg,*
Vsevolod Pudovkin, 1927

Figure 12.11 *The End of St. Petersburg,*
Vsevolod Pudovkin, 1927

thematic or intellectual relationship. Thus, it makes a visual connection between the destruction of the war and the corrupt economic system.

These sequences of fast-paced montage are emblematic of the early Soviet era. They demonstrate critical-practice experiments in style that still influence filmmaking today. It is vital to understand the significance editing has on the way in which audiences view and enjoy films. These early experiments laid the groundwork for the future development of editing.

The critical practice of the French New Wave

In the late 1950s world cinema witnessed a new phenomenon, the French New Wave. Breaking with previous traditions, New Wave filmmakers introduced stylistic and thematic innovations into feature films. Inspired by earlier film movements such as Italian neo-realism, in many ways, it was a reaction against what its proponents saw as the conservative work of the older generation. The French New Wave proved influential in film history, prompting similar developments in many other national cinemas.

The context of the French New Wave

As we learned in Chapter 11, it is important to contextualize any development in national cinema in relation to the social and political culture from which it emerges. The French New Wave developed in the late 1950s. France throughout the 1950s had been recovering from the effects of World War II and particularly the German occupation. Many films from 1945 onwards presented the concerns of reconstruction and the trauma of remembering the devastation of the war, for example, the work of Alain Resnais. His documentary, *Night and Fog* (1955), evokes the horrors of the Holocaust by contrasting the stillness of the abandoned concentration camps with archive footage of them in use during the war, in an effective postwar reconsideration of events. This film also heralds some of the developments to become key in the New Wave; it structures its material in an

Figure 12.12   *400 Blows*, François Truffaut, 1959

innovative, non-linear manner. By 1959, a new generation of filmmakers were ready to emerge and to challenge the practices of the previous generation, a generation associated with the troubled times of war. This was the year when the three most influential films of the movement were released: *Breathless*, directed by Jean-Luc Godard, *400 Blows*, directed by François Truffaut and *Hiroshima Mon Amour*, directed by Alain Resnais.

Following the end of the war, a change in film distribution practices brought the return of Hollywood films to France after they had been banned during the German occupation. For the young filmmakers of the French New Wave, these films had a powerful impact during their early viewing years. Several French New Wave films show the influence of Hollywood style, not so much by imitation as by subversion. In other words, French New Wave filmmakers were aware of the Hollywood style, which they then mined self-consciously for stylistic references. Without trying to imitate Hollywood style, they impersonated it. For example, François Truffaut's film, *Shoot the Piano Player* (1960), is a twist on the Hollywood gangster genre. It uses plot situations and character types common to that genre, but includes specific traits that are more in line with the New Wave style, such as an elliptical narrative and character motivations which are not clearly defined.

The theory of the French New Wave

The French New Wave is an ideal of critical practice. Before its filmmakers began making films, they were writers and critics. Many were associated with a film journal founded in the 1950s called *Cahiers du Cinéma*. In an interview in 1962, Jean-Luc Godard discussed this connection and theorized the role of the critic-artist:

> All of us at *Cahiers* thought of ourselves as future directors. Frequenting cine-clubs and the Cinematheque was already a way of making films, for the difference between writing and directing is quantitative not qualitative …
>
> As a critic, I thought of myself as a film-maker. Today I still think of myself as a critic, and in a sense I am, more than ever before. Instead of writing criticism, I make a film but the critical dimension is subsumed. I think of myself as an essayist, producing essays in novel form or novels in essay form: only instead of writing I film them. Were the cinemas to disappear, I would simply accept the inevitable and turn to television; were television to disappear, I would revert to pencil and paper. For there is a clear continuity between all forms of expression. It's all one. The important thing is to approach it from the side which suits you best. (Godard, 1972: 171)

The editor of *Cahiers du Cinéma* during this period was the critic André Bazin. Bazin is well known for his theories of film, which are grounded in the celebration of realist style. He believed that the primary function of film was to aspire towards a close imitation of reality. This interest in realism was partly a response to the idea that film theorists needed to distinguish which specific qualities of film differentiated it from other arts. One of the distinctive qualities of film was the way it could closely approximate the actual world. Bazin's theories validated certain realist film-makers and movements. In Chapter 7 we encountered Italian neo-realism originating after World War II and using certain stylistic techniques including long takes, non-professional actors and location shooting. Writing in France throughout the 1950s, Bazin championed Italian neo-realism, a style and movement that would in turn influence French New Wave filmmaking.

Another fundamental idea developed in the writing of the *Cahiers du Cinéma* critics was auteur theory, discussed in the previous chapter. This claimed that the director is the author of a film. The auteur's skill can be recognized in a film's mise-en-scène and their directorial choices across a number of films. Recognition of the auteur became a new focus when looking at national cinemas in Europe. Unlike with the commercial, industrial practices of mainstream Hollywood, the perception was that European art-house films could be better defined by the vision of the individual director as author.

As this concept of individual authorship led to directors developing their own unique styles, it is difficult to pinpoint a consistent style within the French New Wave in the same way as one might talk about the innovations of the Soviet montage theorists. What the French New Wave introduced was an attitude to filmmaking rather than a style, the idea that feature films could dispense with the conventions of classical narrative form. Although there was no defined style, it is the stylistic features of the French New Wave that were recognized: the **non-continuity** staging and editing, handheld camera movement and long takes, location shooting.

A key development of the New Wave was its approach to storytelling. Early New Wave films exhibited a narrative style that was less bound by the rules of convention than previous films. These films often featured elliptical narrative structures, where the stories were more disjointed and did not follow the Classical conventions of cause and effect. Frequently New Wave films did not resolve their narratives using the principles of closure that audiences had come to expect. François Truffaut's *400 Blows*, for example, ends enigmatically with the main character running to the sea. Parts of the story remain unresolved but his emotional bid for freedom overrides the need for a traditional ending. The characters in French New Wave films also defy classical conventions. Often the motivations for their actions are not clear to the audience. Complex characters with conflicting attitudes and actions are common in the films of Godard, Truffaut and Resnais. These characters are harder to identify with than the simpler heroes of traditional filmmaking.

French New Wave style often incorporated traits of reflexivity. This involved a heightened awareness of the process of creation with the filmmaker using techniques to remind the viewer that they are watching a film. Thus the audience is not merely caught up in the story but also thinking about how that story is communicated. Stylistic traits, such as direct address, handheld camera work and **freeze frames**, make the viewer conscious of the tools of production, prompting them to think about the film. Reflexivity is linked to another aspect of New Wave style, **intertextuality**. This is the custom of referring to another film, book or work of art. These references, as we will see in the example below, draw the viewer out of the film they are watching. Intertextuality situates a film in a larger cultural context and allows comparisons with or criticisms of other types of art. We will discover some of these features of narrative style and character development, along with many stylistic innovations and reflexivity, in exploring the example of Jean-Luc Godard's *Breathless*.

An example of the French New Wave: Breathless

Jean-Luc Godard's *Breathless* is a key film of the New Wave, embodying many of the characteristics of the movement. It was Godard's first feature, which he shot in a short time span and with a relatively small budget. The film tells the story of Michel Poiccard (Jean-Paul Belmondo), a small-time criminal. Early in the film he steals a car and kills a motorcycle police officer and is on the run. He travels to Paris to see Patricia (Jean Seberg) and tries to persuade her to accompany him to Italy. But in the end she turns him in and he is shot running from the police.

Godard's filmmaking style was informed by his role as a writer and critic. He employed one of the New Wave's important trademarks, **intertexuality**.

> Our first films were all *film de cinephile* – the work of film enthusiasts. One can make use of what one has already seen in the cinema to make deliberate references. This was true of me in particular. I thought in terms of purely cinematographic attitudes. For some shots I referred to scenes I remembered from Preminger, Cukor, etc. (Godard, 1972: 173)

These intertextual references are linked to the film's reflexivity, primarily in the way that it plays with the conventions of genre. *Breathless* references the style of Hollywood gangster films. In one scene the hero stands in front of a cinema looking at a poster advertizing a Humphrey Bogart film. The gangster genre also influences the trajectory of the narrative. Godard saw the fate of Michel bound up in the traditions of the gangster hero and it was these traditions that ultimately determined his destiny:

> What caused me a lot of trouble was the end. Should the hero die? To start with, I intended to do the opposite ... the gangster would win and leave for Italy with his money. But as an anti-convention it was too conventional ... . Finally, I decided that as my avowed ambition was to make an ordinary gangster film, I had no business deliberately contradicting the genre: he must die. (Godard, 1972: 174)

Figure 12.13 *Breathless*, Jean-Luc Godard, 1959

Stylistically, *Breathless* broke with the classical conventions then predominant. The film was shot on a low budget, using an improvizational approach, which led to some unconventional staging choices. Scenes unfold in lengthy takes, without following continuity. This long-take staging can lead to interesting and unusual scenes. For example, at one point Patricia waits in the car, while Michel goes out to talk to a friend. The camera stays with her inside the car and is handheld so the image is shaky. In the distant background, Michel is visible talking to someone on the street, but frequently he is obscured by people walking past. This is unusual as it distances the audience from the action.

Another innovative aspect of the staging in *Breathless* is the use of direct address. At different points in the film, both the main characters look directly into the camera. As the film ends, after Michel has been shot, Patricia is shown facing the camera in close-up. The shot is a fairly long take. Patricia asks the police for an interpretation of Michel's last words. The film ends as she turns away from the camera, turning her back on the audience. The effect of this moment is to break the illusion of the diegetic world and make the audience aware of the film as Patricia looks directly at it. As Michel fails to communicate with Patricia, or she to understand him, the viewer is called upon to reflect on what the film is trying to say in this final scene.

Breathless uses location shooting; the characters move around Paris. A famous sequence shows Michel and Patricia walking along a street as Patricia is selling papers. Like the Italian neo-realists that preceded the French New Wave, location shooting is key to the style of this film. It conveys a sense of immediacy and removes it from the formal staging and artificiality of built sets.

The camera is also used in alternative ways. It is handheld throughout, making the image fairly jumpy. Godard justifies this choice both pragmatically and stylistically:

If we used a handheld camera, it was simply for speed. I couldn't afford to use the usual equipment, which would have added three weeks to the schedule. But this shouldn't be made a rule either: the method of shooting should match the subject … . Seven out of ten directors waste four hours over a shot which should take five minutes work of actual shooting: I prefer to have five minutes work for the crew – and keep the three hours to myself for thought. (Godard, 1972: 173–4)

The innovation for which *Breathless* is perhaps most celebrated is the editing style. Continuity editing is abandoned in favour of long-take sequences, jump cuts and alternative uses of space. For example, in one scene Michel and Patricia are travelling together in a car. A conventional continuity style would cut between the two characters in a shot/reverse shot pattern, maintaining the illusion of the spatial relations between them. Instead the shot stays on Patricia, using jump cuts between different moments. Godard describes his decision to edit this way, abandoning conventional practices:

… we took all the shots and systematically cut out whatever could be cut, while trying to maintain some rhythm. For example, Belmondo and Seberg had a sequence in a car at a certain moment; and there was a shot of one, then a shot of the other, as they spoke their lines. And when we came to this sequence, which had to be shortened like the others, instead of slightly shortening both, the editor and I flipped a coin; we said: 'Instead of slightly shortening one and then slightly shortening the other, and winding up with short little shots of both of them, we're going to cut out four minutes by eliminating one or the other altogether, and then we will simply join the [remaining] shots, like that, as though it were a single shot.' Then we drew lots as to whether it should be Belmondo or Seberg and Seberg remained … (Godard cited in Raskin, 1998)

Cumulatively, all these techniques – non-continuity staging and editing, direct address, handheld camera and long takes – have the effect of making the viewer aware that they are watching a film. Conscious choices increase the audience's awareness of technique. These stylistic choices, as well as the innovations in narrative form and the themes of postwar alienation, were the particular contributions the French New Wave made to global film culture. Many film movements that followed were inspired by the advances of the New Wave and it remains a vital landmark in the development of film style and technique.

The critical practice of Third Cinema

One movement that was influenced by both the Soviet montage practices and the French New Wave was Third Cinema, which developed in Latin America during the 1960s. This inspired the production of a variety of films from different cultures and social situations. Although Third Cinema originated in Latin America, it became an international movement that challenged the rigidity of national boundaries and sought commonalities across nations with similar historical, social and political contexts. Its filmmakers were united in their political goal to challenge conventional filmmaking and empower Third World filmmakers to use cinema as a tool for social change. The work of these filmmakers affords a particularly appropriate model in discussing critical practice, as it encompasses many of the concepts introduced so far: active audience engagement, innovative stylistic techniques and reflexivity.

The context of Third Cinema

During the late 1940s and the 1950s, many countries formerly colonized by European powers gained independence. In the **post-colonial** era, these countries were faced with economic rather than political domination by the first world, a situation described as **'neo-colonialism'**. The theory and practice of Third Cinema were grounded in a critical understanding of these global politics. In particular, Third Cinema is linked to the idea of the Third World. The term 'Third World' was first used during the Cold War to describe countries which were neither affiliated to the Communist bloc nor to NATO. The Third World consists of countries that suffered from the ill effects of the Cold War and would suffer equally in the face of a possible nuclear war, without being participants in either conflict. In the Cold War struggle, the first world meant the capitalist countries of NATO. The second world was the Communist bloc. The Third World was defined as the countries which were affiliated to neither first nor second world. Although the term has its origins in a political definition, it is often used to describe an economic situation as well. These are developing countries that are often economically disadvantaged, with high levels of poverty.

Some of the limits of the term, 'Third World', are apparent. It is not very precise. Since the end of Communism, the second world no longer exists, so the value of the division of the globe into three worlds is questionable. Looking at the atlas you will also notice that the 'Third World' covers a large part of the globe; diverse cultures, languages and traditions are included in this all-embracing term. As we will see, these limitations also extend to the discussion of Third Cinema.

Theories of Third Cinema

A number of critical practitioners working in Latin America in the late 1960s theorized the potential of cinema as a tool for social action and liberation. For example, in Cuba, the documentary filmmaker Julio Espinosa introduced the concept of 'Imperfect Cinema'. This is the idea that popular filmmaking, with its emphasis on technical perfection (and the money required to achieve it), should be replaced by a filmmaking practice that celebrates a rough aesthetic that relates it to the experiences of the people represented. Espinosa was in favour of the democratization of media through technology such as video, which makes media production accessible to a larger group of people.

Around the same time, two Argentinian filmmakers, Fernando Solanas and Octavio Getino wrote a polemical manifesto 'Towards a Third Cinema' (1997). They defined three types of global filmmaking practice:

- The *First Cinema* is the commercial mainstream production associated primarily with Hollywood;
- The *Second Cinema* is the **'auteur'** cinema associated primarily with European art-cinema traditions;

- The *Third Cinema* is a radical, political cinema from the Third World that challenges previous perceptions of filmmaking practice and advocates social change.

These theories of Third Cinema do not proscribe specific stylistic techniques, so much as a political agenda for Third World cinema. However we can summarize some of the underlying features of the movement. First, Third Cinema resisted both first and second cinema. Thus, the films were neither popular entertainment nor the individual vision of a single author. This led to a collective approach to filmmaking, working collaboratively in groups rather than following industrial or artistic models of practice. Often these films blurred the boundaries between different film styles and types, combining documentary and experimental techniques within narrative films. Third Cinema's politics are evident in a left-wing agenda that related to the struggle against neo-colonialism. In order to fulfil these political goals, Third Cinema films used techniques to actively engage the audience in discussion and debate, so that the viewer is inspired to seek social and political change.

Solanas and Getino theorized Third Cinema but they also presented these ideas in the film, *Hour of the Furnaces* (1968). This film adopted the style of a documentary to investigate the issue of neo-colonialism in Latin America. It runs four and a half hours and is divided into three parts. Its experimental outlook allows it to incorporate moments in which the audience is invited to debate and reflect. This engagement with the audience in some senses defines Third Cinema. It is based on the assumption that the filmmaker is communicating with an active viewer who is aware of the political and social issues, rather than just making a film to be passively consumed for entertainment.

Third Cinema influenced the development of national cinemas across the Third World and was significant in the development of political cinema internationally. However, Third Cinema was specific to a time and place and, although influential, it came to an end. One of the critiques it faced was the use of the terms 'Third World' and 'Third Cinema'. These terms are no longer specific enough to embrace the variety of cinema originating from diverse regions of the world such as the continents of South America and Africa. The Third World includes many varied territories, each with different histories, languages, cultures and political concerns.

Current writing on film cultures from the Third World now takes into consideration the cultural specificity of different national cinemas. Filmmaking from Latin America, Africa, the Middle East and Asia is a growing and exciting area of film study. For example, in recent years Iranian film has produced an exciting New Wave film revival. In addition, Burkina Faso in West Africa hosts FESPACO one of the world's largest film festivals, while India is the largest film-producing nation in the world.

An example of Third Cinema: Memories of Underdevelopment

Memories of Underdevelopment (1968) is based on a novel by the Cuban writer Edmundo Desnoes and directed by Tomás Gutiérrez Alea, one of the most respected directors from Cuba. Set in Havana, it follows the character of Sergio (Sergio Corrieri) as he tries to come to terms with the changes to Cuban society brought about by the 1959 revolution. Sergio is alienated from his surroundings and feels isolated from the action of the revolution. As the film starts, we see Sergio parting with his wife (Yolanda Farr) and family as they leave Cuba for the US. His family in general, and his wife in particular, represents an unquestioning assimilation of capitalist values.

Sergio does not embrace these values, but neither is he able to function under the Communist system. Although he chooses not to leave, thus passively accepting the revolution, he lives in Havana and makes a living as a landlord, an occupation that is capitalist in nature, making money through owning property rather than through labour.

There is another level to Sergio's passivity; he is an intellectual and this puts him at odds with his environment and culture. Many of these intellectual ideas are not shared by his fellow Cubans as they stem from European or North American values. For example, at one point, Sergio visits the house where the American novelist Ernest Hemingway lived prior to the revolution. Hemingway represents a colonial intellectual who thought of Cuba as a playground, a space to hunt and fish, away from the restrictions of the US. Sergio calls the house 'a refuge'. Sergio's voice over here is critical of Hemingway, judging him an intellectual colonizer, yet at the same time, when it comes to the action of the scene, he uses the house as a place to hide from his non-intellectual girlfriend Elena (Daisy Granados), passively dismissing her as an inferior, without ever confronting her directly.

Sergio's relationship with Elena embodies much of his conflicted position towards post-revolutionary Cuba. He perceives her to be 'underdeveloped', lacking the intellectual capacity or curiosity that he values. This explains his careless treatment of her. Her position is more complex, although her motivations are not fully revealed nor her actions explained. On the one hand, the film's representation of women could be seen as highly problematic. Sergio's wife is materialistic and shallow, while the maid Naomi (Eslinda Núñez) purely serves the function of a sexual fantasy for Sergio and Elena is shown as stupid, manipulative and only interested in 'trapping' Sergio.

Figure 12.14   *Memories of Underdevelopment*, Tomás Guttiérrez Alea, 1968

These are all common stereotypes of women characters. However these representations could be a result of the film's point of view, which is Sergio's; his sexist and class-biased opinion of the women in his life is reflected in the film.

The film's use of point of view ties to the question of identification, how the viewer relates to the characters in the film. This film is difficult on first viewing because of the way in which the audience's processes of identification are challenged. In the last chapter we saw how, in a film such as *Raiders of the Lost Ark*, we are used to a certain simplified engagement with a character. This process is subverted if we try to directly identify with Sergio. Not only is Sergio deeply conflicted, he is a character whose crises and problems are completely rooted in his situation and his cultural context. In contrast, Indiana Jones is a simple character to understand. His motivations are clear, his cultural context is familiar, not only to an American audience, and he is generalized and stereotypical to the extent that many different viewers can relate to him. The text even invites members of the racial and ethnic groups that he is so happily killing to relate to him as well; this is one of the central conflicts of identification for the post-colonial viewer.

Indy is also a character who is primarily action driven; he moves the plot along through his actions and the narrative centres around him. In this, he again differs from Sergio. Identification with Sergio is problematized as he is not action driven. His surroundings and the political turmoil in which he is caught up move him around, rather than his actions influencing the world around him. This can leave the audience feeling uncomfortable, as the practices of first cinema usually allow the audience to feel in control; characters it identifies with move the story along through their actions. In contrast, this film wants to disrupt and question the audience's process of identification and make it think about the characters in complex ways rather than just passively identifying with them. The director Alea discusses this process of identification:

> In my view, the Sergio character is very complex … . In one sense Sergio represents the ideal of what every man with that particular kind of mentality would like to have been: rich, good-looking, intelligent, with access to the upper social strata and to beautiful women who are very willing to go to bed with him. That is to say, he has a set of virtues and advantages which permit spectators to identify to a certain degree with him as a character …
>
> So then what happens to the spectator? … . Because the spectators feel caught in a trap since they identified with a character who proceeds to destroy himself and is reduced to … nothing. The spectators then have to re-examine themselves and all those values, unconsciously held, which have motivated them to identify with Sergio. They realize that those values are questioned by a reality which is much stronger, much more potent and vital. (Alea, 1990: 189–90)

Another interesting factor is how the film uses documentary techniques within the narrative. For example, at one point Sergio narrates a commentary on the failed 1961 Bay of Pigs invasion (when American-trained and -backed Cuban exiles invaded Cuba through the Bay of Pigs in an attempt to overthrow Castro's Communist regime). The mixing of documentary and narrative styles was a characteristic of the culture of post-revolutionary Cuban film. This era's films sought a way to express the conflicts inherent in establishing a Communist society in a post-colonial Third World country, facing problems of illiteracy, rural underdevelopment and poor communications. As with the Soviet Union of the 1920s, film, as a popular medium, served to bring information and education to the Cuban population. The integration of documentary and narrative styles became a way to combine both information and entertainment.

In addition, this stylistic choice is reflexive; it does not allow the spectator to get so wrapped up in the narrative that they forget to think. The documentary sections of the film require the spectator to, in a sense, take a step back and engage with the theoretical and political issues raised by the film. As usual with Third Cinema of this period, the film inspires an active audience to participate in the political sphere and confront the problems raised, and to engage in discussion, debate and ultimately political action. This combination of political engagement, active audience and collaborative authorship is one of Third Cinema's significant contributions to filmmaking and it continues to influence ideas about critical practices outside the mainstream.

Critical practice in feminist film

Chapter 11 showed how a film can be analyzed or interpreted from a feminist perspective. In this case, we saw how a Classical Hollywood film such as *Gentlemen Prefer Blondes* (1953) represents women in a particular way, tied to the sexist ideology of society at the time. That discussion revealed how feminist critics analyze women characters in film; criticize the negative aspects of their portrayal; identify how the male gaze is structured in film spectatorship; and question how these problematic representations and identifications can still be appealing to women viewers. Feminist filmmaking takes an active part in this critical dialogue by creating representations of women that are alternatives to the mainstream.

Feminist filmmaking is a very important and rich field of critical practice designed to challenge conventional representations. Unlike Soviet montage, the French New Wave or Third Cinema, feminist film practice is not tied to a specific culture or time. Work in this tradition spans different periods, cultures and identities, using a variety of styles and techniques. Rather than a coherent movement, feminist film emerges from fundamental social concerns about the nature of gender, and how it is constructed through culture.

Women have been making films since the early silent period. Feminist criticism has traced the work of women filmmakers through different eras, exploring how they challenge the male dominance of the film industry. For example, feminist theorists, critics and historians have explored the work of early innovators such as Dorothy Arzner, a director in Hollywood during the Classical period, who produced films within the studio system. It is useful to question whether her work demonstrates a sensibility that differs from, or questions, the prevailing patriarchal ideology. Is she a critical-practice filmmaker in the feminist tradition? This is one of the issues we will address in our discussion of feminist filmmaking. Here we will touch on some of the main concerns of feminist film practice and look at the films of Agnès Varda as representative of this approach.

Feminist alternatives to mainstream cinema

Chapter 11 introduced the issues surrounding gender in film, examining how feminist criticism has explored the use of sexist film language. Classical narrative films have often reproduced those gendered stereotypes that have been summed up by critic John Berger (1977) in the phrase 'men act, women appear'. This evaluation of gender stereotypes summarizes two key points about the representation of women. First, women are the object of the male gaze. Second, women are cast in passive roles in the narrative; they don't move the story along. One goal of feminist filmmaking is to question and disrupt these stereotypical representations.

A film such as Dorothy Arzner's *Dance, Girl, Dance* (1940) is a good example of an early feminist style in the Classical Hollywood era; it disrupts conventional viewing pleasures in an interesting way. This musical in the Classical form tells the story of two showgirls who perform in musical halls and are objectified by the male audience. In a memorable scene one of the performers, Judy (Maureen O'Hara), challenges this system of representation by halting her stage performance to look out at the men watching. She then confronts them about their attitude to women and the way they look at her as she dances. This unusual moment for Classical Hollywood has significance beyond its place within the story of *Dance, Girl, Dance*. When Judy steps out in front of the diegetic audience to accuse them of objectifying women, she is also challenging the film audience to think about its role in viewing this film and others in the same tradition.

Another goal of feminist film practice is to develop active roles for women characters in the narrative. The last chapter demonstrated how mainstream film often shows women outside the agency of the narrative, not in control of the story in the same way that male characters are. Feminist film aims to create films that correct this imbalance by focusing on women who are in control of the story and not represented merely as sexual objects. Early feminist film questioned the mainstream system of representation and sought to address this by making films with stronger women characters. This change in ideas about gender then became reflected in mainstream film practices. Since the growth of feminist filmmaking, more women participate in the creative processes of the entertainment industry and there are wider and more diverse images of women in mainstream films. Characters such as Ripley (Sigourney Weaver) in *Alien* (1979) can be seen as emblematic of this development. She is a strong persona and the narrative action centres around her, as it does with a male hero such as Indiana Jones.

Feminism has evolved over time. As the mainstream develops more sophisticated ways of representing women, feminist film practice expands to incorporate issues beyond the initial questions of representation, such as marginalization and difference. Specifically, feminists have taken up the question of how the oppression of women is systematically linked to the oppression of minority and other marginalized groups.

The films of Agnès Varda

One filmmaker whose work is representative of some of the significant changes in feminist styles is Agnès Varda. Feminist filmmaking is an international theoretical tendency and she is one of many filmmakers who represent the diversity of feminist film expression. Agnès Varda is a French filmmaker who has been making films for over fifty years. Looking at two examples of her style, from her earlier and her later work, will demonstrate how feminist concerns and techniques have shifted over the years. Varda was involved in the French New Wave (although she was not affiliated with *Cahiers du Cinéma*), through the rise of an international feminist movement and other significant shifts in film culture.

One of her best-known early films is *Cleo from 5 to 7*, made in 1962 at the height of the New Wave period. The film follows the character of Cleo (Corinne Marchand) for two hours of her life: between 5 and 7 in the evening. During these two hours she is waiting for the results of a medical test that will tell her whether or not she has a terminal illness. Cleo is a successful, professional singer and her life and self-perception are bound up in her success and the way in which she commodifies her appearance. During the film, Cleo undergoes a change, growing in her awareness and her sense of self. This film is a feminist response to the standard way women are represented. Cleo, the singer, is objectified and passive, two of the stereotypes usually associated with women.

As part of the French New Wave, there are parallels between *Cleo from 5 to 7* and *Breathless*. Both use innovative techniques that break with convention: handheld camerawork, location shooting, non-continuity editing, available light and direct address. They also both use intertextuality and reflexivity. Whereas Godard's intertextual references are to Classical Hollywood, Varda's include Godard himself who appears briefly in a silent-film sequence that Cleo watches from the projection booth of a cinema. Some of Varda's feminist concerns are apparent in the differences between these two films. Godard's use of character involves breaking the conventional processes of audience identification with the anti-hero Michel. Varda, on the other hand, presents us with the complex character of Cleo, whose transformation invites the viewer to contemplate the changing role of women.

Like in *Breathless*, location is important in *Cleo from 5 to 7*, perhaps even more so. Cleo's transformation is narrativized by a journey through the streets of Paris. She moves from a visit to the fortune teller at the beginning to a café and then she goes home. She leaves her home again to visit a friend, goes to the park and then finally to the hospital. Her journey of self-realization occurs during her time on the streets. In one memorable sequence, a series of cuts shows her being looked at and, importantly, looking back.

Direct address also features importantly in *Cleo*. In the scene in her home she is visited by her composer (played by the film's actual composer, Michel Legrand) and lyricist (Serge Korber), as they work on their music. At one point she starts to sing and is backed by a non-diegetic band. The camera moves in on her as she sings and she looks directly at the camera. This moment is a major turning point in the film, after which her transformation becomes more apparent. She takes off her wig, dresses more plainly and walks out of her home alone, without the support of the maid, Angèle (Dominique Davray), who has been following her up to this point.

Cleo's change in appearance is significant, as appearance is one of the film's main themes. In one scene, Cleo articulates her concern with appearance and the way people look at her: 'I thought everyone looked at me. I only look at myself.' The mise-en-scène frequently features mirrors and other reflective surfaces. At one point a mirror is broken and Cleo sees herself as a fractured reflection. In this film, Varda is commenting on women's status as object to be looked at, and creating a story that tells of Cleo's shift from this role to that of a more active and self-determined individual.

In her later work, Varda also demonstrates the many ways in which the concerns of the feminist film tradition have developed over fifty years. Contemporary feminist theory examines how women in society are bound to the system that privileges some and excludes others. Varda's later work has represented this growing concern with the relationship between women's oppression and other forms of marginalization. Her 2003 film, *The Gleaners and I*, a documentary in the first-person style discussed in Chapter 4, shows this movement clearly. It focuses on the practice of 'gleaning' or collecting the leftovers after a harvest, an old tradition in France, which Varda traces through to contemporary life where she meets various people who still live off the scraps of others. Many of those she meets live in poverty and outside the mainstream of political and social life.

Varda's French New Wave origins are still evident in the reflexivity of *The Gleaners and I*. Varda is very aware of her role as a filmmaker observing the life of the gleaners. The title shows this connection and she reflects on the process of filmmaking as a form of 'gleaning' images, capturing moments of life that are otherwise disregarded. In one scene, she poses like a classical painting of a woman gleaning, standing beside the hanging image holding a sheaf of wheat. Her voice over explains: 'There is another woman gleaning in this film, that's me. I'm happy to drop the ears of wheat and pick up my camera.' Thus, she incorporates into this reflection the study of herself and her own image. She sees the connections between the women in the traditional paintings of the gleaners and her self-representation.

The Gleaners and I is also evidence of a developing interest within feminist filmmaking in the plight of the economically and politically marginalized, making connections with those who are forced to glean as a way to survive. During her journey, Varda meets people living in poverty on the margins of society, including those from poor and recent immigrant populations. Her encounters with other forms of difference and marginalization forge links between these different groups. Ultimately, the film shows the failings of an economic, political and social system that is wasteful, while leaving others to live on the waste. Although Varda's films present only a small sample of the diversity of feminist practice, they demonstrate significant elements of this critical practice and its shifting politics over the last fifty years. Feminist filmmaking and film theory also remain influential in how we look at many different aspects of human relations, particularly around gender and sexuality and as such, have had a considerable influence on the growth of queer film, to which we will now turn.

Critical practice and the New Queer Cinema

Lesbian and gay filmmaking spans a wide range of movements and styles in its interrogation of its subject and in its approach to representation but we are going to examine a specific moment within the larger tradition of lesbian and gay film – the **New Queer Cinema** movement, dating from the early 1990s – to see how it represents a critical-practice approach, and brings together several different filmmaking and critical traditions at a key political point. Like many of the other movements that we have discussed, New Queer Cinema, named in an article by the critic B. Ruby Rich in 1992, combined theoretical and critical engagement with artistic practice. Rich identified themes and stylistic traits and catalogued the films that she felt gave rise to New Queer Cinema. As she later described it: 'It was meant to catch the beat of a new kind of film- and video-making that was fresh, edgy, low-budget, inventive, unapologetic, sexy and stylistically daring.' (Rich, 2000) We will examine the New Queer Cinema in its historical, political, aesthetic and theoretical context and consider a film that typifies its key aspects, its address to a specific viewership and its progression towards the mainstreaming of lesbian and gay imagery.

At this time, the term 'queer', previously used as pejorative slang, was rehabilitated. 'Queer' was reclaimed by activists and theorists to define a community of resistance and to forge political links between those oppressed by their position outside mainstream sexual identities. Queer politics sought to unite the interests of lesbians, gay men, bisexuals, transgender and intersex people. Thus, New Queer Cinema and theory spoke to a political alliance grounded in resistance to the expectations of an oppressive moral code.

The context of New Queer Cinema

As well as being influenced by feminist practice, New Queer Cinema is also deeply rooted in the traditions of avant-garde or experimental film (studied in Chapter 5), which included such filmmakers as Kenneth Anger, Jack Smith and Andy Warhol who deployed gay imagery to explore the nature of sexuality outside the sanctioned arena of mainstream film. In the US, the strict censorship practices of the Hays Code meant that overt references to gay and lesbian sexuality were disallowed, which meant that gay and lesbian filmmaking remained part of the experimental underground. This allowed a filmmaker like Barbara Hammer to produce work explicitly exploring lesbian sex, relationships and history in such films as *Dyketactics* (1974) and *Nitrate Kisses* (1992). These films were usually exhibited at festivals dedicated to experimental or lesbian and gay film, which constituted an independent circuit for filmmakers to show, and for audiences to see, films that dealt with queer subject matter in a radically different way from the conventions of mainstream film. By the 1990s, the gay and lesbian festival circuit had expanded to provide a platform for aspiring queer filmmakers and their work inspired B. Ruby Rich to identify and name the movement that would become New Queer Cinema.

Emerging from underground film, New Queer Cinema also had political roots in the 1980s. Early in the 1980s, the AIDS virus took a toll on the gay communities in both America (US) and the United Kingdom (UK). As there was no national health system in the US, treatment for the virus was difficult to obtain, provoking an increase in activism to highlight this fact. Out of this crisis grew a grassroots political campaign to raise awareness of AIDS and to destigmatize those with the disease. This new-found political activism was evident in the queer community in organizations such as ACT-UP (AIDS Coalition to Unleash Power) and Queer Nation. These organizations incorporated video technologies to spread awareness. AIDS videos were a grassroots use of accessible technology for political purposes which led to a heightened media sensitivity within the queer community. These videos form an important precursor to the New Queer Cinema movement, much of which thematically or subtextually dealt with the crisis.

As B. Ruby Rich celebrated the founding of New Queer Cinema, she was to lament its end in the article 'Queer and Present Danger', when it came under criticism for several reasons, one of which was even part of Rich's initial argument, that the movement favoured certain members of the gay community. White gay men were more likely to have their work distributed and celebrated at the expense of lesbians, the transgender community and people of colour. Certainly the centrality of directors Todd Haynes and Tom Kalin gave that impression, but as time progressed, the diversity of the films presented under the New Queer Cinema banner increased.

As New Queer Cinema was influenced by previous traditions and movements, so it likewise had an influence on mainstream representations. Hollywood films in the 1990s began to engage with issues of queer sexuality from broader perspectives and incorporate gay and lesbian characters and storylines into films such as *Philadelphia* (1993) and *Jeffrey* (1995).

Queer Theory and New Queer Cinema

New Queer Cinema arose at the convergence of several different cultural and political movements. As the previous section suggests, it was closely linked to queer activism and exploited cheap video technology as a tool in activist protest. Another key intersection was the academic interest in the idea of **Queer Theory**. Queer Theory is a cross-disciplinary debate that contextualizes gender and sexuality within a complex field of thought, drawn from developments in feminism and gender theory. Key writers such as Eve Kosofsky Sedgwick with *Epistemology of the Closet* (1990) and Judith Butler with *Gender Trouble* (1990) theorized gender as performative rather than a fixed biological fact.

As part of a wider interdisciplinary engagement, this period also marks a growth of queer film theory, which revisited mainstream cinema to uncover queer subtextual readings, explore the neglected work of the queer avant-garde and to investigate the role of queer spectatorship in making meaning at the point of reception. New Queer Cinema occurred around the same time as the development of Queer Theory, engaging artistically with the new theoretical ideas. Many of these films question the fixity of previous categories, seeking not only to overturn stereotypes of gay and lesbian characters, but to question the heterosexual basis and bias of characterization itself.

New Queer Cinema in action

The years following the festivals that led B. Ruby Rich to celebrate the birth of New Queer Cinema saw a dramatic increase in films produced for the lesbian and gay market and a growth in dedicated film festivals. A significant film from this time, produced on a small budget but reaching a wider audience, was *Go Fish* (1994), which focuses on a group of lesbians living in Chicago. Central to the film is the love story between Max (Guinevere Turner) and Ely (V. S. Brodie), but aside from this conventional girl-meets-girl plot, the film enlists experimental techniques to explore the lives of contemporary lesbians.

Figure 12.15   *Go Fish*, Rose Troche, 1994

Go Fish demonstrates the critical practice of New Queer Cinema in a number of ways. The film was produced outside the mainstream and grounded in a community-based environment. The initial preproduction and production phases occurred independently, with writer/producer Guinevere Turner and writer/director Rose Troche supported by the local community and working with a crew recruited from students and those involved in activist video. It wasn't until well into the production process that the film received the support of executive producers, Tom Kalin and Christine Vachon. At the Sundance Film Festival, it was picked up for distribution and received a limited commercial release. The film's progression from its origins in an activist community through the sponsorship of established filmmakers in the New Queer Cinema movement to its eventual commercial release parallels the shift of queer filmmaking from an underground to a more mainstream practice.

The opening scene is set in a seminar where a group of Women's Studies students discuss the sexual identity of historical figures, working out who might have been lesbian. This light-hearted scene shows a revisioning of history from a lesbian perspective, seeking to uncover an untold and repressed story. The film goes on to engage with questions of identity, with the protagonists living in a lesbian community and occasionally coming into conflict with their families, particularly the character of Evy (Migdalia Melendez). *Go Fish* works against conventional stereotypes of lesbian life, which focus on the negative, to present a queer positive image of its characters. It does so unapologetically, making no justifications for them, simply showing them living their lives. In some ways this is different from earlier New Queer Cinema films, such as Tom Kalin's *Swoon* (1992), which reject the idea of positive images in favour of more complex representations of the queer subject in society. In response to Rich's critique of New Queer Cinema as centred on white gay male experience, *Go Fish*'s director Rose Troche is a Latina lesbian and the film embraces the racial and cultural diversity of its characters. This undermines the sense of a homogenous lesbian community and gives place to a wider range of experiences.

Go Fish incorporates different experimental techniques. Sequences unfold that do not relate to the central narrative but explore a more subjective space. In this way, it marks a transition from the more experimental practices of the queer avant-garde into a more mainstream gay and lesbian practice, as the experimental passages are contained within the conventional narrative structure of a romance.

Critical practice in popular cult film

The previous sections have examined examples from different points in world film history to see how filmmakers have consciously integrated critical thinking into the creation of their work. Throughout we have seen that many movements – the French New Wave, Third Cinema, feminist filmmakers, New Queer Cinema – often use their filmmaking practice to resist, critique and redefine the stereotypes and limitations of popular filmmaking forms. What about popular films themselves? Do films made within the mainstream entertainment industry engage with critical practice? It is with this question in mind that we will conclude this chapter by investigating the critical practice of popular cult film. **Cult film** reflects many of the societal anxieties and concerns of our time. What entertains us also says something important about us.

'Cult' films often have active and engaged fan communities. Studying the critical practice of cult film involves examining the types of films that garner fan audiences and identifying the strategies and techniques they use to communicate both with their fans and with casual viewers. In contemporary society film is a product that crosses many different media. So for many popular films, you can also buy toys, action figures, computer games, clothing and fast-food meals with film-theme tie-ins. You can read comics or novelizations of the film, watch television interviews or 'making of' specials, look at official and fan websites and participate in online discussion forums. Some fans write and share online fan fiction or make video parodies or tributes to their favourite films, which are shared online via sites such as YouTube.

In an attempt to cater to different audiences, popular films often contain intentional **subtextual** meanings and certain viewers can read and interpret these for added entertainment. So, for example, the films in the *Harry Potter* series are primarily marketed at children, with the teenage heroes, action adventure and magic and mystery appealing to a younger viewing audience. At the same time, however, these films contain other cultural allusions that can interest a more adult and scholarly audience, such as references to mythology.

This use of reference and allusion is one way in which popular film engages with multiple audiences. This is a form of intertextuality similar to that found in the French New Wave, when Godard references Humphrey Bogart as a Hollywood icon in *Breathless*. Intertextuality in popular film becomes a generic code, relating one film, television programme, comic book or other cultural form to another. *The Matrix* (1999), for example, is inspired and influenced by several different cultural texts and styles. These influences include cyberpunk science fiction, videogame culture, kung fu action films and religion. More than just a backdrop, they are fundamental to the way in which the film communicates with the audience, as they are familiar cultural texts.

Film is an act of communication only fully completed when it is viewed. We have seen how proponents of critical practice often try to actively engage the audience. From the direct address of the French New Wave, to the discussion breaks of Third Cinema, a key feature of critical-practice filmmaking is the relationship with the viewer. Popular entertainment film traditionally has a different conception of the viewer, as consumer, enticed to purchase the entertainment product. How the product is consumed is of less interest to the commercial industry. Yet as critical practitioners, both artists and theorists are interested in how viewers interact with films. A cult film is one that may or may not have achieved commercial success, but has inspired a large and devoted following of fans. These fans often respond to the film in more active ways than casual viewers, by writing fan fiction, creating websites, making copies or parodies of the film, dressing in a style to do with the film, attending conventions and special screenings and, in general, participating in a community whose members are all devotees of the film.

Particular genres, such as science fiction, fantasy and horror can inspire cult followings because they have multiple levels of meaning, and are open to different interpretations. These genres often lend themselves to theoretical interpretation. Science fiction, for instance, may address questions about the nature of existence, the power of technology, the differences between humans and non-humans, among others. The following section will show how *The Matrix* (1999) deploys multiple levels of meaning to engage an active audience.

Critical practice in The Matrix

The Matrix was produced by Warner Bros. and written and directed by the Wachowski brothers. Two sequels followed: *The Matrix Revolutions* (2003) and *The Matrix Reloaded* (2003). The directors of this film are well known for their reticence about these films; they rarely give interviews and have not responded to many of the interpretations made of the film. Despite this, the film series is extremely popular and has inspired much writing and reflection on its themes and subtexts. This writing has ranged from popular reviews through fan writing to serious scholarly analysis, often engaging with the film's themes of religion and philosophy.

In the first film we meet Neo (Keanu Reeves), a software programmer by day and a computer hacker by night. He meets a woman called Trinity (Carrie-Anne Moss) and after being arrested he is introduced to Morpheus (Laurence Fishburne), another hacker. Morpheus offers him a choice between taking a blue pill that would keep his life as normal or a red pill that would allow him to see 'the Matrix'. He takes the red pill and wakes to find that the world he thought he knew was a simulation, a computer program powered by human bodies. He learns that his destiny is to help the resistance movement fight the artificial intelligence that controls the humans within the program.

So how can we discuss *The Matrix* as a critical-practice film? There are so many themes and levels of textual meaning that simply to review what has been discussed so far would take up pages. At best we can summarize some key themes and questions raised by the film.

- *Technology*. How does the film's central battle between technology and humanity relate to our fears about the technological control of the world in which we live?
- *Reality*. How does the film's vision of virtual reality and cyberspace speak to our experiences as viewers?
- *Faith and belief*. How does the myth of the saviour resonate with our cultural understanding of faith in individual actions? How does this interact with the film's other uses of religion, in particular the Buddhist references?

The Matrix also resonates with intertextual references that relate to its central themes of technology and the nature of reality. At different points, the film makes direct references to the novel *Alice in Wonderland* by Lewis Carroll, relating Neo's experience of learning about the Matrix to Alice's adventures after she goes down the rabbit hole. The film also alludes to the book, *Simulacra and Simulation* (1994), by the French philosopher Jean Baudrillard. In an early scene before Neo has discovered the false nature of his world, he is visited by friends. He gives them a computer disc that is concealed in a hollow copy of Baudrillard's book; the hollow book is itself a simulation of the 'real' book. In a later scene, Morpheus shows Neo the 'real' world outside the simulation of the Matrix, introducing it with a quotation from Baudrillard, 'the desert of the real'. Through these references, the film engages with its audience on different levels. For those who know Baudrillard, the film can be understood in terms of his philosophical ideas about the nature

Figure 12.16   *The Matrix*, Andy Wachowski and Larry Wachowski, 1999

of reality. For others, it can be seen in relation to the more popularly known children's fable about Alice and her trip into a fantasy world outside the bounds of the 'real' world.

The film is open to religious interpretations. Neo is hailed by many of the characters, particularly Morpheus, as 'the One'. Prophecy has led Morpheus to believe that Neo is a long-awaited saviour whose destiny is to rescue humanity from their enslavement to the artificial intelligence behind the Matrix. This posits the idea of Neo as the 'Messiah' in a Christian allegory, able to release humans trapped in false belief in the virtual world and awaken them to knowledge of the truth.

The Matrix can certainly inspire many and multiple interpretations. Most of what has been written about it is grounded in evidence found in the film itself. In other words, critical analysis and theoretical interpretation of the film have emerged from the film's intertextual references and subtextual levels of meaning. In this way, it demonstrates another way in which critical practice can be seen to operate on the level of both the creation of the film itself and of the appreciation of its fans and the critical writing of those who have analyzed it.

Summary and key questions

The critical-practice approach to filmmaking has influenced filmmakers throughout history. From the Soviet silent era to the recent work of the New Queer Cinema movement, filmmakers have been inspired to combine critical thinking with artistic practice to extend the boundaries of filmmaking form. When viewing films from different eras, you can assess how the filmmakers approached their work, both critically and stylistically.

- What critical or theoretical writing have the filmmakers produced?
- How does their critical work relate to their filmmaking practice?
- Does the film demonstrate the practices of reflexivity or intertextuality, relating their work to a context outside the world of the film itself?
- How do the filmmakers address their audience?
  - Does the film engage the viewer actively, or treat them as a passive recipient of entertainment?
  - What techniques does the film use to ensure an active audience?

Want to learn more?

Think about this ...

Critical practitioners

Objective: To apply the concept of 'critical practice' to the work of specific filmmakers.

Take a film that you enjoy and briefly research the writing and thought of the creative team. How does it engage with critical-practice ideas? Do the filmmakers articulate critical or stylistic ideas about the film? How does the film demonstrate critical-practice ideals?

> **Try this ...**
>
> *The New Wave style*
>
> Objective: To relate the work of critical practitioners to your own creative process.
> You will need: A video camera and a script idea.
>
> Shoot a short film in the style of the French New Wave. How do you work with this particular style? What insights does it give into alternative narrative practice?

Further reading

Each of these film movements has been written about extensively, as a style and as a form of critical practice. For soviet montage, see Eisenstein, *Film Form* and *Film Sense*, Pudovkin, *Film Technique* and for a radical approach to documentary, Vertov, *Kino-Eye*. For the French New Wave, see Godard, *Godard on Godard* and the collection edited by Jim Hillier, *Cahiers du Cinéma*. For Third Cinema, see Jim Pines and Paul Willemen, *Questions of Third Cinema*, Roy Armes, *Third World Filmmaking in the West*, Teshome Gabriel, *Third Cinema in the Third World* and Mike Wayne, *Political Film: The Dialetics of Third Cinema*. For feminist film, see E. Ann Kaplan, *Women and Film: Both Sides of the Camera* and Geetha Ramanathan, *Feminist Auteurs*. For New Queer Cinema, see Michele Aaron, *New Queer Cinema*. For cult film and *The Matrix*, see Glenn Yeffeth, *Taking the Red Pill*.

Films studied in this chapter

400 Blows 1959 François Truffaut (director)
Alien 1979 Ridley Scott (director)
Battleship Potemkin 1925 Sergei Eisenstein (director)
Breathless 1959 Jean-Luc Godard (director)
By the Law 1926 Lev Kuleshov (director)
Cleo from 5 to 7 1962 Agnès Varda (director)
Dance, Girl, Dance 1940 Dorothy Arzner (director)
Dyketactics 1974 Barbara Hammer (director)
The End of St. Petersburg 1927 Vsevolod Pudovkin (director)
The Extraordinary Adventures of Mr. West in the Land of the Bolsheviks 1924 Lev Kuleshov (director)
Gentlemen Prefer Blondes 1953 Howard Hawks (director)
The Gleaners and I 2003 Agnès Varda (director)
Go Fish 1994 Rose Troche (director)
Hiroshima Mon Amour 1959 Alain Resnais (director)
Hour of the Furnaces 1968 Fernando Solanas and Octavio Getino (directors)
Jeffrey 1995 Christopher Ashley (director)
The Matrix 1999 Andy Wachowski and Larry Wachowski (directors)
The Matrix Reloaded 2003 Andy Wachowski and Larry Wachowski (directors)

The Matrix Revolutions 2003 Andy Wachowski and Larry Wachowski (directors)
Memories of Underdevelopment 1968 Tomás Guttiérrez Alea (director)
Night and Fog 1955 Alain Resnais (director)
Nitrate Kisses 1992 Barbara Hammer (director)
October 1927 Sergei Eisenstein (director)
Philadelphia 1993 Jonathan Demme (director)
Raiders of the Lost Ark 1981 Steven Spielberg (director)
Shoot the Piano Player 1960 François Truffaut (director)
Swoon 1992 Tom Kalin (director)

Other examples to explore

There are examples of interesting films from each of the movements studied in this chapter. For Soviet montage, see *Mother* (1926 Vsevolod Pudovkin director) or *Man with a Movie Camera* (1929 Dziga Vertov director). For the French New Wave, see *Jules and Jim* (1962 François Truffaut director) and *Week End* (1967 Jean-Luc Godard director). With Third Cinema there are a variety of films from an international context that have been discussed as representing the principles of the movement. From Senegal, see *Ceddo* (1977 Ousmane Sembene director), from India, see *Pather Panchali* (1955 Satyajit Ray director) and from Bolivia, see *Blood of the Condor* (1969 Jorge Sanjinés director). There is also a wide variety to choose from in relation to feminist practice, but films of interest include *Born in Flames* (1983 Lizzie Borden director), *Daisies* (1968 Vera Chytilová director) and *Daughters of the Dust* (1991 Julie Dash director) as well as Agnès Varda's latest film, *The Beaches of Agnes* (2009). For New Queer Cinema, see *Poison* (1991 Todd Haynes director) and *The Watermelon Woman* (1996 Cheryl Dunye director). There are also many interesting examples of cult film, but see in particular *Bladerunner* (1982 Ridley Scott director) and *Serenity* (2005 Josh Whedon director).

Bibliography

Chapter 1

Bordwell, David, Kristin Thompson and Janet Staiger (1985) *The Classical Hollywood Cinema: Film Style and Mode of Production to 1960*. New York: Columbia University Press.

Burch, Noël (1992) *Theory of Film Practice*. Princeton, NJ: Princeton University Press.

Dancyger, Ken (1999) *The World of Film and Video Production*. New York: Harcourt Brace.

Geuens, Jean-Pierre (2000) *Film Production Theory*. Albany: SUNY Press.

Maltby, Richard (2003) *Hollywood Cinema*. Oxford: Blackwell.

Mast, Gerald (ed.) (1983) *Movies in Our Midst*. Chicago, IL: University of Chicago Press.

Neale, Steve (2000) *Genre and Hollywood*. London: Routledge.

Schatz, Thomas (1998) *The Genius of the System: Hollywood Filmmaking in the Studio Era*. London: Faber and Faber.

Wayne, Mike (1997) *Theorising Video Practice*. London: Lawrence and Wishart.

Chapter 2

Aumont, Jacques (1997) *The Image*. London: BFI.

Barbagallo, Ron (2005) 'From Concept Art to Finished Puppets: An Interview with Graham G. Maiden, Puppet Fabrication Supervisor on *Tim Burton's Corpse Bride*'. *Animation, Art, Conservation*. http://www.animationartconservation.com/?c=art&p=corpse_bride, accessed 20 March 2010.

Byrne, Eleanor and Martin McQuillan (1999) *Deconstructing Disney*. London: Pluto Press.

Furness, Maureen (2008) *The Animation Bible*. London: Laurence King.

Laybourne, Kit (1979) *The Animation Book*. New York: Three Rivers Press.

Mannoni, Laurent (2000) *The Great Art of Light and Shadow: Archaeology of the Cinema*. Exeter: University of Exeter Press.

Millerson, Gerald and Jim Owens (2008) *The Video Production Handbook*. Burlington, MA: Focal Press.

Murphy, Mary (2008) *Get Started in Animation*. London: A. C. Black.

Musburger, Robert (2005) *Single Camera Video Production*. Burlington, MA: Focal Press.

Pilling, Jayne (1999) *A Reader in Animation Studies*. New Barnet: John Libbey.

Pincus, Edward and Steven Ascher (2007) *The Filmmaker's Handbook*. New York: Plume.

Smoodin, Eric (1994) *Disney Discourse: Producing the Magic Kingdom*. New York: Routledge.

Wells, Paul (2008) *Re-imagining Animation: The Changing Face of the Moving Image*. Worthing: AVA.

Chapter 3

Aristotle (1996) *Poetics*. London: Penguin Books.

Aronson, Linda (2001) *Screenwriting Updated: New (and Conventional) Ways of Writing for the Screen*. Los Angeles, CA: Silman-James Press.

Bordwell, David (1985) *Narration in the Fiction Film*. Madison: University of Wisconsin Press.

Bradley, Jane (2009) *Screenwriting 101: Small Steps While Thinking Big*. Dubuque, IA: Kendall Hunt.

Chatman, Seymour (1990) *Coming to Terms: The Rhetoric of Narrative in Fiction and Film*. Ithaca, NY: Cornell University Press.

Dancyger, Ken and Jeff Rush (2007) *Alternative Scriptwriting: Successfully Breaking the Rules*. Burlington, MA: Focal Press.

Field, Syd (2005) *The Screenplay: The Foundations of Screenwriting*. New York: Delta.

Fleishman, Avrom (1992) *Narrated Films: Storytelling Situations in Cinema History*. Baltimore, MD: Johns Hopkins University Press.

Genette, Gérard (1980) *Narrative Discourse: An Essay in Method*. Ithaca, NY: Cornell University Press.

Hart, John (2008) *The Art of the Storyboard: A Filmmaker's Introduction*. Burlington, MA: Focal Press.

Katz, Steven D. (1991) *Film Directing Shot by Shot: Visualizing from Concept to Screen*. Studio City, CA: Michael Wiese Productions.

Maras, Steven (2009) *Screenwriting: History, Theory and Practice*. London: Wallflower Press.

McKee, Robert (1999) *Story: Substance, Structure, Style and the Principles of Screenwriting*. London: Methuen.

Propp, Vladimir (1968) *The Morphology of the Folk Tale*. Austin: University of Texas Press.

Rimon-Kenan, Shlomith (1983) *Narrative Fiction: Contemporary Poetics*. London: Methuen.

Thompson, Kristin (1999) *Storytelling in the New Hollywood: Understanding Classical Narrative Technique*. Cambridge, MA: Harvard University Press.

Todorov, Tzvetan (1977) *The Poetics of Prose*. Ithaca, NY: Cornell University Press.

Chapter 4

Barbash, Ilsa and Lucien Taylor (1997) *Cross-Cultural Filmmaking: Handbook of Making Documentary and Ethnographic Films and Videos*. Berkeley: University of California Press.

Bruzzi, Stella (2006) *New Documentary*. London: Routledge.

Chanan, Michael (2007) *The Politics of Documentary*. London: BFI.

Else, Jon (2005) Interview: *All Things Considered*. National Public Radio, 29 March.

Grierson, John (1966) 'First Principles of Documentary', in *Grierson on Documentary*, Forsyth Hardy (ed.) London: Faber.

Nichols, Bill (1994) *Blurred Boundaries: Questions of Meaning in Contemporary Culture*. Bloomington: Indiana University Press.

Nichols, Bill (2001) *Introduction to Documentary*. Bloomington: Indiana University Press.

Rabiger, Michael (2004) *Directing the Documentary*. Oxford: Focal Press.

Renov, Michael (2004) *The Subject of Documentary*. Minneapolis: University of Minnesota Press.

Rosenthal, Alan (1996) *Writing, Producing and Directing Documentary Film and Video*. Carbondale: Southern Illinois University Press.

Chapter 5

Brakhage, Stan (1989) *Film at Wit's End*. Kingston, NY: Documentext.

Buñuel, Luis (1983) *My Last Breath*. London: Jonathan Cape.

Deren, Maya (1965) 'Notes, Essays, Letters'. *Film Culture* no. 39.

Freeman, Judi (1996) 'Bridging Purism and Surrealism: The Origins and Production of Fernand Léger's *Ballet Mécanique*', in Rudolf E. Kuenzli (ed.) *Dada and Surrealist Film*. Cambridge, MA: MIT Press.

Hall, Doug and Sally Jo Fifer (1991) *Illuminating Video: An Essential Guide to Video Art*. New York: Aperture.

Hamlyn, Nicky (2003) *Film Art Phenomena*. London: BFI.

Knight, Julia (1996) *Diverse Practices: A Critical Reader on British Video Art*. Luton: University of Luton Press.

Kuenzli, Rudolf E. (1996) *Dada and Surrealist Film*. Cambridge, MA: MIT Press.

LeGrice, Malcolm (2001) *Experimental Cinema in the Digital Age*. London: BFI.

Rees, A. L. (1999) *A History of Experimental Film and Video from the Canonical Avant-Garde to Contemporary British Practice*. London: BFI.

Renov, Michael and Erika Suderburg (1996) *Resolutions: Contemporary Video Practices*. Minneapolis: University of Minnesota Press.

Rush, Michael (2003) *Video Art*. London: Thames and Hudson.

Sitney, P. Adams (1974) *Visionary Film: The American Avant-Garde*. Oxford: Oxford University Press.

Stern, Fred 'Fernand Léger's *Mechanical Ballet*'. *Artnet*. http://www.artnet.com/magazine_pre2000/features/stern/stern2-24-98.asp, accessed 20 February 2010.

Wees, William Charles (1992) *Light Moving in Time: Studies in the Visual Aesthetics of Avant-Garde Film*. Berkeley: University of California Press.

Youngblood, Gene (1970) *Expanded Cinema*. New York: Dutton.

Chapter 6

Balazs, Bela (1970) *Theory of the Film: Character and Growth of a New Art*. New York: Dover Books.

Bergery, Benjamin (2002) *Reflections: Twenty-One Cinematographers at Work*. Hollywood, CA: ASC Press.

Brown, Blain (2002) *Cinematography: Theory and Practice: Imagemaking for Cinematographers, Directors and Videographers*. Burlington, MA: Focal Press.

Cook, Pam (1978) 'Duplicity in *Mildred Pierce*', in E. Ann Kaplan (ed.) *Women in Film Noir*. London: BFI.

Dyer, Richard (1997) 'The Light of the World', in *White*. London: Routledge.

Geuens, Jean-Pierre (2000) 'Lighting', in *Film Production Theory*. Albany: SUNY Press.

Lowell, Ross (1999) *Matters of Light and Depth*. New York: Lowell-light Manufacturing.

Malkiewicz, Kris (1986) *Film Lighting*. New York: Prentice Hall.

Malkiewicz, Kris (1989) *Cinematography*. New York: Prentice Hall.

Mascelli, Joseph V. (1965) *The Five Cs of Cinematography*. Los Angeles, CA: Silman-James Press.

Schaefer, Dennis and Larry Salvato (1984) *Masters of Light: Conversations with Contemporary Cinematographers*. Berkeley: University of California Press.

Shohat, Ella and Robert Stam (1994) *Unthinking Eurocentrism: Multiculturalism and the Media*. New York: Routledge.

Zettl, Herbert (2011) *Sight, Sound, Motion: Applied Media Aesthetics*. Belmont, CA: Wadsworth.

Chapter 7

Affron, Charles and Mirella Jona Affron (1995) *Sets in Motion: Art Direction in Film Narrative*. New Brunswick, NJ: Rutgers University Press.

Baron, Cynthia, Diane Carson and Frank P. Tomasulo (2004) *More than a Method: Trends and Traditions in Contemporary Film Performance*. Detroit, MI: Wayne State University Press.

Blum, Richard A. (1984) *American Film Acting: The Stanislavski Heritage*. Ann Arbor: UMI Research Press.

Gaines, Jane and Charlotte Herzog (1990) *Fabrications: Costumes and the Female Body*. London: Routledge.

Geuens, Jean-Pierre (2000) 'Staging', in *Film Production Theory*. Albany: SUNY Press.

Gibbs, John (2002) *Mise-en-Scène: Film Style and Interpretation*. London: Wallflower Press.

Katz, Steven D. (1991) *Film Directing Shot by Shot: Visualizing from Concept to Screen*. Studio City, CA: Michael Wiese Productions.

Olson, Robert L. (1993) *Art Direction for Film and Video*. Burlington, MA: Focal Press.

Rabiger, Michael (2008) *Directing: Film Techniques and Aesthetics*. Burlington, MA: Focal Press.

Chapter 8

Alten, Stanley R. (2001) *Audio in Media*. Belmont, CA: Wadsworth.

Altman, Rick (1992) *Sound Theory, Sound Practice*. London: Routledge.

Belton, John and Elisabeth Weis (1985) *Film Sound: Theory and Practice*. New York: Columbia University Press.

Chion, Michel (1994) *Audio-Vision: Sound on Film*. New York: Columbia University Press.

Chion, Michel (1999) *The Voice in Cinema*. New York: Columbia University Press.

Jackson, Blair (2004) 'Surrounded by Dr. Octopus!', *Mix: Professional Audio and Music Production*. mixonline.com/mag/audio_surrounded_dr_octopus/, accessed 22 February 2010.

Sider, Larry (2003) *Soundscape: The School of Sound Lectures, 1998–2001*. London: Wallflower Press.

Yewdall, David Lewis (2007) *Practical Art of Motion Picture Sound*. Burlington, MA: Focal Press.

Chapter 9

Dancyger, Ken (2006) *The Technique of Film and Video Editing: History, Theory and Practice*. Burlington, MA: Focal Press.

Eisenstein, Sergei (1975) *Film Sense*. New York: Harcourt Brace.

Eisenstein, Sergei (1977) *Film Form*. New York: Harcourt Brace.

Geuens, Jean-Pierre (2000) 'Editing', in *Film Production Theory*. Albany: SUNY Press.

Murch, Walter (1995) *In the Blink of an Eye. A Perspective on Film Editing*. Los Angeles, CA: Silman-James Press.

Oldham, Gabriella (1992) *First Cut: Conversations with Film Editors*. Berkeley: University of California Press.

Ondaatje, Michael (2002) *The Conversations: Walter Murch and the Art of Editing Film*. London: Bloomsbury.

Pearlman, Karen (2009) *Cutting Rhythms: Shaping the Film Edit*. Burlington, MA: Focal Press.

Reisz, Karel and Gavin Millar (1982) *The Technique of Film Editing*. Burlington, MA: Focal Press.

Chapter 10

Cooke, Mervyn (2008) *A History of Film Music*. Cambridge: Cambridge University Press.

Flinn, Caryl (1992) *Strains of Utopia: Gender, Nostalgia, and Hollywood Film Music*. Princeton, NJ: Princeton University Press.

Gorbman, Claudia (1987) *Unheard Melodies: Narrative Film Music*. Bloomington: Indiana University Press.

Gorbman, Claudia (2000) 'Scoring the Indian: Music in the Liberal Western', in Georgina Born and David Hesmondhalgh (eds) *Western Music and Its Others*. Berkeley: University of California Press.

Kalinak, Kathryn (1992) *Settling the Score*. Madison: University of Wisconsin Press.

Kassabian, Anahid (2001) *Hearing Film: Tracking Identifications in Contemporary Hollywood Film*. New York: Routledge.

Laing, Heather (2007) *The Gendered Score: Music in 1940s Melodrama and the Woman's Film*. Aldershot: Ashgate.

Powrie, Phil and Robynn Stilwell (2006) *Changing Tunes: The Use of Pre-existing Music in Film*. Aldershot: Ashgate.

Tincknell, Estella and Ian Conrich (2006) *Film's Musical Moments*. Edinburgh: Edinburgh University Press.

Wierzbicki, James (2008) *Film Music: A History*. London: Routledge.

Chapter 11

Anderson, Benedict (1983) *Imagined Communities*. London: Verso.

Arbuthnot, Lucie and Gail Seneca (1990) 'Pretext and Text in *Gentlemen Prefer Blondes*', in Patricia Erens (ed.) *Issues in Feminist Film Criticism*. Bloomington: Indiana University Press.

Berger, John (1977) *Ways of Seeing*. London: Penguin.

Boorman, John (1985) *Money into Light*. London: Faber and Faber.

Corrigan, Timothy (1998) *A Short Guide to Writing about Film*. New York: Longman.

Ebert, Roger (2004) 'Eternal Sunshine of the Spotless Mind', *Chicago Sun Times*, 19 March. http://rogerebert.suntimes.com/apps/pbcs.dll/article?AID=/20040319/REVIEWS/403190302/1023, accessed 31 August 2009.

Erens, Patricia (ed.) (1990) *Issues in Feminist Film Criticism*. Bloomington: Indiana University Press.

Geertz, Clifford (1973) 'Thick Description: Toward an Interpretive Theory of Culture', in *The Interpretation of Cultures: Selected Essays*. New York: Basic Books.

Julien, Isaac and Colin MacCabe (1991) *Diary of a Young Soul Rebel*. London: BFI.

Maland, Charles J. (2003) 'Powered by a Ford?: Dudley Nichols, Authorship and Cultural Ethos in *Stagecoach*', in Barry Keith Grant (ed.) *John Ford's* Stagecoach. Cambridge: Cambridge University Press.

Modleski, Tania (1988) 'The Woman Who Was Known Too Much', in *The Women Who Knew Too Much*. New York: Routledge.

Moscowitz, John E. (2000) *Critical Approaches to Writing about Film*. Upper Saddle River, NJ: Prentice Hall.

Mulvey, Laura (1975) 'Visual Pleasure in Narrative Cinema', *Screen* vol. 16 no. 3.

Penley, Constance (ed.) (1988) *Feminism and Film Theory*. New York: Routledge.

Propp, Vladimir (1968) *The Morphology of the Folk Tale*. Austin: University of Texas Press.

Shohat, Ella and Robert Stam (1994) *Unthinking Eurocentrism: Multiculturalism and the Media*. New York: Routledge.

Snead, James (1994) *White Screens, Black Images: Hollywood from the Dark Side*. New York: Routledge.

Stutesman, Drake (1999) '"Gives Good Face": Mr John and the Power of Hats in Film', *Framework* no. 41. http://www.frameworkonline.com/Issue41/41ds.htm, accessed 31 August 2009.

Turim, Maureen (1990) 'Gentlemen Consume Blondes', in Patricia Erens (ed.) *Issues in Feminist Film Criticism*. Bloomington: Indiana University Press.

Chapter 12

Aaron, Michele (2004) *New Queer Cinema: A Critical Reader*. Edinburgh: Edinburgh University Press.

Alea, Tomás Gutiérrez (1990) 'Memories of *Memories*', in Michael Chanan (ed.) *Memories of Underdevelopment*. New Brunswick, NJ: Rutgers University Press.

Armes, Roy (1987) *Third World Filmmaking in the West*. Berkeley: University of California Press.

Baudrillard, Jean (1994) *Simulacra and Simulation*. Ann Arbor: University of Michigan Press.

Bazin, André (1972) *What Is Cinema?* Berkeley: University of California Press.

Berger, John (1977) *Ways of Seeing*. London: Penguin.

Burton, Julianne (1990) 'Individual Fulfilment and Collective Achievement: An Interview with Tomás Gutiérrez Alea', in Michael Chanan (ed.) *Memories of Underdevelopment*. New Brunswick, NJ: Rutgers University Press.

Butler, Judith (1990) *Gender Trouble: Feminism and the Subversion of Identity*. London: Routledge.

Eisenstein, Sergei (1975) *Film Sense*. New York: Harcourt Brace.

Eisenstein, Sergei (1977) *Film Form*. New York: Harcourt Brace.

Espinosa, Julio (1979) 'For an Imperfect Cinema', *Jump Cut* no. 20.

Gabriel, Teshome (1982) *Third Cinema in the Third World: The Aesthetics of Liberation*. Ann Arbor: UMI Research Press.

Godard, Jean-Luc (1972) *Godard on Godard*, Tom Milne (ed.) New York: Viking Press.

Hillier, Jim (1985) *Cahiers du Cinéma*. London: Routledge and Kegan Paul.

Kaplan, E. Ann (1983) *Women and Film: Both Sides of the Camera*. London: Methuen.

Pines, Jim and Paul Willemen (1989) *Questions of Third Cinema*. London: BFI.

Pudovkin, V. I. (1959) *Film Technique*. New York: Bonanza.

Ramanathan, Geetha (2006) *Feminist Auteurs: Reading Women's Film*. London: Wallflower Press.

Raskin, Richard (1998) 'The Art of Film Editing: Five Explanations for the Jump Cuts in Godard's *Breathless*'. *P.O.V.: A Danish Journal of Film Studies* no. 6. http://pov.imv.au.dk/Issue_06/section_1/artc10.html, accessed 27 August 2009.

Rich, B. Ruby (1992) 'New Queer Cinema', *Sight and Sound* vol. 2 no. 5 (September), reprinted in B. Ruby Rich (2004) *New Queer Cinema: A Critical Reader*. Edinburgh: Edinburgh University Press.

Rich, B. Ruby (2000) 'Queer and Present Danger', *Sight and Sound*, March. http://www.bfi.org.uk/sightandsound/feature/80, accessed 25 February 2010.

Sedgwick, Eve Kosofsky (1990) *Epistemology of the Closet*. Berkeley: University of California Press.

Solanas, Ferdinand and Octavio Getino (1997) 'Towards a Third Cinema', in *New Latin American Cinema*, Detroit, MI: Wayne State University Press.

Vertov, Dziga (1984) *Kino-Eye: The Writings of Dziga Vertov*. Berkeley: University of California Press.

Wayne, Mike (2001) *Political Film: The Dialectics of Third Cinema*. London: Pluto Press.

Yeffeth, Glenn (2003) *Taking the Red Pill: Science, Philosophy and Religion in* The Matrix. Chichester: Summersdale.

Glossary

8mm The smallest gauge of film, used mostly for home movies and in 'artist' film.

16mm A film gauge often used in educational settings, independent films and previously for documentary or industrial production.

30° rule In **continuity editing**, the convention that the camera should be moved at least 30° between shots (or change lens position) in order to avoid a **jump cut**.

35mm The standard professional gauge of film.

70mm A large-gauge format used to produce professional films of a particularly high quality.

180° rule/180° space In **continuity** staging or editing, the camera is placed on one side of the **axis of action** so that the spatial relations between characters remain clear.

absorb A property of both lighting and sound (which travel in waves). In sound, the **acoustics** of a space are changed when soft surfaces are present as these surfaces absorb the sound-waves and reduce **reverberation**. Darker colours absorb the light rather than reflect it.

Abstract Expressionism A 1950s **modernist** movement of art associated with artists such as Jackson Pollock.

academy ratio The 3 x 4 **aspect ratio** common to films made up to the 1950s, named after the Academy of Motion Picture Arts and Sciences, for which it was standard.

acousmatic A sound that is heard without its source being seen.

acoustics The property of an environment that relates to how the sound-waves travel.

Act 1 In narratives using the **three-act structure**, the first act introduces the characters and sets up the principal action of the scene.

Act 2 In narratives using the **three-act structure**, the second act contains the main or **rising action** of the film.

Act 3 In narratives using the **three-act structure**, the third act is the **climax** and the **denouement** of a film.

action line See **axis of action**.

ambient track/ambience The characteristic room noise audible in a location.

analogue The predigital method of recording audio and video.

anamorphic A system used to shoot and project in **widescreen** format. During shooting, the image is compressed vertically and during projection, the anamorphic lens expands the width of the image.

animation reference In the creation of **CGI**, when an actor performs a scene in place of a computer-generated character, the actor's performance is known as the animation reference.

antagonist In conventional narrative, the character who stands in opposition to the hero or **protagonist**, usually the 'bad guy'.

anthropomorphism/anthropomorphic An animal that takes on the characteristics of a human being.

aperture The small hole in the front of the camera, behind the lens, through which the light passes to create exposure.

armature In figure animation, a metal skeletal form with movable joints over which the figure or animated character is constructed.

art director The member of a film's crew responsible for coordinating elements of design and décor.

artist film and video A contemporary name for **experimental film**, for those using film and video for a fine-art-based practice.

aspect ratio The height and width of the projected image of a film.

assistant director An assistant to the **production manager**, responsible for organization and management of the **production** phase of a film.

asynchronous sound Sound that does not match the visual action of a scene, for example when an actor's words are heard slightly before or after his or her lips move.

atmos track See **ambient track**.

aural perspective Similar to a visual **point of view**, this gives the perspective of what a character hears.

auteur theory The theory that the director has authorial control over a film.

available light The light that is available in a given location without the addition of extra lighting units.

avant-garde film See **experimental film**.

axis of action In the **continuity** system, an imaginary line between characters in a scene that is used as a guide to where the camera can be placed in order to maintain clear spatial relations.

back light A light source placed behind the subject being lit. Commonly used as part of a **three-point lighting** set-up to create the appearance of depth.

Betamax A format of consumer video popular in the 1980s.

bird's-eye angle A camera angle that comes from directly above a scene, looking down on the action.

boom The large pole to which a microphone is attached to bring it close to the actors in a scene, while staying out of the frame of the shot.

B-Roll In documentary, the additional illustrative visual material that is played as background to an interview.

Cahiers du Cinéma A French film journal from the 1950s, associated with auteur theory, in which many of the filmmakers of the **French New Wave** published film criticism.

camera angle The angle at which a camera is placed to capture the action, for example a **high angle** or **low angle**.

camera assistants Assistants who work with the **camera operator**.

camera obscura A darkened room with a small aperture to the daylight (sometimes supplemented with a lens), so that an image is projected from outside onto a screen inside.

camera operator The person on a crew designated to look after the running of the camera, under the direction of the **cinematographer**.

camera position The proximity of the camera to the action, for example, in a **long shot** or **close-up**.

cardiod microphone A microphone with a heart-shaped **pick-up pattern** used for isolating individual sounds, such as the voice of a single speaker.

casting director The crew member responsible for supervising the audition and casting process.

catalyst In narrative structure, the element that initiates the conflict in the **plot**.

catharsis/cathartic In narrative theory, the viewer's feeling of emotional release that accompanies the resolution of the story's conflict.

cause and effect In narrative theory, the way events in the **story** relate to each other, so that one action or event is the result of a previous action or event.

CCD (charged couple device) The computer chip inside a video camera that collects visual and colour information.

cel Short for celluloid, cel refers to a single image of animation, a drawing on clear plastic.

cel animation An animation style that uses drawings on layers of clear plastic.

celluloid The plastic material on which a strip of film is based.

CGI (computer-generated images) Computer-generated special effects, including characters animated by computer and incorporated into the live action of a film.

character narrator In narrative theory, a narrator who is also a character participating in the story's action.

character profile In scriptwriting, an outline of the elements of a character developed by the writer as part of the scripting process.

cinematographer The crew member responsible for supervising all elements of the camera and lighting crew.

cinematography All the elements of a film that involve the camera, including lighting and exposure.

cinéma vérité A 1960s movement of **documentary** film that responded to changes in technology, including lighter cameras and sound-recording equipment. **Cinéma vérité** films are associated with observational techniques and rough, handheld camerawork, **available light** and location sound.

Classical Hollywood cinema The period of film from the late 1920s to the early 1960s. During this time many conventions of narrative film practice were developed that still influence film-making today.

claymation An animation style using figures made from a malleable substance such as clay or plasticine.

clear leader See **leader**.

climax In narrative structure, the point where a **story** reaches the height of the action and the principal conflicts are resolved.

close-up A **camera position** that is close to the subject, for example showing a face.

closure The ending of a fiction film, when the conflicts raised in the narrative are resolved.

colour temperature The colours of different types of light sources; daylight has a blue tinge and incandescent light an orange tinge.

compiled score Music for a film that is drawn from sources outside the film.

composed score Music that is created specifically for a film.

composer The person responsible for writing the music for a film.

condenser microphone A microphone type that is sensitive to sound, delicate and needs an internal power source.

continuity Can refer to the **continuity system** of shooting and editing, or to the maintenance of a consistent image from take to take in order to avoid mistakes in a scene.

continuity editing Editing in the style of the **continuity system**.

continuity system The system of staging and editing a film so that the spatial relations remain clear. Continuity staging and editing involves shooting and editing in **180° space**, where the camera is placed on one side of the action.

costume designer The crew member responsible for the design and supervision of the creation of a film's costumes.

costume drama A drama set in a historical period, requiring costumes suitable and appropriate to that era.

counterpoint Derived from musical terminology, counterpoint refers to different **melodies** working separately but in conjunction with each other. In film, it is often used to describe a non-literal relationship between sound and image.

coverage A practice of the **continuity system** that involves shooting the same action multiple times from different **camera positions**.

crane A hydraulic lift for a camera that allows it to move on a vertical axis during the course of a shot.

cross cutting See **parallel editing**.

Cubism A movement of modern art, associated with artists such as Pablo Picasso.

cue See **musical cue**.

cue sheet The list of points at which the music will enter a film

cult film A film that is popular with a fan audience, who engage with the film more actively than conventional viewers.

cutaway A shot that shifts out of a scene to show something illustrative of the action.

cutting on movement A technique of editing that uses movement within the frame to make an edit point smooth.

Deep Canvas A software program used to add three-dimensional space to animation.

denouement In narrative theory, the point of the plot after the **climax**, when the conflicts are resolved.

depth composition A visual composition choice that implies the three-dimensionality of space by placing action in the foreground, midground and background.

depth of field How much of an image is in focus.

diegetic/diegesis In narrative theory, the diegesis is the world of the narrative. Elements in that world, things that the characters can see or hear are described as 'diegetic'.

dialectics A Marxist term (drawn from the philosopher Hegel) for the process of conflict between two opposing ideas or social forces. The idea is applied to **montage** by Sergei Eisenstein.

diffused light/diffusion Soft light that is created by placing something between the light source and the subject that will disperse the light-waves. Clouds in front of the sun serve to diffuse the sunlight and create **soft light** conditions.

digital video/DV A video format introduced in the mid-1990s that records digital video and audio signals to tape.

direct address When a character or subject talks directly to the camera/audience.

Direct Cinema A movement of documentary film dating from the early 1960s in North America that responded to increased mobility in production equipment by developing a more **realist** style. Sometimes known as **cinéma vérité**.

director The person responsible for coordinating all aspects of the **production** phase, supervising the overall look and working with the actors. The director has responsibility for the creative side of a film.

dissolve An editing **transitional device** which replaces one image with another.

distribution The way a film is sent out into the world to be seen. This includes the marketing and the preparation and presentation for exhibition in different media.

documentary A non-fiction film presenting real events or arguments outside the conventions of fictional style.

dolly A vehicle used to move a camera around a scene.

dramatic score Music that does not have a direct source within the **diegesis**, also known as **non-diegetic** music.

dub Replacing one type of audio with another.

Dutch angle A canted angle, which places elements in a scene diagonally.

DVD A disc-based digital-video format used commercially for the distribution of home entertainment.

dynamic microphone A microphone type (as opposed to a **condenser microphone**) which is rugged, not very sensitive and frequently used for outdoor recording situations where it is not easily affected by wind noise.

early cinema The period of cinema before the full development of narrative form, dating from the invention of film in the mid-1890s to around 1905.

editor The crew member responsible for editing a final film from all the shot footage.

ellipsis See **temporal ellipsis**.

elliptical narrative A narrative style with a disjointed **plot** that does not follow the classical conventions of **cause and effect**.

embedded narrator A narrator who appears within the plot, recounting part or all of the story.

emotional memory A technique of **Method acting** when the actor uses the memory of a previous emotional experience to motivate a performance.

ENG Electronic news gathering, using video to shoot news and current events.

establishing shot The opening shot of a scene that establishes the location and the position of the characters.

exhibition The presentation of a film, either in the cinema or through other media.

Expanded Cinema A term made popular in **experimental film** in the 1970s by Gene Youngblood. Expanded Cinema was inclusive of other forms of media such as video and live performance.

experimental film A film type unlike narrative or documentary film, based in art practices, which challenges the form of film and experiments with technique and style.

exposure/exposed Film that has passed through the camera and been exposed to light. Exposure relates to the calculation of all the factors of how the light reaches the image, including **aperture** and **shutter speed**.

exposition In narrative and screenwriting, the explanation of story events that occurred before the main action of the film.

Expressionism/Expressionistic A movement of modern art, and of film, prevalent in Germany in the 1920s; Expressionistic work projects internal emotions externally, so that the **mise-en-scène**, design and lighting, reflect the characters psychological and emotional states.

exterior light Lighting for scenes shot outdoors.

extra An actor with a non-speaking role, usually part of the background of a scene or in a crowd.

extreme close-up A very tight **close-up** shot centred on some detail in an image, for example, a partial face or hand.

extreme long shot A camera position that includes a landscape, group or crowd shot at a distance.

eye-level shot A **camera angle** positioned at the level of a character's face.

eyeline match An editing technique that matches a **shot/reverse shot** pattern following a character's gaze from one shot to the next.

fade/fade in/fade out An editing **transitional device** that dissolves a scene or sequence in or out of black or another colour. Often, this marks the end of a sequence or a shift in time and space.

fade to black see **fade**.

fast motion A film played back at in increased speed. With film, this is created in-camera by shooting fewer **frames per second** then projecting at normal fps, and with video it is created as an editing effect.

feminism/feminist theory In film terms, a theoretical tradition which explores the representation of women and the way in which films encode gendered spectatorship.

fill light A **soft light** that is used to support the main light of a scene and reduce the shadows created by other lights. One of the lights in a **three-point lighting** set-up.

film This term can mean a number of things. On the basic technical level, it is the photo-chemical material that passes through a camera to capture images and through a projector to play them back. On a more general level, it refers to the completed product of the filmmaking process.

film noir A movement or style of filmmaking originating in the 1940s, film noir is associated with detective stories and stylistically shot with **low-key lighting**, urban landscapes and distinguishable character types.

film stock The material on which a film is captured.

flashback The point in a **plot** where the action moves back to a previous point in the **story**.

flashforward The point in a **plot** where the action moves forward to a later point in the **story**.

flipbook A pre-animation toy with images drawn on the pages of a book. When flipped through by the reader, it creates the appearance of motion.

foam latex A material used in the creation of special-effects make-up and in creating puppets for figure animation.

focus The part of an image that is clear and crisp.

Foley/Foley artist Named after the innovator in sound techniques, Foley refers to the creation of sound effects, mostly in a studio setting.

footage Originating from a reel of film where certain lengths are equivalent to amounts of time, footage refers to shot images, with or without sound.

frame The area of a screen in which the image of a film or video appears.

frame narrator A narrator whose telling of the story frames the whole plot, in opposition to an **embedded narrator**.

frames per second/fps The speed at which film (or video) passes through a camera. The standard **fps** for normal speed sound film is 24, **PAL** video is 25 and **NTSC** video is 30.

freeze frames A point where a moving image freezes into a still image, usually created as a **post-production** effect.

French New Wave An influential French film movement dating from the late 1950s, which broke with many previous narrative conventions and with the expectations of the **continuity system**.

F-stops The units that measure how far the **aperture** on a **lens** is open.

FX A shortened term for 'effects' it refers to the special effects in a film.

gate The area of a camera or projector where a film passes through and is held in front of the **aperture** for exposure.

gauges The different film formats based on the width of the film strip.

genre A type of film such as a Western or a musical.

golden hour See **magic hour**.

graphic matching A technique of editing focusing the viewer's attention on a similar point in the frame from shot to shot with the area of interest remaining in the same part of the frame.

handheld When a camera is used without a stabilizing device such as a tripod, it is literally held by hand.

hard light When light-waves travel directly from the source to a subject being lit, creating a harsh effect and distinct shadows.

harmony In music, harmony is created when different, but compatible, notes are played at the same time.

Hays Code A method of self-censorship adopted by the Hollywood studios in 1934, the Hays Code defined what could or could not be shown in the Classical period.

headroom In the composition of a shot of a person, the amount of space from the top of the head to the upper edge of the **frame**.

heightened realism A performance style of acting between a **realist** performance and a **stylized** performance.

high angle A camera angle that looks down on a subject.

high definition/HD A contemporary video format with a high-quality image.

high-key lighting A lighting style that is bright, evenly lit, with few shadows in the frame. Often associated with melodrama or comedy.

homoerotic The reading of the **subtext** of a conventional film to acknowledge the presence of same-sex desire.

iconography The design elements in **mise-en-scène**.

identification The psychological process of relating to a character within a film.

ideology/ideological Ideology refers to a system of beliefs or ideas held by a society.

Imax A specialized large-gauge film format, that needs to be projected in specifically equipped cinemas.

indirect address When a character or subject does not talk directly to the camera/audience.

ingénue A young female lead character.

in media res In narrative theory, a Latin term meaning 'in the middle of the action' that acknowledges that the action of a **plot** always starts somewhere in the middle of the **story**, thus certain actions have preceded the start of the plot.

insert See **cutaway**.

installation In video or film, an artwork that contains the projection or screening of video and/or film within a larger sculptural or three-dimensional form.

instrumentation In film music, the types of instruments used to perform a given **cue**.

intensity The brightness of a light source.

interior A scene shot inside.

interior light An indoor lighting set-up.

intermittent motion The stop-start process whereby a film moves through a camera or projector.

intertexuality When a film (book or other text or art form) refers to elements in another.

iris The opening at the front of the camera, which includes the **aperture** and the **shutter**. It can also refer to a circular-shaped **wipe**.

Italian neo-realism A post-World War II movement that used an increase in realist techniques, such as location shooting, long takes and non-professional actors, to explore post-war struggles in Italy.

jump cut An edit that is created when the **30° rule** is broken and the shots do not move more than 30° or change lens position. Jump cuts move the image around the frame and break the illusion of the **continuity system**.

key In music terms, key refers to either a **major** or **minor** key in which music is played.

key light In a lighting set-up, such as **three-point lighting**, the key light is the principal light source for a scene.

key-to-fill ratio In **three-point lighting**, the key-to-fill ratio is the ratio between the fill light, and key and fill light together, which defines whether a scene is lit **high key** or **low key**.

Kinetograph A camera first invented by Thomas Edison to be used in conjunction with his **Kinetoscope**.

Kinetoscope A way of viewing film, patented by the Edison company, before the development of the projector. The Kinetoscope was designed so that one viewer at a time could see the image by looking through a peephole in the Kinetoscope box where the image was projected.

Kuleshov effect/Kuleshov experiment Named after the Soviet filmmaker Lev Kuleshov, the Kuleshov experiments tested editing different shots together to explore the effects of **montage** in creating meaning for the audience.

lavalier A small microphone that is used to capture sound from one person at a time, often clipped to a jacket or piece of clothing.

leader A strip of **celluloid**, either clear, black or coloured that is placed at the beginning or end of a **reel** of film.

lead room In visual composition, the space in front of a walking figure.

leitmotiv A term coined by opera composer Richard Wagner to describe a musical theme or **melody** that accompanies a particular character, location or idea.

lens The series of optics at the front of a camera that focuses the light onto the film or videotape capturing the image.

line animation An animation style based on simple line drawings.

location scout The crew member responsible for finding and securing the locations for a film.

location shooting The production of a film outside a studio setting.

logical light source In a lighting set-up, the placement of the **key light** in a position that gives the appearance that an **offscreen** light source comes from that area.

long shot A camera position that includes a figure's full body, or a group of characters.

long take A style of shooting and editing where the shot is of a long duration, often associated with a **realist** style.

look space In composition, the framing of a subject to the opposite side of their gaze, so that they do not appear to be looking at the edge of the frame.

low angle A camera angle that looks up at a subject.

low-key lighting A high-contrast lighting style, with areas of light and shadow in the frame, often associated with **film noir** or horror.

magic hour The time of day around dawn or dusk when the natural daylight has a pleasing golden colour.

magic lantern An invention popular before the development of film, a form of slide projector, showing still images of painted scenes.

major key One of the two standard musical keys in western composition. A major key is associated with a bright, positive-sounding **melody**.

main title In film music, the **cue** played over the opening credits.

married print A film print that has an optical soundtrack to the side of the area with the image frame.

masking The process of creating a widescreen format by covering the top and bottom of the frame.

master shot In continuity staging, the shot that shows all the characters in the scene and that covers all the action, often used as the **establishing shot**.

matched action In editing, cutting from one point in the action in one shot, to the same point in the action of the next shot.

materialism See **structuralism**.

medium long shot A shot that covers the subject from nearly full body length, for example from the knees up.

medium shot A shot that is fairly close to its subject, for example a shot of a person from the waist up.

melody In music, an identifiable tune.

melodrama A genre that centres around heightened emotions, often associated with women, and taking place in a domestic environment.

Method acting A style of acting that focuses on **emotional memory** and an internal, psychological development of the performance.

MiniDV A small version of the **DV** format of digital video tape.

minor key One of the two standard musical keys in western composition. A minor key is associated with a melancholy **melody**.

mise-en-scène All the elements that appear in front of a camera, the different aspects of design as well as the placement and movement of characters on screen.

mode of address The way in which a subject talks to the audience either in **direct address** or **indirect address**.

modernism A movement in arts and culture dating from the early part of the twentieth century.

montage An editing style that has its origins in the Soviet Union of the 1920s, **montage** makes meaning through the combination of images and sounds edited together, which are not necessarily linked temporally or spatially.

montage sequence In **Classical Hollywood** style, the use of montage to summarize events occurring over a period of time into a brief sequence.

motion capture In **CGI** animation, the use of an actor performing in a plain costume with **motion points** on it, to guide the computer animation.

motion points The points on an actor's costume used for **motion capture**.

multi-plane camera An advanced form of animation stand developed by the Disney studio to shoot **cel animation** with a three-dimensional appearance.

music editor The crew member responsible for supervising the addition of the music to a film during **postproduction**.

musical A **genre** of film that includes the characters singing and dancing.

musical cue The point where music enters a scene. Film composers work in cues, composing specific selections of music to accompany prearranged moments in a film.

musical theme See **leitmotiv**.

narration The voice telling the story of the film or providing rhetorical information in a documentary.

narrative In film terms, a story-based or fictional film. More generally, it refers to story forms and styles.

narrator The person or agency that tells a story. In written or spoken narratives, the narrator is the person speaking or a writer writing in the first person. In film terms, the narrator can be telling the story through **voice over**, or the narrator's functions can be seen through filmic techniques.

national cinema An approach to film criticism which examines films from a particular country and cultural context.

neo-colonialism A **post-colonial** form of imperial domination which is economic rather than political.

neo-realism see **Italian neo-realism**.

New Queer Cinema A movement of the early 1990s that introduced an increased acceptability of and complexity to lesbian, gay, bisexual and transgender imagery in film.

non-character narrator In narrative theory, a narrator who does not appear as a character in the story,

non-continuity A form of staging and editing that does not follow the conventions of the **continuity system**.

non-diegetic Elements in a film that come from outside the world of the story, so that the characters neither see nor hear them.

non-simultaneous sound Sound that occurs at a different temporal point in the narrative from the image.

normal lens A lens that is neither **telephoto** nor **wide angle**, and which reproduces images in a normal perspective.

NTSC (National Television Standards Committee) The video playback system of North America, based on the number of vertical scanning lines of the image.

objectification/objectified The process of turning someone into an object to be looked at, rather than a character with full subjectivity.

observational documentary A 'fly-on-the-wall' documentary style, without the use of rhetorical techniques such as interviews or **voice over**.

offscreen/offscreen space The space outside the frame, where action is implied to continue.

omnidirectional sound/omnidirectional microphone The way of hearing sound from all directions rather than just in relation to what can be seen. Also refers to a microphone with this type of **pick-up pattern**.

omniscient A narrator who is in a position to know everything about a story, including the thoughts and feelings of the characters.

optical soundtrack Sound on film that is printed to the side of the film strip and plays back by contact with a special light source.

out-of-synch See **asynchronous sound**.

over-exposure Images shot when the **aperture** is open too wide, so that the frame or parts of the frame appear too bright.

over-the-shoulder shot A shot of one character, for example in a conversation scene, with the character they are talking to visible in the frame. The camera literally shoots one character over the shoulder of the other.

PAL A video playback system common in much of Europe, based on the number of vertical scanning lines of the image.

pan The movement of a camera on a horizontal axis.

pan and scan A technique used for transferring a **widescreen** film image to **academy ratio** video, where part of the image is cut off.

parallel editing Editing between two different spaces following the same narrative time.

patriarchy/patriarchal The sexist system of male-dominated control.

pencil test A line-drawn animation that is the first stage in the process of a more complex **cel animation**.

performance art A **modernist** practice of art that combines theatrical performance with traditions of fine art in a manner designed to blur the boundaries between theatrical practice and **installation**, and between audience and performer.

period drama A dramatic film set in a historical time period.

pick-up pattern The direction in which a microphone is sensitive to sound.

Pixelvision A very low-cost and poor-quality video format, designed as a children's toy, which became popular with video artists.

plot The way in which a story is told, all the events as they unfold in the film, in the order in which they are presented.

plot outline A stage of scripting a film, the plot outline presents the events of the story in the order they will appear in the film.

plot point A decisive moment in the narrative that signals the end of one of the three acts.

point of view The subjective position of a character, for example, a camera position that shows what a character sees.

Portapak A portable video recorder introduced in the late 1960s that allowed video cameras to be used outside the studio.

post-colonial The period following the decolonization of large parts of the Third World by European powers. The term refers to the political, economic and cultural after effects of imperialism both on the colonizing countries as well as those that were colonized.

postproduction The stage of completing a film, including editing, sound mixing and adding music.

preproduction The stage of preparing to shoot and edit a film. Preproduction involves the scripting, the financing, the casting and rehearsal, the location scouting and everything that needs to occur before shooting starts.

presentational A type of **stylized performance**, where the performer faces the audience in **direct address**.

processing/processed After a film has been exposed, it is sent to a laboratory where the image is put through a chemical process allowing it to be viewed.

producer The producer of a film is responsible for the overall management of the business and administration side of production.

production The production phase of a film is when the material is shot.

production designer The crew member responsible for supervising all the design elements in a film.

production manager The production manager assists the **producer** of a film in the day-to-day administration and scheduling of shooting activities.

projection The way in which a film or video can be presented to an audience. A film projector works similarly to a camera in reverse, the film runs through and the light projects the image onto a screen.

props Short for 'properties', the props of a film are the small items needed in a scene.

prosthetics A type of special-effects make-up, often artificial body parts or skin moulded out of latex or foam rubber and added to the actor.

protagonist The main character of a **story**.

psychoanalysis/psychoanalytical Psychological theories based on ideas developed by Freud. Psychoanalytical theories have been applied to film to explore how film's apparatus communicates with the ideal spectator.

pull focus See **rack focus**.

queer theory A theoretical tradition, developed out of **feminist theory**, that explores the nature of same-sex desire and culture within the larger context.

rack focus A shift in focus from one plane to another during the course of a shot.

reaction shot A shot that shows a character listening and reacting to what is said/done.

reading script A preliminary script for a film that does not include the directorial information.

realist/realism Realism is a complicated term, but in general refers to a method of filmmaking practice which attempts to imitate reality by reducing elements of stylization. It can refer to particular techniques, such as acting, or the overall aim of a film. Often films that are considered realist in style use conventions such as handheld camera, location shooting or available light.

reels The containers onto which film is wound.

reflexivity A film's acknowledgement of its own status as a film, making the viewer conscious of its production and showing an awareness of the existence of the audience.

reframing The small shifts in framing during a shot that maintain the principles of composition.

restricted narration A narrator who only knows parts of the story.

reverberation Part of the **acoustics** of sound-waves as they bounce off a hard surface and produce an echo.

reverse shot see **shot/reverse shot**.

revisionist Western A Western, late in the development of the genre, that questions previous interpretations of history.

rhythm The temporal structure of music, the timing in which different notes are played. Rhythm can also relate to editing.

rising action In narrative theory, the action leading up to the **climax**, which increases the suspense or conflict of the story.

room noise see **ambient track**.

rotating shutter The shutter behind the camera lens that opens in front of the **aperture**.

rough cut In editing, the first preliminary draft of an edited film.

rule of thirds A method of composing an image, where imaginary lines divide the frame horizontally and vertically, and the graphically strong points are at the intersections of these lines.

running time The length of a film.

scene In scriptwriting terms, a scene is a section of the script where the action occurs in one location.

scene heading In scriptwriting, the introduction of a scene that indicates the location and time of day.

score The musical 'script'.

screenwriter The person (or people) responsible for writing the film script.

script supervisor During production, the script supervisor checks that the film maintains **continuity** and that all the necessary shots are covered.

SECAM The video system used in most of Europe based on the number of vertical scanning lines of the image.

second unit A production team separate from the main one, that is scheduled to do secondary shooting in another location, while the main production continues.

sequence analysis A written analysis of a section of a film, that pays close attention to the details of style and technique and how they communicate the film's meaning.

series photography Before the development of motion-picture film, series photography used some of the same principles with still cameras. A number of still cameras were set up to take pictures in a series when triggered by movement. The photographs could then be viewed sequentially to give the impression of motion.

set designer The crew member responsible for the overall design of a location.

SFX See **sound effects**.

shooting script A script that includes directorial annotations, such as shot selections and camera positions.

shot/reverse shot In **continuity editing**, a way of shooting a dialogue scene, where a shot of one character looking at or talking to another is followed by the shot of the character (or thing) they are talking to or looking at.

shotgun microphone see **super-cardiod microphone**.

shutter The mechanism at the front of a camera, behind the lens, that opens and shuts to admit light into the camera.

shutter speed The length of time that a **shutter** opens to allow light in through the **aperture** of a camera, in order to **expose** the film.

simultaneous sound Sound that is running in the same time frame as the image of a scene.

slow motion A film played back at a decreased speed. With film, this is created in-camera by shooting at a higher rate of **frames per second** then playing back at normal fps, and in video, it is created during editing.

soft light Light that is either diffused or reflected when travelling from the source to the subject, so that it produces less distinct shadows and an evenly lit appearance.

sonic flashback A scene where the image continues in the present and we hear sound from a previous moment in the narrative.

sound bridge The linking of one scene to another through the sound continuing over; either the sound of the second scene starts before the visuals of the first have ended, or the sound of the first scene continues after the visuals of the second have started.

sound effects The elements of a soundtrack that are not dialogue or music.

sound recorder The member of a film crew responsible for recording the production audio.

source music Music that appears from a source within the story, a form of **diegetic** sound.

Soviet montage see **montage**.

spotting session In film music, the process where the **director**, **composer** and **music editor** view the **rough cut** of a film to decide when music will be included and how it might sound.

staging The placing and movement of the performers within a scene.

star system During the Classical period, the system whereby stars were under contract to a studio, who decided on their roles and organized their publicity.

Steadicam A camera mount that attaches to the operator's body, moving the camera's centre of gravity away from the operator to produce fluid results.

stereotype A generalized, oversimplified image of a character or group, often negative.

stinger A film music **cue** that features a sudden burst of music to accompany a dramatic point in the action.

stop motion A method of animating three-dimensional figures, where a few frames are shot, the figure is moved slightly and the sequence is repeated.

story In narrative structure, a sequence of events presented in chronological order. The story includes many elements that are not directly seen within the course of a film, but are implied through the action and dialogue.

storyboard The preplan for a film presented as it will appear on screen in a series of drawings with notes on how the shots will be realized.

straight cut An edit without a **transitional device**.

structuralist/materialist film A genre of experimental film which foregrounds the apparatus of filmmaking itself.

studio system During the Classical period in Hollywood, production was dominated by five **vertically integrated** companies. These studios defined the style of Classical Hollywood practice.

stylized performance A method of acting that shows awareness of the performance and the audience, rather than maintaining the illusion of a closed world of the narrative.

subjective Coming from the perspective of an individual's **point of view**. Camerawork or sound can be subjective, representing what a character sees or hears.

subtext A level of meaning deeper than the obvious surface meaning.

Super 8 A particular type of the 8mm gauge of film, popular with artists and for home movies.

super-cardiod microphone A more directed form of **cardiod microphone**.

Surrealism/Surrealist A movement of modern art associated with dreamlike images representing the unconscious and often featuring radical and unexpected juxtapositions.

surround sound Sound systems that play back sound from all directions.

synchronous sound/Synchronization/synch Sounds that match the images.

talking head A conventional interview style where the subject talks to the camera either in **direct** or **indirect address**.

tapering When shooting a scene with either a camera movement or a **zoom**, the operator starts the movement slowly, builds up to the required speed then slows down again before stopping. This gives the movement a smooth appearance.

telephoto lens A lens that makes objects appear smaller in the frame by shooting with a narrower angle of view. A telephoto lens also shifts the perspective so that objects appear closer to each other in depth.

tempo Usually refers to the speed of a music track.

temporal ellipsis In narrative and editing, a moment when time is contracted, leaving out part of the action.

temp track A music track used during **postproduction** before the final **score** is completed, standing in for the actual **cues**.

text Text can refer to a number of things, the most basic being written material on screen. On another level, the text can refer to any artistic product such as a film. When reading a film's text, one is looking at the most basic level of meaning, what the film is about.

thick description Borrowed from anthropology, thick description incorporates analytical and contextual information.

Third Cinema A movement of film originating in Latin America in the 1960s that advocated a politically radical cinema opposed to the commercial mainstream or the auteur cinema traditions.

thirds lines The imaginary lines in a frame that mark the points of the **rule of thirds**.

three-act structure A common narrative structure for films, consisting of a beginning, middle and end.

three-point lighting A conventional lighting set-up which illuminates a subject from three positions, a **key light**, **fill light** and **back light**.

tilt The movement of a camera on a vertical axis.

track/tracking shot A movement of a camera on a **dolly** sideways across a scene.

transition/transitional device In editing, how one shot replaces another, such as **dissolves**, **fades** or **wipes**.

tubes In older analogue television and video systems, before the development of **CCDs**, tubes were used to capture and play back the images.

two-inch quad An early format of videotape, on reels rather than an enclosed cassette.

two-shot A shot containing two characters and often used as a **master shot** in the set-up of a conventional conversation scene.

Umatic A professional format of **analogue** video tape.

under-exposure Images shot without the **aperture** being sufficiently open, so that the frame, or parts of the frame, appear dark.

unexposed Film that has not passed through the camera or been exposed to light.

unreliable narrator/narration In narrative theory, a narrator who may or may not be telling an accurate version of the story.

vertical integration A practice of the studio system of the **Classical Hollywood** period, whereby studios owned the means of production, distribution and exhibition.

VHS The most common format of analogue home video.

video art An art-based practice of video, experimenting with the form, similar to **experimental film**.

voice over (VO) Used in both documentary and fiction situations, voice over refers to narration from a source that may be part of the **story** of the film but that is not occupying the same time and space as the images.

voyeurism Gaining sexual pleasure from illicit viewing.

Western A genre of film set historically during the late 1800s in the Western part of America. This genre was popular during the Classical period.

white balance A setting on a video camera that adjusts the **colour temperature** by selecting a white surface and aligning the other colours relative to this reference point.

wide-angle lens A lens (or a setting on a **zoom lens**) which allows for the widest angle of view. A wide-angle lens also shifts the perspective so that objects in depth appear further from each other.

widescreen A format of film of television screen that is wider that the traditional 3 x 4. There are a variety of widescreen formats including the now standard 16 x 9 and the **anamorphic lens** process.

wipe An editing transitional device that replaces one image with another in a number of patterns.

Zoetrope A cylinder with a series of pictures on the inner surface that, when viewed through slits with the cylinder rotating, gives an impresssion of continuous motion.

zoom lens A lens that moves between **wide-angle** and **telephoto** positions.

Index